PENGUIN HANDBOOKS

PH36

THE PENGUIN HOYLE

HUBERT PHILLIPS

Hubert Phillips has long been recognized as our leading authority on indoor games. Within the limits of what is possible in one volume, the *Penguin Hoyle* covers the whole field.

The book has three main sections. The first is devoted to card games. There is a full explanation, with illustrative deals, of our most popular card games: Bridge, Solo Whist, Poker, Black Maria, Cribbage, and about thirty others. There are brief notes on another forty card games and a fine selection of Patience games. The second section covers Games of Encounter. These include Draughts and Backgammon, both of which are very fully dealt with, and two fascinating games of the author's own invention: a variant of the Chess War Game (*Kriegsspiel*) and a new and exciting Naval War Game. This game can be played with enjoyment by everyone who likes a battle of wits. The element of skill predominates, but there's also (as in war itself) an element of chance. In the third section, the author presents more than thirty Party Games; many of these, too, are of his invention.

If you want your guests to enjoy themselves, and if they want, not only a lot of fun, but a modicum of mental stimulus, the *Penguin Hoyle* will provide it.

Cover design by John Miles

THE PENGUIN

HOYLE

A Book of Indoor Games

HUBERT PHILLIPS

PENGUIN BOOKS

Penguin Books Ltd, Harmondsworth, Middlesex
U.S.A.: Penguin Books Inc., 3300 Clipper Mill Road, Baltimore 11, Md
AUSTRALIA: Penguin Books Pty Ltd, 762 Whitehorse Road,
Mitcham, Victoria

—

First published 1958

—

Made and printed in Great Britain
by The Whitefriars Press Ltd
London and Tonbridge

CONTENTS

CONTENTS

FOREWORD

THE great Edmond Hoyle was born in 1672, when the Merry Monarch was king, and lived to be nearly a hundred; when he died, in 1769, John Wilkes was fighting his battle for free speech and George III was in process of losing the American colonies. Hoyle was nearly seventy when he published his famous *Treatise on Whist*. In later editions he added other games: Piquet, Quadrille, Backgammon, Chess. His *Laws of Whist* stood unchallenged for over a hundred years, and Hoyle's name, like that of Edward Cocker, became a household word. 'According to Cocker', said the schoolmasters; the clubmen, 'according to Hoyle'. And for many years now *Hoyle* has been a generic term for collections of indoor games.

My *Hoyle* is the fruit of many years' labour. Before I was ten I played Chess, Draughts, Whist; and I have devoted much thought, from my schooldays onwards, to the *rationale* of games of skill and chance. I should like to say a little about the three sections of this book.

CARD GAMES. Here I have made no attempt to cover the whole field. There are literally hundreds of card games; new ones are being invented almost every week. I have confined myself to games that I know to be popular in this country. If you want to know how to play Contract Bridge, you will find set out here the mechanics of the game, a summary of its laws, a selection of illustrative hands which will prove, I hope, a source both of entertainment and instruction. I have also dealt at length with a number of other games. These include Poker (the most difficult game of all), Booby and Black Maria (the best games for three players), Option and Piquet (the best games for two). And if you like Patience, which America calls Solitaire, you will find here a number of its more challenging variants.

GAMES OF ENCOUNTER. This section does not include Chess, the greatest of all indoor games, since Chess is the subject of Harry Golombek's admirable Penguin Handbook (PH 24). I have, however, included my own variant of the Chess War Game (*Kriegsspiel*). Here is a game which, once you have mastered its rules, can be played with as much enjoyment by novices as by those who have devoted years to the study of Chess theory. I have played, or umpired, hundreds of games of *Kriegsspiel*, and can't recall one that wasn't exciting as well as being good for a laugh. There's an element of luck in the game, but a great deal of skill too; the better of two players will win nine times out of ten.

In this section, too, I include Draughts and Backgammon, and have, I hope, said enough about both games to render recourse to any other book unnecessary.

Finally, there is my Naval War Game: a favourite game with schoolboys of all ages. Here you get a faint simulacrum of that much grimmer exercise, a naval battle. I might add that, while this book was going through the press, I invented another game, which many may think the more exciting of the two. This game, like *Kriegsspiel*, is played on one board under the supervision of an umpire. I regret very much that I can't include it; you will find it, however, in my book, *Games of Skill for Two*.

PARTY GAMES. These call, I think, for no special word of explanation. Their classification in the Table of Contents gives a fair idea of their scope. I should like, however, to commend the reader's attention to the last section (Quiz Games). Such games are followed on the radio and TV with an almost passionate interest – I know that from my own experience on quiz panels – but it's much better fun, surely, to 'have a go' oneself than to listen to other people.

It would not be fair to Messrs H. F. and G. Witherby, the publishers of my *Indoor Games Compendium*, not to say how extensively I have drawn on three of its four volumes. *Party Games* was published in 1952; *Card Games* in 1953. *Games of Skill for Two* has not yet gone to press; I have held up its publication to include my new war game. My fourth volume, incidentally, is *Chess*, written in collaboration with Harry Golombek.

I must also mention my great indebtedness to my late secretary, Mrs C. R. Bennett, who has performed, with her customary care and efficiency, the exacting task of reading the proofs of this book. *Hoyle* is, I believe, about the tenth of my books to benefit from her co-operation.

HUBERT PHILLIPS

October 1957

Card Games

CARD GAMES

THERE is an infinitude of card games. Any recognized game, by some slight alteration in its rules, can become another one; the games which have rules followed by everyone who plays them can be counted on the fingers of two hands. For example, I have invented a number of games – more or less derivative – most of which have only been played privately. Two or three of them, however, have been given considerable publicity.

No one, therefore, could hope to list all the card games there are. Brave attempts at doing so have been made, but without any hope of success. Between the completion of this book, and its appearance in print, there will, no doubt, be new games in circulation.

For this reason, I have given much thought to the question of my presentation of card games. By confining myself to an exposition of the mechanics of the games listed, I could have included a larger number. But to do that is, as the old saying goes, to empty out the baby with the bath-water. Many readers are unable to follow a merely mechanical statement of how a game is played. To arouse their interest, one must make the game come to life; one must illustrate its strategy and tactics. And this makes heavy demands upon one's space.

All the same, I am sure my plan is the right one. I have dealt as fully as possible with the games which, I know, command a wide measure of support – Contract Bridge; Solo Whist; Piquet; Poker; Cribbage – and to games which, if not so well known, have been widely publicized and are popular: Black Maria; Bezique; Option; Canasta; and various other games of the Rummy family. I have also treated fairly fully a number of popular round games. For the rest, I have offered a brief account of the best-known card games not more fully treated, which will at least (I hope) make intelligible what kind of games they are.

Let us, for a moment, consider the nature of a pack of cards. Reduced to its fundamentals, what is it? Four sets of cards which are numbered: either from 1 to 13 (as in Misère pots at Poker) or from 2 to 14 (Contract Bridge) or, optionally, in both ways (Rummy). Three of the numbers – the 11, 12, and 13 – are presented pictorially: these are the Knaves, Queens, and Kings. The court cards add a touch of colour and excitement to games which, played purely with sets of numbers, would lose much of their attractiveness.

What can one do with these four sets of numbered cards? One can amuse oneself in countless ways. The simplest games are pure games of chance, in which one bets on what cards will be turned up (Fan Tan), or on how closely the cards which are turned up will approximate to an arbitrary number (Baccarat). Or one can combine this purely gambling element with the exercise of a moderate degree of skill (Vingt et Un). Or, again, one can devise games which involve the melding of cards of like denomination (Canasta), or which combine the business of melding with the arrangement of cards in sequences (Rummy; Bezique; Piquet). These last two games – Bezique and Piquet – involve also a trick-taking factor; and now we are well in the field where the play of one's cards – the order in which one presents them – becomes significant. And so to those games – for the most part derivative of Whist, which itself has a long history – in which one of the four suits is given priority over the others, and in which success depends on so organizing the play of one's cards as to secure the maximum number of tricks. These 'trump and partnership' games have long been the aristocrats of the card world; they are not only exciting; they have a high intellectual content.

Even now I have not exhausted the possibilities of the world of cards. Cribbage, for example, is like no other game: its basic idea is arithmetical. Poker, a development of the simpler game Brag, demands a combination of two factors: a knowledge of probability, and a capacity to assess how the minds of other players are working. Nor is this all. There are, for example, the stop games (Parliament; Newmarket); the avoidance games (well illustrated by Black Maria); and the wide range of games for one player called Patience. I hope that the selection which I have given in this book will fairly illustrate how much mental stimulus, how much entertainment, how much solace for barren hours, a pack of cards can offer.

Contract Bridge

Contract Bridge derives from the great game of Whist, which dominated the fashionable card-clubs throughout the nineteenth century. Whist is a 'trump and partnership' game, and so are its descendants: Bridge; Auction Bridge; Contract Bridge. Bridge was first played about 1890; in its original form it is dead and now only of historical interest. Auction Bridge, if not quite dead, is no longer of any significance. But Contract Bridge, first played about 1930, has become the standard card game in all card-clubs and in tens of thousands of homes, and has acquired a literature which far exceeds that of all other card games put together. Several new books on Contract * are published every year; its theory is the subject of continuous study by professional writers on the game; and there is an almost incessant round of national and international tournaments; in the latter, some twenty countries compete. I do not think that any other card game will rival it in popularity or interest for many years to come.

I cannot hope in this compendium to present the principles of Contract exhaustively; to do so, one would need an encyclopaedia. But, in what follows, an attempt will be made to make the mechanics of the game intelligible; to explain the technical terms which are in general use; and to present a selection of illustrative deals from the study of which much that is of value may be learned.

I. THE MECHANICS OF THE GAME

Contract is a game for four players, played with the standard pack of 52 cards. The 13 cards of the four suits rank in their normal order: Ace; King; Queen; Knave (or Jack); Ten; Nine; Eight; Seven; Six; Five; Four; Three; Two. That is to say, when

* Writers on Contract Bridge seldom give the game its full title: it can be called either 'Contract' or 'Bridge'. I use both terms in my exposition: they mean exactly the same thing.

all four cards of the same suit are played to a trick, the highest-ranking card wins it.

A session at Contract consists of one or more rubbers. Each rubber constitutes an independent event. Before each rubber those taking part 'cut' for partners and choice of seats, i.e. each of the four players draws a card from the pack, which is spread face downwards on the table. For this purpose, cards rank in the order given above, and the suits rank: Spades; Hearts; Diamonds; Clubs. Thus, if A draws the ♥ 5: B, the ♠ Q; C, the ♠ 5; D, the ♦ 3; B and C will be partners against A and D, for the ♠ 5 ranks higher than the ♥ 5. B and C will also have choice of seats.

For convenience, it is usual to call the positions at the table North, South, East, and West. Players may be referred to by reference to the seats which they occupy. So N – S are always partners against E – W.

The *object* of the game is to score more points than one's opponents. A *rubber* is the best of three games, i.e. the side which first wins two games has won the rubber, and the score is then added up. But it is possible to win the rubber and yet to be a loser, for points are scored both in attack and in defence. An important element in the strategy of the game is deciding when it is worth while to incur loss rather than surrender a game. Bridge is normally played for stakes, calculated on the basis of so much per hundred points. You can play for as little as a penny a hundred or for £5 a hundred or even more. But if you are in the £5 a hundred class you will at least know how Bridge is played! Club stakes are usually 3d, 6d, or 1s a hundred.

Each game consists of one or more deals. Players deal in succession, the rotation being clockwise. The first dealer is the player who has drawn the highest card. Let us suppose that this is South. Then West deals next; after West, North; and so on.

Before the *deal* the pack is well shuffled by the player to the dealer's left, and cut to the *dealer* by the player to his right. He then deals out the whole pack, one at a time (i.e. 13 cards to each player), beginning with the player to his left. The cards are dealt face downwards and no player should touch them until the deal is complete. Each player then picks up his cards, arranges them in any way he wishes in his hand (taking care not to show any of them to other players) and the *bidding* of the hand begins.

There are two elements in the operation of each deal. The first is the *bidding*. The second is the actual *play*.

I will explain the *play* first. The *bidding* (or *auction*) precedes it, but the bidding is meaningless unless we know what it is all about.

II. THE PLAY

When the auction is complete, one of the four players will have become the *declarer*. He 'plays the hand', and the hand of his partner (who is now *dummy*) is displayed face upwards on the table as soon as a *lead* has been made to the first *trick*. This first lead is made by the player on declarer's left.

The player who leads to this first trick plays a card face upwards on the table. Now Dummy's hand goes down. Declarer plays a card from Dummy; then the player to his right plays a card; finally, Declarer plays one himself. This completes the trick. The cards are gathered by Declarer, if he has won the trick, or by one of the defending side, if they have won the trick; and this and subsequent tricks, as they are completed, are stacked neatly (face downwards) in front of whoever is collecting them. Dummy takes no part in the play, and should not even collect the cards when his side has won the trick.

The player who has won a trick leads the first card to the next one.

As already mentioned, a trick is won by the highest card played to it, if all four cards are of the same suit. If not, it is won by the highest card of the suit led, unless someone has played a *trump*. If there is a *trump suit* (as is the case in about two deals out of three) any card of the trump suit takes precedence over any card of any other suit. Thus, if Spades are trumps, the ♠ 2 will win against the Ace of any other suit.

A player must 'follow suit' if he can. If a Diamond is led, he must play a Diamond if he has one. If he has no Diamond, and (say) Spades are trumps, he can either trump or *discard* a Heart or Club.

Now the object of the play is to take as many tricks as possible. The *bidding* (or *auction*) which precedes the play is to determine which shall be the declaring side. It is important to secure the *declaration* if possible. For only the declaring side can score points which count towards game; and the declaring side also nominates the trump suit, or decrees that the game shall be played at *No Trump*, i.e. without a trump suit at all.

III. THE BIDDING

Before the play begins, the two sides pit their wits against one another for the right to play the hand. The successful side is that which *contracts* to make the higher score. Every contract carries with it a score which – if the contract is made – will count towards game. But, if the contract is not made, the declaring side is penalized and points are scored by the defenders.

The bidding takes the form of an *auction*. The dealer has the right to bid first; the player to his left bids next; and so on. Each side tries to contract for enough points to prevent the other side from securing the declaration. If one side has achieved a *game declaration*, the other side may think it worth while to contract for more tricks than it can make; this is a *sacrifice bid*.

These are the scores which count towards game if the number of tricks contracted for is made by the declaring side:

Where the bid is One Club: 20 points
Where the bid is Two Clubs: 40 points
Where the bid is Three Clubs: 60 points

and so on up to Seven Clubs, scoring 140 points.

But if Six or Seven Clubs are bid, and made, there are also – as we shall see – substantial bonuses for a *Slam*.

One, Two, Three, etc. refer to tricks made *in excess of six*. Thus a bid of One Club means that whoever makes the bid contracts (on behalf of his side) to take seven tricks if Clubs are trumps.

One Diamond is a superior bid to One Club; Two Diamonds 'overcalls' Two Clubs; and so on. But the scoring value of Diamonds and Clubs is the same.

Hearts overcall Diamonds; Spades overcall Hearts. In both these suits trick-values are 30 per trick.

Bids at No Trump overcall suit bids. At No Trump, the first trick (i.e. the first over six) is worth 40 points. Subsequent tricks are worth only 30 points each.

Hence in the auction, the sequence of possible bids (each a legitimate overcall of the one before) is as follows:

One Club: 20 points
One Diamond: 20 points
One Heart: 30 points
One Spade: 30 points
One No Trump: 40 points
Two Clubs: 40 points

and so on up to Seven No Trump (220 points). A bid of Two always overcalls a bid of One; a bid of Three overcalls a bid of Two, etc. Four Clubs only scores 80 points; but a bid of Four Clubs will overcall a bid of Three No Trump, although that scores 100.

To secure a game, 100 points must be scored. So a *game contract* is a contract of Five Clubs or Five Diamonds; Four Hearts or Four Spades; or Three No Trump.

Bidding Systems

Thousands of books have been written – the majority of them worthless – to publicize various systems of bidding at Contract Bridge. It is impossible to summarize here even the more significant of them. But a fairly good idea of how competent players bid can be gained by studying the illustrative hands which follow; the sixteen boards at Duplicate especially are designed to throw light on critical bidding situations. I believe that it is a great mistake for the beginner to follow slavishly *any* system. If he remembers, throughout the auction, that he is bidding, not on thirteen cards, but on twenty-six; and if he can contrive, as each successive bid is made, to build up a reasonably accurate picture of the cards his partner holds, he cannot go far astray. And, with every bid he makes, he should weigh *potential gains* against *potential losses*.

A Competitive Auction

Here is an example of a competitive auction. South is the dealer and has the right to bid first. We will suppose it is the first deal of the rubber.

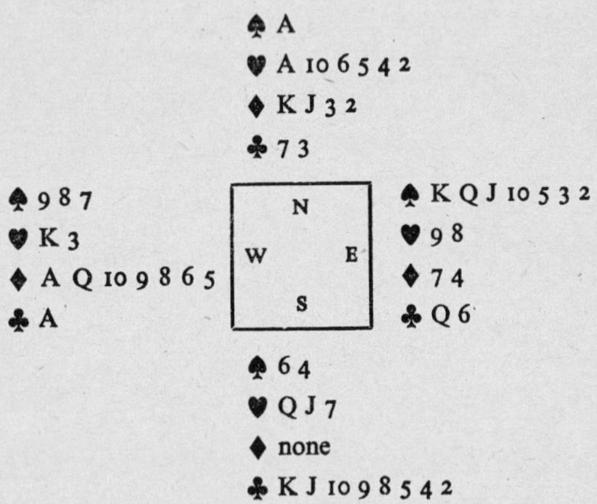

♠ 6 4
♥ Q J 7
♦ none
♣ K J 10 9 8 5 4 2

THE BIDDING

South	*West*	*North*	*East*
No (1)	1 ♦	1 ♥	2 ♠ (2)
3 ♣	3 ♦	3 ♥	3 ♠
4 ♥	4 ♠	4 N.T.	5 ♠
6 ♣ (3)			

Note

(1) A player is not obliged to bid. He can *pass*, which he does by saying 'No Bid'. He can also *double* a contract, but of this more anon. If, as often happens, all four players pass, the hand is 'thrown in', and the deal passes to the next player in the ordinary way.

(2) A player is not obliged to make a minimum overcall. East can bid Two Spades (as he does here) or any greater number.

(3) After this bid, the players all say 'No Bid'. The auction is now closed, and South becomes declarer at a contract of Six Clubs. He has undertaken to take twelve tricks with Clubs as trumps.

Let us now play this hand through. West leads to the first trick; his lead is the ♠ 9. North (Dummy) places his cards face upwards on the table. He arranges them in suits, as shown below; the trump suit (Clubs) should, strictly speaking, be placed at Dummy's right:

♣ 7 3 ♥ A 10 6 5 4 2 ♠ A ♦ K J 3 2

Here now are the 13 tricks in sequence. The card in italics wins the trick, and whichever hand wins this trick leads to the next one:

Trick	*West*	*North*	*East*	*South*
1	♠ 9	♠ *A*	♠ 2	♠ 4
2	♦ 5	♦ 2	♦ 4	♣ *2*
3	♠ 7	♣ *3*	♠ 3	♠ 6
4	♣ *A*	♣ 7	♣ 6	♣ 8
5	♠ 8	♥ 2	♠ 5	♣ *4*
6	♦ 6	♥ 4	♣ Q	♣ *K*
7	♥ 3	♥ 5	♥ 8	♥ *Q*
8	♥ K	♥ *A*	♥ 9	♥ J
9	♦ 8	♥ *10*	♠ 10	♥ 7

There is no need for further play. Declarer lays his cards face upwards on the table, claiming the remainder of the tricks. A player should not do this unless he is certain beyond cavil that his claim is valid. In this case South's claim is incontestable; he holds the four remaining trumps.

Note that each player follows suit unless he has no card of the suit led. Declarer wins tricks 2, 3, and 5 by *trumping* (or *ruffing*) a card of another suit. It is a simple hand, but the play is not without interest; it needs to be carefully planned.

On the deal which we have just analysed, N – S score 120 points for Six Clubs bid and made, which is more than enough for game. But this is not all they score: there is also a bonus for bidding and making six tricks. So at this point it will be advisable to explain the various ways in which points can be scored.

Points made by winning games are supplemented by points scored for winning the rubber; and by various bonus and penalty points.

The scoring seems, at first blush, very complicated: I know a good many 'family' Bridge players who have never mastered it! But without an exact knowledge of the score it is impossible to play really well; if you make a point of keeping your own score, every time you play, you will very soon become familiar with its intricacies.

To score at Bridge, you need two columns; we will call them WE and THEY. In the left-hand column we score the points that 'we' make; in the right-hand column, the points that 'they' make. Towards the bottom of the column a line is drawn. Points which count towards game are entered 'below' the line; all other scores 'above' the line. At the end of the rubber, the scores are totalled, and settlement, on whatever basis has been agreed, is made on the difference between them.

IV. SCORING AT CONTRACT BRIDGE

(1) *Below the Line*

Tricks bid and made are scored 'below the line', since they count towards game. If the successful contract is worth 100 points or more, another line is drawn to show that a game has been won. If partners have already scored, say, 60 points towards game (this is called a *part score*), 40 more will complete the necessary 100 and the line is drawn in just the same way. If the contract is for, say, Three Hearts, and ten tricks are made, the 90 points contracted for are scored below the line and the remaining 30 points above the line.

DOUBLED CONTRACTS. A player who thinks that his opponents will not make their contract can, when it is his turn to bid, *double* the contract instead of passing or offering a higher contract of his own. The *double* ranks as his bid. If the double is accepted by the declaring side (i.e. if no one else makes a bid) the points scored per trick are doubled; tricks in Clubs count 40;

tricks in Hearts, 60; and so on. But if the declarer fails to make his contract, the penalties for failure are increased (see below).

If a player makes his doubled contract, he scores, above the line, a bonus of 50 points. If he makes more tricks than he has contracted for, he also scores a bonus above the line in respect of each of these tricks. How big these bonuses are, depends on whether he has, or has not, already won one game.

We must now introduce the element of *vulnerability*. A side which has won one game towards the rubber becomes *vulnerable*. A vulnerable side scores, above the line, higher premiums or bonuses, and incurs heavier penalties, than a side which is non-vulnerable.

REDOUBLED CONTRACTS. A player whose contract has been doubled can *redouble*. Now the points per trick are doubled again. A contract of One Diamond, redoubled and made, scores 80 below the line. And, as before, there are bonuses if extra tricks are made, and heavier penalties if the contract is defeated.

But the *only* points scored 'below the line', and counting towards game, are points in respect of tricks made which have been contracted for.

(2) *Above the Line*

These points are scored *above the line:*

BY THE DECLARING SIDE. (i) *Honours*. If a player holds four 'Honours' in the trump suit (i.e. any four of the top five cards, A, K, Q, J, 10), he scores100 points. If he holds all five of them, he scores 150 points. If, in a No Trump contract, a player holds all four Aces, he scores 150 points.

(ii) The point-value of tricks made but not contracted for (i.e. overtricks).

(iii) *Where a contract has been doubled:* 100 points if declarer is not vulnerable, and 200 points if declarer is vulnerable, in respect of each overtrick.

(iv) *Where a contract has been redoubled:* 200 points if declarer is not vulnerable, and 400 points if declarer is vulnerable, in respect of each overtrick.

(v) In addition to the above, a bonus of 50 points where declarer has made a doubled or redoubled contract.

(vi) *Slam bonuses.* Where 12 tricks are bid and made (Small Slam) a bonus of 500 points if not vulnerable, or of 750 points if vulnerable.

Where 13 tricks are bid and made (Grand Slam), a bonus of 1,000 points if not vulnerable, or of 1,500 points if vulnerable.

(vii) *Rubber points.* For winning a two-game rubber (i.e. taking two games without the adversaries' taking any), 700 points. For winning a three-game rubber, 500 points.

BY THE DEFENDING SIDE. (i) *Where an undoubled contract is defeated:* 50 points, if the declarer is not vulnerable, for every trick by which he falls short of his contract. 100 points for each such trick if the declarer is vulnerable.

(ii) *Where a contract has been doubled and defeated:* If the declarer is not vulnerable, 100 points for the first trick by which he falls short of his contract, and 200 points for every subsequent trick. If the declarer is vulnerable, 200 points for the first undertrick, and 300 points for every subsequent one.

(iii) *Where a contract has been redoubled and defeated,* double the above penalties. Thus a player who, being vulnerable, has been doubled in a contract of Three No Trump, has redoubled, and has made only five tricks, is penalized 400 + 600 + 600 + 600, or no less than 2,200 points. Doubling and redoubling, especially where the declaring side is vulnerable, are weapons which are not to be lightly handled.

Here is the score-sheet of an actual rubber, consisting of eight deals, which illustrates the various elements in the scoring table. In the ordinary way, of course, the scores would not be spaced out and itemized as they are here: that has been done to make the whole thing crystal-clear. These are the eight deals to which the numbers in the left-hand column refer.

An Example

DEAL	WE	THEY
8	500	
8	750	
8	150	
7		400
6	800	100
5		500
5		50
5		100
4		500
3	90	
2	50	
1	30	
	THE LINE	
1	60	
3	40	
5		360
8	190	
	2,660	2,010
	2,010	
WE win by	650	

(1) WE bid Two Hearts and made Three. So WE scored 60 below the line and 30 for our overtrick (not bid) above the line.

(2) THEY bid Four Spades and failed by one trick. So WE scored 50 above the line.

(3) WE bid One No Trump (enough to give us the game) and made ten tricks, 40 below the line; 90 above the line. WE now had won a game and so became *vulnerable*.

(4) WE bid Three No Trump (an attempt to snatch a quick rubber); were doubled and 'set' two tricks. So THEY scored 500 above the line.

(5) THEY bid Six Spades (Small Slam), were doubled, and made all 13 tricks. So THEY scored 360 below the line, 100 for their overtrick, 50 for making a doubled contract (sometimes called '50 for

the insult'), and 500 for a Small Slam bid and made. Now BOTH SIDES were *vulnerable.*

(6) THEY bid Four Hearts, were doubled, and 'set' three tricks; Declarer held ♥ Ace, K J 10. So WE scored 800 above the line (200 + 300 + 300) and THEY scored 100 for Honours.

(7) WE bid Five Clubs, redoubled, and were defeated by (or 'set') one trick. So THEY scored 400 above the line.

(8) WE bid Six No Trump and made the contract; declarer held all four Aces. So WE scored 190 below the line; 150 for Aces; 750 for a vulnerable Small Slam, bid and made; and 500 points for a three-game rubber. We had won this exciting rubber by 650 points. For purposes of settlement 650 ranks as 600.

ILLUSTRATIVE HANDS

Now that we know all about the scoring, let us play through two or three illustrative hands; they will not only throw further light on the mechanics of the game, but will offer one or two glimpses of the principles of bidding and play.

1. *An Ill-advised Double*

Score: love all *Dealer:* South

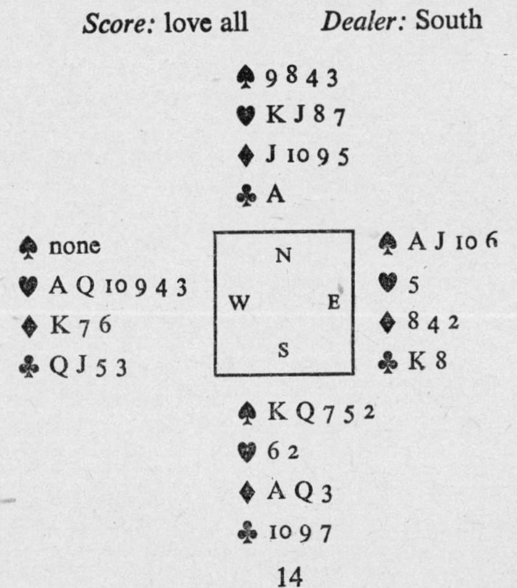

THE BIDDING

South	*West*	*North*	*East*
1 ♠	2 ♥	3 ♠	Double
No	4 ♥	Double	No
No	No		

West becomes declarer at a contract of Four Hearts doubled.

Note on the bidding. South is just about strong enough to open with One Spade. (He is contracting – knowing nothing, so far, about North's hand – to make seven tricks with Spades as trumps.) West has a perfectly good 'overcall' of Two Hearts. North now bids Three Spades, to tell his partner that, if Spades are trumps, his hand is about two tricks better than the average. East's double is not good. He has strong trumps, but he must know that his partner has none; in defence, therefore, he is only worth two or three tricks. And his double, if unsuccessful, will have given away a game.

Now West panics. He thinks it unlikely – on the bidding – that Three Spades will be defeated, and that a 'sacrifice' in Four Hearts will be cheaper. This is a bad bid, because it shows lack of confidence in his partner. And mutual confidence is the first essential of a successful partnership.

THE PLAY (with a running commentary).

The card in *italics* takes the trick. I advise beginners to set out the four hands and play the deal through. If they do this repeatedly, with hands that they come across in the Press, they cannot fail to benefit.

Trick	*North*	*East*	*South*	*West*
1	♠ 3	♠ *A*	♠ 5	♦ 6

North attacks at the outset, leading his partner's suit. Declarer (West) goes up at once with East's ♠ Ace. He suspects that trumps are massed to his left, and does not want to weaken his suit prematurely. Dummy's hand is now almost valueless

Trick	*North*	*East*	*South*	*West*
2	♥ *J*	♥ 5	♥ 2	♥ 9

Declarer takes a double *finesse*. The play of the ♥ Q would have been a simple finesse. To 'finesse' is to make a favourable assumption, which may or may not be correct, about the position of an adverse card. There is a faint hope (which proves illusory) that South holds the ♥ J.

3	♠ 9	♠ 10	♠ Q	♥ *3*

The attack in Spades is resumed. West has to part with a trump, and now launches a counter-attack in Clubs.

4	♣ *A*	♣ 2	♣ 7	♣ Q
5	♠ 8	♠ J	♠ K	♥ *4*

Another trump gone! Declarer, though conscious of impending defeat, can only carry on with his play.

6	♥ *7*	♣ 4	♣ 9	♣ J
7	♠ 4	♠ 6	♠ 7	♥ *10*

That North has no second Club is another blow to Declarer's hopes. The attack in Spades is continued, reducing Declarer's trumps to two.

8	♦ 5	♣ *K*	♣ 10	♣ 5
9	♦ 9	♣ 8	♥ *6*	♣ 3

A blunder by Declarer which loses a trick. He had forgotten that South might still have a trump. If a Diamond is led from Dummy's hand N – S can only make the ♦ Ace and a trump.

10	♥ *K*	♦ 2	♠ 2	♥ Q

Spades are led against Declarer for the fifth time. This shows how powerful an offensive weapon a strongly-held suit can be. Declarer, hoping against hope, tries another trump finesse.

11	♥ 8	♦ 4	♦ 3	♥ *A*

Excellent play by North. He is sure that his partner holds ♦ Ace; for without it, South would not have had an opening bid. So he throws Declarer in with the ♥ Ace to lead away from his guarded ♦ K. Now N – S take the last two tricks.

12	♦ 10	♦ 8	♦ *Q*	♦ 7
13	♦ J	♣ 6	♦ *A*	♦ K

Declarer is four tricks down on his doubled contract, i.e. N – S score 700 points. A favourable situation has been well exploited by the defence.

2. *Intelligent Defence to a Three No-Trump Contract*

Score: North – South vulnerable *Dealer:* West

This deal is adapted from one published in Mr John Brown's excellent book, *Winning Defence.*

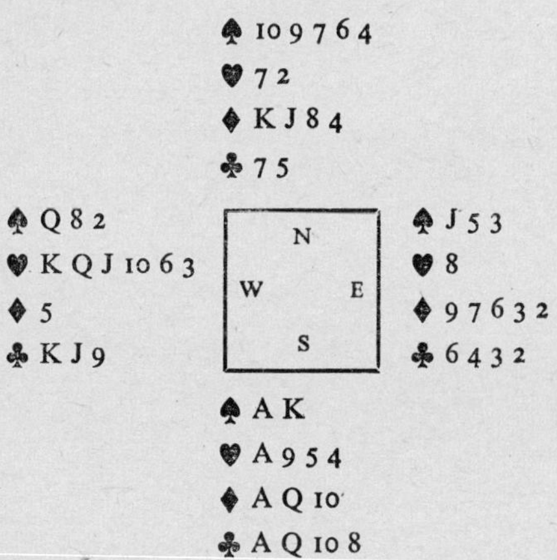

THE BIDDING

West	*North*	*East*	*South*
1 ♥	No	No	Double
No	3 ♠	No	3 N.T.
No	No	No	

Note on the bidding. South's double is a *conventional* bid. It does not tell North that South can defeat a contract of One Heart, but tells North that South has a powerful hand and invites him (North) to make a bid. Since North would make some sort of bid, however weak his hand, he shows that it is not without strength by bidding *Three* Spades instead of Two. South, whose hand is 'gappy', should have accepted this suggestion and bid

Four Spades: a contract which (as the cards lie) can easily be made. But South succumbed to the lure of his four Aces (with their bonus of 150 points) and settled for Three No Trump.

THE PLAY. (South is Declarer at a contract of Three No Trump)

Trick	*West*	*North*	*East*	*South*
1	♥ *K*	♥ 2	♥ 8	♥ 4

Declarer holds up his ♥ Ace to be sure of exhausting East's Hearts.

Trick	*West*	*North*	*East*	*South*
2	♥ Q	♥ 7	♣ 2	♥ *A*
3	♠ 2	♠ 4	♠ 3	♠ *A*

An exploratory play by Declarer. It is just possible that one defender holds ♠ Q, J only.

Trick	*West*	*North*	*East*	*South*
4	♦ 5	♦ 4	♦ 2	♦ *A*
5	♥ 3	♦ 8	♦ 3	♦ *Q*
6	♥ 6	♦ *J*	♦ 6	♦ 10
7	♥ 10	♦ *K*	♦ 7	♥ 5

Plain sailing so far. But Declarer needs three more tricks. He has no hope of another trick from Dummy. He can only make the contract, therefore, if he can compel West to lead away from the guarded ♣ K.

Trick	*West*	*North*	*East*	*South*
8	♠ Q	♠ 6	♠ 5	♠ *K*

West throws his ♠ Q under Declarer's ♠ K. This *unblocking* play is the key to the defence. West, if he is put in with a Heart, can transfer the lead to his partner.

Trick	*West*	*North*	*East*	*South*
9	♥ *J*	♣ 5	♣ 3	♥ 9
10	♠ 8	♠ 9	♠ *J*	♣ 8

Declarer's downfall is now in sight.

Trick	*West*	*North*	*East*	*South*
11	♣ 9	♣ 6	♦ *9*	♣ 10
12	♣ *K*	♠ 7	♣ 6	♣ Q
13	♣ J	♠ 10	♣ 4	♣ *A*

The defence have taken five tricks and South is 'set' one trick. 100 points to E – W, though Declarer scores his 150 for Aces. South can make certain of his contract if, at trick 7, he discards, not a Heart, but a Club. Now West must discard a Club also, and

Declarer 'establishes' a second Club trick by leading the ♣ Ace and then another Club. He makes one Heart trick; four Diamond tricks; two Spades; and two Clubs.

SIXTEEN BOARDS AT DUPLICATE

Duplicate Bridge, played between two teams of four, is the form of Bridge adopted in international contests and in nearly all tournaments. The members of each team occupy the N – S seats in one room, and the E – W seats in another room. The 'boards' played are either pre-dealt or (more usually) dealt in one of the two rooms; each player, when he plays to a trick, places the card he has played in front of him; so the four hands as dealt can then be reassembled and transferred to the other room. Hence the luck of the deal is eliminated, for the cards held by North in one room will be those held by the opposing team's North in the other room; and the same holds good of the other three pairs of players. So Duplicate Bridge affords, in the long run, a fair test of the comparative skill of the two teams.

I say 'in the long run', for, while the luck of the deal is eliminated, a considerable element of luck remains. For example, what is theoretically the best contract may fail, owing to abnormal distribution, where a less sound contract succeeds; or the (theoretically) 'best' lead may fail against a slam contract where an indifferent lead succeeds in breaking it. Hence sheer luck may produce a favourable 'swing' of 1,000 points or more. But, under rigorously competitive conditions, the best teams will, in course of time, assert their superiority, so that, by and large, the duplicate game serves its purpose.

Normally, each deal is a separate event. The position as regards vulnerability is predetermined, in accordance with a prescribed sequence. For a non-vulnerable game, 300 points are scored; for a vulnerable game, 500 points; for a part-score, 50 points. The match score is determined either by the aggregate of points (as in the example which follows) or by 'match points': a somewhat arbitrary, but more 'scientific' method, which lies outside the scope of this book.

In this section we follow the fortunes of a short match of sixteen 'boards', played between the Tenace Club and Singleton's. These, of course, are purely imaginary institutions.

Throughout this match, the players are seated as under:

Mr Ruff
(*Tenace Club*)

N

Lady Grandcoup (*Singleton's*) W E Mr Thinkwell (*Singleton's*)

S

Mrs Yarborough
(*Tenace Club*)

Dr Diehard
(*Singleton's*)

N

Miss System (*Tenace Club*) W E Mr Flutter (*Tenace Club*)

S

Mrs Hazard
(*Singleton's*)

So, throughout the match, Mr Ruff holds the same cards as Dr Diehard; and similarly with the other players.

The sixteen hands presented are not at all typical. (I once played in a 32-board match in which seven of the 32 hands dealt were thrown in.) Here I have selected hands which are interesting in themselves, and which all illustrate one or more critical points in bidding or play. Moreover, for the reader's convenience, I have so arranged the cards that, in a high proportion of cases, South secures the final contract.

The beginner who wishes to improve his game cannot do better than take part in some of the innumerable duplicate contests organized by the various national Bridge unions, by county associations, and by clubs.

The addresses of these Bridge organizations, and some account of their current activities, will be found in the two monthly magazines, *The British Bridge World* and *Bridge*.

Board 1

Deceptive Lead against a Slam Contract

Score: love all *Dealer:* South

North
♠ J 10 8 2
♥ A
♦ K 8 3
♣ A K 7 6 4

West
♠ 6 5
♥ 10 3 2
♦ Q J 9 7 6 5
♣ 10 8

East
♠ 4 3
♥ K Q 9 8 7 4
♦ none
♣ Q J 9 5 2

South
♠ A K Q 9 7
♥ J 6 5
♦ A 10 4 2
♣ 3

THE BIDDING

Room 1

South Mrs Yarborough	*West* Lady Grandcoup	*North* Ruff	*East* Thinkwell
1 ♠	No	3 ♣	3 ♦
Double	No	No	3 ♥
3 ♠	No	4 ♥	No
5 ♦	No	6 ♠	Double

North's bid of Three Clubs is a force to game. Thinkwell, anticipating a high contract, makes a bluff bid of Three Diamonds to ensure a Diamond lead. Doubled, he retreats to Three Hearts. Now North shows his control of the Heart suit, and South her control of Diamonds. The contract of Six Spades is duly arrived at.

Thinkwell's double cannot be commended.

Room 2

South Mrs Hazard	*West* Miss System	*North* Diehard	*East* Flutter
1 ♠	No	3 ♣	3 ♥
3 ♠	No	4 N.T.	No
5 ♥	No	6 ♠	

In this Room the hand is bid on orthodox lines. Diehard's Four No Trump bid is 'Blackwood'; the Five Hearts response shows two Aces.

THE PLAY

Room 1. Lady Grandcoup made the cunning lead of the ♦ J. Mrs Yarborough played the ♦ K from Dummy, and Flutter, ruffing, returned a trump. South cannot now make the contract. Trumps are drawn; two Hearts can be ruffed in Dummy; but the Club suit fails to 'break' and there is no way of disposing of a losing Diamond. Had Mrs Yarborough stopped to think, she would have realized that East cannot have a genuine Three Diamonds bid, and that the lead of the ♦ J may well be 'bogus'. If she plays a low Diamond from Dummy she makes her contract.

N – S make 11 tricks   100 points to E – W (Singleton's)

Room 2. The ♥ 10 was led and the contract made without difficulty. Two Hearts were ruffed in Dummy and one of Declarer's losing Diamonds discarded on Dummy's ♣ K. So only one Diamond trick was lost.

N – S make 12 tricks   980 points to N – S (Singleton's)

(180 for tricks; 300 for game; 500 for the slam)

Match score: 1,080 points to Singleton's.

Where a team gains points in both rooms in a duplicate match there is said to be a 'swing'. In this short match Singleton's team, playing the better Bridge, secured a 'swing' on eight of the sixteen boards played. The Tenace Club had only two swings.

Board 2

An Impossible Contract, and a Dilemma in Defence

Score: North – South vulnerable *Dealer:* West

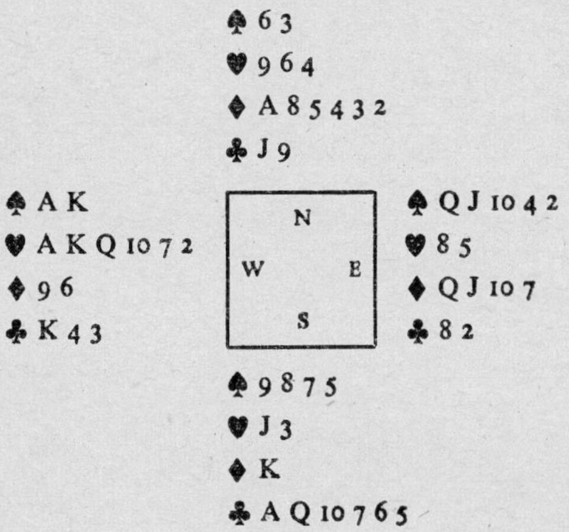

THE BIDDING

Room 1

West	*North*	*East*	*South*
Lady Grandcoup	Ruff	Thinkwell	Mrs Yarborough
1 ♥	No	1 ♠	No
3 ♥	No	3 N.T.	No
4 N.T.			

Lady Grandcoup bids badly here. She was playing the Two Club system, and should have opened with Two Hearts. Her partner then responds with Two No Trump (negative), and the final contract may be Four Hearts, Four Spades, or Three No Trump. West's Four No Trump is based on the unjustified assumption that East holds one or two high cards. Although suspecting that this is a slam try, East wisely closes the auction.

Room 2

West	*North*	*East*	*South*
Miss System	Diehard	Flutter	Mrs Hazard
2 ♥	No	2 N.T.	No
3 ♥	No	3 ♠	No
4 ♥			

This is the orthodox bidding of these hands.

THE PLAY

Room 1. South led the ♣ 7. Declarer (East) played Dummy's ♣ K (a somewhat hazardous venture) and ran off the next eight tricks (six Hearts and two Spades). But the remaining tricks fell to the adversaries.

E – W make 9 tricks 50 points to N – S (Tenace Club)

Room 2. West, somewhat luckily, made her contract. North led the ♠ 6. Declarer ran off all her winners.

Now she led the ♦ 6. North, suspecting a trap, put up the ♦ Ace - for, if the lead is from ♦ K 6, and North does not play the ♦ Ace, the trick is won in Dummy, and the ♦ K can be discarded on Dummy's ♠ Q. So the ♦ Ace and ♦ K fell together, and now N – S could only make the ♣ Ace.

E – W make 11 tricks 450 points to E – W (Tenace Club)

Score on this board: 500 to Tenace Club.
Match score: 580 to Singleton's.

The next Board (Board 3) introduces another slam hand; six slams in all are bid in the course of this short match. This is, of course, a higher proportion than is likely to occur in ordinary play. Beginners are apt to be chary of bidding their slams: they seem to think that there is some *mystique* in contracting for twelve tricks which can only come with experience. This is to be deprecated. If one knows that one has the cards, it's just as easy to make twelve tricks as to make eleven. Slams should, in my opinion, be bid whenever there is a reasonable chance of making them; not only because of the points that accrue, but because slam hands offer, as a rule, valuable experience in the planning of one's play.

Board 3

A Well-played Slam; Cute Defence to Three No Trump

Score: East – West vulnerable *Dealer:* North

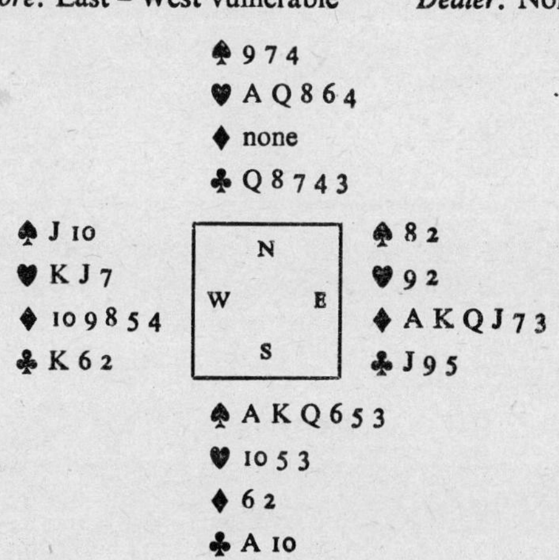

THE BIDDING

Room 1

North	*East*	*South*	*West*
Ruff	Thinkwell	Mrs Yarborough	Lady Grandcoup
1 ♥	2 ♦	3 ♠	4 ♦
No	No	4 ♠	No
5 ♦	No	6 ♠	

North's Five Diamonds shows control of the suit, and invites his partner to consider slam possibilities. South accepts the invitation.

Room 2

North	*East*	*South*	*West*
Diehard	Flutter	Mrs Hazard	Miss System
No	1 ♦	2 ♣	2 N.T.
3 ♣	3 N.T.	Double	

Mrs Hazard has recourse to a very hoary ruse. Anticipating a bid of No Trump by West, she conceals her real strength (Spades) and the No Trump bid materializes. Knowing that her partner will lead a Club, South can now safely risk a double.

Successful though South's gamble is, there is nothing wrong with her adversaries' bidding. They are unlucky in that both are strong in Diamonds.

THE PLAY

Room 1. The ♦ 10 was led. Mrs Yarborough played the hand well. She could see that, to make her slam, the ♥ K must lie with West and that the Hearts must be divided 3 – 2. She therefore provides against contingencies by giving up a Heart trick at the outset. Ruffing the ♦ 10 in Dummy, she led the ♥ 4; her ♥ 10 fell to West's ♥ J. Another Diamond was led and ruffed. Now Declarer drew trumps; finessed Hearts against West's ♥ K, and discarded her losing Club on one of her established Hearts.

N – S make 12 tricks 980 points to N – S (Tenace Club)

Room 2. South's ruse worked to perfection. A Club was led, and South ran off seven tricks. The lead of the ♥ 10 at trick 8 brought the total to nine. So Miss System was set five tricks, doubled – which more than counterbalances Mrs Yarborough's success in Room 1.

E – W make 4 tricks 1,400 points to N – S (Singleton's)

Score on this board: 420 points to Singleton's.
Match Score: 1,000 to Singleton's.

The bidding in Room 1 (Board 3) illustrates one use of what is, properly handled, a powerful weapon: the bid of an adversary's suit. It has various uses. A player holding a hand strong in every suit except Spades may bid Two Spades over an opening bid of One Spade. This is commonly regarded as a force to game, and invites partner to choose his suit. Or again (as here) an adversary's suit may be bid to show either a void or an Ace: in either case, first-round control.

Board 4

Crafty Defence Defeats a Slam Contract

Score: Both vulnerable *Dealer:* East

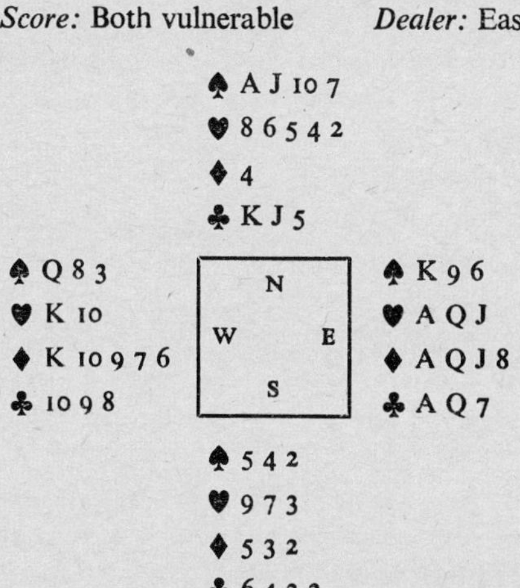

THE BIDDING

Room 1

East	*South*	*West*	*North*
Thinkwell	Mrs Yarborough	Lady Grandcoup	Ruff
3 N.T.	No	6 N.T.	–

East, with only three certain tricks, should be content with a Two No Trump opening. The final contract will be Three No Trump or Five Diamonds. Exchange the N – S hands, and it isn't too easy to make either of these contracts.

Room 2

East	*South*	*West*	*North*
Flutter	Mrs Hazard	Miss System	Diehard
2 N.T.	No	3 ♦	No
3 N.T.			

West bids correctly in showing her suit; since, for all she can tell, there may be a Diamond slam.

THE PLAY

Room 1. The ♣ 2 was opened, and Ruff, realizing that East must hold the ♣ Ace, cunningly played the ♣ J. Thinkwell, winning with the ♣ Q, led a Spade to the ♠ Q; Ruff allowed this card to win. Believing now that South held both ♣ K and ♠ Ace, Declarer, having cashed all his winners, led a Spade at the eleventh trick; South, he thought must then perforce lead from the minor tenace in Clubs. But, alas, North now made the ♠ Ace and ♠ J to set the contract one trick.

E – W make 11 tricks   100 points to N – S (Tenace Club)

Room 2. The defence showed no guile corresponding to Mr Ruff's, and Flutter, finessing Clubs twice, made 12 tricks.

E – W make 12 tricks   690 points to E – W (Tenace Club)

Score on this board: 790 to Tenace Club.
Match score: 210 to Singleton's.

Board 5

Creating an Entry

Score: North – South vulnerable   *Dealer:* South

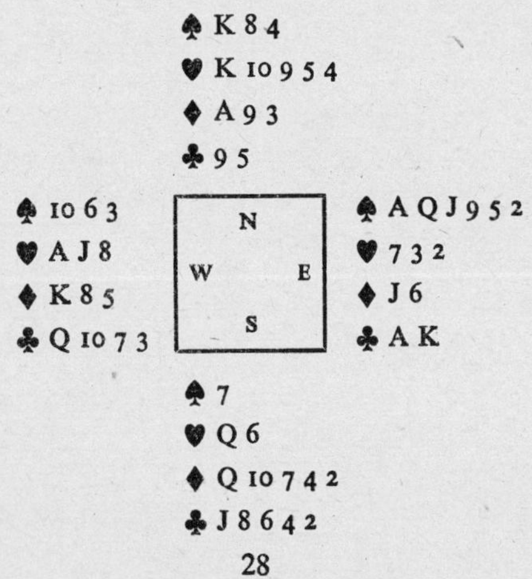

THE BIDDING

Room 1

South	*West*	*North*	*East*
Mrs Yarborough	Lady Grandcoup	Ruff	Thinkwell
No	No	No	1 ♠
No	2 N.T.	No	3 ♠
No	3 N.T.		

Many players, holding West's cards, would raise East's bid of Three Spades to Four Spades. It is a close decision. But West has no short suit, and 'tenace positions' in three suits; Three No Trump is therefore the better bid.

Room 2

South	*West*	*North*	*East*
Mrs Hazard	Miss System	Diehard	Flutter
No	No	1 ♥	2 ♠
No	2 N.T.	No	3 ♠
No	4 ♠		

North's bid of One Heart (vulnerable) is bad. It might lead to a heavy penalty. As it happens, however, it serves the purpose of telling South which suit to lead.

THE PLAY

Room 1. Lady Grandcoup, not without anxiety, contrived to land her contract. The ♥ 10 was opened; South played the ♥ Q, and, when the ♥ Ace was held up, continued the suit. The ♥ Ace was held up again and Ruff established his suit. Everything now turned on the Spade finesse. At trick 4 Declarer led the ♠ 10 and, when North played low, finessed. Another Spade followed. Six Spade tricks, two Clubs and the ♥ Ace gave Lady Grandcoup her nine tricks.

E – W make 9 tricks   400 points to E – W (Singleton's)

Room 2. The same nine tricks were made as in Room 1 – which makes all the difference in a ten-trick contract! South led the ♥ Q; Flutter won in Dummy and (as in Room 1) led Dummy's ♠ 10. Declarer cashed his trump winners and the ♣ Ace, K; but he has no entry for the ♣ Q stranded in Dummy. However, he now plays, the contract is set one trick.

The contract can be made if, placing the ♠ K with North, Declarer concedes a trump trick. At trick 2 he leads a low trump from Dummy. He wins with his ♠ Q; leads out the ♠ Ace; cashes the ♣ Ace and ♣ K; and throws the lead to North with a Spade. Now, whether North next leads a Heart or a Diamond, Dummy's hand must take two tricks. But only an expert player would have the foresight to gauge the situation correctly.

E – W make 9 tricks 50 points to N – S (Singleton's)

Score on this board: 450 to Singleton's.
Match score: 660 to Singleton's.

Board 6

Errors in Bidding

Score: East – West vulnerable *Dealer:* West

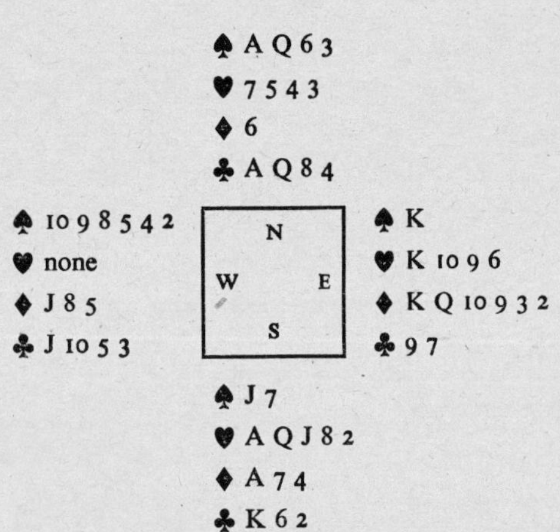

THE BIDDING

Room 1

West	*North*	*East*	*South*
Lady Grandcoup	Ruff	Thinkwell	Mrs Yarborough
No	1 ♠	2 ♦	2 ♥
No	4 N.T.	No	5 ♥
No	6 ♥	Double	

East's double is bad in principle and in practice proves disastrous. It tells Declarer that the adverse Hearts are massed to her right. This enables her to plan her play successfully.

Room 2

West	*North*	*East*	*South*
Miss System	Diehard	Flutter	Mrs Hazard
No	No	1 ♥	No
1 ♠	No	2 ♦	No
2 ♠	No	2 N.T.	No
3 ♠	Double	4 ♦	Double

Here E – W pile error upon error. After North's 'trap' pass, East opens with a 'funny' bid of One Heart: pointless at any score, and highly dangerous when vulnerable. East, having already deceived his partner, should have left One Spade alone; this might well have been the final contract! But instead, East lures his partner to destruction. His Two No Trump bid (the sequel to his own misleading opening) is particularly foolish.

THE PLAY

Room 1. Thanks to East's misguided double, Mrs Yarborough made all thirteen tricks. The ♦ J was led, won with Declarer's ♦ Ace. She entered Dummy by ruffing a Diamond; led the ♥ 7; and, when East played the ♥ 6, played low. A second finesse followed; then a Club was played to Dummy's ♣ Ace and the Heart finessed once more. Now the ♥ Ace dropped the ♥ K. The lead of the ♣ K at the next trick, to which East followed, enabled Declarer to deduce that Thinkwell held the Singleton

♠ K. So the ♠ 7 was led and the ♠ Ace played from Dummy. The last four tricks are obvious.

N – S make 13 tricks   1,310 points to N – S (Tenace)

Room 2. The luckless Flutter made just five tricks – all in trumps. Mrs Hazard made the obvious lead of the ♦ Ace, followed by another Diamond. Declarer should have won in his own hand, and ruffed a Heart in Dummy. Instead, he won in Dummy and tried to steal a Spade trick. But Diehard went up with the ♠ Ace, and put his partner in with a Club to kill Dummy's last trump.

E – W make 5 tricks   1,400 points to N – S (Singleton's)

Score on this board: 90 points to Singleton's.
Match Score: 750 to Singleton's.

Board 7

A Defensive 'Swindle'

Score: Both vulnerable   *Dealer:* North

West		East
	♠ J 10 9 5 ♥ Q 10 5 4 ♦ A Q J ♣ A 2	
♠ Q 3 2 ♥ A K 8 ♦ K 9 7 4 ♣ 10 8 5	N W E S	♠ 7 ♥ J 9 3 ♦ 8 6 5 2 ♣ 9 7 6 4 3
	♠ A K 8 6 4 ♥ 7 6 2 ♦ 10 3 ♣ K Q J	

THE BIDDING

Room 1

North	*East*	*South*	*West*
Ruff	Thinkwell	Mrs Yarborough	Lady Grandcoup
1 N.T.	No	3 N.T.	–

South, having adequate support for No Trump, does not disclose her strength in Spades. Why give free information to the adversaries? And why, without some strong reason, contract for ten tricks instead of nine?

Room 2

North	*East*	*South*	*West*
Diehard	Flutter	Mrs Hazard	Miss System
1 N.T.	No	3 ♠	No
4 ♠			

Mrs Hazard – wrongly, as has been hinted – prefers a Spade contract to No Trump. Her bid of Three Spades, moreover, is barely warranted by her holding.

THE PLAY

Room 1. The play presented little difficulty. Thinkwell led a Club. Declarer won in his own hand; led ♠ J, and finessed. Lady Grandcoup won with the ♠ Q; her best return is the ♥ 8, but she made things simple for Ruff by leading the ♦ 4. He finessed; cashed four Spade winners and two Clubs, and again finessed Diamonds for ten tricks. But a better player than Ruff would not have taken this second Diamond finesse. If East produces the ♦ K, Declarer may be one down on his contract.

N – S make 10 tricks 630 points to N – S (Tenace)

Room 2. Mrs Hazard was neatly outmanoeuvred by Flutter. Miss System led the ♥ K, and Flutter observing Dummy's ♥ Q 10 5 4 – began what looked like a 'peter' by dropping the ♥ 9. The ♥ Ace was next led, and Flutter played the ♥ 3. When, at trick 3, the ♥ 8 appeared, Declarer was in a quandary. Apparently Flutter was now void of Hearts. So Mrs Hazard played Dummy's ♥ 10, and the ♥ J took the trick. And, of course, West's ♠ Q set the contract.

N – S make 9 tricks   100 points to E – W (Tenace)

Score on this board: 730 points to Tenace.
Match score: 20 points to Singleton's.

Board 8

Timid Bidding; Imaginative Play

Score: love-all   *Dealer:* East

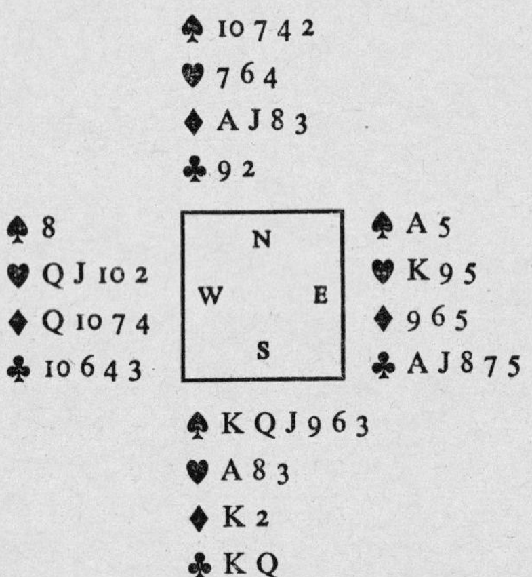

THE BIDDING

Room 1

East	*South*	*West*	*North*
Thinkwell	Mrs Yarborough	Lady Grandcoup	Ruff
1 ♣	2 ♠	3 ♣	–

The Tenace Club players bid pusillanimously. Mr Ruff (no vulnerable) can well afford to bid Three Spades. And Mr Yarborough would be risking little in bidding Three Spades her self. E – W buy a very cheap contract.

Room 2

East	*South*	*West*	*North*
Flutter	Mrs Hazard	Miss System	Diehard
1 ♣	3 ♠	No	4 ♠

Mrs Hazard signals the possibility of game, and silences the opposition, by a pre-emptive Three Spades overcall. Dr Diehard's hand is well worth his raise to Four Spades.

THE PLAY

Room 1. The ♠ K was led. Declarer, winning with the ♠ Ace, led the ♣ Ace followed by another trump. Mrs Yarborough, unwilling to lead a Diamond, played another Spade. Declarer ruffed in Dummy and led a low Diamond. Ruff played the ♦ J, but there was now no chance of breaking the contract. This would only have been effected by the lead of the ♦ K at trick 4.

E – W make 9 tricks   110 points to E – W (Singleton's)

Room 2. Mrs Hazard played well to land her ten tricks in Spades. The ♥ Q was led and won with Declarer's ♥ Ace. If, now, trumps are led, the contract must fail: E – W will make the ♠ Ace, the ♣ Ace, and two Hearts. So Mrs Hazard took her only chance of getting rid of a loser. Postponing the lead of trumps, she played the ♦ K at trick 2 and then took the Diamond finesse. On the ♦ Ace she discarded a Heart, thus making sure of her contract.

N – S make 10 tricks   420 points to N – S (Singleton's)

Score on this board: 530 points to Singleton's.
Match score: 550 to Singleton's.

This last Board (Board 8) emphasizes a point which cannot be stressed too often: the necessity to *plan one's play* (as Declarer) before playing from Dummy to the first trick. In this situation a 'huddle' is always excusable. Mrs Hazard (Room 2) began by counting her potential losers: One Spade; Two Hearts; One Club. She could only get rid of one of them by the line of play which she adopted.

Board 9

Two Difficult Contracts

Score: East – West vulnerable   *Dealer:* South

	♠ K ♥ 10 8 7 6 4 ♦ K Q J 6 ♣ Q 8 7	
♠ Q ♥ K 3 ♦ A 10 9 8 5 4 2 ♣ K J 9	N W E S	♠ 7 6 4 3 2 ♥ 9 5 ♦ 7 3 ♣ A 6 4 3
	♠ A J 10 9 8 5 ♥ A Q J 2 ♦ none ♣ 10 5 2	

THE BIDDING

Room 1

South	*West*	*North*	*East*
Mrs Yarborough	Lady Grandcoup	Ruff	Thinkwell
1 ♠	2 ♦	Double	No
2 ♠	No	2 N.T.	No
3 ♥	No	4 ♥	

North's double of Two Diamonds is a doubtful proposition. West can make this contract: North therefore throws upon his partner the onus of taking the double out. Not everyone would have Mrs Yarborough's strength of mind. Disliking No Trump, Mrs Yarborough next makes a preference bid in Hearts, and Ruff has no hesitation in bidding game.

Room 2

South	*West*	*North*	*East*
Mrs Hazard	Miss System	Diehard	Flutter
3 ♠	No	4 ♠	-

Mrs Hazard, non-vulnerable against vulnerable opponents, decides to pre-empt. Since her bid suggests that she does not need trump support, Dr Diehard promptly produces a game contract. Flutter, holding five small trumps, has the good sense not to double.

THE PLAY

Room 1. The contract looks almost foolproof, but Lady Grandcoup found the one lead which breaks it. There are obvious objections to a Diamond lead, a Heart lead, or a Spade; so Lady Grandcoup tried the ♣ J. This happy inspiration gave her side four tricks: three in Clubs and the ♥ K.

N – S make 9 tricks 50 points to E – W (Singleton's)

Room 2. The same lead (♣ J) would, of course, have set Four Spades. But Miss System, knowing nothing of North's Diamond strength, opened with the ♦ Ace. Trumping the opening lead, Declarer entered Dummy with the ♠ K; led the ♦ K, and discarded a Club. The ♦ Q followed. East ruffed and Declarer discarded a second Club. Flutter now made the mistake of leading a Heart, thus losing an all-important tempo. Declarer finessed; West won with the ♥ K and cashed the ♣ K, but now Declarer was home. A Club lead at trick 4 sets the contract.

N – S make 10 tricks 420 points to N – S (Singleton's)

Score on this board: 470 to Singleton's.
Match score: 1,020 to Singleton's.

Board 10

When Not to Hold Up at No Trump

Score: Both sides vulnerable *Dealer:* West

	North	
	♠ A 6 4	
	♥ 8 3	
	♦ Q 5 3	
	♣ Q J 7 6 4	
West		**East**
♠ Q 5	N	♠ 10 9 8 3 2
♥ A J 9 7 6 2	W E	♥ 10 5
♦ J 10 2	S	♦ 8 7 6 4
♣ K 5		♣ 8 3
	South	
	♠ K J 7	
	♥ K Q 4	
	♦ A K 9	
	♣ A 10 9 2	

THE BIDDING

Room 1

West	*North*	*East*	*South*
Lady Grandcoup	Ruff	Thinkwell	Mrs Yarborough
1 ♥	No	No	2 N.T.
No	3 N.T.		

This is more or less routine bidding and calls for no special comment.

Room 2

West	*North*	*East*	*South*
Miss System	Diehard	Flutter	Mrs Hazard
1 ♥	No	No	2 ♥
No	3 ♣	No	3 N.T.

I prefer the bidding in Room 1. South's take-out overcall in Hearts virtually commits her side to a contract at the level of three; which – if North's hand is trickless – may be doubled and severely penalized.

THE PLAY

Room 1. Mrs Yarborough made a hash of her contract. The ♥ 7 was led; the ♥ 8 played from Dummy; Thinkwell produced the ♥ 10. Now Declarer decided to hold up her ♥ K, Q, and played low. Thinkwell returned his ♥ 5; the ♥ Q fell to West's ♥ Ace, and another Heart lead cleared the suit for West. Entering Dummy with the ♠ Ace, Declarer led the ♣ Q and finessed – unsuccessfully – against East. Lady Grandcoup, winning, ran off her three established Hearts to set the contract two tricks.

Had it been necessary to take the Club finesse, not against East, but against West, the hold-up would have been correct; for there is a reasonable chance that East, even if he has the ♣ K, will have no third Heart to lead.

N – S make 7 tricks   200 points to E – W (Singleton's)

Room 2. The opening lead was again the ♥ 7, but here Declarer played the hand correctly. Mrs Hazard won the first trick, crossed over to Dummy with a Spade, and took the Club finesse. West won and led the ♥ Ace, but Declarer had still a stopper in the suit. She thus made her contract and two overtricks.

N – S make 11 tricks   660 points to N – S (Singleton's)

Score on this board: 860 to Singleton's.
Match score: 1,880 to Singleton's.

Mrs Hazard's bid in Room 2 is an example of the overcall of an opponent's suit to signify a game-going hand. But here (as mentioned) so strong a bid is dangerous, because partner *must* make some response, and may be obliged to make it on a virtually trickless hand. The result might have been a swingeing penalty.

Board 11

Bad Bidding and Good Defence

Score: love all *Dealer:* North

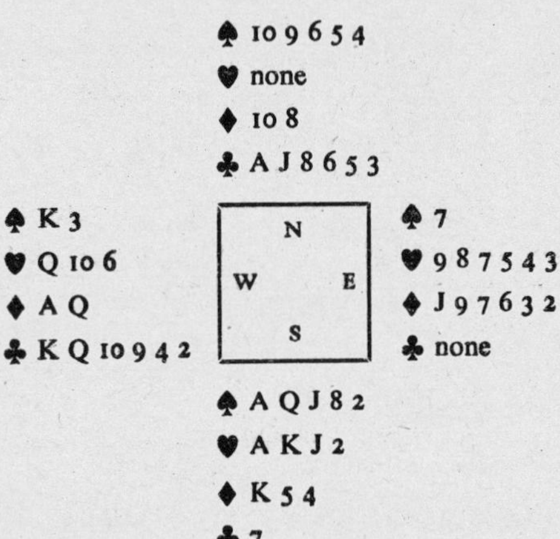

THE BIDDING

Room 1

North	*East*	*South*	*West*
Ruff	Thinkwell	Mrs Yarborough	Lady Grandcoup
1 ♣	Double	Redouble	No
No	1 ♥	1 ♠	2 ♥
2 ♠	3 ♥	Double	

It is on 'unbalanced' hands of this type that the swings at Duplicate occur. Each side is trying to outwit the other, and some 'funny' bidding results. North should not make any opening bid. East's take-out double is hazardous – what happens if West's strength is in Spades? – and South's redouble, in preference to a strong Spade bid, gives North a completely false picture of South's hand. North naturally thinks that his partner holds most of the missing Clubs. Now East unmasks his tenuous Heart battery; South continues to underplay her Spades, and North – conscious that his first bid was deceptive – gives only minimum support. The result of all this is that, when Three Hearts is bid, Mrs Yarborough thinks she has the double of a lifetime. North, with a virtually worthless hand on which he has already made two bids, should, of course, take the double into Three Spades.

Room 2

North	*East*	*South*	*West*
Diehard	Flutter	Mrs Hazard	Miss System
No	No	1 ♠	Double
4 ♠			

This is better bidding, though it is hard to explain why Miss System prefers a take-out double to a straightforward Two Clubs.

THE PLAY

Room 1. South should, of course, have opened with the ♥ K, but she elected to lead her singleton Club. Dummy's ♣ K drew North's ♣ Ace, and Declarer ruffed. Thinkwell next led a Diamond and finessed Dummy's ♦ Q. The ♣ Q followed, on which Thinkwell discarded his ♠ 7. Mrs Yarborough ruffed and now (too late) took three rounds of trumps, the third won by Dummy's ♥ Q. The ♦ Ace was played; then a Club which Declarer ruffed. Conceding a Diamond, he laid down his cards; he had made just nine tricks and his contract.

E – W make 9 tricks   530 points to E – W (Singleton's)

Room 2. The ♣ K was led. Mrs Hazard, after a protracted huddle, played low from Dummy. This play makes certain of the contract if West's ♣ K is allowed to hold the trick. But the hold-up of the ♣ Ace gave Flutter the key to Declarer's intentions. Ruffing the ♣ K with his solitary trump (what point is there in conserving it?) he shot back a Diamond at trick 2 to defeat the contract by one trick. A good example of imaginative card-reading.

N – S make 9 tricks   50 points to E – W (Tenace)

Score on this board: 480 points to Singleton's.
Match score: 2,360 to Singleton's.

Board 12

Mrs Yarborough was Lucky

Score: North – South vulnerable *Dealer:* East

West		North / South		East
		North		
		♠ K 10 5 3		
		♥ J 10 7 4		
		♦ Q J 5 2		
		♣ 9		
♠ 8 2				♠ Q 6
♥ A Q 6 3				♥ 9 8 5
♦ 10 9				♦ 8 7 4 3
♣ K Q J 7 4				♣ A 10 5 2
		South		
		♠ A J 9 7 4		
		♥ K 2		
		♦ A K 6		
		♣ 8 6 3		

THE BIDDING

Room 1

East	*South*	*West*	*North*
Thinkwell	Mrs Yarborough	Lady Grandcoup	Ruff
No	1 ♠	3 ♣	3 ♠
5 ♣	5 ♠		

Mrs Yarborough's Five Spades is a precarious contract: it would be better bidding to accept the Club sacrifice, and double. Lady Grandcoup must be set three tricks. Mrs Yarborough makes her contract, but this does not justify her bidding.

Room 2

East	*South*	*West*	*North*
Flutter	Mrs Hazard	Miss System	Diehard
No	1 ♠	3 ♣	4 ♠

The 'optimum' contract is East's Five Club sacrifice (Room 1). Flutter fails to rise to the occasion.

THE PLAY

Room 1. The ♣ K was led. West then switched to the ♦ 10. Declarer won with the ♦ Ace; ruffed a Club in Dummy; returned to her hand with the ♠ Ace and ruffed another Club. Now the ♠ K was led out, dropping East's ♠ Q, and one of Declarer's Hearts was discarded on the fourth round of Diamonds.

N – S make 11 tricks 650 points to N – S (Tenace)

Room 2. Again the ♣ K was led. But Flutter (more alert than Thinkwell in Room 1) overtook with the ♣ Ace and led back a Heart to West's major tenace. On getting in, Declarer led out the ♠ Ace and then (unsuccessfully) finessed the ♠ J against West.

N – S make 9 tricks 100 points to E – W (Tenace)

Score on this board: 750 points to Tenace.
Match score: 1,610 to Singleton's.

Board 13

Failure of a Slam Contract

Score: Both vulnerable *Dealer:* South

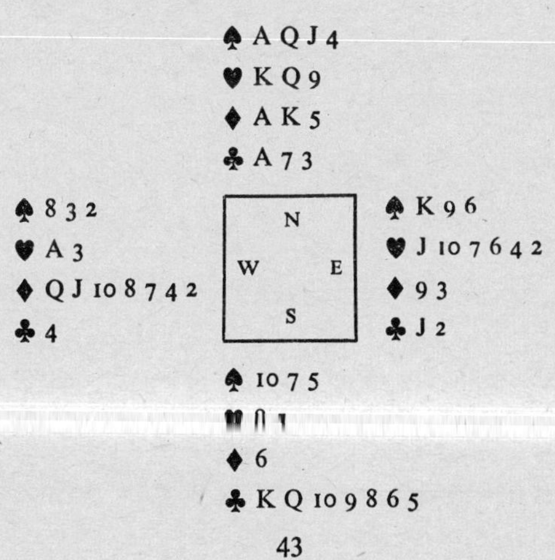

THE BIDDING

Room 1

South	*West*	*North*	*East*
Mrs Yarborough	Lady Grandcoup	Ruff	Thinkwell
No	No	2 N.T.	No
5 ♣	No	6 ♣	

Mrs Yarborough need not have rushed matters. If she bids Three Clubs her partner is pretty sure to bid again. However, the optimum contract is attained.

Room 2

South	*West*	*North*	*East*
Mrs Hazard	Miss System	Diehard	Flutter
No	3 ♦	Double	–

Miss System's pre-emptive Three Diamonds has merit: she has six certain tricks, and, if her partner has none, there must be a slam for the adversaries. Diehard doubles for penalties (for a take-out he would bid Three No Trump).

THE PLAY

Room 1. Mrs Yarborough failed to make her contract. The ♦ Q was led; she won the trick; drew trumps; and finessed unsuccessfully against the ♠ K. But the contract could, and should, have been made. After drawing trumps, Declarer leads a Heart. West must go up with the ♥ Ace. Now Spades can be discarded on the ♦ K and ♥ Q, and it is not necessary to take the finesse at all.

N – S make 11 tricks 100 points to E – W (Singleton's)

Room 2. Miss System made 7 tricks: which tricks these were is obvious. A distinct coup for the Tenace Club had Mrs Yarborough played correctly in Room 1.

E – W make 7 tricks 500 points to N – S (Singleton's)

Score on this board: 600 points to Singleton's.
Match score: 2,210 to Singleton's.

Board 14

A Well-bid No Trump Contract

Score: Love all *Dealer:* West

West		North / South		East
		♠ A 5		
		♥ 9 8 3		
		♦ A K J 6		
		♣ K J 8 5		
♠ K J 6 4 2		N		♠ Q 8
♥ K J 6		W E		♥ 7 4
♦ 9 4		S		♦ 10 7 5 3 2
♣ A 9 3				♣ 10 6 4 2
		♠ 10 9 7 3		
		♥ A Q 10 5 2		
		♦ Q 8		
		♣ Q 7		

THE BIDDING

Room 1

West	*North*	*East*	*South*
Lady Grandcoup	Ruff	Thinkwell	Mrs Yarborough
No	1 N.T.	No	2 ♥
No	3 ♥	No	4 ♥

Mr Ruff's is not a good Three Hearts bid. His partner may only hold (say) J *x x x x* of the suit. Two No Trump would be better; Mrs Yarborough can then bid Three No Trump if (as in this case) her strength in Hearts is adequate.

Room 2

West	*North*	*East*	*South*
Miss System	Diehard	Flutter	Mrs Hazard
No	1 ♦	No	1 ♥
No	2 ♣	No	2 N.T.
No	3 N.T.		

This, in my opinion, is unexceptionable bidding.

THE PLAY

Room 1. The ♠ 4 was led, and West – inevitably – made one Spade trick, the ♣ Ace, and two trumps, to set the contract one trick.

N – S make 9 tricks 50 points to E – W (Singleton's)

Room 2. Mrs Hazard played well to land her contract. The ♠ 4 was led and Declarer (correctly) went up with Dummy's ♠ Ace. If she fails to do so, she cannot stop the suit twice. Flutter threw his ♠ Q, to avoid blocking the suit. Declarer now led Dummy's ♣ 5, since two Club tricks can be established while the Spade suit is still held. Miss System, winning, continued Spades. Declarer won the fourth round of the suit and now cashed two Clubs, four Diamonds and the ♥ Ace to give her nine tricks.

N – S make 9 tricks 400 points to N – S (Singleton's)

Score on this board: 450 points to Singleton's.
Match Score: 2,660 to Singleton's.

Board 15

Ducking Play

Score: North – South vulnerable *Dealer:* North

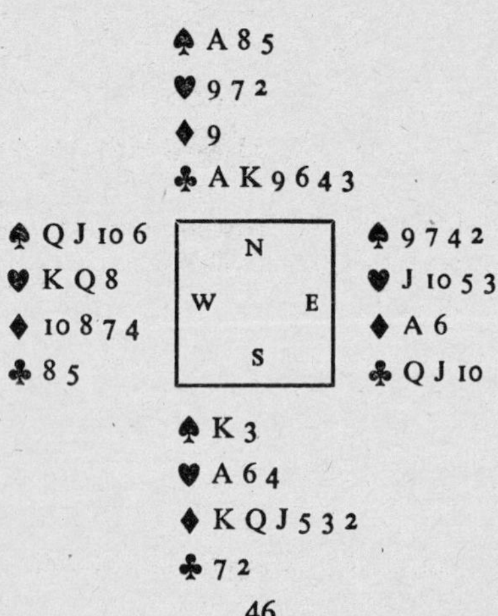

THE BIDDING

Room 1

North	*East*	*South*	*West*
Ruff	Thinkwell	Mrs Yarborough	Lady Grandcoup
1 ♣	No	3 ♦	–

Mrs Yarborough's Three Diamond bid puzzled her partner. If she has defensive strength, why not *Two* Diamonds? Ruff decided that to bid again on his unbalanced hand might land him in unnecessary difficulties.

Room 2

North	*East*	*South*	*West*
Diehard	Flutter	Mrs Hazard	Miss System
1 ♣	No	1 ♦	No
2 ♣	No	2 N.T.	No
3 N.T.			

This is more constructive bidding. After two positive bids from his partner Dr Diehard can reasonably contract for game.

THE PLAY

Room 1. Mrs Yarborough's contract cannot fail, even at Double Dummy. She loses two trump tricks and two Hearts.

N – S make 9 tricks   110 points to N – S (Tenace)

Room 2. The best lead, as the cards lie, is the ♥ K, but Miss System chose the ♠ Q. Declarer handled a difficult contract admirably. She put up Dummy's ♠ Ace and immediately led the ♦ 9. East ducked, of course, and Declarer, winning in her own hand, led a Club and played low from Dummy. East won and led a Spade, but Declarer was now home, taking 5 Club tricks, two Spades, one Diamond and the ♥ Ace.

N – S make 9 tricks   600 points to N – S (Singleton's)

Score on this board: 490 points to Singleton's.
Match Score: 3,150 to Singleton's.

Board 16

Trump Coup Lands a Slam Contract

Score: East – West vulnerable *Dealer:* East

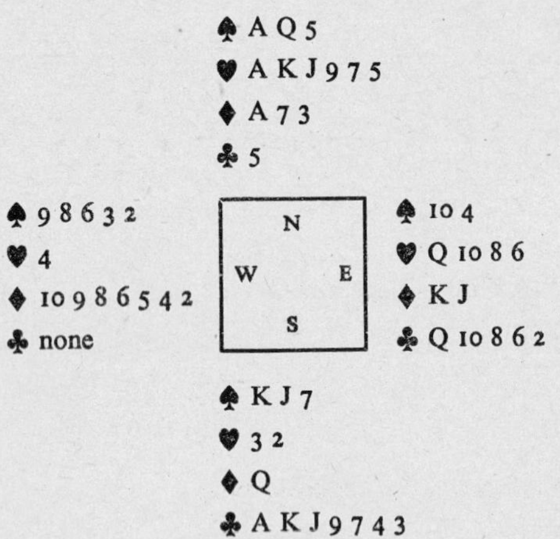

THE BIDDING

Room 1

East	*South*	*West*	*North*
Thinkwell	Mrs Yarborough	Lady Grandcoup	Ruff
No	1 ♣	No	2 ♥
No	3 ♣	No	4 N.T.
No	5 ♦	No	6 ♥
Double			

This final deal shows unbalanced distribution; the strength massed in the N – S hands; and Nemesis lying in wait for North. It illustrates also the element of luck which the mechanics of Duplicate Bridge do not eliminate. Exchange the E – W hands, and North cannot miss his Six Hearts contract, while South would come hopelessly to grief in Six Clubs. Six Hearts, as bid in Room 1, is, in fact, the better of the two contracts.

Room 2

East	*South*	*West*	*North*
Flutter	Mrs Hazard	Miss System	Diehard
No	1 ♣	No	2 ♥
No	3 ♣	No	3 ♥
No	4 ♣	No	4 N.T.
No	5 ♦	No	6 ♣
Double			

Mrs Hazard's obstinate insistence on her Club suit almost suggests the exercise of a sixth sense! East's double looks cast-iron. But (unlike Thinkwell in Room 1) he is seated on the wrong side of the Declarer.

THE PLAY

Room 1. Thinkwell made the inspired lead of a small Club. Lady Grandcoup, of course, ruffed; and – since nothing could prevent the loss of two trump tricks – the unfortunate Ruff was set 300 points.

N – S make 10 tricks 300 points to E – W (Singleton's)

Room 2. Mrs Hazard atoned for her erratic bidding by admirable play.

Trick	Miss System *West*	Diehard *North*	Flutter *East*	Mrs Hazard *South*
1	♦ 10	♦ *A*	♦ J	♦ Q
2	♦ 2	♦ 3	♦ K	♣ 3
3	♥ 4	♥ *K*	♥ 6	♥ 2
4	♦ 4	♣ 5	♣ 2	♣ 9
5	♠ 5	♥ *A*	♥ 8	♥ 3
6	♦ 5	♥ J	♥ Q	♣ 4
7	♠ 3	♠ *A*	♠ 4	♠ 7
8	♦ 6	♥ 9	♥ 10	♣ 7
9	♠ 6	♠ 5	♠ 10	♠ *K*
10	♠ 8	♠ Q	♣ 6	♠ J

and South must win the last three tricks.

N – S make 12 tricks. 1,090 points to Singleton's.

Score on this Board: 1,390 to Singleton's.

Match Score: 4,540 to Singleton's.

The summarized score of the match follows.

SCORE SHEET OF THE DUPLICATE MATCH

T= Tenace Club   S= Singleton's

Board	Vul:	Room 1					Room 2					Net Score		Running Score	
		Con't	Dec:	R'lt	T	S	Con't	Dec:	R'lt	T	S	T	S	T	S
1	neither	6 ♠ d	S	− 1	—	100	6 ♠	S	+ 6	—	980	—	1,080	—	1,080
2	N − S	4 N.T.	E	− 1	50	—	4 ♥	W	+ 5	450	—	500	—	—	580
3	E − W	6 ♠	S	+ 6	980	—	3 N.T. d	W	− 5	—	1,400	—	420	—	1,000
4	both	6 N.T.	E	− 1	100	—	3 N.T.	E	+ 6	690	—	790	—	—	210
5	N − S	3 N.T.	W	+ 3	—	400	4 ♠	E	− 1	—	50	—	450	—	660
6	E − W	6 ♥ d	S	+ 7	1,310	—	4 ♦ d	E	− 5	—	1,400	—	90	—	750
7	both	3 N.T.	N	+ 4	630	—	4 ♠	S	− 1	100	—	730	—	—	20
8	neither	3 ♣	E	+ 3	—	110	4 ♠	S	+ 4	—	420	—	530	—	550
9	E − W	4 ♥	S	− 1	—	50	4 ♠	S	+ 4	—	420	—	470	—	1,020
10	both	3 N.T.	S	− 2	—	200	3 N.T.	S	+ 5	—	660	—	860	—	1,880
11	neither	3 ♥ d	E	+ 3	—	530	4 ♠	S	− 1	50	—	—	480	—	2,360
12	N − S	5 ♠	S	+ 5	650	—	4 ♠	S	− 1	100	—	750	—	—	1,610
13	both	6 ♣	S	− 1	—	100	3 ♦ d	W	− 2	—	500	—	600	—	2,210
14	neither	4 ♥	S	− 1	—	50	3 N.T.	S	+ 3	—	400	—	450	—	2,660
15	N − S	3 ♦	S	+ 3	110	—	3 N.T.	S	+ 3	—	600	—	490	—	3,150
16	E − W	6 ♥ d	N	− 2	—	300	6 ♣ d	S	+ 6	—	1,090	—	1,390	—	4,540

Laws of Contract Bridge

The official Laws of Contract Bridge run to about 10,000 words and it would be a waste of space to reproduce them here. But there are some Laws which every player should know:

REDEAL. There must be a redeal if the cards are not properly dealt, e.g. one player picks up a card belonging to one of the others.

MISSING CARD. If a player has a card too few (e.g. he has dropped one on the floor) the missing card, when found, is deemed to be his.

IRREGULARITIES. Any player (including Dummy, unless Dummy has looked at another player's cards) may draw attention to an irregularity, and may ask for, or give, information as to the appropriate penalty.

ENFORCEMENT OF PENALTY. Either opponent may enforce a penalty against Declarer, but opponents may not consult as to what penalty (if there is more than one) should be enforced.

CHANGING A CALL. A player must stand by any call he has made (provided it is a legitimate call) unless he changes it in the same breath.

INSUFFICIENT BID. If a player makes an insufficient bid (e.g. Two Clubs over Two Spades) he must substitute a sufficient bid or pass.

If he makes the lowest sufficient bid in the suit already mentioned (in this case, Three Clubs) there is no penalty.

If he makes any other sufficient bid (e.g. Two No Trump) his partner may take no further part in the auction.

If he passes, his partner may take no further part in the auction, and, if the offending side secure the contract, Declarer may demand, or forbid, the lead of a particular suit.

CALLING OUT OF TURN. If a player says 'No Bid' out of turn, he must pass when next it is his turn to call. Thenceafter, if the auction continues, he may call. The auction reverts to the player whose turn it is to call.

If any call, other than a pass, is made out of turn, the auction reverts to the player whose turn it is to call, and the offender's partner may take no further part in the auction.

REVIEWING THE AUCTION. A player may ask for a call to be repeated. When it is his turn to call, he may ask what the previous bids were, and also after the auction has closed and before the opening lead.

DUMMY'S RIGHTS. Dummy takes no active part in the play (e.g. he should not play a card, however obvious the play may be) and should refrain from comment, except that:

(*a*) he may give or obtain information on any question of fact or law.

(*b*) may question any player who appears to have revoked. (He should automatically say to his partner 'No Heart, partner?' etc., to guard against a revoke by Declarer.)

(*c*) he may draw attention to an irregularity, and may warn his partner if the latter is about to commit one.

For example, Dummy may correct his partner if the latter is about to lead from the wrong hand.

PREMATURE LEAD OR PLAY BY A DEFENDER. If a defender leads to the next trick before his partner has played, or plays out of turn before his partner, Declarer may call on the offender to play his highest or lowest card of the suit led, or a card of another specified suit.

LEAD OUT OF TURN. This may be treated as the correct lead. If Declarer has led out of turn from the wrong hand, he can be made to lead from the correct hand, and must (if possible) lead a card of the same suit. If a defender leads out of turn when the lead is with Declarer or Dummy, the card led out of turn becomes a penalty card. If it was the other defender's turn to lead, Declarer may either forbid the lead of the suit, or may treat the card led out of turn as a penalty card.

PENALTY CARD. This is laid face upwards on the table, and must be played at the first opportunity.

Any card improperly exposed by either defender becomes a penalty card. There is no penalty against Declarer for showing any or all of his cards. But if he lays down all his cards, by inference claiming the rest of the tricks, he may be called on to explain how he proposes to play the hand.

WHEN DUMMY BECOMES DECLARER. If the wrong defender

leads to the first trick, and Declarer thoughtlessly spreads his hand as Dummy, Dummy becomes Declarer.

REVOKE (*i.e. failure to follow suit when one is able to do so*)

(*a*) if the revoke is *established* (i.e. the trick has been turned and the lead made to the next trick) two tricks are transferred to the non-offending side if these are tricks won after the revoke. One trick only, if but one is won after the revoke. No penalty, if the revoking side wins no more tricks. The revoke trick ranks as a trick won after the revoke.

(*b*) The above rules only apply to the first eleven tricks. For a revoke in the twelfth trick, there is no penalty.

(*c*) If the revoke is not established, a card of the proper suit is substituted for the revoke card. The revoke card, if played by a defender, becomes a penalty card.

Whist and its Derivatives

Whist – Sarah Battle's game – was, throughout the nineteenth century, the principal game of the West End clubs. Its mechanics are essentially those of Contract Bridge, except that there is no Dummy; one has to deduce, not how 26 cards are distributed, but how 39 cards are distributed. There is no No Trump call, and the trump suit is determined arbitrarily. To learn to play Whist really well demands a high order of intelligence, and a great deal of experience; but it is no longer taken seriously; the Whist of our village Whist Drives is little more than a gamble.

Whist was killed, as a serious game, partly by the ever-growing complexity of its conventions (the celebrated 'Cavendish', dictator of the cards clubs in the eighties, gives eight pages of leads which players were expected to memorize); partly by the meteoric rise of Bridge about the turn of the century. The original Bridge had no competitive bidding element; the dealer nominated the trump suit or left it to his partner. Auction Bridge – similar to Contract, except that one could make game or slam without having to contract for it – came in about 1910; Contract Bridge, the game we now know (except that its rules have been several times revised) came in in 1930. There may of course be further developments presently; for example, I tried many years ago to popularize Contract Whist. This is a magnificent game, but much more difficult than Contract Bridge, from which it only differs in that Dummy's hand doesn't go down.

Other derivatives of Whist are: *Solo Whist*, which I have dealt with at some length; Bridge for two, which I have named *Option;* Bridge for three (*Booby*). Another game I have experimented with is *Baby Whist*, played with a 28-card pack (seven tricks instead of thirteen); this affords good practice in card play.

Solo Whist

Solo Whist is an excellent game for four players and calls for a high degree of skill. But it has never acquired the social standing attaching to Whist and its successors. It is not played in the West End Clubs; it has next to no literature; and, in consequence, its possibilities as a game have not been explored by writers on cards as fully as they deserve to be. But there are thousands of good Solo players who derive much satisfaction from the subtlety and intricacy of their game, and who regard it as intellectually superior to Contract.

It has also the advantage, over Bridge and similar games, that each deal is a separate event. Hence five players can participate, each of them standing out in turn.

The Deal

Solo is not primarily a partnership game, though it embodies – as we shall see – a partnership element. The four players, having taken their seats, draw cards to decide who shall deal first. Each player deals in turn, the rotation, as in Bridge, being clockwise. The first dealer is the player who draws the lowest card. For this purpose, the Ace ranks as the lowest card of its suit, and, conventionally, suits rank in their Bridge order: Clubs (lowest); Diamonds; Hearts; Spades.

The pack is shuffled by the dealer and cut to him by the player on his right. He then deals the cards, face downwards, three at a time to each player, beginning with the player to his left. This leaves four cards, which are dealt singly. The last card, which, of course, is the dealer's, is turned up to indicate the trump suit. It is taken up at the completion of the first trick.

The Play

When the deal is completed, the players take up their cards and look at them. The object of the game is to win *tricks* – as in Whist or Bridge – and the player who leads to the first trick will be the Eldest Hand, i.e. the player on the dealer's left.* A trick is won by the highest card of the suit led, unless the cards played to it include one or more *trumps;* in that case the trick is won by whoever has played the highest trump. The winner of a trick leads to the next one.

As in Whist, a player must follow suit if he can; if he has no card of the suit led, he can either discard or trump.

The play continues until the fate of the hand has been decided. It may be necessary to complete all thirteen tricks; but sometimes (as we shall see) there is no occasion to do so.†

The Calls

Each player, beginning with the Eldest Hand, is entitled, in his turn, to make one or more *calls*. These calls decide who is playing with, or against, whom; and the number of tricks which the caller is trying to make. Calls rank in a pre-determined order. A player is not obliged to make a call; he can pass. If he passes, he is not allowed to speak again (there is, as we shall see, one exception to this rule). A player whose call has been overcalled by another player can, in his turn, make a call which is higher than that made against him.

A *call* is a statement of the player's willingness to attempt to

* Except (see below) where the call is Abondance Déclarée.

† i.e., where the call is Misère, Misère Ouverte, or Abondance Déclarée.

take a specified number of tricks – either in partnership with another player, or 'solo', i.e. in opposition to the other three.

Calls rank in the following order:

(1) *Proposal and Acceptance* (colloquially known as 'Prop and Cop'). A player who 'proposes' offers, playing in partnership with any other player, to take eight of the thirteen tricks. In this call the trump suit is that of the card originally turned up. Any player, in his turn, can accept; it is not necessary for partners to be seated opposite one another. The first caller (Eldest Hand) can accept another player's proposal even if he has passed originally; this is the only exception to the rule that a player who has passed may not speak again.

(2) *Solo*. This call supersedes a Proposal (whether accepted or not). It is a statement of the player's willingness to attempt to take *five* tricks against the opposition of the other three players. The trump suit is that of the turned-up card.

(3) *Misère*. A player calling Misère undertakes to *lose* all thirteen tricks, against the combined efforts of the others to make him take one. There is no trump suit at Misère.

(4) *Abondance*. Here the caller announces his willingness to try to take nine tricks out of the thirteen. He may, however, name his own trump suit. But he does not mention the trump suit until his call has been *ratified*; i.e. until the other three players have passed.

(5) *Abondance in Trumps* (i.e. in the suit indicated by the turned-up card). This overcalls an Abondance declaration with one of the other suits as trumps. But note: a player proposing an Abondance in the suit of the card turned up does not disclose that this is his trump suit unless he is overcalling another Abondance. And in that case, the first Abondance declarer does not disclose what his trump suit would have been.

The object of these rules is to avoid, so far as possible, prejudicing the chances of a player who overcalls Abondance with Misère Ouverte.

(6) *Misère Ouverte* (Open Misère). As with an 'ordinary' Misère, the caller undertakes to try to lose all the tricks. But, in addition, he places his twelve remaining cards face upwards on the table as soon as the first trick has been completed.

(7) *Abondance Déclarée.* The highest call. The caller's objective is to take all thirteen tricks. Here there is no trump suit. This call differs from all the others in that the opening lead is made, not by the Eldest Hand, but by the Declarer himself.

It should now be clear why it is not always necessary to play a hand right through. Where the final call is an accepted Proposal, Solo, or Abondance in Trumps, each side tries to take as many tricks as possible. But a Misère hand is finished as soon as the caller takes a trick, and Abondance Déclarée is finished if the caller loses a trick.

SOME EXAMPLES OF CALLING SEQUENCES. We will call the players South (dealer), West (Eldest Hand), North and East. West in each case calls first.

1. *Proposal and Acceptance*

West	*North*	*East*	*South*
Pass	Propose	Accept	Pass

North and East now play in partnership against West and South.

2. *Proposal accepted by Eldest Hand*

West	*North*	*East*	*South*
Pass	Pass	Propose	Pass
Accept			

West and East play in partnership against North and South.

3. *Proposal, not accepted, amended to Solo*

West	*North*	*East*	*South*
Pass	Pass	Propose	Pass
Pass	Pass	Solo	

No one accepts East's proposal, so he decides to try Solo.

4. *Competitive Calling*

West	*North*	*East*	*South*
Pass	Propose	Accept	Solo
Pass	Misère	Pass	Pass

North, despite his original proposal, is prepared to play to lose all thirteen tricks.

5. *Competitive Calling*

West	*North*	*East*	*South*
Propose	Solo	Misère	Pass
Pass	Abondance	Pass	Pass
Pass			

North has contracted for nine tricks. He will not disclose his trump suit until the other players have passed.

The Stakes

Solo scores could, of course, be kept on paper, and an agreed settlement made when play ended. But, since each hand is a separate event, and since the game is almost invariably played for stakes, it is an almost universal practice for settlement to be made after each hand. There is, of course, no need for money to change hands after each deal; counters will do perfectly well. But the game is not likely to give much satisfaction – because of the obvious temptation to overcall a good hand – unless money stakes, however small, are played for.

Solo has no generally accepted code of laws. Players should agree their own stakes beforehand. The following scale of stakes is recommended:

PROPOSAL AND ACCEPTANCE. If Proposer and Acceptor make their eight tricks, they receive one unit each, plus one quarter-unit for each trick made over eight. If they fail, they each pay one unit, plus one quarter-unit for each trick lost in excess of six.

SOLO. The caller, if he makes five tricks, receives one unit from each of the other three players, plus one quarter-unit for each extra trick that he makes. Similarly, if he fails, he pays one unit to each of the others, plus one quarter-unit for every trick in excess of nine made by the opponents.

MISÈRE. The caller receives two units from each of his opponents if he succeeds in fulfilling his contract. If he fails, he pays each opponent two units.

ABONDANCE (AND ABONDANCE IN TRUMPS). Three units are received from, or paid to, each of the other players; plus one half-unit for every trick made in excess of nine, or for every trick in excess of five made by the adversaries.

MISÈRE OUVERTE. Four units are received from, or paid to, each of the three opponents.

ABONDANCE DÉCLARÉE. Six units are received from, or paid to, each opponent.

Suppose that the agreed 'unit' is one shilling, we might have the following series of transactions:

Call	*Payments Received* (+) *or Made* (−)			
	West	*North*	*East*	*South*
1. West proposes; North accepts. They make ten tricks	+ 1s 6d	+ 1s 6d	− 1s 6d	− 1s 6d
2. North proposes; East accepts. They only make four tricks	+ 1s 9d	− 1s 9d	− 1s 9d	+ 1s 9d
3. West attempts Solo and makes nine tricks	+ 3s	− 1s	− 1s	− 1s
4. East tries Misère and fails	+ 2s	+ 2s	− 6s	+ 2s
5. South calls Abondance and makes eleven tricks	− 4s	− 4s	− 4s	+ 12s
6. West fails to make Misère Ouverte	− 12s	+ 4s	+ 4s	+ 4s
7. South calls Solo; makes only three tricks	+ 1s 3d	+ 1s 3d	+ 1s 3d	− 3s 9d
8. North makes an Abondance Déclarée	− 6s	+ 18s	− 6s	− 6s
Net result	− 12s 6d	+ 20s	− 15s	+ 7s 6d

The pluses and minuses must, of course, balance. My example shows that even a modest shilling unit could prove quite expensive to an indifferent or unlucky player.

Illustrative Deals

1. Proposal and Acceptance

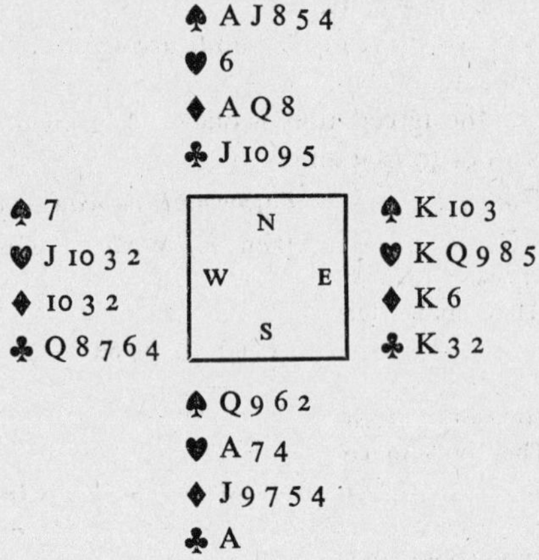

The ♠ 9 was turned up to indicate the trump suit.

THE CALLS

West	*North*	*East*	*South*
Pass	Propose	Accept	Pass

To propose, a player should have four probable tricks (at least) in his hand, and fairly well distributed strength. North's hand is a minimum; cautious players would say, below the minimum. But West has passed already; North has five trumps – which suggests that, with the aid of the acceptor, three tricks at least should be taken in the trump suit – and his Diamonds and Clubs should be worth rather more than two tricks.

East has no hesitation about accepting. He has good supporting trumps; a strong second suit; and two more Kings. He estimates that his hand is worth five tricks at least.

As the cards lie, ten tricks should be made against any opening lead.

2. *Solo*

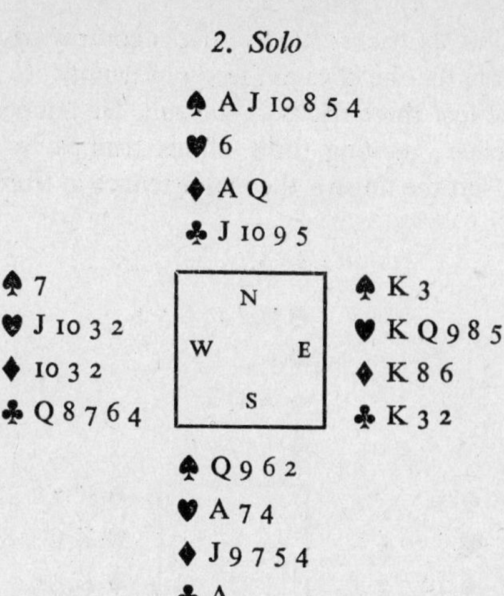

The ♠ 9 was turned up to indicate the trump suit.

West	*North*	*East*	*South*
Pass	Solo	Pass	Pass

This deal is the same as the last one, except that North's ♦ 8 has been exchanged for East's ♠ 10. This addition to North's trump holding makes all the difference to his hand. He ought, with ordinary luck, to make four of his trumps; the ♦ Ace gives him his fifth trick. There are also outside chances of making the ♦ Q or a Club.

Trick	1	2	3	4	5	6	7
W	♦ 10	♦ 2	♥ 2	♥ 3	♣ 4	♠ 7	♥ 10
N	♦ *A*	♦ Q	♥ 6	♠ *4*	♣ 5	♠ 10	♠ *5*
E	♦ 6	♦ *K*	♥ *K*	♥ 5	♣ 2	♠ *K*	♥ Q
S	♦ 4	♦ 5	♥ 4	♥ A	♣ *A*	♠ 2	♥ 7

Trick	8	9	10	11	12	13
W	♣ *Q*	♣ 8	♥ J			
N	♣ 10	♣ 9	♠ *8*	♣ J	♠ *J*	♠ *A*
E	♣ 3	♣ *K*	♥ 9			
S	♦ 7	♦ 9	♦ J	♠ *6*	♠ 9	♠ Q

North makes six tricks: the five tricks contracted for, and one overtrick. Note that he does not lead out trumps: to do so would mean that he lost three tricks in the suit. He adopts a policy of 'passive defence', making three of his trumps by ruffing; the ♦ Ace; and – at the finish – the major tenace in trumps.

3. Misère

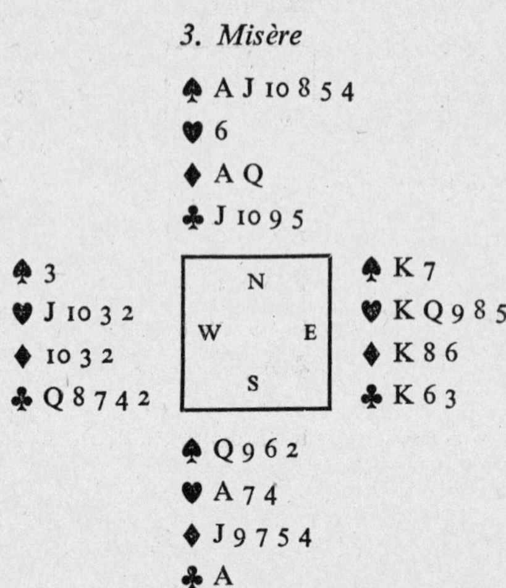

The ♠ 9 was turned up to indicate the trump suit.

West	*North*	*East*	*South*
Misère	Pass	Pass	Pass

West's is a somewhat 'sketchy' Misère; he is vulnerable in two suits. But all calls should be made on a calculation of risks, and West considers that he has an odds-on chance. His opening lead is a bold one, yet this is a 'calculated risk': the odds are 7 to 2 against all three opponents being able to play under the ♣ 7. The play:

Trick	1	2	3	4	5	6	7
W	♣ 7	♦ 3	♦ 10	♥ 3	♠ 3	♥ J	♥ 2
N	♣ 5	♦ *A*	♦ *Q*	♥ *6*	♠ *A*	♠ 4	♣ J
E	♣ 6	♦ K	♦ 8	♥ 5	♠ K	♠ *7*	♥ *9*
S	♣ *A*	♦ 7	♦ J	♥ 4	♠ Q	♠ 6	♥ 7

Trick	8	9	10	11	12	13
W	♥ 10	♦ 2				
N	♣ 10	♣ 9	and now, obviously, West is home.			
E	♥ *8*	♦ *6*				
S	♥ A	♦ 4				

The play illustrates the difficulties of the defence. South's Diamond lead (trick 2) would have defeated the call if East had not thrown his ♦ K under North's ♦ Ace. For East could then have taken the second Diamond trick and compelled West to take the third. Similarly, the Heart suit could have been so played as to defeat West's hazardous call. But, of course, the caller at Misère relies on the difficulties of inter-communication between his three opponents.

4. Misère

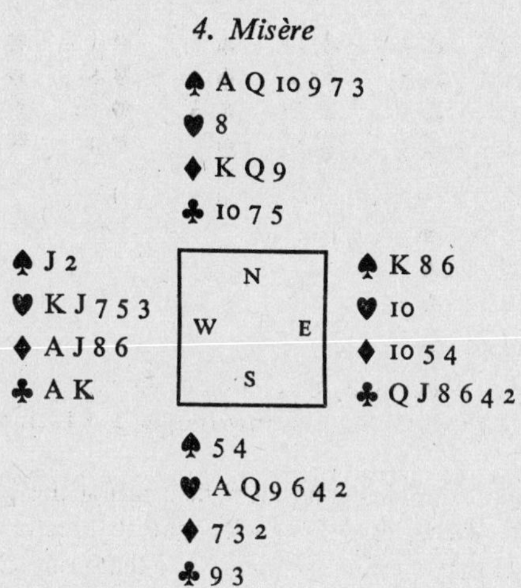

The ♦ 3 *was turned up to indicate the trump suit.*

West	*North*	*East*	*South*
Propose	Accept	Pass	Misère
Pass	Pass		

South's is a passable Misère hand, despite the vulnerability of his Clubs, and in play he made his call:

Trick	1	2	3	4	5	6	7
W	♣ *A*	♣ *K*	♦ J	♠ J	♥ *K*	♦ *A*	♠ 2
N	♣ 10	♣ 7	♦ *Q*	♠ 10	♥ 8	♦ K	♠ *A*
E	♣ Q	♣ J	♦ 10	♠ *K*	♥ 10	♦ 5	♠ 8
S	♣ 9	♣ 3	♦ 7	♠ 4	♥ 9	♦ 3	♠ 5

Trick	8	9	10	11	12	13
W						
N						
E						
S						

and South is now out of danger.

But the call could have been defeated had East played more imaginatively after winning trick 4 with the ♠ K. He should have tried to create the opportunity to discard his remaining Spades.

Trick	1	2	3	4	5	6	7
W	♣ *A*	♣ *K*	♦ J	♠ J	♥ *J*	♥ *K*	♥ *7*
N	♣ 10	♣ 7	♦ *Q*	♠ 10	♥ 8	♦ K	♦ 9
E	♣ Q	♣ J	♦ 10	♠ *K*	♥ 10	♠ 8	♠ 6
S	♣ 9	♣ 3	♦ 7	♠ 4	♥ 9	♥ Q	♥ 6

Trick	8	9	10	11	12	13
W	♥ *5*	♠ 2				
N	♠ A	♠ 3				
E	♣ 8	♣ 6				
S	♥ 4	♠ *5*				

At trick 8 it becomes clear that East has no more Spades. West's only possible lead is now the ♠ 2, which sinks South's contract.

These two examples show how fascinating the Misère call at Solo can be. Declarer pits his wits against three opponents. But the very fact that there are so many, and that none of them knows at the outset what cards the other two holds, gives him his opportunity. Contract Bridge, where one is trying to visualize two unseen hands, is difficult enough; here each of the defenders is trying to visualize three.

Incidentally, the *etiquette* of Solo must be most scrupulously observed. To play a card with undue emphasis, or to register disapproval of another player's lead, may wreck Declarer's chance of making a Misère contract.

5. *Abondance*

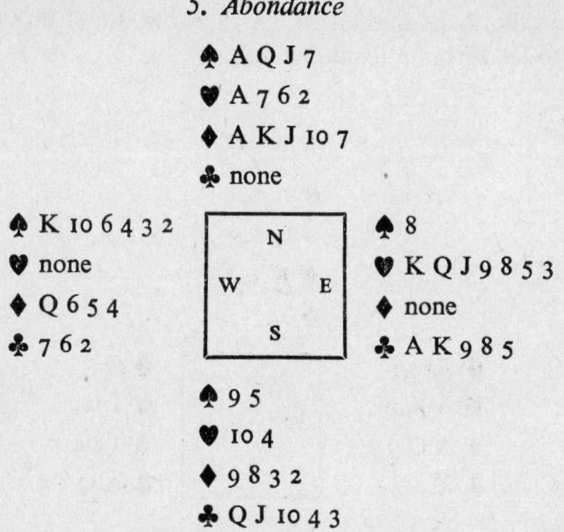

The ♥ 10 is turned up to indicate the trump suit.

West	*North*	*East*	*South*
Pass	Solo	Abondance	Pass
Pass	Pass	Pass	

East now announces that his Abondance is in the trump suit. This is a slightly hazardous call, in view of North's solo; but a critical trump, the ♥ 10, is known to be in the South hand. East hopes for six Heart tricks and three tricks (at least) in Clubs. He plays well and makes his nine tricks:

Trick	1	2	3	4	5	6	7
W	♠ 4	♠ 2	♣ 2	♠ 3	♦ 4	♦ 5	♠ 6
N	♠ *A*	♠ Q	♥ *A*	♠ J	♥ 2	♥ 6	♥ 7
E	♠ 8	♥ *3*	♥ K	♥ *J*	♥ *Q*	♥ *9*	♥ *8*
S	♠ 5	♠ 9	♥ 4	♦ 2	♥ 10	♦ 3	♦ 8

Trick	8	9	10	11	12	13
W	♣ 6	♦ 6	♣ 7	♠ 10	♠ K	♦ Q
N	♦ 7	♦ 10	♠ 7	♦ J	♦ K	♦ A
E	♣ *A*	♥ *5*	♣ 9	♣ *K*	♣ 8	♣ *5*
S	♣ 3	♦ 9	♣ *10*	♣ Q	♣ *J*	♣ 4

Note the end-play in the Club suit. If East leads out the ♣ Ace and then the ♣ K, his call will be defeated. In effect, he compels South to lead from a losing tenace.

6. Misère Ouverte

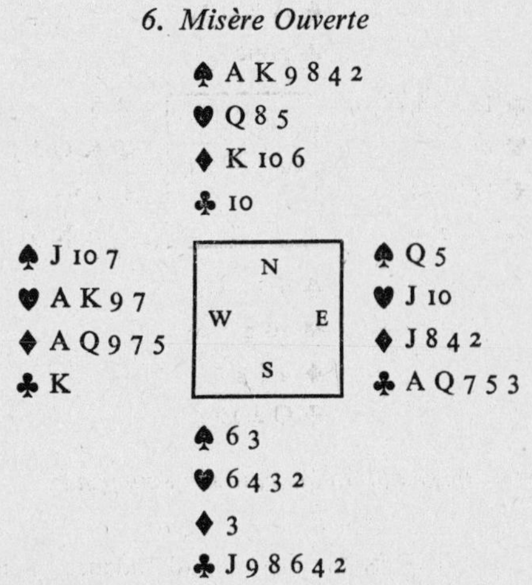

The ♥ 6 was turned up to indicate the trump suit.

West	*North*	*East*	*South*
Propose	Accept	Pass	Misère Ouverte
Pass	Pass		

Against South's call, West led the ♠ J. There was now no possible way of defeating South; for if Clubs are led (the most feasible plan) West can only get rid of four of his Diamonds. But the call could have been defeated by the 'blind' lead of the ♣ K. South's hand is exposed at the conclusion of the first trick:

Trick	1	2	3	4	5	6	7
W	♣ K	♥ *K*	♥ *A*	♥ *9*	♦ 5	♠ J	♠ 10
N	♣ 10	♥ Q	♥ 8	♥ 5	♦ 6	♦ 10	♦ K
E	♣ *A*	♥ J	♥ 10	♠ Q	♦ *J*	♣ *Q*	♣ *7*
S	♣ J	♥ 6	♥ 4	♥ 3	♦ 3	♣ 9	♣ 6

Trick	8	9	10	11	12	13
W	♠ 7	♦ 7				
N	♠ A	♠ 8	♠ 2			
E	♣ 5	♠ 5				
S	♣ 4	♠ 3	♠ 6			

7. Misère Ouverte

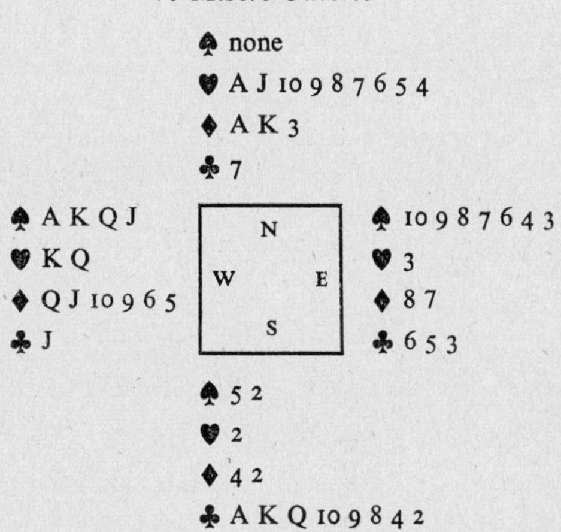

The ♠ 5 was turned up to indicate the trump suit.

West	*North*	*East*	*South*
Solo	Abondance	Pass	Misère Ouverte
Pass	Pass		

West might perhaps have tried Abondance, since he has the lead. As the cards lie however his contract will fail. The ♦ Q is led; North wins and leads the ♥ Ace; then another Heart gives East an immediate ruff.

Against Misère Ouverte, West led the ♣ J; now the call cannot be defeated. But a different line of attack would have proved successful:

Trick	1	2	3	4	5	6	7
W	♠ *A*	♠ *K*	♠ *Q*	♠ *J*	♦ 5	♣ J	
N	♣ 7	♥ J	♥ 10	♥ 9	♦ 3	♦ A	
E	♠ 10	♠ 9	♠ 8	♠ 7	♦ *7*	♠ *6*	♣ *6*
S	♠ 5	♠ 2	♣ A	♣ K	♦ 4	♣ 10	♣ 4

Trick	8	9	10	11	12	13
W						
N						
E	♣ *5*	♣ 3				
S	♣ 2	♣ *9*				

This example, and the last one, show the perils which accompany a call of Misère Ouverte, but how nice a combination of judgement and *flair* is necessary to defeat it. There are few more fascinating situations in any card game than those which this call offers.

8. Abondance Déclarée

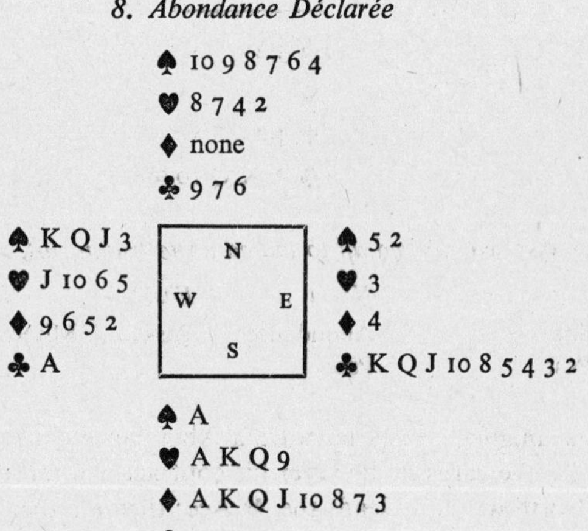

The ♠ Ace was turned up to indicate the trump suit.

West	*North*	*East*	*South*
Propose	Accept	Misère Ouverte	Abondance Déclarée

South has twelve certain tricks; he is taking a chance on the Heart suit. The adverse Hearts may (improbably) be divided 3 – 3 – 3; or the ♥ J and ♥ 10 may both be unguarded; or, if either is guarded, whoever holds it may be compelled to unguard it to retain a guard in Spades or Clubs. (This is the situation known in Bridge as a pseudo-squeeze.) South began by leading out his Diamonds and succeeded in fooling West:

Trick	1	2	3	4	5	6	7
S	♦ *A*	♦ *K*	♦ *Q*	♦ *J*	♦ *10*	♦ *8*	♦ *7*
W	♦ 2	♦ 5	♦ 6	♦ 9	♠ 3	♠ J	♣ A
N	♣ 6	♣ 7	♣ 9	♠ 4	♠ 6	♠ 7	♠ 8
E	♦ 4	♥ 3	♠ 2	♠ 5	♣ K	♣ Q	♣ J

Trick	8	9	10	11	12	13
S	♦ *3*	♥ *A*	♥ *K*	♥ *Q*	♥ *9*	♠ *A*
W	♥ 5	♥ 6	♥ 10	♥ J		
N	♠ 9					
E	♣ 2					

West has, of course, carefully noted the discards of North and East. He knows that East has only Clubs left; in any case, South must be void in Clubs. He knows also that South holds the ♠ Ace, and assumes (correctly) that he also holds the ♥ Ace K Q. But what is South's thirteenth card? The ♠ 10 or a Heart? West puts his money on the ♠ 10 and loses. His decision is, logically, a bad one; since for South to call Abondance Déclarée with only a 10 of a suit would surely be courting disaster. North however is more to blame than is West. North should have thrown his four Hearts instead of four of his Spades. Moreover, he should have played them from the top downwards, when the position could not have been misread.

Abondance Déclarée is, of course, a very rare call; and when it does occur, gives little opportunity for interesting play.

AUCTION SOLO

This 'streamlined' version of Solo Whist was introduced about sixty years ago. It probably owes something to the American game of Boston.

The mechanics of the game are basically those of Solo Whist. There is a turned-up trump; a prescribed sequence of calls; an opening lead by the Eldest Hand. But (*a*) there is no Proposal and Acceptance, the lowest declaration being a five-trick Solo; and (*b*) there is a much more extensive range of calls. These calls, beginning with the lowest – each call supersedes those which precede it – are as follows:

(1) 5-trick Solo.
(2) 5-trick Solo in the trump suit.*
(3) 6-trick Solo.
(4) 6-trick Solo in the trump suit.
(5) 7-trick Solo.
(6) 7-trick Solo in the trump suit.
(7) 8-trick Solo.
(8) 8-trick Solo in the trump suit.
(9) Misère.
(10) 9-trick Abondance.
(11) 9-trick Abondance in the trump suit.
(12) 10-trick Abondance.
(13) 10-trick Abondance in the trump suit.
(14) 11-trick Abondance.
(15) 11-trick Abondance in the trump suit.
(16) 12-trick Abondance.
(17) 12-trick Abondance in the trump suit.
(18) Misère Ouverte.
(19) Abondance Déclarée, with no trump.
(20) Abondance Déclarée in the trump suit.

This last call supersedes a normal Abondance Déclarée because it is more difficult to make. At an ordinary Abondance Déclarée, the caller leads to the first trick, just as he does at Solo Whist. But, at the last call listed, the first lead is made by the Eldest Hand. Hence the caller must be prepared to win the first trick, whatever the opening lead.

As in Solo Whist, a caller can start anywhere in the scale; and any call can be superseded by one which is higher in the scale. A player who has passed must thereafter remain silent, but a player

* i.e. the suit indicated by the turned-up card.

who has made a call may go on calling, as long as his call supersedes the call last preceding it.

Stakes

A reasonable scale of stakes would be:

Solo. One unit received from, or paid out to, each opponent, plus $\frac{1}{4}$ unit received for every trick made above the number contracted for, or paid out for every trick, in excess of one, by which the contract fails.

Misère. Two units received from, or paid out to, each opponent.

Abondance. Three units received from, or paid out to, each opponent; plus $\frac{1}{2}$ unit in respect of each overtrick or additional undertrick.

Misère Ouverte. Four units received from, or paid out to, each opponent.

Abondance Déclarée. Six units received from, or paid out to, each opponent.

If there is a 'kitty', contributions might be half a unit from each player, wherever a hand is 'passed out.'

Illustrative Deals at Auction Solo

1. A Seven-trick contract

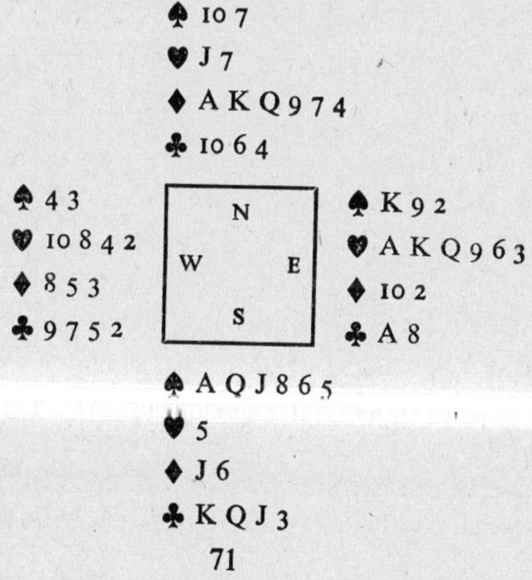

The ♠ 8 was turned up to indicate the trump suit.

West	*North*	*East*	*South*
Misère	Solo (5)	Solo (6)	Solo (6) in trumps
Pass	Pass	Solo (7)	Solo (7) in trumps
Pass	Pass	Pass	

West considers Misère Ouverte but decides not to risk it. As the cards lie, he could almost certainly make this contract, but the ♣ 4, 3 in one hand could well break it.

South makes his call without difficulty. He has just enough trumps to establish two tricks in Clubs.

2. An Eight-trick contract fails

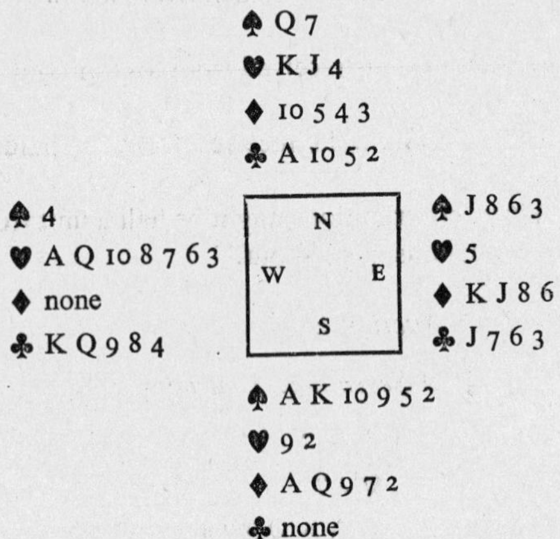

The ♠ 9 was turned up to indicate the trump suit.

West	*North*	*East*	*South*
Solo (5)	Pass	Pass	Solo (5) in trumps
Solo (6)	Pass	Pass	Solo (6) in trumps
Solo (7)	Pass	Pass	Solo (7) in trumps
Solo (8)			

West and South each have two good suits. In the competitive auction which results, West is pushed one trick farther than he really wants to go. But he takes a chance on making five tricks in his trump suit (Hearts) and three tricks in Clubs. The adverse distribution of the latter suit (4 – 4 – 0) just foils his contract:

Trick	1	2	3	4	5	6	7
W	♥ *A*	♥ 10	♠ 4	♥ *3*	♣ K	♥ *6*	♣ *Q*
N	♥ 4	♥ *J*	♠ *Q*	♠ 7	♣ *A*	♦ 3	♣ 2
E	♥ 5	♠ 3	♠ 6	♠ 8	♣ 3	♦ 6	♣ 6
S	♥ 2	♥ 9	♠ 9	♠ K	♠ 2	♦ A	♦ 2

Trick	8	9	10	11	12	13
W	♣ 9	♥ *7*	♣ 4	♥ *8*	♣ 8	♥ *Q*
N	♣ *10*	♦ K	♣ 5	♦ 5	♥ *K*	
E	♣ 7	♦ 7	♣ *J*	♦ 8		
S	♠ 5	♦ 4	♦ 9	♦ Q		

3. *Competitive Auction*

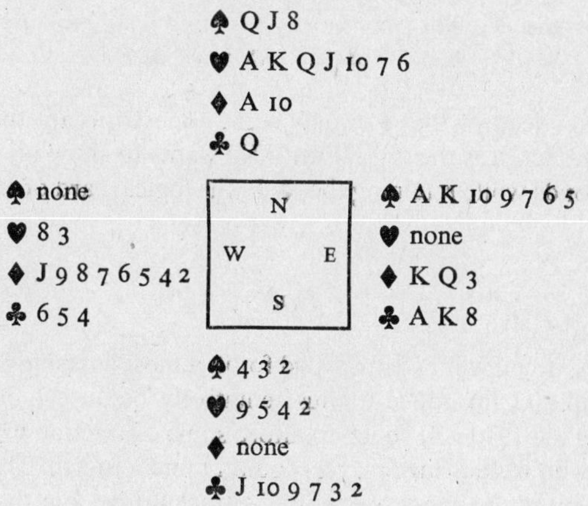

The ♠ 3 was turned up to indicate the trump suit.

West	*North*	*East*	*South*
Misère	Abondance (9)	Abondance in trump suit (9)	Misère Ouverte
Pass	Pass	Pass	

This is a most interesting deal, with all four suits irregularly distributed. North has a cast-iron Abondance; so has East; and South has an excellent chance of making Misère. This contract can only fail if one adversary holds the 6, 5, 4 of Clubs, and the suit is not led until the four higher adverse Clubs have been discarded. But West, as it happens, does hold the three low Clubs, and intelligent co-operation by South's three adversaries bring about his downfall:

Trick	1	2	3	4	5	6	7
W	♦ 9	♥ 8	♥ 3	♦ 2	♦ 4	♦ 5	♦ 6
N	♦ *A*	♥ *A*	♥ *K*	♥ *Q*	♠ Q	♠ J	♠ 8
E	♦ K	♣ A	♣ K	♣ 8	♠ *K*	♠ *A*	♠ *10*
S	♣ J	♥ 9	♥ 5	♥ 4	♠ 4	♠ 3	♠ 2

Trick	8	9	10	11	12	13
W	♦ 7	♦ *J*	♣ *6*	♣ *5*	♣ 4	
N	♣ Q	♦ 10				
E	♠ *9*	♦ 3				
S	♣ 10	♣ 9	♣ 3	♣ 2	♣ *7*	

West's lead of the ♦ 9 may seem almost too apt to be true! But, in fact, it is the logical lead. He wants to show his length in Diamonds while retaining the ♦ J: the logical card of entry.

Booby

This is, if you will take my word for it, a most amusing card game for three; I introduce it thus tentatively because I invented it during the 1940 – 41 'blitz' to afford some distraction where three of us who were Bridge players couldn't find a fourth. The bidding and play of the hands are as in Contract Bridge, but there is also a Nullo call: a contract to lose seven or more tricks. This call ranks above Hearts but below Spades. Thus, a player overcalling Three Hearts with Three Nullos has contracted to take not more than four tricks.

The dealer gives each player seventeen cards, and deals the fourth (face downwards) as a first contribution to Dummy. Each player now selects four cards from his own hand, which also go, face downwards, to Dummy. Competitive bidding then begins and whoever secures the contract gets the Dummy. So, obviously, you won't be throwing all your 'dud' cards into Dummy unless you have made up your mind not to bid for it yourself.

Two or three illustrative hands should suffice, I think, to give you the general idea.

We will call the players South, West, and North; South is the dealer. Dummy's cards are parked in the East position. If North secures the contract, South occupies the East chair; if South is the declarer, it is occupied by North. So the three players are always in the same relative positions. They are determined originally by cutting.

First Illustrative Deal

	South	*West*	*North*
Cards	♠ A K 6 4 2	♠ Q 5	♠ J 10 9 8 7 3
as	♥ 7 5 4 3	♥ A 10 8 6 2	♥ K Q J
dealt:	♦ J 10 8	♦ A K 5 4 3 2	♦ Q 9 7 6
	♣ K 10 8 7 6	♣ A Q J 2	♣ 9 5 4 3

Dealt to Dummy: ♥ 9

For Dummy, South throws ♥ 7 5 4 3
West throws ♠ Q 5 ♦ 5 4
North throws ♣ 9 5 4 3

The hands are now:

♠ A K 6 4 2	♠ none	♠ J 10 9 8 7 3
♥ none	♥ A 10 8 6 2	♥ K Q J
♦ J 10 8	♦ A K 3 2	♦ Q 9 7 6
♣ K 10 8 7 6	♣ A Q J 2	♣ none

(Each of the players has voided one suit.)

THE AUCTION

South	*West*	*North*
2 ♠	4 ♥	Double
No	No	

North leads the ♠ J to the first trick, and Dummy's hand is exposed:

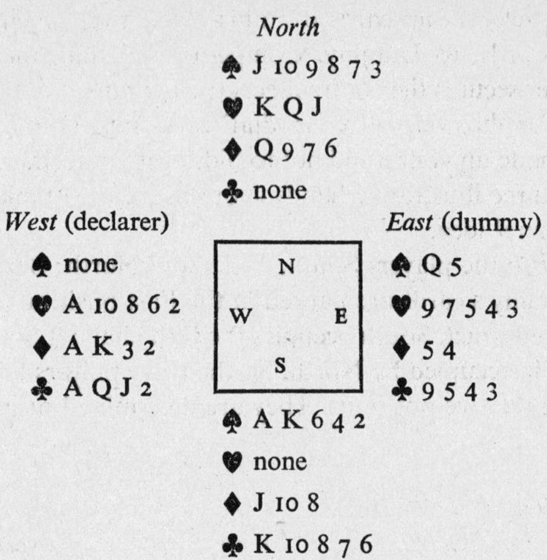

Declarer is not unlucky here. He finds five Hearts in Dummy and just makes his contract, losing two trump tricks and a Club. All the same, a rash double on North's part. South had bid Spades, which made it highly probable that West would be void of the suit.

Second Illustrative Deal

	South	*West*	*North*
Cards	♠ J 10 5 4	♠ A Q *7* 2	♠ *K 9 8* 6 3
as	♥ 10 8 5 3	♥ K Q J 7 4	♥ A 9 6 2
dealt:	♦ Q 10 5	♦ K 9 8 7 6	♦ A J 4 3 2
	♣ A K *Q 9 7 5*	♣ *10 8 6*	♣ J 4 2

The ♣ 3 has been dealt to Dummy, and the cards in *italics* are contributed by the players.

THE AUCTION

South	*West*	*North*
No	1 ♥	Two Nullos
No	No	

South moves to the East position. He leads the ♠ J to the first trick:

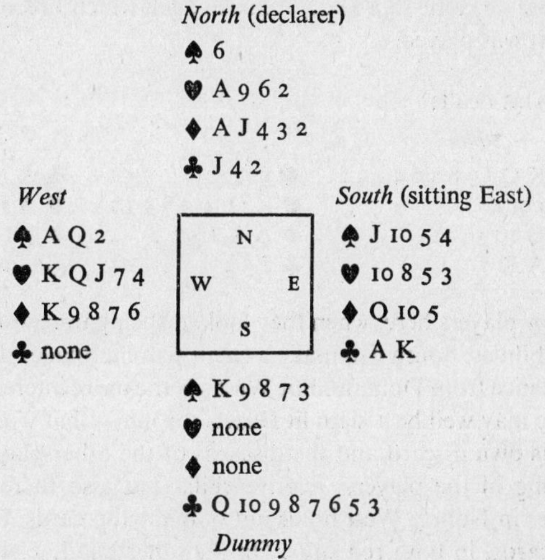

The trick-by-trick play is interesting:

Trick	*South*	*Dummy*	*West*	*North*
1	♠ J	♠ 9	♠ *A*	♠ 6
2	♠ 10	♠ 8	♠ *Q*	♥ A
3	♠ 5	♠ *K*	♠ 2	♥ 9
4	♠ *4*	♠ 3	♦ K	♥ 6
5	♣ *A*	♣ Q	♦ 9	♣ J
6	♣ *K*	♣ 8	♦ 8	♣ 2

and Declarer loses, easily, the remainder of the tricks.

Once again Declarer was fortunate in his Dummy. He actually makes six Nullos. He had planned to bid Four Nullos, and, pusillanimously, changed his mind at the last moment.

The play of a Nullo hand at Booby bears a generic resemblance (*a*) to the play of a Misère hand at Solo, and (*b*) to the play at Black Maria. In each case success turns on the possession of one or more long suits, in which it is nearly always essential to hold the lowest cards. Declarer was fortunate in that neither opponent held five Spades to the two.

Third Illustrative Deal

Now we come to a really freakish deal, which I recorded at the time it was played.

Cards as dealt:

South	*West*	*North*
♠ K Q J 9 8 7 6 5 4 3 2	♠ none	♠ A 10
♥ none	♥ K Q 10 9 8 5 3 2	♥ A J 7 6
♦ Q 10 5	♦ A K J 4 3 2	♦ 9 8 7 6
♣ A K 7	♣ J 5 2	♣ Q 10 9 8 6 4 3

Two players here, when they look at their cards, visualize slam possibilities. South can make a small slam in Spades without any assistance from Dummy. But West's is the more interesting hand. There may well be a slam in Hearts for him – that would depend on his own discard and the discards of the other players, to say nothing of the players' relative skill – but also there are possibilities in Nullos. West holds not only the top cards, but also the low cards, in both red suits. On the other hand, a Nullos call – unlike a suit call – can be wrecked by a bad dummy. How lucky West was the bidding and play will show.

The ♥ 4 was dealt to Dummy. South discarded his three Diamonds and the ♣ 7 (leaving himself with twelve certain tricks at a Spade contract). West discarded his three Clubs and the ♥ 3; he hoped to make at least game in Hearts, and didn't want Dummy to be void of trumps. North threw his four Diamonds.

THE AUCTION

South	*West*	*North*
3 ♠	6 ♥	No
6 ♠	7 ♥	Double
No	7 Nullos	Double

South's first bid was 'cagey'. He felt fairly sure that Hearts would be bid against him, and wanted his Six Spades to look like a 'sacrifice'. But West, as we are aware, had a second string to his bow.

North led the ♣ Q to trick 1, and the Dummy was exposed.

THE PLAY

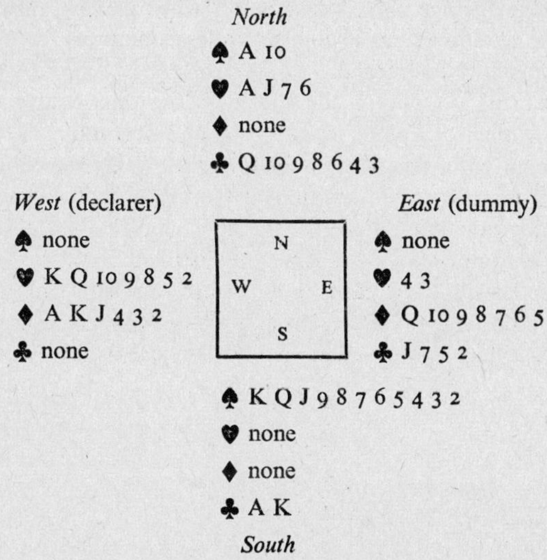

The ♣ J was thrown from Dummy under North's ♣ Q. South won and led his second Club. The ♣ 7 was of course played from Dummy's hand. If North could have continued to lead at this point! But South, perforce, led a Spade, and Dummy's ♣ 5 was promptly ditched, bringing Declarer safely home.

This deal – not altogether untypical, where each player starts with 17 cards – may serve to show that Booby, apart from being a fair test of skill, can be good for many a laugh.

Option

This is the name which I give to a variety of Double Dummy Contract which has recently attained a considerable vogue. There is a good deal of luck in Option, as you will see, but there is also ample scope for the exercise of skill. It's a much more exciting game than is any other form of Double Dummy, and also affords excellent practice in the handling of the cards. All but the best Bridge players lose points when playing against the declarer; Option brings to light countless situations from which there is much to be learned.

The scoring at Option is the same as at Contract Bridge, except that the winner of a game gets a bonus of 300 points.

To begin with, the players cut for seats. Whoever wins deals first and nominates his position at the table. In the diagram I have made South the dealer of the first hand. He has chosen to sit with his opponent to his right; this is the more advantageous position. He deals the cards as in Bridge, one at a time to four 'players': himself; his adversary and the two dummies. The hand opposite to him is exposed as soon as the deal is completed.

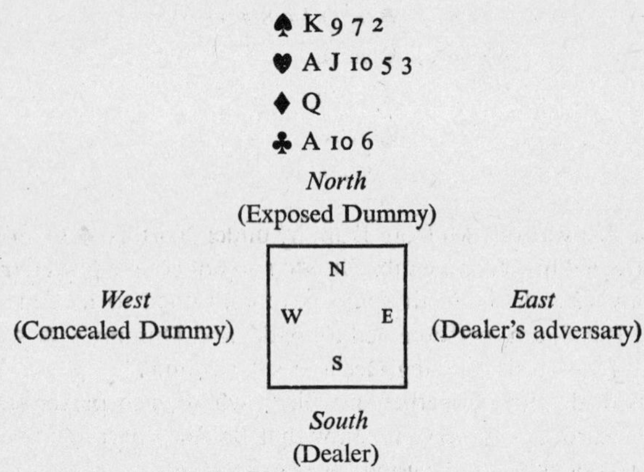

The players now look at their cards and a competitive auction begins, conducted exactly as in Bridge. The dealer has the right to speak first. He also has what is worth a good deal more: the right to determine which Dummy will go to the player who makes the final declaration. If he bids (say) Four Spades, nominating the exposed Dummy, any bid made against him – say, Five Hearts – will mean that (if South now passes) the nice array of cards exposed will be taken over by East. And similarly with the concealed Dummy. If South secures the final contract, nominating the exposed Dummy, West's cards are turned over and sorted into suits, and the lead to the first trick is made from West's hand. If South secures the contract, nominating the concealed Dummy, North's exposed hand is moved to the West position and West's cards to the North position. Similarly, if East secures the contract and the exposed Dummy has been nominated, the North and West hands are exchanged.

On what principles should one bid in this fascinating game? I can best demonstrate them, I think, by considering various typical situations. We will assume, to begin with, that neither player is vulnerable.

Case 1

The exposed Dummy is that set out above.

South's hand is: ♠ 10 6 5 3
♥ Q 8 4
♦ A K 8
♣ 7 4 2

South decides (somewhat rashly) to take a chance on a bid of Four Spades. He considers that he has an odds-on chance of making ten tricks. He does not give enough thought to the fact that, with so attractive a Dummy exposed, East may well overcall him.

East's hand is: ♠ A J
♥ 9
♦ J 7 6 4 2
♣ K Q J 9 8

He bids Six Clubs, with a very good chance of getting home, and so scoring 120 below the line, with bonuses of 500 for the Small Slam and 300 for the game. Now the unfortunate South realizes that he has blundered. The best he can do now is to bid Six Hearts, Six Spades, or Six No Trump. He will be doubled, of course, and must lose at least 300 points.

So South would have done better to choose the concealed Dummy, making some such modest bid as One Diamond. South holds A K 8 of the suit, and the concealed Dummy should include four or five Diamonds. East sees no point in contesting the call. The four hands, with both Dummies exposed, are:

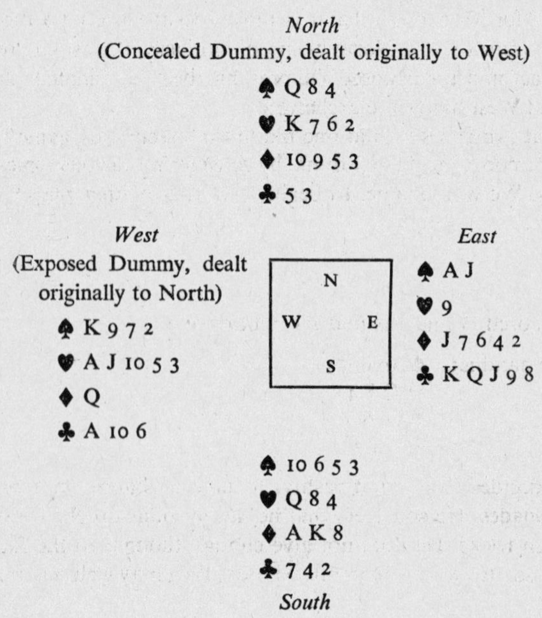

Before North's cards are turned up, East leads (say) the ♣ 6 from the exposed Dummy. South makes five tricks: 100 points to East, who mentally kicks himself for not having had the courage to double.

Case 2

Again neither player is vulnerable. The exposed Dummy (dealt to *North*) is:

♠ A 5 3
♥ none
♦ J 10 5 3 2
♣ 10 8 7 6 3

South holds: ♠ J 10 7
♥ 8 7
♦ A K 8 6
♣ K Q 5 2

South considers that, if the luck is with him, he may well make game in Diamonds, so opens the proceedings with a Five Diamonds bid, nominating the exposed Dummy. He considers it most unlikely that East can make any successful over-bid.

East holds:

♠ K Q 9 6 2
♥ K 9 2
♦ 9 7 4
♣ J 9

He makes a sacrifice bid of Five Spades. South doubles, and the four hands are:

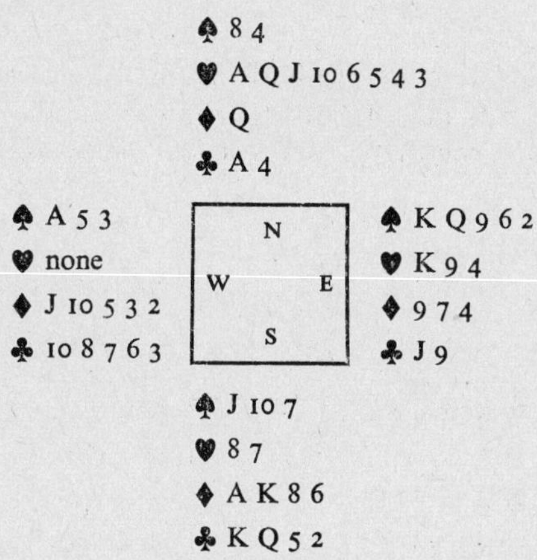

Before the North hand is exposed, South leads the ♦ Ace from his own hand. The cards are awkwardly placed for East, who takes only seven tricks (it's an interesting Double Dummy hand, with several possible lines of play: set the cards out and see if you can do better). So South, who would not have succeeded in making Five Diamonds, clocks up 700 points.

Case 3

Let us now suppose that South only is vulnerable. The exposed Dummy is: ♠ Q J 7
♥ 4 2
♦ K J 8 7 5 4 2
♣ 4

South holds: ♠ A 5 4 3
♥ K 9 7
♦ 3
♣ A J 10 8 6

He prudently bids One Club, nominating the concealed Dummy. *East* has: ♠ 8
♥ A Q 10 8 6 5 3
♦ Q 10 9
♣ K 7

As East is not vulnerable, his hand (in his opinion) justifies a gamble. He bids Four Hearts. South, who can see three tricks and a probable fourth, doubles. The four hands are:

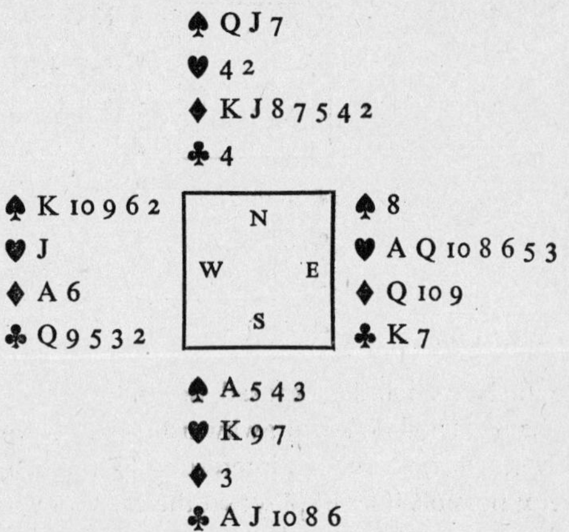

South leads the ♣ Ace.

East is set two tricks: 300 points. A very proper penalty for over-bidding. Part-scores are valuable at Option, and East should have been content to bid Two Hearts. South would not have risked an over-bid of Three Clubs.

Case 4

This time South is not vulnerable; East is. The exposed Dummy is:

♠ K 9 6 2
♥ Q 8 3
♦ 7 2
♣ Q 7 6 5

South holds:

♠ A Q J 10
♥ K 10 6
♦ A 8 5 4
♣ K 10

With the exposed Dummy, South can probably make Four Spades. But, knowing East to be an impetuous bidder, who enjoys the Poker element in Option, he decides to try for an even better score. He bids One Diamond, nominating the concealed Dummy.

East promptly bids Four Hearts, which South doubles. The four hands are:

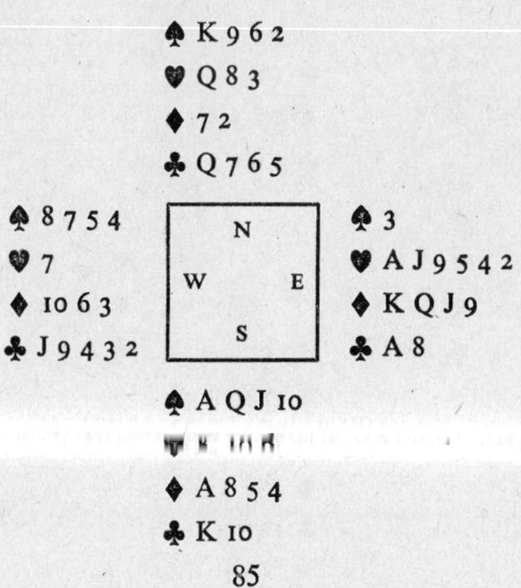

South leads the ♠ Ace; the cards of the concealed Dummy are turned up; and East sees at once that he has fallen for a 'swindle'. He makes only seven tricks, losing 800 points to his enterprising opponent. I need hardly underline the moral.

Case 5

Strenuous competition can occur when both South and East have good hands and there is a really attractive Dummy. Both players were vulnerable, and the exposed Dummy produced:

♠ A K J ♥ A Q J 8 ♦ A 7 ♣ K Q J 9

South had dealt himself:

♠ Q 10 8 5 4 ♥ K 7 ♦ K J 3 ♣ 10 7 4

South went into a long huddle before deciding what to bid. At ordinary Contract he and his partner would (or should) bid and make Six Spades. But South decided it more than likely that East, if he held the ♣ Ace, would over-bid with Six No Trump. So, with twelve tricks on top, he bid Six No Trump himself.

It was now East's turn to huddle. Deducing from South's confident bid that the latter held good Spades (headed by the Queen), the ♦ K, and quite probably the ♥ K as well, he bid Seven No Trump over South's Six. South wisely refrained from doubling.

The four hands were:

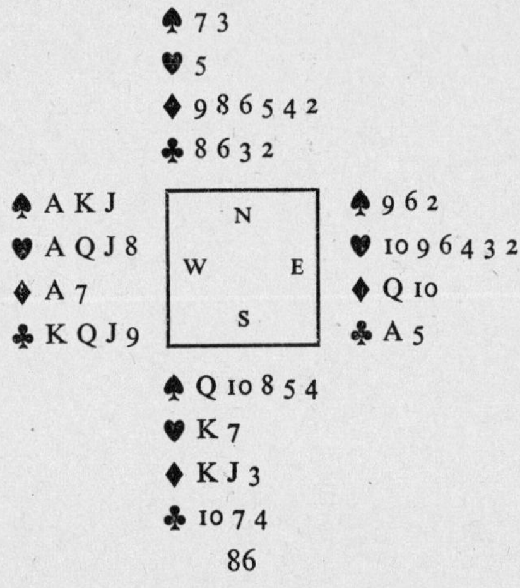

South, hoping against hope that East's bid was a sacrifice, led the ♣ 4 and the contract was made without difficulty.

A more cautious South would have opted for the concealed Dummy, and accepted an 800 penalty with as good a grace as possible. There are situations – like this one – in which a player who has to bid first is doomed whatever he does. All he can do is to try to lose as little as possible.

Case 6.

Here again both players were vulnerable. The exposed Dummy showed:

♠ Q 8 ♥ Q 9 8 5 2 ♦ 8 7 6 ♣ 8 3 2

South had dealt himself a very good hand:

♠ A K J 10 7 2 ♥ none ♦ K Q 5 3 ♣ K J 6

His obvious bid appears, at first blush, to be Four Spades with the exposed Dummy. South carefully considered this bid. He can almost certainly make ten tricks in Spades. But also he is void of Hearts. If East holds the Heart suit in strength, and has both the ♦ Ace and ♣ Ace, he can bid Five Hearts with a fair chance of making the contract. So South took his courage in both hands and bid Four Spades with the concealed Dummy. East cannot make any possible overbid.

East had also a good hand; nettled by South's bid, he doubled. The four hands were:

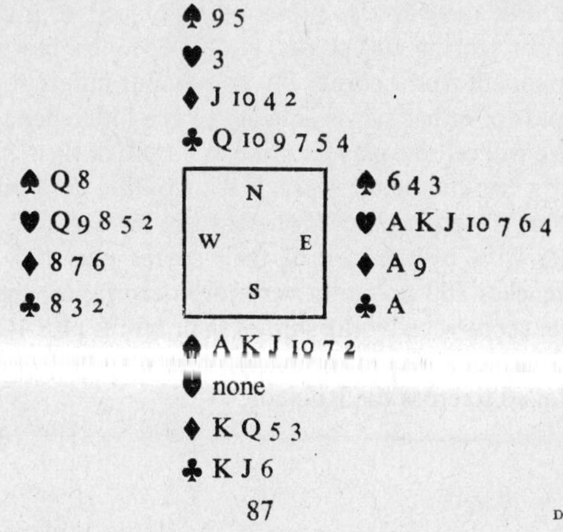

The ♥ 2 was led from West's hand and South made his contract with an overtrick.

These illustrative hands will have shown, I trust, what a good game Option is. Almost every deal can produce a battle of wits. I advise any Bridge player, who is thinking of playing this game for substantial stakes, to deal himself a number of trial hands, and thoroughly explore their possibilities, before he pits his wits against those of an experienced player.

Piquet

Piquet is one of the best of card games for two: with one exception – Option – I prefer it to any other. Though played with only thirty-two cards, it offers an endless variety of interesting situations; it has a high skill factor; and one knows exactly how long a game will take to play, as it consists of only six deals. A game, by the way, is known as a *partie;* this is one instance of its 'Frenchified' terminology. The game, in its original form, was known as Sant or Cent, but the French terms are said to have been adopted in compliment to Charles I's queen, Henrietta Maria.

The object of the game is to score points – as many points as possible. But there is also a secondary object: to make sure (if one can) of scoring 100 points, and to do one's best to prevent one's opponent from scoring 100 points. For failure to score 100, on the part of either player, makes all the difference to the final score. We will call the players A and B. If both of them have scored 100, but A has the better score, A wins by the *difference* in their scores plus 100 points. But if one of them has failed to reach 100, the other wins by the *sum* of their scores plus 100. If neither player reaches 100 points (a very rare occurrence) the one with the better score wins by the sum of their scores plus 100. In these last two instances the losing player is said to be 'rubiconed' i.e. he has failed to cross the Rubicon.

Examples

A scores 119 points; B scores 104. A wins by 115 points.
A scores 87 points; B scores 283. B wins by 470 points.
A scores 92 points; B scores 84. A wins by 276 points.

It is often touch and go whether a player makes the target of 100 points or not, and it is in these crucial situations that there is most scope for the exercise of skill.

If the game is played for stakes, they are usually calculated at so much a hundred points. The game is interesting enough in itself to render quite modest stakes – or no stakes at all – satisfactory.

How Points are Scored

Points are scored in two ways: in the calls (or declarations) before play begins, and in play. To this end, the mechanics of the game involve two distinct operations: (1) discarding from one's hand and taking in new cards, and (2) playing out the hand.

The Deal

The game is played with a pack of thirty-two cards, i.e. a standard pack from which have been removed all cards from the 6 to the 2 inclusive. The remaining cards rank in their Bridge order: A K Q J 10 9 8 7. There is no trump suit, all four suits having an equal status throughout.

The *partie* consists of six deals. The players take it in turn to deal. At the outset, they cut the pack to decide who shall deal first. Whoever cuts the higher card has the option of dealing or not dealing; he will normally elect to deal. If both players cut, say, a King, they reshuffle the pack and cut again.

To deal first is held to confer a (very slight) advantage, the reason being that, when it comes to the sixth deal, the score may be in a critical position, and the non-dealer has (as we shall see) greater scope for the exercise of judgement.

The deal having been decided, the dealer shuffles the pack and the non-dealer cuts it to him. The dealer then gives each player twelve cards, dealing them face downwards; it is usual to deal them either two at a time, or three at a time, the non-dealer receiving cards first. When each player has his twelve cards, the remainder are set aside, face downwards, to form the *talon* or *stock*.

Discarding and Taking in Cards

When the deal is complete, each player takes up his twelve cards and looks at them. Each is now entitled to replace a specified number of his cards by cards taken from the stock. The non-dealer, who is known as *Elder Hand*, may replace as many as five of his cards, and must replace one. If he does not want to replace as many as five, he may inspect the cards which he would have taken had he replaced the whole number. He does not show these cards to the dealer, who is known as

Younger Hand

The cards which a player replaces are not added to the stock, but are set aside (face downwards). At any time during the play either player can look at his own discards.

The Younger Hand takes in three cards, where the Elder Hand has taken in five, i.e. he takes the remaining three cards of the stock. He must take in one. If the Elder Hand decides to take fewer than five cards, the Younger Hand may take in any number up to the number left in the stock, e.g. if the Elder Hand takes in only two cards (inspecting the next three cards of the stock) the Younger Hand can take any number up to six. He must first take the cards left by the Elder Hand.

If the Younger Hand does not take the whole of the stock, he can, if he wishes, look at the remainder. He must decide whether he wants to do so after Elder Hand has led to the first trick. If he looks at them, Elder Hand is entitled to see them too; i.e. in practice Younger Hand will turn them face upwards. If Younger Hand decides not to look at them, Elder Hand cannot see them either; these cards remain face downwards.

The number of cards that either player takes will depend, of course, on what he has in his hand, and how he is planning his play. Intelligent discarding is one of the most important features of the game.

Declaration

When the exchange of cards has been completed, each player calls or declares his hand. Declarations are called in the following order: Point; Sequences; Quatorzes or Trios. They take the form of a conversational interchange. Its character can best be illustrated by an example.

Suppose that, when the exchange of cards for cards from the stock has been completed, Elder Hand holds:

♠ A K J 10 9 ♥ A K ♦ A J 9 ♣ J 10

while Younger Hand holds:

♠ Q 8 ♥ Q J 10 ♦ K Q 7 ♣ A K Q 8

the calling might proceed as follows:

E.H. 'Point of five.'

Y.H. 'Good.'

E.H. 'Five. A tierce to the Knave.'

Y.H. 'Not good.'

E.H. 'Five. Three Aces.'

Y.H. 'Not good.'

E.H. 'Then my score is still Five.' He leads to the first trick and Younger Hand declares: 'Tierce major, three; tierce to the Queen, six; fourteen Queens, twenty', and play proceeds.

This verbal counting, and repetition of the score at each stage, are a characteristic feature of the game, and after a few *parties* the beginner will have acquired the knack of it.

Let us now interpret the conversation to which we have just listened.

Elder Hand, who declares first, begins by naming his *point*. This is (normally) the number of cards in his longest suit; 'point of five' means 'I have a five-card suit'. When Younger Hand says 'Good' he means that he is not contesting the point, so Elder Hand scores five for it. If Younger Hand has a six-card suit or better he will say 'Not good'. If he also has a five-card suit, he will say 'How many?' This means: 'What is the point-count?' The point-count is: 11 for an 10 for Ace; a court card, other cards their pip value. So, in this case, Elder Hand, to the question 'How many?' would reply 'Fifty', and Younger Hand would then say: 'Good', or 'Not good', or 'Equal'. The holder of the better Point scores one for each card in the suit; if there is equality, neither player scores.

After the Point, Elder Hand declares sequences. If he has more than one, he declares his best sequence first. A sequence is three or more consecutive cards of the same suit. A sequence of three cards is called a Tierce, and counts 3 points if it is good. A sequence of four cards is a Quart, and counts 4 points. But sequences of more than four cards are worth a good deal more. A sequence of five cards (Quint) scores 15; a sequence of six cards (Sixième), 16; a sequence of seven cards (Septième), 17; a sequence of eight cards (Huitième), 18.

Whoever has the best sequence can score for any other sequences he holds, but only one of the players can score. Thus, if Elder Hand holds:

♠ A K Q ♥ A K Q ♦ A K Q J ♣ A K

and Younger Hand holds:

♠ J 10 9 8 7 ♥ J ♦ none ♣ Q J 10 9 8 7

Elder Hand has a Quart and two Tierces, but scores nothing for them, Younger Hand has a Sixième and a Quint, and scores both (31 points in all).

After the sequences, Quatorzes and Trios. A player has a Quatorze when he holds all four Aces, Kings, Queens, or Tens. (Four Nines, Eights or Sevens count nothing.) A Trio, similarly, is a holding of three Aces, Kings, Queens, Knaves, or Tens. As with the sequences, only one of the players can score for Quatorze and/or Trio. But he can score for as many as he holds. Thus we might find Elder Hand holding:

♠ A K Q ♥ A K Q ♦ A K Q 9 8 7 ♣ none

while Younger Hand held:

♠ J 10 ♥ J 10 ♦ J 10 ♣ A K Q J 10 9

This would be a maddening deal for Elder Hand. His Point of Six is not good; it is eclipsed by Younger Hand's Point of Six, which totals 60 to his 55. His four Tierces (there are two in the Diamond suit) are worthless, because Younger Hand has a Sixième. And his three Trios – Aces, Kings, Queens – also score nothing, since Younger Hand has a Quatorze of Knaves (usually called 'Fourteen Knaves') also a Quatorze of Tens. I might add – anticipating a little – that on this deal Elder Hand, though he scores nothing in the calling, takes all twelve tricks and scores a Capot (53); while Younger Hand scores 6 for his point; 16 for his Sixième; 14 for his Knaves; 14 for his Tens; and – because Elder Hand has scored nothing in the declaration – gets 60 more for a Repique. A total, on this deal, of 110 points.

THE PLAY. After the declaration of hands comes the *play* There are twelve tricks in all. Elder Hand leads to the first trick (a great advantage). Younger Hand must follow suit if he can, and there is no trump suit. The trick is won by the higher card of the suit played. A player who cannot follow suit may discard any card he wishes.

Scoring in the play is conducted, as in the declaration, conversationally. A player scores one point every time he leads to a trick; one point every time he takes a trick; one extra point for taking the last trick. And a player who has won the majority of tricks (seven or more) scores another 10 points.

ADDITIONAL SCORES. What gives Piquet an added piquancy is the scoring of Carte Blanche, Repiques, Piques, and Capots.

Carte Blanche is worth 10 points. These points can be claimed by any player who is dealt a hand containing no court card (K, Q or J). He establishes his *carte blanche* by counting his cards rapidly face upwards on the table. The value of *carte blanche* lies not so much in the 10 points scored as in the fact that they take precedence of any other score. Hence a *carte blanche* bars an adverse Repique.

A *Repique* is scored (in the absence of an adverse *carte blanche*) when one player clocks up a total of 30 points before he has led or played to the first trick, while his opponent fails to score. Either Elder Hand or Younger Hand can score a Repique.

A Repique counts 60 points.

A *Pique* is scored, by Elder Hand only, when he has amassed 30 points in the declaration and play before his opponent has scored anything. A Pique is worth 30 points.

Examples. (1) Elder Hand holds:

♠ A K Q J 10 9 ♥ A K Q ♦ none ♣ A K Q

Younger hand holds:

♠ none ♥ J 10 9 8 7 ♦ A K Q J 10 ♣ J 10

Elder Hand has a Point of six and Sixième; a Tierce in Hearts and another in Diamonds; three Aces, three Kings, and three Queens. All these are good. So his score in hand is 37 and he scores 60 more for his Repique: 97 in all. (Incidentally, he has a Capot, as will shortly become apparent.)

(2) Elder Hand holds:

♠ A K Q J 9 ♥ A K Q J ♦ A K Q ♣ none

This, on the face of it, is a more than useful hand. But Younger Hand holds:

♠ 10 ♥ 10 ♦ 10 9 8 7 ♣ A K Q J 10 9

He has a Point of Six and Sixième (both good); a Quart in Diamonds; and fourteen tens. He scores $6 + 16 + 4 + 14 = 40$, and 60 for a Repique.

(3) Elder Hand holds:

♠ A K Q J 10 ♥ A K Q J ♦ A 8 7 ♣ none

Younger Hand holds:

♠ none ♥ 10 9 8 7 ♦ K Q J ♣ K Q J 10 9

Elder Hand scores 5 for his Point; 15 for his sequence in Spades; 4 for his Quart in Hearts; 3 for his Aces. So far, 27. Now play begins. He leads to the first three tricks, which brings his total up to 30, and now adds 30 for his Pique.

An *equality* in the declaration does not bar a Repique or Pique. Thus, Elder Hand holds:

♠ A K Q 10 8 ♥ A ♦ 8 ♣ A K Q 10 8

Younger Hand holds:

♠ J ♥ K Q J 10 9 ♦ K Q J 10 9 ♣ J

Elder Hand has a Point of five totalling 49. So has Younger Hand. But Younger Hand has also two Quints, each worth 15 points, and fourteen Knaves, making 44 in all. He duly scores another 60 for his Repique.

Capot. This is scored by either player when he takes all twelve tricks. The Capot is worth 40, and takes the place of the 10 scored for the majority of tricks. A Capot is always worth 53 (12 for tricks, plus one for the last trick, plus the 40).

A Capot cannot count towards a Pique.

An Illustrative Partie at Piquet

We will call the players A and B. They cut for deal and A cuts the higher card. He elects to deal first.

First Hand

A deals: to B: ♠ 9 8 ♥ J 9 7 ♦ Q 10 9 8 ♣ K Q 9

to himself: ♠ K J 10 ♥ A 10 8 ♦ J 7 ♣ A J 10 7

B discards ♠ 9 7 ♥ 9 7 ♣ 9 and takes in ♠ A Q ♥ K Q ♦ K.

His hand is now: ♠ A Q ♥ K Q J ♦ K Q 10 9 8 ♣ K Q.

A throws ♥ 10 8 and ♦ 7. He takes in ♠ 7 ♦ A ♣ 7. So his hand is: ♠ K J 10 7 ♥ A ♦ A J ♣ A J 10 8 7

The declarations

B: 'Point of five.'

A: 'How many?'

B: 'Forty-seven.'

A: 'Good'.

B: 'Five. Tierce to the King.'

A: 'Good.'

B: 'Eight. And a tierce to the ten, eleven. Fourteen Queens: twenty five.'

(Play now begins)

B (playing ♦ K) 'Twenty-six.'

A (winning with ♦ Ace) 'One' (Leads ♣ Ace) ' Two'

. . . and so the play goes on. B wins seven tricks, including the last, and scores 45 points to 6 on the deal.

I will set out the remaining five deals more briefly.

The cards **in bold type** are discarded.			B's score			A's score		
Deal	B	A	Dec'n	Play	Total	Dec'n	Play	Total
2	(Y.H.) ♠ K 8 ♥ K J 10 9 8 7 ♦ Q ♣ **Q J 9** (a difficult discard) After discarding: ♠ K 8 ♥ K J 10 9 8 7 ♦ Q ♣ K 10 7 (Unlucky! Had he kept his Clubs he would have had the better sequence)	(E.H.) ♠ **Q J 9 7** ♥ Q ♦ A J 10 9 7 ♣ A **8** After discarding: ♠ A 10 ♥ A Q ♦ A K J 10 9 8 7 ♣ A	–	2	2	21	23	44
			Score so far:		47			50
3	(E.H.) ♠ **Q 9 7** ♥ none ♦ K Q **10 9** ♣ A J 10 9 8 After discarding: ♠ K 10 ♥ 10 9 ♦ K Q ♣ A J 10 9 8 7	(Y.H.) ♠ A J **8** ♥ A K Q 7 ♦ A **J 8** ♣ K Q After discarding: ♠ A J ♥ A K Q J 8 7 ♦ A 7 ♣ K Q	15	3	18	9	11	20
			Score so far:		65			70

Deal	B	A	Dec'n	Play	Total	Dec'n	Play	Total
4	(Y.H.) ♠ none ♥ A K Q J 8 ♦ K J 8 7 ♣ J 10 9	(E.H.) ♠ A K Q J 10 9 ♥ 10 ♦ A Q ♣ A Q 8 (leaves one card)	–	–		29	30 53	112
	♠ none ♥ A K Q J 9 8 ♦ K J 9 ♣ K J 7	♠ A K Q J 10 9 8 7 ♥ 7 ♦ A 10 ♣ A						
			Score so far:					
					65			182

B is massacred here. A (who has just missed a Repique, scoring 29 in hand) begins by playing out his eight Spades. B throws all his Hearts, keeping two guarded Kings. Now A produces the ♥ 7 and – as there is no indication what his last card is – B can only take a chance. He throws the ♦ J on the ♥ 7 and so loses all the tricks. A has Pique and Capot; and, in the remaining two hands, B must score 35 to save the 'Rubicon'.

Deal	B	A	Dec'n	Play	Total	Dec'n	Play	Total
5	(E.H.) ♠ A K J 10 9 8 7 ♥ J ♦ 10 8 ♣ Q 8	(Y.H.) ♠ Q ♥ A Q 9 7 ♦ A Q ♣ A J 10 9 7						
	After discarding: ♠ A K J 10 9 8 7 ♥ K 10 ♦ K 9 ♣ K	♠ Q ♥ A Q 8 ♦ A Q J 7 ♣ A J 10 9	96	20	116	—	6	6
			Score so far:					
	(B's worries are over. He has a Repique against the cards).				181			188

Deal	B	A	Dec'n	Play	Total	Dec'n	Play	Total
6	(Y.H.) ♠ A K Q 9 ♥ A 9 8 ♦ 10 9 ♣ A 9 8	(E.H.) ♠ J 10 7 ♥ Q J 7 ♦ A K ♣ K J 10 7 (No clear indication as to what should be thrown. In view of the score, A keeps all his high cards.)						
	After discarding: ♠ A K Q 9 8 ♥ A 9 ♦ Q 10 9 ♣ A Q	After discarding: ♠ J ♥ K Q J 10 ♦ A K J 8 7 ♣ K J	5	19	24	21	6	27
		Final score:			205			215

A's Quatorze just saves him from defeat on the last hand. He wins a well contested *partie* by 10 points, i.e. 110 points in all.

Throughout this illustrative game, the discarding and play have been of a high standard. If you are unfamiliar with Piquet, you will – I think – learn quite a lot about it by setting out these hands and playing them through.

Bezique

This is one of our standard card games for two players. I prefer Piquet, with which Bezique has some affinity, as having a higher skill factor and presenting more interesting problems in play. But Bezique has always had its devotees, and the Six Pack game, which will be described shortly, requires a very good brain indeed.

'Ordinary' Bezique is played with two Piquet packs (64 cards in all). You can buy Piquet sets with the type of marker that is traditionally used. But it will do perfectly well to remove from two ordinary packs the Twos, Threes, Fours, Fives and Sixes, and shuffle them together.

The player cutting the highest card deals; Ace ranks high. Eight cards are dealt, face downwards, to each player; they are normally dealt 3 – 2 – 3. The stock is then placed between the two players and the top card turned up to indicate the trump suit. If this card is a 7, the dealer scores 10.

Play is in two parts (as in Piquet): the Preliminary Play and the Play-Off. During the Preliminary Play each player's object is to score as many points as possible by acquiring, and declaring, scoring combinations. In the Play-Off the object is to take tricks which carry bonus points.

The Preliminary Play

The turned-up card (indicating the trump suit) is placed face upwards beside the stock. Now the non-dealer leads to the first trick; the dealer plays a card to it. He does not have to follow suit. The winner of the trick draws the top card from the stock; the non-winner draws the next card. Whoever won the trick leads to the next one. And so playing to tricks, and replenishing one's hand with cards (so that one always has eight), goes on until the stock is exhausted. In play, the Ten of a suit ranks next below the Ace, and higher than the King.

As long as this part of the game continues, there are only two objectives in winning tricks. They are (*a*) to score Aces and Tens, each of which counts 10 to the player who wins a trick containing one or both of them; and (*b*) to make *declarations*. A declaration can only be made by a player who has just won a trick. When he makes a declaration, he lays the cards concerned on the table.

The declarations, and the points which each carries, are:

(1) *Common Marriage* (King and Queen of a plain suit): 20.
(2) *Royal Marriage* (King and Queen of trumps): 40.
(3) *Bezique* (Queen of Spades and Knave of Diamonds): 40.

(4) *Double Bezique* (both Queens of Spades and Knaves of Diamonds): 500.
(5) *Four Knaves:* 40.
(6) *Four Queens:* 60.
(7) *Four Kings:* 80.
(8) *Four Aces:* 100.
(9) *Sequence* (A 10 K Q J of the trump suit): 250.

There is one other bonus score. A player who is dealt, or draws, the 7 of trumps, may, immediately after taking the trick, exchange it for the turned-up trump card. This ranks as a declaration.

Only one declaration can be made at a time.

Thus, suppose that the turned-up trump card is the ♥ Q. A player is dealt originally:

♥ A K 9 7 ♠ Q J ♦ Q J.

This is a nice hand: almost embarrassingly so. The hand includes two cards towards a sequence; Bezique; and the ♥ 7. The ♥ Q, if secured in exchange for the ♥ 7, will be a third card towards a sequence and a third card towards four Queens. The best lead would be the ♥ 9, which would probably win the trick. Then the ♥ 7 is exchanged. After next winning a trick, Bezique would be declared, and the ♠ Q and ♦ J laid on the table.

Do not forget that, after taking a trick, one can only make *one* declaration. Moreover, a subsidiary declaration must be made before a higher-scoring one. Thus, one cannot lay down the five top cards of the trump suit, claim a Sequence, and subsequently score the Royal Marriage. The latter must be scored first. If the sands were running out, and there were small prospect of taking tricks, one would, of course, score the Sequence at once and forfeit the points for a Royal Marriage.

The same card may figure in more declarations than one, provided they are of different kinds. Thus, the same ♦ J can figure in declarations of Bezique, Double Bezique, Four Knaves, and a Sequence. But it cannot be combined with two separate Queens of Spades to form two Beziques, or with three more Knaves to form a separate set of Four Knaves.

A card once declared remains on the table until it has been played.

Towards the end of the game, both players may well have a number of cards exposed on the table. Play can then become very interesting, since it is possible to calculate the maximum number of tricks that one's adversary can take, and perhaps to prevent his making any more declarations.

The Play-Off

The winner of the last trick, before the exhaustion of the stock, lead to the first of the eight tricks now to be played. In the play-off it is compulsory to follow suit. Only Aces and Tens now count; so the simplest plan is to collect the tricks one has won and count the Aces and Tens which they contain.

Element of Skill in Bezique

It will be seen from the above summary that the element of skill is far from negligible. You have to decide how far you should conserve good cards for declarations and how far you should use them for winning tricks. You must have a coherent plan, based on the declarations you hope to be able to make. As the end of the game draws near, you may find it necessary to try to win all the tricks, e.g. if the adversary has declared Bezique and you suspect that he has at least one more Bezique card. So don't part, without good reason, with the high trumps. Finally, a good memory plays an important part in success. A player with a first-class memory will, at the end of the game, know almost exactly what cards his opponent holds.

SIX PACK BEZIQUE

If memory, the power of concentration, and the capacity to frame a flexible plan of campaign, play their part in the comparatively simple game of Bezique, how much more is this true of the game when played with six packs: 192 cards in all.

Fundamentally, Six Pack Bezique is a glorified version of the game I have just described, but there are several important differences in the rules and scoring. Here they are:

(1) Twelve cards are dealt to each player instead of eight.

(2) A player who is dealt no King, Queen, or Knave, and shows his hand to his opponent, may score 250 for Carte Blanche. Carte Blanche can be scored again, after the first trick has been played, if the player holding it fails to draw a court card. And so on indefinitely, until a court card appears.

(3) No card is turned up to indicate the trump suit, and the exchange of the 7 plays no part in the game. The trump suit is that of the first Marriage Declared. So a player dealt (say) ♠ A A A K Q Q, among other cards, will make every effort to win the first trick and make Spades trumps.

(4) *Scoring*. The scores can run into almost astronomical figures. The various ranking items are:

Carte Blanche: 250.
Marriage in the trump suit: 40.
Common marriage: 20.
Sequence in trumps: 250.
Sequence in other suits: 150.
Bezique: 40.
Double Bezique: 500.
Treble Bezique: 1,500.
Quadruple Bezique: 4,500.
Four Aces of Trumps: 1,000.
Four Aces: 100.
Four Tens of Trumps: 900 (no score for other Tens).
Four Kings of Trumps: 800.
Four Kings: 80.
Four Queens of Trumps: 600.
Four Queens of 60.
Four Knaves of Trumps: 400.
Four Knaves: 40.
Winning the last trick: 250.

(5) There is no score for taking tricks containing Aces or Tens.

(6) In the Play-Off, these rules must be followed:

(*a*) One must follow suit if possible.
(*b*) If one can't follow suit, one must trump.
(*c*) One must win the trick if possible.

(7) Available cards can figure in comparable scoring combinations over and over again. Thus, one has scored 4,500 for Quadruple Bezique. One draws another ♠ Q, wins a trick, and can score Quadruple Bezique again. It is thus theoretically possible to score Quadruple Bezique five times.

The *Game* is not (as in Two-Pack Bezique) so many points up (usually 1,000). It ends when all the cards have been played. The points scored by the player with the lower total are deducted from his opponent's score, and the latter wins by the difference in points plus 1,000. But if the loser has failed to clock up 3,000 points, loses by the sum of the two scores plus 1,000.

In this case, as in Piquet, the player with the lower score is *rubiconed.* If neither player reaches 3,000, the player with the lower score is rubiconed.

Examples:

(*a*) A: 8,540, B: 4,900. A wins by 3,640 plus 1,000=4,640 points.
(*b*) A: 11,220, B: 2,940. A wins by 14,160 plus 1,000 = 15,160 points.
(*c*) A: 2,700, B: 2,530. A wins by 5,230 plus 1,000 = 6,230 points.

Obviously it may be worth incurring considerable sacrifices of material to make sure of rubiconing an opponent.

Cribbage

Cribbage is a purely English game, different in character from any other, and without any of the variants that more cosmopolitan games have produced. It is quite a good game to teach to young people; for while – in its simplest form – it involves little mental effort, it does inculcate the habit of rapid and accurate calculation.

Its object is simple: to achieve a prescribed number of points – 61 in Five-Card Cribbage – before one's opponent. Scoring is usually effected by 'pegging' on a special board; this enables both players to see at a glance that the last score has been correctly recorded. But, in the absence of a board, the scoring can be done on a piece of paper.

Normally there are two players. A full pack of 52 cards is used. The players cut for deal; the player with the lower card deals. Ace is low; if both players cut cards of the same denomination, they cut again. The non-dealer begins the scoring by pegging 'three for last'.

Five cards are dealt, face downwards, to each player, beginning with the non-dealer. They take up their cards and each discards two, face downwards, which are set aside; these four cards constitute the dealer's 'crib'. The non-dealer will throw cards which are no use to him and which (he hopes) won't much help the dealer either. The dealer, who will presently score the 'crib', will endeavour to contribute good cards to it without detriment to the remaining three.

Now the non-dealer cuts the remainder of the pack to the dealer. The latter turns up the top card of the bottom half of the pack. This card is called the 'start'. If the 'start' happens to be a Knave, the dealer at once pegs 'two for his heels'.

The Play

The play of the hand now begins. The non-dealer leads off by laying a card face downwards on the table. He announces its pip-value. The dealer then plays a card, endeavouring, if possible, to score. Then the non-dealer plays again; and so on; until all six cards have been played. But if the play of a card will bring the aggregate pip-value above 31, it is not playable. The pip-value of all court cards is 10; of the Ace, one.

Points Scored in Play

Pairs

A player duplicating a card played by his opponent scores two for a 'pair'. Should a third card of that denomination follow, 6 points are scored for a Pair Royal. And if yet a fourth card of that denomination can be played, a Double Pair Royal (12 points) is scored.

Runs

If three cards in succession form a sequence of three, 3 points are scored for a 'run'. A run can be extended to four, five, or even six cards. The cards constituting a run need not be played in any particular order; 2 3 4 make a run of three; so do 4 3 2. Similarly 5 4 2 3 counts as a run of four; 3 7 5 4 6 as a run of five. As this example shows, it is not necessary for a run of four to be preceded by a run of three.

Fifteens. Scoring at Cribbage revolves largely round the magic number *fifteen.* A player who brings the aggregate score in play to 15 at once pegs 'fifteen two'. He may score a run or pair at the same time.

Thirty-one. A player who brings the aggregate score to 31 exactly scores two.

'*One for Last.*' A player who cannot play a card without making the total more than 31 says 'Go'. If his opponent is similarly placed, he too says 'Go'. The play is now over. If the second player can contribute one or more cards, he does so. In any case he scores 'one for last'.

Examples of Scoring in Play

(1) A (dealer) holds J 8 5. B (non-dealer) has 7 6 4. B leads the 7. A plays the 8 ('fifteen two'). B plays the 6 '(three for a run'). The total is now 21. A plays the 5, scoring 4 for his run of four. B plays his 4, scoring 5 for his run of five. A says 'Go'. B says 'Go'. B scores one for 'last'.

(2) A (dealer) has 6 5 4. B has 6 6 4. B leads a 6. A plays a 6 (two for a pair). B plays his second 6 (six for a pair royal). A plays his 5. B plays his 4 (three for a run). A says 'Go'. B plays his 4, scoring two for a pair and two for 31.

The Show

The players' cards are now taken up again, and each 'shows' his hand. Scoring in the 'show' is on the same lines as in the play, except that the 'start' now becomes part of each 'show', and also of the 'crib'. Thus the show is a count of the scoring value of four cards; the crib, of five. In scoring the show, points are always scored in a definite order: (*a*) fifteens; (*b*) pairs; (*c*) runs; (*d*) flush; (*e*) 'his nob'.

We have already met with fifteens, pairs, runs. A flush scores (3 points) if all three cards in a player's hand are of the same suit. If the 'start' is of that suit also, 4 points are scored. 'His nob' counts 1. This is scored when a player holds a Knave of the same suit as the 'start'.

Examples

(1) The 'start' is a 10. B (non-dealer) shows first. He holds 8 7 5. This is a very poor hand. He scores 'fifteen four' (10 plus 5, and 8 plus 7) and that is all.

A (dealer) holds 10 5 5. A nice collection. He scores 'fifteen eight' (for each 10 can be paired with each 5 to make 15); 2 for the pair of Tens; 2 for the pair of Fives. Total: 12.

(2) The 'start' is a 5. B holds 4 4 6. He scores 'fifteen four' (4 5 6 plus 4 5 6); 2 for his pair of Fours; 6 for two runs of three. (The same card can be counted, over and over again, in every scoring combination of which it forms a part.) Total: 12.

A holds J J J. He scores 'fifteen six', plus 6 for his pair royal. One of his Knaves is of the same suit as the 'start', so he scores one more for 'his nob'. Total: 13.

When each player has scored his show, the dealer turns up his crib. This is scored on the same lines as the show, except that no flush is scored unless (a rare event) all five cards are of the same suit. But there are, of course, five cards that count in the crib, as against four in the show, so higher scores are possible. The maximum scorable in the crib is, as we shall see, 29.

FIVE CARD CRIBBAGE: SCORING COMBINATIONS IN THE CRIB

With a little practice these will soon become familiar. I don't, of course, give them all; a crib can be worth 20-odd points or nothing. But these are the ones that score most, or are most difficult to assess:

(a) 10-card and 5 combinations

Cards held	*Fifteens*	*Pairs*	*Total*
Q Q Q Q 5	8	12	20
Q Q Q 5 5	12	6 + 2	20
(Each Q scores 15 with each 5)			
Q Q 5 5 5	14	6 + 2	22
(The three Fives make another 15)			
Q 5 5 5 5	16	12	28

(There are eight fifteens here. Four consist of Q + 5, and four of 5 5 5.)

If the combination is as above, except that it consists of J 5 5 5 5, and if the J is of the same suit as the 5 which is the 'start', the total score is 29. And this, of course, is a most unlikely combination to hold; for no player is likely to contribute two Fives to his opponent's crib. But it might happen if the start were, say, a 6 and he himself began with 6 6 5 5 3.

(b) 9, 6 and 3 combinations

9 + 6 = 15. 9 + 3 + 3 = 15. 6 + 6 + 3 = 15.
6 + 3 + 3 + 3 = 15.

Cards held	*Fifteens*	*Pairs*	*Total*
9 9 9 9 6	8	12	20
9 9 9 6 6	12	6 + 2	20
9 9 6 6 6	12	2 + 6	20
9 6 6 6 6	8	12	20
9 9 9 3 3	6	6 + 2	14
9 9 3 3 3	12	2 + 6	20
9 3 3 3 3	12	12	24
6 6 6 6 3	12	12	24
6 6 6 3 3	12	6 + 2	20
6 6 3 3 3	10	2 + 6	18
6 3 3 3 3	8	12	20
9 9 6 6 3	10	2 + 2	14
9 9 6 3 3	8	2 + 2	12
9 6 6 3 3	12	6	18
9 6 3 3 3	10	6	16

(*c*) *8, 4, 3 in combination*

8 + 4 + 3 = 15. 4 + 4 + 4 + 3 = 15.

Cards held	*Fifteens*	*Pairs*	*Total*
8 8 8 4 3	6	6	12
8 8 4 4 3	8	2 + 2	12
8 8 4 3 3	8	2 + 2	12
8 4 4 4 3	8	6	14
8 4 4 3 3	8	2 + 2	12
8 4 3 3 3	6	6	12
4 4 4 4 3	8	12	20

(*d*) *7 and 4 in combinations*

7 + 4 + 4 = 15.

Cards held	*Fifteens*	*Pairs*	*Total*
7 7 7 4 4	6	6 + 2	14
7 7 4 4 4	12	6 + 2	20
7 4 4 4 4	12	12	24

(The double pair royal of Fours produces *six* pairs of Fours to make 15 with the Seven.)

(*e*) *6, 5, 4, 3 in combination*

Here there are runs to be taken into consideration, as well as pairs and fifteens.

Cards held	*Fifteens*	*Pairs*	*Runs*	*Total*
6 6 6 5 4	6	6	9	21
6 6 5 5 4	8	4	12	24
6 6 5 4 4	8	4	12	24
6 5 5 5 4	8	6	9	23
6 5 5 4 4	8	4	12	24
6 5 4 4 4	6	6	9	21
5 5 5 4 3	2	6	9	17
5 5 4 4 3	–	4	12	16

(Why 12 for runs? Because there are four combinations of 5 and 4, each, with the 3, making a run of three.)

Cards held	*Fifteens*	*Pairs*	*Runs*	*Total*
5 5 4 3 3	4	4	12	20
5 4 4 4 3	2	6	9	17
5 4 4 3 3	4	4	12	20
5 4 3 3 3	6	6	9	21

Hints to Beginners at Cribbage

(1) When discarding for your opponent's crib avoid, if possible, giving him a pair or a Five. High discards are to be preferred to low ones. But don't, of course, give him Tens or court cards if the start is a 5.

(2) When discarding for your own crib remember that it will have five cards in it, so it's worth while contributing good cards. But don't go all out to put your best cards into crib if it means wrecking your show.

(3) Pay special attention to the *play*, and plan it carefully. This is where indifferent players throw most points away.

(4) Always score in the prescribed sequence: fifteens; pairs; runs; flush (if any); 'his nob'.

(5) Familiarize yourself with the scoring combinations set out above, and make sure that you understand how each of the totals is arrived at.

SIX AND SEVEN CARD CRIBBAGE

In these games six (or seven) cards are dealt to each player instead of five. Otherwise they are played in the same way as Five-Card Cribbage, with the following exceptions:

(1) There is no 'three for last'.

(2) Six Card Cribbage is 121 points up ('twice round the board') and Seven Card Cribbage is 181 points up ('three times round the board').

(3) Play does not stop at, or before, the total pip-value of the cards played has reached 31. When a player scores for 31 or for 'go', the other player leads off again with one of his remaining cards. Here is an example from Seven Card Cribbage:

A (dealer), having thrown out two cards for crib, holds Q Q Q 9 9. B holds 8 7 7 6 4.

B plays 8. A plays Q (18). B plays 7 (25). A: 'Go'. B plays 6, scoring 'two for Thirty-one'.

A now plays Q. B plays 7 (17) A plays Q (27). B plays 4, again scoring 'two for Thirty-one'.

A now plays 9. B's cards are exhausted, so A plays his second 9, scoring two for a pair and 'one for last'.

Scoring Combinations at Seven Card Cribbage

The show at Six Card Cribbage, like the crib in all three games, involves five cards in all, and the most important of the relevant scoring combinations have already been given. But at Seven Card Cribbage, the show involves six cards (five in hand plus the start); hence there are some very high scoring combinations. Here are a few of the more significant:

Cards held	*Fifteens*	*Pairs*	*Runs*	*Total*
Q Q Q Q 5 5	16	14	–	30
Q Q Q 5 5 5	20	12	–	32
Q Q 5 5 5 5	24	14	–	38
Q Q Q Q 3 2	8	12	–	20
Q Q 3 3 3 2	12	8	–	20
Q 3 3 3 2 2	12	8	–	20
(Similarly with combinations of, say, 10 4 Ace.)				
9 9 9 9 6 6	16	14	–	30
9 9 9 6 6 6	18	12	–	30
9 9 9 6 6 3	14	8	–	22
9 9 6 6 6 3	18	8	–	26
9 9 3 3 3 3	24	14	–	38
6 6 6 6 3 3	24	14	–	38
8 8 8 4 3 3	12	8	–	20
8 4 4 4 4 3	16	12	–	28
4 4 4 4 3 3	16	14	–	30
7 7 4 4 4 4	24	14	–	38

Cards held	*Fifteens*	*Pairs*	*Runs*	*Total*
5 5 5 4 3 3	8	8	18	34
5 5 4 4 3 3	8	6	24	38
5 4 3 3 3 3	12	12	12	36
6 6 6 5 4 4	12	8	18	38
6 6 5 5 5 4	14	8	18	40
6 6 5 5 4 4	16	6	24	46
(This is the highest possible combination.)				
6 5 5 4 4 4	12	8	18	38
6 5 4 4 4 4	8	12	12	32
6 5 4 3 3 3	10	6	12	28
5 4 3 3 3 2	8	6	12	26

Cribbage for Four Players

This makes a good partnership game. The players are seated as in Bridge, with N – S partners against E – W. The game is almost identical with the two-handed game, the only difference being that each player throws one card instead of two into the crib. Hence one card fewer is dealt to each player; i.e. Five Card Cribbage becomes Four Card Cribbage; the six card game becomes a five card game; the seven card game becomes a six card game.

Here are two illustrative deals. This is the five card game (corresponding to Six Card Cribbage where there are only two players).

Deal 1

West deals first. The cards dealt are:

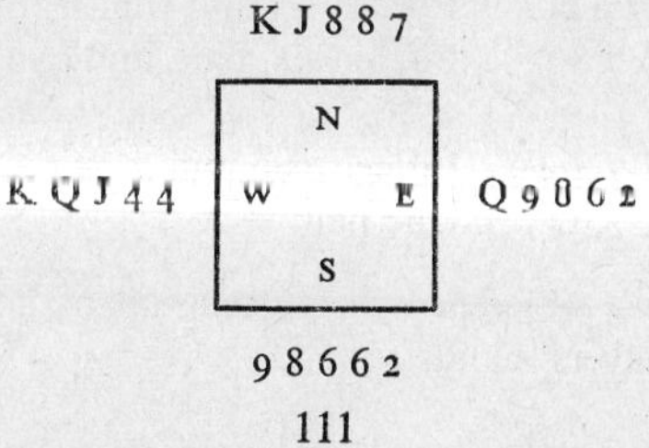

DISCARDING FOR CRIB

North throws K
East throws Q
South throws 3
West throws K

These cards having been discarded, West presents the pack to North to be cut, and turns up a 7 as the 'start'.

THE PLAY. (The running count is shown in brackets.)

North	*East*	*South*	*West*
J (10)	9 (19)	9 (28) a	Go
Go	2 (30) b	8 (8)	Q (18)
8 (26)	Go	Go	4 (30) c
Go	Go	Go	J (10)
8 (18)	8 (26) d	Go	4 (30) e
Go	Go	Go	–
7 (7)	6 (13)	6 (19) f	–
–	–	6 (25) g	

a: *North – South* score 2 for a pair.
b: *East – West* score 1 for last.
c: *East – West* score 1 for last.
d: *East – West* score 2 for a pair.
e: *East – West* score 1 for last.
f: *North – South* score 2 for a pair.
g: *North-South* score 6 for a pair royal and 1 for last.

North – South: 10 *East – West* 15

THE SHOW. (The start forms part of each hand and of the crib.)

North has: J 8 8 7 7. Fifteen eight and two pairs = 12.
East has: 9 8 7 6 2. Fifteen six and run of four = 10.
South has: 6 6 7 8 9 Fifteen six, pair, and two runs of four = 16.
West has: Q J 7 4 4 Fifteen two and a pair = 4.
West's crib: K K Q 7 3. One pair = 2.

(Note what a difference the turning-up of a 7 for the start made to all players' hands.)

Score so far (including play): *North – South* 38   *East – West* 33.

Deal 2. North deals. The cards dealt are:

East: 5 4 4 A A
South: Q J 7 7 7
West: 10 4 3 2 A
North: K 9 8 5 A

DISCARDING FOR CRIB:

East throws 5 (reluctantly)
South throws Q
West throws 10
North throws K

THE START: *North* turns up 6.

THE PLAY

East	*South*	*West*	*North*
4 (4)	J (14)	A (15) a	A (16) b
A (17) c	7 (24)	4 (28)	Go
A (29)	Go	2 (31) d	9 (9)
4 (13)	7 (20)	3 (23)	8 (31) e
–	7 (7)	–	5 (12) f

a: *East – West* score 2 for 15.
b: *North-South* score 2 for a pair.
c: *East-West* score 6 for a pair royal.
d: *East – West* score 2 for 31.
e: *North – South* score 2 for 31.
f: *North – South* score 1 for last.

Score so far: *North – South* 43   *East – West* 41 ('level pegging').

THE SHOW

East has: 6 4 4 A A   Fifteen four and two pairs = 8.
South has: J 7 7 7 6   A pair royal = 6
West has: 6 4 3 2 A   Fifteen two and run of four = 6.
North has: 9 8 6 5 A   Fifteen six = 6.
North's crib: K Q 10 6 5 Fifteen six = 6.

Score so far: *North – South* 55   *East – West* 55.

The rival partnerships have all but reached the half-way mark and, so far, have clocked up identical scores. This shows how important it is that the 'play' should be carefully planned.

AUCTION CRIBBAGE

This variant of the six card game was devised partly to add a little extra excitement, and partly to meet those maddening situations where the non-dealer holds (say) 9 9 6 6 5 5, and so can only keep a promising hand at the risk of losing more than he stands to gain. If he were dealer he could keep his 9 9 6 6 and throw the 5 5 into the crib, with every chance of two good scores.

So the crib is put up for auction as soon as the two hands have been dealt. The dealer has the right to bid first. He offers, say, 2 points for the crib. The non-dealer can let this bid stand or can over-bid with 3. Then the dealer can bid again if he likes; and so on till both parties are satisfied.

Points offered by the successful bidder are deducted from his score. So whoever secures the first crib starts the game with a minus.

There is an element of Poker in this game, of course. A player who does not particularly want the crib can, if he has flair, extract points from an over-eager opponent. Towards the end of the game the crib can become increasingly valuable, and one may pay as much as 6 or 7 points to wrest it from an opponent who is threatening to peg out. To add to the piquancy of these critical situations, the player who secures the crib has, in Auction Cribbage, the first show.

Suppose (for example) that A has scored 115 points and B 112 points. A holds J 5 5 5 3 A. B holds Q 10 8 7 7 6. Neither particularly wants the crib, but each player will bid up to maybe 10 points for the right to show first.

Black Maria

This is an 'avoidance' game: a development of the ancient game of Hearts. I invented it during World War I, and it has since received a good deal of publicity. On the whole it is, I think, the best card game for three players. It has inevitably an element of luck, but also a very high skill factor. The essentials of success are (*a*) good judgement in discarding; (*b*) an accurate memory; every suit must be counted down to the 2; (*c*) the capacity to plan one's end-play.

HOW BLACK MARIA IS PLAYED

The three players cut for deal; the lowest card is the dealer's. The ♣ 2 is removed from the pack; the remaining 51 cards are dealt out one at a time and face downwards to the three players. Each player then will have 17 cards in his hand.

Passing Cards

The players now inspect their hands. Each takes three cards and passes them, face downwards, to his right-hand neighbour. A player must choose the cards he means to pass before inspecting those he has taken in. When all have passed their cards, play begins.

The Play

The deal consists of seventeen tricks. The player to the dealer's left leads to the first trick; the others must follow suit if they can. A player who can't follow suit may discard whatever he likes. The trick is won by whoever has played the highest card of the suit led. The winner of the trick leads to the next one.

Penalty Cards

The winning of a trick is, in itself, of no importance. The object of the game is *not* to win tricks containing one or more penalty cards. The penalty cards are:

The ♠ Q (Black Maria) which counts 13 points against whoever wins it.

The ♠ K which counts 10 points against whoever wins it.

The ♠ A which counts 7 points against whoever wins it.

All the Hearts, which count 1 point each against those who win them.

Thus penalties totalling 43 points are incurred every deal. The game consists of an agreed number of deals – nine is a good number, as each player deals three times – and the adverse scores are then totalled and settlement made on the differences. Suppose, for example, that nine deals have been played and the adverse scores are:

A: 184 points.
B: 38 points.
C: 165 points.

A loses 146 points to B and 21 points to C, a total of 167 points.

B wins 146 points from A and 127 points from C, a total of 273 points.

C loses 127 points to B and wins 21 from A, an adverse difference of 106 points.

So, if (say) penny points are being played for, B will receive 13s 11d from A and 8s 10d from C.

We will now play through a few illustrative hands, designed to illustrate the finer points of this fascinating game.

Deal 1

(All these deals are hands from actual play.)

C has dealt and A leads to the first trick.

A's initial holding	*B's initial holding*	*C's initial holding*
♠ J 9	♠ A Q 10 7 6 2	♠ K 8 5 4 3
♥ Q 10 8 6 3	♥ K 7	♥ A J 9 5 4 2
♦ 8 7 2	♦ A 10 6 5 4 3	♦ K Q J 9
♣ A K Q 9 7 6 5	♣ 10 4 3	♣ J 8

Comment: A has a most unpromising hand. He has only two Spades: an insufficient guard should he be passed one or more penalty cards. And his long Club suit, from which the 4 and 3 are missing, is also a heavy handicap.

A passes to C	*B passes to A*	*C passes to B*
♦ 8 7 2	♥ K 7 ♣ 10	♦ K Q J

Comment: A decides that his best chance is to void a suit. Then, if he is passed the ♠ Q and ♠ K, he may be able to discard them. C is well satisfied with both his Spades and his Hearts. But I think he is running a risk in hanging on to the ♠ K, although it is four times guarded.

The Reconstituted Hands

♠ J 9	♠ A Q 10 7 6 2	♠ K 8 5 4 3
♥ K Q 10 8 7 6 3	♥ none	♥ A J 9 5 4 2
♦ none	♦ A K Q J 10 6 5 4 3	♦ 9 8 7 2
♣ A K Q 10 9 7 6 5	♣ 4 3	♣ J 8

Comment: C has the best chance of avoiding trouble.

The Play

The winner of each trick (card in italics) leads to the next one.

Trick	*A*	*B*	*C*
1	♣ *Ace*	♣ 4	♣ J
2	♣ 5	♣ 3	♣ *8*
3	♥ 3 (1)	♠ Q (13)	♥ *5* (1)
4	♥ *K* (1)	♠ Ace (7)	♥ 4 (1)
5	♠ *J*	♠ 10	♠ 8
6	♥ 6 (1)	♣ Ace	♥ *Ace* (1)
7	♥ Q (1)	♦ *K*	♦ 9
8	♠ *9*	♠ 7	♠ 5
9	♥ 8 (1)	♦ Q	♥ *J* (1)
10	♥ 7 (1)	♠ J	♥ *9* (1)
11	♥ *10* (1)	♦ 10	♥ 2 (1)

and A's six Clubs take the remaining tricks, which include the ♠ K (10).

SCORE: against A: 21
against B: 1
against C: 21

Comment: A, with his almost hopeless hand, took the bold course of leading Clubs in the hope of a 2 – 2 break. This gamble came off. C, at trick three, decided that a Heart lead was safest and duly collected the ♠ Q. He would have done better to lead a Spade. A, in spite of his initial *coup*, could not avoid being landed with the lead at the finish. But, in view of his initial holding, he might well have fared worse.

Deal 2

A's initial holding	*B's initial holding*	*C's initial holding*
♠ Ace	♠ Q 9 6 2	♠ K J 10 8 7 5 4 3
♥ Q J	♥ A 9 7 5 4 2	♥ K 10 8 6 3
♦ 10 9 8 7 5 4 2	♦ K Q J 6 3	♦ Ace
♣ A K Q 9 7 6 5	♣ J 10	♣ 8 4 3

Comment: Once again the danger to A lies in his long Club suit, from which the ♣ 4 and ♣ 3 are missing. B dislikes the Spade situation; he can get rid of the ♠ Q, but will probably receive one of the other penalty cards. C would feel happier if his Hearts included the 2.

A passes to C	*B passes to A*	*C passes to B*
♠ Ace ♥ Q J	♠ Q ♦ K Q	♥ K 10 8

The Reconstituted Hands

♠ Q	♠ 9 6 2	♠ A K J 10 8 7 5 4 3
♥ none	♥ A K 10 9 8 7 5 4 2	♥ Q J 6 3
♦ K Q 10 9 8 7 5 4 2	♦ J 6 3	♦ Ace
♣ A K Q 9 7 6 5	♣ J 10	♣ 8 4 3

Comment: A faces the future with misgiving. B is quite happy. C doesn't at all like not having the ♠ 2.

But C need not have worried. As so often happens, one of the other players – in this case A – had a more obdurate problem to contend with.

The Play

Trick	*A*	*B*	*C*
1	♦ K	♦ J	♦ *Ace*
2	♠ *Q*	♠ 9	♠ J
3	♦ 2	♦ *6*	♠ K
4	♣ 9	♣ *J*	♣ 8
5	♣ 7	♣ *10*	♣ 4
6	♦ *Q*	♦ 3	♠ Ace

And A must take the remainder of the tricks.

SCORE: against A: 33
against B: 10
against C: nil

Comment: A was almost defenceless, as the cards lay. His lead at trick three showed flair; it landed B with the ♠ K, but it deprived A of his only card of exit. Nor – since he had no Heart – could he save even a few points by leading out this suit.

Deal 3

A's initial holding	*B's initial holding*	*C's initial holding*
♠ A Q 10 6 5 3	♠ 8 7 4	♠ K J 9 2
♥ Q 10 5	♥ J 8 7	♥ A K 9 6 4 3 2
♦ 10	♦ A 9 8 7 5 4 2	♦ K Q J 6 3
♣ A K Q 9 7 6 5	♣ J 8 4 3	♣ 10

Comment: Again we find A with an obdurate Club suit. But this time he is more or less in command of the Spade situation, B would have an almost perfect hand were it not for his poor Spade holding. C's is a good, though not a very good, hand.

A passes to C	*B passes to A*	*C passes to B*
♣ A K Q	♥ J 8 7	♠ K ♦ K ♣ 10

The Reconstituted Hands

♠ A Q 10 6 5 3	♠ K 8 7 4	♠ J 9 2
♥ Q J 10 8 7 5	♥ none	♥ A K 9 6 4 3 2
♦ 10	♦ A K 9 8 7 5 4 2	♦ Q J 6 3
♣ 9 7 6 5	♣ J 10 8 4 3	♣ A K Q

Comment: For A, danger now lurks in his ponderous Heart suit. For B, in his ill-guarded ♠ K. C looks forward with some confidence to the outcome of the deal.

The Play

Trick	*A*	*B*	*C*
1	♦ 10	♦ *Ace*	♦ Q
2	♣ 9	♣ J	♣ *Ace*
3	♠ 6	♠ 8	♠ *J*
4	♥ *5*	♠ K	♥ 2
5	♣ 7	♣ 10	♣ *K*
6	♥ *Q*	♦ K	♥ 3
7	♣ 6	♣ 8	♣ *Q*
8	♠ 5	♠ 7	♠ *9*
9	♠ 3	♠ *4*	♠ 2
10	♣ *5*	♣ 4	♦ J
11	♥ *J*	♦ 9	♥ 9
12	♥ 10	♦ 8	♥ *K*
13	♥ *8*	♦ 7	♥ 6
14	♥ *7*	♦ 5	♥ 4

and A's high Spades take the last three tricks.

SCORE: against A: 41
against B: nil
against C: 2

Comment: A's Hearts, as he had expected, proved his undoing; for he knew that the rest of the suit was massed in C's hand (he had received three Hearts from B). His opening lead, however should have been the ♠ 10. But this, as the cards lay, would not have helped; C wins and returns a low card in the Heart suit, exactly as he did at trick four. The result shows that B had played wisely in passing his Hearts at the outset of the game. Once B's last Spade is played, A is doomed. B's ♣ 4 is a card of exit, and a battle develops in Hearts between A and C; C is bound to get the better of this if he has memorized A's cards. His lead at trick fourteen is the *coup de grâce*.

Canasta

This elaborate variation of Rummy first became popular about eight years ago. It is played with two packs of cards mixed together plus four Jokers (108 cards in all). As the twos are also 'wild' there are in effect eight Jokers.

Two, three or four players participate. The four-handed game is the most popular and affords most scope for skill. I will describe this first.

Values of the cards:		
	Jokers – – –	50 points each
	Twos – – –	20 points each
	Aces – – –	20 points each
	K Q J 10 9 8 – –	10 points each
	7 6 5 4 and black threes	5 points each

Red threes count 100 points each. But a side with all four red threes scores 800 for them.

Players cut for deal and partners as at Bridge. Partners – also as at Bridge – sit opposite to one another. The first deal is made by the player to the right of whoever, in drawing, drew the highest card.

Eleven cards are dealt to each player. The remainder form the *stock pile*. To this, as in all Rummy games, will be added a *discard pile*.

The players look at their hands. Anyone who has a red three must at once place it face upwards on the table. These cards play no part in the game; they just mean bonus points for those who draw them. A player who has laid one or more red threes on the table replaces them in his hand from the stock pile.

The *object* of the game is to score as many points as possible. Points are scored by *melding* cards, i.e. laying them face upwards on the table. A *meld* consists of three cards of a kind, of which two at least must be *natural*. Thus valid melds are A A A, A A Joker, A A 2. But A 2 Joker, A 2 2, A with two Jokers, are not valid melds.

High scores depend on melding seven cards of a kind. Each such meld is a *canasta* (basket). A canasta must include four natural cards at least. Thus 9 9 9 9 2 2 Joker would be a valid meld. A *natural canasta* (one which contains no twos or Jokers) carries a bonus of 500 points; a mixed canasta (containing one or more twos or Jokers) carries a bonus of 300 points. Cards of the appropriate denomination can be added to a completed canasta.

Let me now resume my account of the play. The top card of the stock pile will (as in Rummy) have been turned up. Each player in turn takes a card from the stock pile, discarding one card which he doesn't want. This may, of course, be the card he has taken in, or in certain circumstances he can take the whole of the discard pile, which to begin with consists of only one card but may soon attain sizable proportions.

Before a side makes its first meld the discard pile can be taken by a player who holds a natural pair matching its top card, together with the necessary count. The count to be shown before making the first meld depends on the score. A side which has not yet reached 1,500 can make its first meld with a count of 50. From 1,500 to 2,995 the count for the first meld must be at least 90. After 3,000 the count required is 120. Game is usually 5,000 up.

Suppose, then, it's the beginning of the game and you have not so far melded. Your cards include 9 9 and a Joker, and the player to your right discards a 9. You show your pair of nines and Joker, take the discard pile, and put down the three nines and Joker (count: 80) for your first meld. After that you can meld freely.

Competition to secure the discard pile is keen, as big scores depend upon getting possession of it. A first essential in good play, therefore, is not – if you can avoid doing so – to throw a card which will enable your left-hand adversary to collect the discard pile.

So the game proceeds, each side endeavouring to meld so far as is tactically sound and, of course, to build up canastas. Each player can contribute to his partner's melds.

After the first meld the pack can be taken, not only with a natural pair corresponding to the top card, but with one natural card and a wild card. So the side that melds first has a decided advantage. The *riposte* to this is the device of 'freezing the pack'.

Stop Cards

The four black threes, like the red threes, play a unique part in the game. A black three is a 'stop card'. If played to the discard pile the next player cannot in any circumstances take it. Hence black threes should be carefully conserved for use when there is a big discard pile and a risk that the next player may be able to take it. Also, of course, a discard pile containing one or more black threes is a very useful capture.

A card matching a completed canasta is also a stop card so far as the adversaries are concerned unless one of them can produce a natural pair of the same denomination as the cards of the canasta.

Freezing the Pack (i.e. the Discard Pile)

The pack is 'frozen' by the discard of a Joker or a 2. This is placed transversely across the other cards so that the card underneath it remains visible. A 'frozen' pack can only be taken by a natural pair matching the top card of the discard pile. The other side is thus temporarily deprived of two advantages which accrue as soon as it has melded: the privilege of taking the pack with a natural card plus a wild card, and the privilege of taking the pack if the top card corresponds to any of one's own melds.

Going Out

A hand ends when a player has melded all his cards, provided he has made at least one canasta. Going out carries a bonus of 100 points unless the whole hand of eleven cards is melded at one turn (including, of course, a canasta). This is called 'going out concealed' and carries a bonus of 200 points.

Of course, going out is not the primary object of the game. If, as may well happen, you are in a dominating position and building up canasta after canasta, to go out would be very foolish. In the four-handed game a player who is in doubt whether to go out or not may ask his partner: 'May I go out?' before drawing his last card from the stock. In this case he must abide by his partner's decision.

Scoring. Bonuses are scored first:

Natural canastas (each)	500 points
Mixed canastas (each)	300 points
Red threes (each)	100 points
All four red threes	800 points
Going out	100 points
Going out concealed	200 points

The values of the cards melded are then added. Thus a canasta of (say) nine Kings, of which one is a Joker and two are deuces, counts 60 plus 50 plus 40 = 150. A meld of three natural sevens counts a modest 15. Black threes cannot be melded except at the final turn by a player who is going out. They then score 5 each.

Cards left in a player's hand and not melded count against the partnership: their value is subtracted from the combined count of bonuses and melds. Moreover, red threes count against a partnership if neither of its members has melded. So it is possible to start with a minus score. If a partnership has a minus score it need observe no minimum in making its first meld.

Hints to Beginners

The tactics and strategy of Canasta have been reduced by experts to something of a fine art. I have not space to discuss them in this book. But don't forget that, as in Contract Bridge, the first essential for success is *good partnership understanding*.

Do all you can to facilitate your partner's game, and make your own plan of campaign intelligible to him so that he can help you.

Concentrate at the start on winning the first pack. Pay special attention to the discards of your left-hand adversary, or you may present this important pack to the opponents.

If your opponents are apparently building up a winning advantage go out as quickly as possible. This means you must concentrate on getting at least one canasta.

On the other hand don't go out if the advantage is with you. Every time you can take the discard pile that advantage is enhanced. This is eminently a game where Providence is on the side of the big battalions.

Don't freeze the pack on any and every possible occasion. Freeze only – unless you can't help yourself – when you have the better chance of taking the discard pile.

Finally, this is a game in which misunderstandings with partner are very liable to occur. You may be doing the very thing that he doesn't want. So courtesy, tolerance and, above all, equanimity are assets which those with whom you play will appreciate.

CANASTA FOR TWO PLAYERS

The game is as described above, except that each player is dealt fifteen cards instead of eleven and must have two canastas to go out.

I do not myself care for this game. It tends to be too one-sided. A player who gets an initial advantage can, if he plans intelligently, keep on freezing the pack for his opponent while he himself piles up half a dozen or more canastas.

CANASTA FOR THREE PLAYERS

Thirteen cards are dealt to each player; two canastas are needed to go out. The score is 'all against all'. The only way to win is to go all out for a good score, and not worry about freezing the pack to impede one's left-hand neighbour.

Poker

Poker is, historically, a derivative of the much older game of Brag. But, in its modern form, it has come to us from America. During the last fifty years it has gained enormously in popularity. And it would no doubt be even more widely played – especially in clubs – if its legal status had not been prejudiced by the chaotic state of our gaming laws. There is some reason to hope, however, that, by the time this book appears, it will no longer be permissible for the police to take arbitrary action against an otherwise respectable club because poker is played on its premises.

The prejudice against poker derives from the belief, rooted in pure ignorance, that this is a gambling game comparable to chemin-de-fer or baccarat. There is no comparison whatever. In the opinion of every card expert who has ever given evidence in a court of law the 'skill factor' of Poker is higher than that of any other card game, not excepting Contract Bridge. By this I mean that it is more certain that, over a given period, good players will win and bad players will lose than is the case with Bridge or with any other game. (The only exception is the game I call Challenge, which is too difficult and too limited in its appeal to find a place in the repertory of games played in card clubs.)

Poker is eminently suited for adoption as a club game because it cannot be played satisfactorily by fewer than five players, while a full table requires seven. And why is it so popular? For a number of reasons.

(1) Its mechanics are very simple. Anyone can learn *how Poker is played* in, maybe, half an hour. But to learn to play Poker well demands not only a sound knowledge of its relevant mathematics but months, if not years, of practice.

(2) Poker is a game in which each player is operating 'on his own'. He can thus play as erratically as he likes without provoking antagonism. Indeed, since Poker *must* be played for stakes (however minute), the more erratically he plays the more popular he is likely to be!

(3) Each deal is a separate event. Hence, if there is a vacancy at a table one can join it at any time; and, if there is a sufficiency of players, one can quit the table at any time without spoiling the game for others.

(4) Finally – and herein lies the secret of Poker's popularity – it can be very exciting. Every deal may produce a battle of wits. One needs not only a knowledge of the mathematics of the game, but a capacity to judge how other players' minds are working. For the 'psychological' element of the game is just as important as the 'mathematical'; they are very nicely balanced. No one playing for the first time in a new 'school' can hope to do

more than hold his own till he has had some opportunity of judging what type of game its other members play.

Why Poker must be Played for Stakes

Poker is almost the only game in which money stakes are essential. They can of course be quite small, just as the stakes at Bridge can be quite small. But stakes there must be, because the game consists, in essence, in competitive betting on the value of the hands held. If one player is prepared to bet more than any of the others, he wins the whole of the money staked *without showing his hand.* He may, in fact, hold nothing at all (hence the popular delusion that Poker is 'just bluff'). Obviously, if there were in fact no money at stake, competitive betting could go on indefinitely and there would be no skill factor at all.

'Bluffing' is an intrinsic part of the game, but the player who thinks that he can win much, or win often, by bluffiing against good players will very rapidly be disillusioned.

How Poker is Played

There are two varieties of Poker as it is normally played in clubs: 'Straight' Poker and 'Pots'. I will first explain 'straight' Poker.

(1) The number of players is from five to seven. They are seated at a circular table. One full pack of cards is required. (In clubs two are used, the pack being changed at prescribed intervals.) The arrangement of seats is determined by drawing cards, the player in the lowest-numbered seat having the first deal. After the first deal it passes in rotation to the left.

(2) Before the deal the player to the dealer's left puts up one chip (the *ante*). (Chips of various colours are provided for club play; playing at home one can of course use matches or anything else. I shall expound the game in terms of chips won and lost, since it makes no difference what the value of one chip is.) The player next to the *ante* puts up two chips; this is the *straddle.* Only these two players – the *ante* and the *straddle* – need, unless they wish to do so, risk any money on the deal.

(3) The dealer now shuffles the pack, which is cut to him by his right-hand neighbour. He then deals five cards face downwards and one at a time to each player. The players take up their hands and inspect them, taking care not to show their cards to any of the other players. Competitive betting now begins.

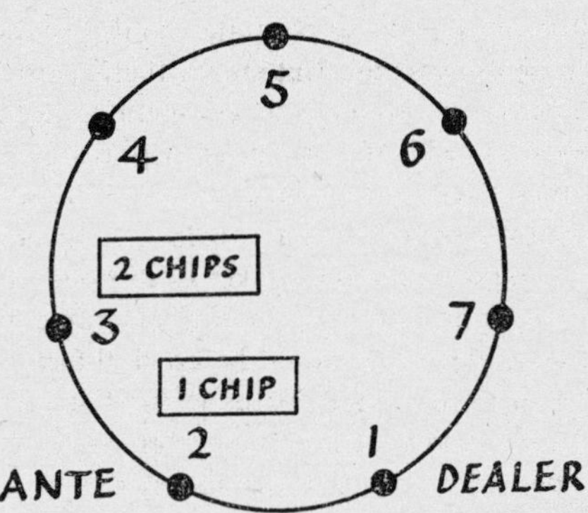

(4) The player next to the straddle (No. 4 in the diagram) is the one who is 'first to speak'. If he thinks he has a reasonable chance of eventually holding the best hand, he says 'Play' and puts up four chips. If he thinks little of his chances he throws his cards face downwards on the table and has no further interest in the deal. If he has elected to play the next player can either say 'Play', also putting up four chips, or can increase the total by any number of chips up to eight, or can throw his hand in.* And so on with the remaining players. If the initial bet of four chips has been increased to eight, the player next coming in may, if he wishes, make the total sixteen; thenceafter it cannot be increased by more than eight chips at a time.* Betting continues until (*a*) one player has wagered more than anyone else is prepared to put up, in which case he takes all the chips staked without any of the hands being shown, or (*b*) two or more players have staked the same amount, in which case the game continues.

* These are the normal club rules. In private play the school itself will determine to what extent it is permissible, in competitive betting, to increase the stakes.

I have not yet explained what constitutes a winning hand; this must stand over till I have finished expounding the mechanics of the deal.

Meanwhile, here is an example of the way the betting might go when the seven players have looked at the cards.

No. 4: ('first to speak'). 'Play' (puts up 4 chips).
No. 5: 'No' (throws his hand in).
No. 6: 'Play' (puts up 4 chips).
No. 7: 'No' (throws his hand in).
No. 1: 'Double' (puts up 8 chips).
No. 2: 'No' (throws his hand in, abandoning his chip).
No. 3: 'Play' (puts up another six chips).
No. 4: 'Make it 16' (puts up another 12 chips).
No. 6: 'No' (throws in, abandoning 4 chips).
No. 1: 'Play' (puts up 8 more chips).
No. 3: 'Play' (puts up another 8 chips).

There are 53 chips staked, which will go to the eventual winner plus such other chips as may be staked after the *draw*.

(5) *The Draw*. There are three players left in the game: Nos. 3, 4, and 1. Each of these, in the order in which cards were first dealt to them, discards as many cards as he likes from his hand (he can, if he is crazy enough, throw all five) and receives the corresponding number from the dealer. These also are dealt face downwards. Thus No. 3 (who will receive cards first) may ask for two cards; No. 4 (who next receives them) for three cards; No. 1 (the dealer, who gives himself cards last) may say 'I'm taking one'. Now the betting begins again.

(6) The player who reopens the betting is the one who spoke first of those who have survived. In this case No. 4, who was actually first to speak. He can either bet or 'check', which means that he is not increasing the stake.* If he bets he can bet up to a maximum of eight chips and this, again, applies to subsequent bets. In the case we are considering we will suppose that No. 4 checks. No. 1 also checks. No. 3 says 'Twenty-four', putting up another eight chips. No. 4 throws his hand in. No. 1 says 'See

* This is the practice at most clubs. At others whoever reopens the betting must stake at least one more chip.

you at 24', also putting up another eight chips. No. 3 now announces what he holds, at the same time laying his hand face downwards on the table. No. 1 also lays his hand face downwards on the table, announcing what he holds. Whoever has the better hand takes all the chips that have been staked.

In the (very rare) event of two players holding equal hands the chips staked are divided between them.

This description of the mechanics of the deal has taken me a good deal longer to write than the deal would in fact take. The average deal at 'straight' Poker lasts about a minute. For it may well happen that only one player is prepared to bet, in which case he collects the ante and straddle; or that no one has a hand good enough to bet on, in which case the straddle (last to speak) collects the ante.

(7) *Ranking of Hands.* A player bets before the draw if he thinks he stands a reasonable chance of finishing with the best hand. After the draw he continues to bet as long as he thinks his chance justifies the risk, or because he is deliberately staging a bluff. In making their initial bets players will have in mind the ranking order of the hands eventually shown. This ranking order of hands is as follows:

i. *Royal Straight Flush.* The five top cards (Ace highest) of a suit, e.g. ♥ A K Q J 10.

ii. *Straight Flush.* Five cards of a suit in sequence: e.g. ♠ 9 8 7 6 5 or ♣ 5 4 3 2 A. Here the Ace ranks as the lowest card; it can be high or low at Poker as one chooses. But it cannot serve both purposes at once; 3 2 A K Q is not a straight.

iii. *Fours.* Four cards of the same denomination together with any fifth card: e.g. ♠ 8, ♥ 8 5, ♦ 8, ♣ 8. If two players both hold fours (a not uncommon occurrence) the higher denomination of fours wins.

iv. *Full Hand* (*or Full House*). Three cards of one denomination with two of another denomination: e.g. K K K 5 5; 7 7 7 A A. Should these two hands be opposed to one another the former is the better.

v. *Flush.* Five cards, not in sequence, in the same suit: e.g. ♦ A 8 5 4 2. If there are two competing flushes their relative rank depends on the highest card in each, or on the next highest card if their highest cards are the same. ♦ A 8 5 4 2 beats ♣ K Q J 9 6 and ♦ A K 7 6 3 beats ♣ A Q J 10 4.

vi. *Straight.* Five cards, not in the same suit, in sequence: e.g. ♠ 9, ♥ 8, ♦ 7, ♦ 6, ♥ 5. If two straights meet one another the higher one wins.

vii. *Threes.* Three cards of the same denomination, with any two others of different denominations; e.g. 9 9 9 A 4. Here again 'three nines' must win against 'three eights'. If three players finish with 'threes' there is likely to be keen competitive betting.

viii. *Two Pairs.* Two cards of one denomination and two of another, with a fifth card of a third denomination: e.g., A A 3 3 9 or K K Q Q 6. The former hand would win, as the Aces rank higher than the rival Kings. Similarly, A A 4 4 2 will win against A A 3 3 K.

ix. *One Pair.* Two cards of the same denomination, with three others: e.g. A A 7 5 2; Q Q J 9 6. The former would win.

x. *Hands Containing Not Even One Pair.* These may participate in the final 'showdown' and may on occasion win. Thus, two players have drawn one card to a flush and both have failed to make it. They both check after the buy; other players have already thrown in. A holds ♠ K 7 4 3, ♦ 6; B holds ♥ Q J 10 8, ♣ 5. A wins because his hand is 'King high', where B's is only 'Queen high'. Had B drawn the ♣ A he would have won. He would also have won had he drawn the ♣ K, since while both players have Kings, B has the next highest card, a Queen.

Equality. Players divide the chips staked where they both hold Royal Straight Flushes (a thing I have never seen, or ever expect to see) or identical Straight Flushes, or Straights headed by cards of the same denomination. They also divide if they both hold (say) A A J J 6 or A K 9 3 2.

(8) *Division.* If there are only two players left in the game either may invite the other to divide the 'kitty' before they have shown their hands.*

(9) *Penalties.* It is usual in club play for Royal Straight Flushes, Straight Flushes, and Fours to carry 'penalties'. The holder of a Royal Straight Flush receives (say) 16 chips from each of the other players at the table (whether they drew cards

* In some clubs, however, this is not permissible.

or not); the holder of a Straight Flush, 8 chips; the holder of Fours, 4 points. Should two players qualify they are both paid. A player who is dealt one of these high hands 'pat' and can find no one to play against it may claim penalties by showing his cards.

Relative Frequency of the Various Hands

The table of precedence of Poker hands, as we may call it, is based upon the *a priori* chance that a particular type of hand will be dealt 'pat'. There are 2,598,960 ways in which a hand of 5 cards can be dealt from a pack of 52 cards. They are made up as follows:

Royal Straight Flushes	4
Straight Flushes	36
Fours	624
Full Houses	3,744
Flushes (other than Straight Flushes)	5,108
Straights (other than Straight Flushes)	10,200
Threes	54,912
Two Pairs	123,552
One Pair	1,098,240
Hands containing one Pair or better	1,296,420
Hands containing no Pair	1,302,540
	2,598,960

Hence (given a perfect shuffle) it is an almost even money chance that any given hand will start worth at least one Pair.

Let us now consider three examples from actual play.

Illustrative Deal 1

We will call the seven players A B C D E F G. A is 'first to speak'. E is dealer. F is the 'ante' and has put up one chip. G is the 'straddle' and has put up two chips.

The hands dealt are:

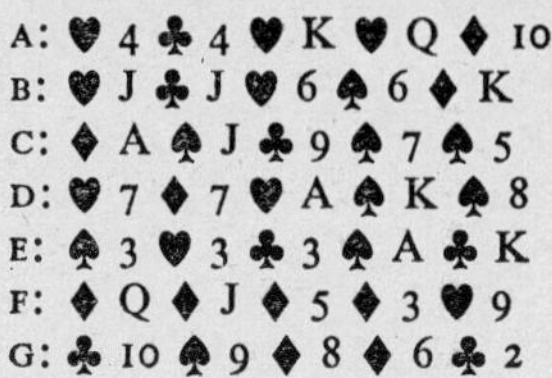

A: ♥ 4 ♣ 4 ♥ K ♥ Q ♦ 10
B: ♥ J ♣ J ♥ 6 ♠ 6 ♦ K
C: ♦ A ♠ J ♣ 9 ♠ 7 ♠ 5
D: ♥ 7 ♦ 7 ♥ A ♠ K ♠ 8
E: ♠ 3 ♥ 3 ♣ 3 ♠ A ♣ K
F: ♦ Q ♦ J ♦ 5 ♦ 3 ♥ 9
G: ♣ 10 ♠ 9 ♦ 8 ♦ 6 ♣ 2

BETTING BEFORE THE DRAW. A has only a Pair of Fours. This is nothing like good enough to play on; with seven players, the 'first to speak' should not open on less than a pair of Aces. A throws in.

B has pairs of Knaves and Sixes ('Knaves up'). He says 'Play' and puts up four chips.

C's hand is worthless and he throws in; so does D, who has only a pair of Sevens.

E has three Threes. This hand is good enough to double on. He says 'Make it eight' and puts up eight chips.

F has four Diamonds. If he can buy a fifth he will have a Flush: probably the winning hand. The odds against his drawing a fifth Diamond are roughly four to one; the stakes so far subscribed do not offer him these odds. Nevertheless E, who is of an optimistic temperament, decides to play and puts up seven more chips. In the long run such play will lose.

G's hand is worthless. He abandons his two chips.

B says 'Play' and puts up another 4 chips.

There are thus three players left in, and 26 chips, so far, to play for.

THE DRAW AND SUBSEQUENT BETTING. F draws one card, throwing the ♥ 9. He receives the ♣ Q. He now has merely a pair of Queens.

B throws the ♦ K and receives the ♦ 9. He still has his two Pairs.

E draws two cards to his Threes and does not improve.

There is no betting. B 'checks' and both the other players see him. E takes the 26 chips.

Illustrative Deal 2

The hands as dealt:

A: ♥ 4 ♦ 4 ♣ A ♣ Q ♣ 8
B: ♣ 10 ♣ 9 ♣ 7 ♣ 4 ♦ 5
C: ♥ K ♦ K ♣ 5 ♠ 3 ♦ 2
D: ♥ 3 ♣ 3 ♣ J ♥ 9 ♠ 6
E: ♥ A ♦ A ♠ 9 ♦ 9 ♣ K
F: ♠ A ♠ 7 ♠ 5 ♠ 4 ♠ 2
G: ♥ 10 ♥ 8 ♥ 6 ♥ 5 ♣ 6

BETTING BEFORE THE DRAW. A, with a pair of Fours, throws in. B throws in. Some players speak first on four to a Flush and to do so, very occasionally, has something to be said for it; because such play keeps the other players guessing, when one draws one card, as to what one's original holding is. But the play is mathematically indefensible and B is a cautious player.

C has a pair of Kings. As two players have already thrown in he is justified in playing on Kings and he puts up 4 chips.

D (a pair of Threes) throws in.

E has pairs of Aces and Nines ('Aces up'). He elects to double, putting up 8 chips.

F has a very fine hand: a 'pat' Flush headed by the Ace. He decides not to double again, however, as G has yet to speak and it is not certain that C will play for the double. He says 'Play', putting up seven more chips.

G, with two chips already staked, decides to draw to his Flush in Hearts and puts up six more chips.

C puts up four more chips. He would be better advised to retire. Two players have come in after the stake has been doubled. C's hand must be potentially the worst of the four.

THE DRAW AND SUBSEQUENT BETTING. F, asked what cards he wants, says 'Play these'.

G draws the ♠ Q to his four Hearts. His hand is now worthless.

C keeps his two Kings and draws ♠ K, ♠ 8, ♥ 2. He has now 'improved' to three Kings. Even so, against a declared 'pat' hand, this isn't good enough.

E (dealer), drawing last, throws the ♣ K and gets the ♥ J in exchange.

The four competing hands now are:

C (first to speak): Three Kings.
E: Aces and Nines.
F: An Ace Flush.
G: A 'bust'.

C checks. E checks without looking at his fifth card. This is a practice often adopted. He may have made a Full House (though the odds are nearly 11 to 1 against his having done so). But if he has done so, and if F raises him, he can of course raise again.

F ignores the chance that E has made his Full House, and bets eight more chips. The remaining players throw their hands in, and F collects the 40 chips staked.

Illustrative Deal 3

This is as exciting a deal as I can recall. It is, of course, very rare indeed for five really promising hands to come up against one another.

The cards dealt were:

A: ♥ 3 ♣ 3 ♠ 10 ♣ 6 ♦ 2
B: ♠ 6 ♠ 5 ♠ 4 ♦ 3 ♠ 2
C: ♠ A ♥ A ♣ A ♣ 5 ♣ 4
D: ♥ 7 ♦ 7 ♣ 7 ♠ 3 ♥ 2
E: ♦ K ♣ K ♦ 9 ♠ 9 ♦ A
F: ♣ Q ♣ J ♣ 10 ♣ 9 ♦ 5
G: ♠ K ♠ Q ♥ J ♦ 10 ♥ 9

BETTING BEFORE THE DRAW. A threw his hand in, of course.

B, with a 'pat' Straight (6 5 4 3 2) was only too pleased to open.

C, with three Aces, doubled, putting up 8 chips.

D, with three Sevens, said 'Play', also putting up 8 chips.

E has a difficult decision. 'Kings up', as it stands, is hardly likely to win and the stake may yet be further increased. E decided to throw in.

F has a wonderful chance: four cards to a Straight Flush, open at both ends. The odds are slightly worse than two to one against his making a straight or better. He said 'Play' and put up another 7 chips.

G has a Straight to the King (a better hand than B's). He raised the stake to 16 chips.

B, somewhat reluctantly, put up 12 more chips. C, D and F each put up 8 more. There were thus, before the draw, 80 chips to play for.

THE DRAW AND SUBSEQUENT BETTING. F (the ante) drew first, throwing his ♦ 5. The odds are 45 to 2 against his making a Straight Flush, but the minor miracle was effected: he drew the ♣ 8. He could be virtually certain of success, whatever the other players drew.

G, of course, drew no cards.

B was in something of a dilemma. He suspected that G had a better 'pat' hand than his own. But if he threw the ♦ 3, drawing one card, he had slightly worse than one chance in five of converting his Straight into a Flush; he had also an outside chance of a Straight Flush. He decided to draw, and (unluckily for him) was rewarded with the ♠ 8, making him a Flush.

C kept his three Aces and drew the ♥ 4 and ♦ 4. This gave him a three-Ace Full House: enough to win perhaps ninety-nine times in one hundred.

But D, as well as F, was to finish with a better hand than C's. He drew to his three Sevens, and received the ♠ 7 and ♥ K. He thus had four Sevens.

There was some heavy betting on this hand. B checked; he was prepared to 'see' at least one raise. C raised the stake to 24 chips; D promptly made it 32. F said: 'Play for 32.'* G, remarking 'What's going on here?', threw his hand in; B reluctantly followed suit. Both players were satisfied that at least one player, and probably two, held a Full House or better.

C, as F had anticipated, made the stake 40 chips; D, cautiously, said 'See you'. Now F made the stake 48 chips and both C and D saw him. He thus collected the 176 chips staked plus 8 chips from

* In some club circles exception is taken (quite improperly) to a player's 'lying low' on what is almost certainly a winning hand. But the avowed object of the game is to win as many chips as possible, and F, sensing that there might be another raise somewhere, was perfectly within his rights in waiting to see if the stake would be raised again. 'Sporting' play may, of course, pay in the long run; but every player must decide for himself about that.

each player for his Straight Flush. D, who had lost 48 chips, was recouped to the extent of 24 chips for his Fours.

Very, very few deals provoke as much competition as this one. Sometimes the play can be remarkably dull for a long sequence of deals: that is why infinite patience is among the many qualities that serious Poker demands. And – let me repeat – no player can hope to win in the long run whose decisions, before the draw, do not conform to the mathematical chances of the situation.

Elementary Mathematics

In 'straight' Poker, unlike 'Pots', only two of the seven players *must* put up any money. Therefore any player who risks more than he stands to gain is playing badly. That is why it is so important that he should know whether he is, or isn't, risking more than he is likely to get back.

All play should be based on the (mathematical) expectation of a profit. When that expectation disappears, a good player will cut his losses and not throw good money after bad.

These generalizations only apply to betting *before* the draw. After the draw, the game is primarily psychological. The element of 'bluff' is introduced. (Of course, a bluff may be planned before cards are bought, but only where it offers a possible alternative to losing money already staked.) After the draw betting will depend not only on calculations of chances, but on calculations as to the way different players react in varying situations. That is why one must learn to know one's 'school'.

A full analysis of the mathematical aspects of Poker would demand far more space than I have at my disposal. But here are a few simple facts which every player should know. Not all players, by any means, do in fact know them; for example I am constantly being asked, by players who have been playing for years, what the odds are against getting Threes or better if one draws three cards to a pair

ENTERING THE GAME. The player who is first to speak should not play on a worse hand than a pair of Aces. If he has thrown in the next player should not play under a pair of Kings. For the next player the minimum should be a pair of Queens; for the next, a pair of Tens. The dealer, if those in front of him have thrown in, can reasonably play on a pair of Eights; the ante can challenge the straddle on any pair, however small, or on an Ace and a King.

SUBSEQUENT BETS. Here mathematical theory will not take us very far; with more than two players, calculations become very complicated. But, first, it is a sound rule to assume that all players are observing the minimum requirements set out above. Hence, if the player 'first to speak' has put up four chips, it is foolish to put up four on a pair of Kings. One is risking more than one is likely to gain. What should one do on two pairs? Some players always double; some never do. The best plan is to vary one's game; double occasionally, especially if one's higher pair is a good one (Knaves or better); on other occasions be content to put up four chips and see how the betting develops.

One should constantly vary one's style of play to keep other players guessing.

THE ODDS AGAINST IMPROVEMENT. Let us now look at what I may call the basic odds, which anyone having mathematical knowledge can work out for himself from the table given on page 132. Here they are.

IMPROVING A PAIR. If one draws three cards to a pair, the chances are that, in 100 draws, one will finish with:

Two pairs	16 times.
Threes	11·4 times.
Full House or better	1·3 times.
	28·7 times.

So the odds against improving a pair, if one draws three cards, are 71·3 to 28·7, or almost exactly five to two. That is to say, one can expect to improve twice out of seven times.

If one keeps a 'kicker' with one's pair, drawing two cards only (this is often done for tactical reasons), the odds against improvement are lengthened. They are very nearly three to one. But one's chance of getting two pairs is very slightly increased.

IMPROVING TWO PAIRS. Here there is only one possible

'improvement': one's two pairs can develop into a Full House. The odds against this are $10\frac{3}{4}$ to 1.*

IMPROVING THREES. Drawing two cards to Threes, one may expect to get, in every 100 draws:

Full house	6·1 times
Fours	4·3 times.
	10·4 times.

So the odds against improving one's Threes, if one draws two cards, are better than 9 to 1.

If one draws only one card to one's Threes (which again is a very frequent tactical play) one's chances of a Full House are slightly improved; one's chances of Fours only half as good. Taking the two together, the odds against improvement are nearly 11 to 1.

DRAWING TO A STRAIGHT. An 'open-ended' Straight consists of four cards in sequence where there is room to complete the sequence of five at either end: e.g. 10 9 8 7; either a J or a 5 will complete the Straight. The odds against success are 38 to 9, or slightly less than 5 to 1.

If the Straight is not open-ended (e.g. A K Q J, 4 3 2 A, or 10 8 7 6), the odds against success are just under 11 to 1.

DRAWING TO A FLUSH. With four cards to a Flush, the odds against 'filling' the Flush are 38 to 9, or slightly over 4 to 1. Players are sometimes tempted to draw two cards to a Flush, especially where three of the five highest cards are held. This, however, is seldom a rewarding gamble; the adverse odds are 23 to 1.

POTS

'Pots' are more exciting than 'straight' Poker, and in some clubs only pots are played. In others, one or more pots are

* This is an extremely simple calculation. Suppose one holds A A 9 9 3. One throws the 3. There are 47 unknown cards, any one of which may be drawn. Four – the remaining two Aces and two Nines – will produce a Full House. Hence the adverse odds are 43 to 4, or $10\frac{3}{4}$ to 1.

played at stated intervals, e.g. every ten minutes. A 'pot' is a deal to which every player must contribute; hence the ultra-cautious player, who at straight poker can throw his hand in five times out of seven without risking anything, must at least play sufficiently often to give himself a chance of getting his money back. The pots most often played are (*a*) Jack Pots; (*b*) Freak Pots; (*c*) Misère Pots. There are many others, but I shall only be able to make passing reference to them.

JACK POTS

Each player puts two chips into the 'pot', i.e. these stakes are segregated in the centre of the table. But such chips as a player subsequently stakes he must place in front of him so that every player can see at a glance how much in all has been staked.

The cards are dealt in the ordinary way. The player on the dealer's left speaks first, as there is no ante or straddle. This player has the right of 'opening' the pot. He can only do so if he holds a pair of Knaves or better. He is not obliged to open, however strong his hand; indeed it is theoretically unsound for the player who is first to speak to open on a pair of Knaves only. If he can open, and wishes to do so, he says 'I open'; if not, he says 'Pass'. The opener of a pot puts up 4 chips. If a player doesn't open, the right to open passes to the player to his left and so on round the table. If no one opens, the hands are thrown in and the pot is 'sweetened' by the addition of half a chip from each player. The cards are then shuffled and dealt again.

A player who has passed does not throw his hand in; he still has the right to play in the pot. When it is opened it is opened with four chips. The player next to the opener now says 'Play' (putting up four chips), or 'Double' (putting up eight chips), or immediately throws in his hand. Competitive betting continues, as in straight poker, until everyone is satisfied.

Now cards are drawn and betting begins again, the opener of the pot being the first to speak.

Before drawing cards the opener may, if he wishes, 'split' his openers; but if he does so he must announce the fact to the table. This situation occurs where opener holds, say, ♠ J ♥ J 9 8 7 and the initial stake has been raised and perhaps re-raised. In such a situation the opener may not think it worth while to put up another 12 chips; he can throw his hand in but must keep his cards (face downwards) in front of him so that he can show his openers at the conclusion of the deal. Alternatively he may say 'Splitting openers'. He then places one of his Knaves face downwards in front of him, and draws one card to his straight flush.

An Illustrative Jack Pot

We will call the players A B C D E F G. G is the dealer; A is first to speak. The cards dealt are:

A: ♠ 5 ♥ 5 ♦ 10 ♣ K 3
B: ♠ K Q J ♥ 7 ♦ 5
C: ♠ 9 8 ♥ 3 ♣ A 5
D: ♠ 7 ♥ 6 ♦ Q ♣ 7 2
E: ♥ 10 2 ♦ 6 2 ♣ 10
F: ♠ A 4 3 ♦ A ♣ 4
G: ♥ K 9 8 4 ♦ 3

A, B, C, D cannot open. E opens on his two pairs. F, with Aces up, could (and in my opinion should) raise the pot; but F does not want to drive other players out. He says 'Play' and, like the opener, puts up four chips.

G, who has four to a flush, decides – correctly – to play. A plays (foolishly) on his pair of fives; B plays on his open-ended straight. C throws in, and D, though he holds a pair, very sensibly throws in also.

There are five players left in the pot. So far there are 14+20=34 chips to play for. I will set out the rest of the play in tabular form:

	E	F	G	A	B
Throws out	♦ 6	♠ 3	♦ 3	♦ 10 ♣ K 3	♦ 5
Draws (A is first served)	♦ 7	♥ J	♠ 10	♠ 6 ♦ 4 ♣ 6 (makes two pairs)	♥ A (makes top straight)

	E	F	G	A	B
Bets (E bets first)	Check	Check	Check	Check	Double (8 chips)
	Throws in	Sees B (8 chips)	Throws in	Throws in	

B, who has made a top straight, wins the pot against F's Aces up. E shows his openers. B collects 42 chips. (14 chips contributed to the pot and 28 chips subsequently staked.)

FREAK POTS

In Freak Pots, all Twos are 'jokers' or 'freaks'; they can represent any card. So it takes a much better hand to win a Freak Pot than is needed to win a Jack Pot; one should not play, as a rule, unless one has a reasonable chance of finishing with high Threes. And there are few hands on which one stands much of a chance of winning if one's hand contains no Freak.

In these pots also there is a new class of hands: Fives. For example, K K K 2 2 would be declared as Five Kings. Fives rank below a Royal Straight Flush, but higher than any other Straight Flush.

The pot consists, as before, of two chips contributed by each player. There are no opening requirements; a player can open on anything.

An Illustrative Freak Pot

As before, G is the dealer and A is first to speak. The hands dealt are:

A: ♥ 5 3 ♦ 6 ♣ J 6
B: ♠ K 10 ♥ A ♦ 3 ♣ 8
C: ♠ 6 ♦ J 5 ♣ K 9
D: ♠ J ♥ 7 ♦ 10 9 8
E: ♠ 5 ♥ Q ♦ K 4 ♣ 3
F: ♥ 10 2 ♦ 2 ♣ 10 7
G: ♠ A 4 ♦ A 7 ♣ 4

Only two of the four 'freaks' have been dealt, and F has both of them. His pair of Tens therefore give him four Tens to draw to; he has every expectation of winning the pot.

A speaks first and passes; B passes; C passes. D, who has a 'natural' straight, is tempted to open but prudently decides to wait. E passes; F opens; G decides (not wisely) to play on his two pairs. A, B and C throw their hands in; D plays; E throws his hand in. So there are three players and 26 chips (14 + 12) to play for.

CARDS DRAWN. They are first offered to D who, however, says 'No cards'.

F throws his ♣ 7 and receives the ♥ 9. He ends, as he began, with four Tens.

G keeps his two Aces and draws ♠ 9 8, ♣ A. His three Aces would be very nice in a Jack Pot (though if this were a Jack Pot they would lose to D's straight) but they are not likely to win against a player who has opened the pot and then bought only one card. He *may* have drawn to concealed threes, or to a straight flush, but it's much more likely that he has opened the pot on fours.

F (opener) bets first. He says 'Double', putting up four chips. G sees him, throwing good money after bad. D, who is certain that one or other of the players can beat him, wisely throws in his straight.

F wins against G, collecting 34 chips.

MISÈRE POTS

These pots have in recent years become very popular; in many clubs they are played more frequently than any of the others. The reason for their popularity lies in the fact that a good hand, unless it is a 'pat' 8 or better (what this means will shortly be made apparent) can be ruined in the draw; while an unpromising hand can quite easily win. A Misère is therefore more of a gamble than other Poker deals; the 'imponderables' tend to outweigh the 'ponderables', and the laws of chance operate with less certainty than is the case in Freak Pots or Jack Pots.

The objective in Misère is the holding of the *worst* hand, judged by the standards which normally apply. The Ace ranks as the lowest card; hence the worst possible hand is 6 4 3 2 A, not all of the same suit. This holding is often called a 'royal' Misère. It is not nearly so rare as a Royal Straight Flush. There are only four possible ways of dealing a 'pat' Royal Straight Flush, but there are 1,020 ways in which a 'pat' royal Misère can be dealt.*

As with a Freak Pot, a Misère Pot can be opened on any hand. But not more than three cards can be drawn. (This is not a harsh restriction; no one but a lunatic would draw four.) It is considered poor play to open a Misère, with the intention of drawing more than one card, unless one is last to speak. And even this is dubious policy, since someone with a better hand may be lying in wait, perhaps with the intention of doubling.

An Illustrative Misère Pot

There are, as before, 14 chips in the pot.

The cards dealt by G are:

To A: J 10 9 7 6
To B: K 8 5 2 A
To C: K Q 8 5 2
To D: Q 10 9 3 2
To E: J J 9 6 A
To F: Q 10 7 5 2
To G: K Q 8 3 A

I do not give the suits of the various cards. Unless a player holds a flush, these are irrelevant.

A (first to speak) passes. B has a good hand; if he throws his King and draws 7 6 4 or 3 he will stand a good chance of winning. So B opens. C plays; D and E throw their hands in. F plays; so does G; both these players are proposing to take two cards. A now throws in, so there are four players in the pot. Each has put up 4 chips.

* This is a very simple calculation. There are four cards of each denomination; four multiplied by itself four times is 1,024. Of these deals four are flushes and therefore do not qualify.

THE DRAW AND SUBSEQUENT BETTING:

	B	C	F	G
Cards thrown:	K	K Q	Q 10	K Q
Cards drawn:	6	7 3	10 5	6 4
Held after the draw:	8 6 5 2 A	8 7 5 3 2	10 7 5 5 2	8 6 4 3 A
Betting (B, as opener, bets first):	Check	Check	Throws in	Double (puts up 4 chips)
	Sees G	Throws in		

G's is a forward double. It is by no means certain that his is the best hand. But he knows B's play sufficiently well to be fairly sure that the latter would double on a 7-high hand or better and believes the same to be true of C. He calculates, therefore, that his double is worth the risk. When B sees G, C decides that one or other of the hands against him is better than his 8 7 5 3 2. He is right, too; and G is right – but only just right – in believing that his hand will beat B's. His 8 6 4 3 A wins by a short head (the third card) against 8 6 5 2 A, and G collects 14 + 16 + 8 = 38 chips.

Misère: Second Illustrative Deal

G (dealer) distributes these cards:

To A: 8 8 6 4 3
To B: K J 9 6 5
To C: 9 8 7 5 2
To D: K K Q 4 2
To E: 8 6 4 3 A
To F: J 10 9 7 7
To G: K 6 5 3 A

A (first to speak) opens. He has 8 6 4 3 to draw to. B, obviously, throws in. C doubles. This is a tactical double. C is proposing to 'stand' on his cards, which may well win if there is no better 'pat' hand out; and he wants to limit competition. D throws in. E doubles again, guessing C's tactics correctly; had C held a really good hand (7 high or better) he would probably not have tried to freeze his competitors out. F throws in. G is a gambler. He holds four cards to a 6-high hand; a 4 or 2 will probably win the pot, and a 7 may do so. In spite of the risk that A or C will raise the pot still further, G puts up his 16 chips.

A is more cautious; he throws in. C stays in the pot, putting up 8 more chips. He thinks that E's redouble may be a bluff: an attempt to make him throw one of his cards.

There are now chips 14+52=66 in the pot.

CARDS DRAWN. C says 'No cards'. E says 'No cards'. G throws his K and draws a 4. The rival hands are: C: 9 8 7 5 2
E: 8 6 4 3 A
G: 6 5 4 3 A

THE BETTING. C speaks first, as the opener (A) has thrown in. He checks. E, aware that there may be a 'royal' to his left, also checks. G, of course, doubles (putting up 8 more chips). C throws his hand in. E sees G, since the latter is well placed for a bluff. G wins and takes a pot of 82 chips.

Seven-Card Stud Poker

This is a fascinating variant of the game. It can be very exciting – and very expensive too. The rules vary from 'school' to 'school'. I give those followed in one of the better-known clubs.

HIGH-CARD STUDS

Before the deal each player contributes 1 chip to the 'kitty'. This is his maximum liability if he decides not to play.

The objective in a High-Card Stud is to finish with the best hand. The dealer begins by dealing three cards to each player, two of them face downwards, the third face up. The players look at the cards which have been dealt face downwards, placing them again face downwards in front of them after they have seen what cards they are.

Betting now begins. The player with the highest exposed card bets first; if two players have equally high cards, the player who bets is the one nearest to the dealer's left. Only one chip at a time can be bet, but this can be raised – one chip at a time – up to a maximum of four. There is no obligation to bet and any player can at any time throw in.

When everyone is satisfied, the dealer gives each player still in the game a fourth card, face upwards. There is a second round of betting, on the same lines as before; then a fifth card is dealt to those players who are left in, again face upwards. From now onwards each player who has not thrown in will have five cards in front of him: two concealed, the other three exposed.

After the third round of betting each player left in may discard one card. He can either throw an exposed card, or a concealed card (which he does not expose). If a player is prepared to 'stand' on his five cards he says so; if he 'stands', however, he may not change his mind and discard next time. When all have decided whether to discard or not, a card is dealt to each player who has asked for one, and betting proceeds as before. A player who has thrown a concealed card gets another one face downwards; otherwise the cards are exposed. This process is repeated, when the betting is over, for one round more.

When cards have been dealt for the last time, betting on the final hands begins. Now a player can check, or can bet any number of chips up to four. Bets can be raised by four chips at a time.

It should now be apparent why the game can be so expensive, and why a prudent player will retire if his hand is unpromising. Each player, before the final round of betting begins, may have staked 16 chips.

High Card Studs: An Illustrative Hand.

(The concealed cards are shown in brackets.)

The dealer (G) gives these cards:

A: (♠ J 7) ♠ 8
B: (♦ A ♣ 9) ♠ K
C: (♣ 8 3) ♦ 9
D: (♦ 7 [illegible]) ♣ 6
E: (♠ Q ♦ 5) ♣ K
F: (♦ K ♣ 5) ♦ 4
G: (♥ K 10) ♦ 6

B, who has the first exposed K, opens the betting. He bets one chip. C and D throw their hands in. E, F, G, A each put up one chip.

Another card is dealt to each player. The hands are now:

A: (♠ J 7) ♠ 8 ♥ 5
B: (♦ A ♣ 9) ♠ K 9
E: (♠ Q ♦ 5) ♣ K ♠ 5
F: (♦ K ♣ 5) ♥ 8 ♦ 4
G: (♥ K 10) ♣ J ♦ 6

Again B bets first. He checks; so do E, F, G, A.

More cards are dealt and the hands are:

A: (♠ J 7) ♠ 8 ♣ 7 ♥ 5
B: (♦ A ♣ 9) ♠ K 9 ♥ J
E: (♠ Q ♦ 5) ♣ K ♥ 9 ♠ 5
F: (♦ K ♣ 5) ♥ 8 ♦ 8 4
G: (♥ K 10) ♦ J 6 ♣ J

G, with a pair of Knaves showing, bets first. He raises the one-chip bet to 2 chips, and A, B, E, F all put up one chip more.

Now those players who wish to do so can discard. No one has a very good hand. A has a pair of Sevens and the faint hope of a Spade flush. B has a pair of Nines, fortified by an Ace and a King. E has nothing better than a pair of Fives. F has a pair of Eights. G, with a pair of Knaves, is, at the moment, leading the field.

A throws his exposed ♥ 5 and receives (face upwards) the ♣ 10. B throws the ♥ J and receives ♥ 4. E throws ♥ 9 and gets ♥ 3. F throws his (concealed) ♣ 5 and receives (face downwards) the ♦ 10. He now has four Diamonds. G throws ♦ 6 and receives ♣ Q, which gives him four cards to an open-ended straight as an alternative draw to his pair of Knaves.

G again bets first. He puts up one more chip, making three. A throws his hand in. B puts up another chip; E throws in; F puts up a chip. There are three runners for the final draw.

B is served first. He throws ♥ 4 and receives ♠ 10. F (aiming at his flush) throws ♥ 8 and gets ♠ 6. G decides to keep his pair. He throws ♣ Q and receives ♥ 7. So the final hands are:

B: (♦ A ♣ 9) ♠ K 10 9
F: (♦ K 10) ♦ 8 6 ♠ 6
G: (♥ K 10) ♦ J ♣ J ♥ 7

F must bet first. For all he can tell, B may have a flush. So he checks; B checks; E checks. The hands are shown and F collects 7 + 13 = 20 chips.

MISÈRE STUDS

Here, as in ordinary Misère pots, the objective is the 'worst' hand. Play is on exactly the same lines as are followed in High Card Studs, so I need do no more than give a couple of illustrative hands. In both hands G is the dealer; the player whose bet is in bold type speaks first; the card in bold type is discarded. To simplify matters, I have not specified the suits of the cards dealt, as these are throughout irrelevant.

Illustrative Hand 1

A	B	C	D	E	F	G
(9 2) K	(2 A) 7	(5 4) 2	(J 10) 7	(6 3) 4	(3 A) 9	(J 9) 6
throw in	2 4	***Bets 1*** 3 4	throw in	2 4	2 4	throw in
	(2 A) 7 4	(5 4) 3 2		(6 3) 4 4	(3 A) 9 5	
	 5	***Bets 4*** 5		4 5	4 5	
	(2 A) Q 7 4	(5 4) Q 3 2		(6 3) 10 4 4	(3 A) 9 5 A	
	 6	 6		throw in	***Bets 5*** 6	

A	B	C	D	E	F	G
	(2 A) *K* 7 4	(5 4) 5 3 2			(3 A) Q 5 A	
	 7	*Bets 6* 7			throw in	
	(2 A) 7 5 4	(7 4) 5 3 2				
	 11	Bets 11				

B wins 7 + 33 + 40 chips (12 of which were his own contribution).

N. B. The number of chips as having been staked represents the total for each player, including his last bid.

COMMENT ON ILLUSTRATIVE HAND 1. This was a typically exciting deal. Three players (B, C, E) began with excellent prospects; F would have done better not to compete. He should certainly not have 'lingered' when the betting became competitive. B and C both improved their chances when the fourth card was dealt to them, though C – with an open-ended straight – has not nearly so good a hand to draw to as B. Neither benefits from the next two cards dealt, but both finish with good hands. After the last deal, C has to bet first. C holds 7 5 4 3 2. B is showing 7 5 4, so C can only lose if B's concealed cards are 2 A or 3 A. Hence he risks the maximum. B sees him, of course, but does not raise, since C's hand may be 6 5 3 2 A. A well-fought battle.

Illustrative Hand 2

This is an example of a hand won on a bluff. F, with 6 3 2 showing, decides to bluff when he throws his second card. His 6 3 2 make a formidable show on the table. E makes a pair and is clearly out of the running. Even so, G decides that it isn't worth while to see F. He is 10 high, and doesn't care to risk 4 chips on an outside chance of winning 22. F throws his hand unseen, and wins 7 + 15 chips = 22, of which 8 are his own.

A	B	C	D	E	F	G
(5 2) K 1	(J J) 7 throw in	(J A) 10 throw in	(4 2) Q 1	(9 3) 4 1	(10 6) 3 Bets:check 1	(Q 4) 7 check 1
(5 2) K 2 throw in			(4 2) K Q throw in	(9 3) 5 4 2	(10 6) 3 2 Bets 2	(Q 4) 7 6 2
				(9 3) J 5 4 3	(10 6) 6 3 2 Bets 3	(Q 4) 7 6 5 3
				(9 3) 9 5 4 3	(10 3) 6 3 2 Bets 3	(7 4) 7 6 5 3
				(9 3) 5 5 4 throw in	(K 10) 6 3 2 Bets 7	(10 4) 7 6 5 throw in

THE LAWS OF POKER

These laws are adapted (by permission) from those in force at a well-known card club.

Introductory

1. The game of Poker is played by five, six, or seven players. Seven players form a complete table.

2. A single pack of fifty-two cards is used, containing four suits of equal value. The cards of a suit, except as stated otherwise in these rules, rank as follows: Ace (highest), King, Queen, Jack, Ten, Nine, Eight, Seven, Six, Five, Four, Three, Deuce (lowest).

3. Poker is played with counters which consist of chips, and half chips.

4. The game comprises plain Poker, and Pots.

The Deal

5. At the formation of a table the first dealer is the player occupying the lowest numbered seat. The deal passes in regular rotation to the left.

6. Every player has the right to shuffle the cards before the cut. The dealer has the right to shuffle last.

7. After the cards have been shuffled, the dealer hands the pack to the player on his right to cut.

8. The player entitled to cut may waive his right and run the cards. If he cuts the pack it must be divided into two packets each containing at least five cards.

9. If a card is exposed when cutting, the pack must be re-shuffled and again cut.

10. The cards must be dealt one at a time, face downwards in rotation from left to right, beginning at the dealer's left hand and continuing until each player has received five cards.

11. If a player deals out of turn he must be stopped before the last card is dealt, or the deal stands good.

12. If any card is exposed in dealing the player must accept the exposed card provided that it was not faced in the pack. If two cards are exposed in the same deal, whether dealt to the same or different players, there must be a fresh deal.

13. There must be a fresh deal if any card is found faced in the pack when dealing the original hands.

14. There must be a fresh deal if too many, or too few, hands are dealt.

15. If the right number of cards is off the pack at the conclusion of

the deal, and there is a doubt about the particular cards any player is entitled to receive, the dealer may adjust the cards so that each player has his correct number of cards.

16. If at the conclusion of the deal one card too many is off the pack, the dealer may return this card to the top of the pack, and the deal stands good if otherwise in order. If more than one card too many is dealt, there must be a fresh deal.

17. If at the conclusion of the deal too few cards are off the pack and the dealer has not seen his hand, he may continue the deal if able to ensure that each player has his correct cards. Otherwise there must be a fresh deal.

18. If a player picks up the wrong hand he must hand it to the player entitled to receive it, and his own hand is dead, provided that the other player may, if he wishes, agree to accept the unseen hand before seeing either hand; in which case the exchange holds good.

19. If a player finds that he has more or less than the correct number of cards he may call attention to the fact before looking at his hand. If his neighbour also has the wrong number the dealer shall adjust.

20. If a player with the wrong number of cards has looked at his hand, his hand is dead, except as provided in Laws 22 and 23.

21. A player whose hand is dead may take no part in the play that deal, and forfeits any counters he may have put up, except that if his hand becomes dead before the draw, he may play on putting up the necessary stake and draw five fresh cards.

22. If a player has only four cards, and his neighbour, who has looked at his hand, has six cards, the hand of six cards is dead, but the dealer should choose one of the six cards at random and give it to the player with four cards.

23. If a player has six cards in front of him which he has not seen, and his neighbour has four cards which he has seen, the dealer must give the player with four cards one of the unseen cards to complete his hand.

Plain Poker

24. The player on the dealer's left is known as the first ante. He must make a contribution of one chip, known as the first ante or blind.

25. The player on the left of the first ante is known as the second ante. He must put up two chips, known as the second ante or straddle.

26. The amounts contributed before the deal by the first and second ante are compulsory. No other player may put up chips before the deal. There is no optional straddle.

27. The player on the left of the second ante must indicate that he will play or pass. If he passes he discards his hand. If he plays he must put up a stake.

28. If the first to speak throws in his hand his rights pass to the player on his left. If all the other players throw in their hands the second ante takes the chips on the table, and the deal passes.

29. When a player enters the game by putting up the necessary stake, the player on his left may enter by putting up the same stake, or may raise the stake, or may throw in his hand. If he throws in his hand his rights pass to the next player on his left, and so on round the table.

30. Any subsequent player entering the game may do so for the value of the stake already put up, or may raise the stake. If either ante takes part in the hand he adds counters to those in front of him so as to make up the necessary amount.

31. If a player speaks out of turn the player whose turn it was to speak is not deprived of his rights. So long as a player holds his cards and has not signified his intention to throw in, his rights remain.

32. A player who enters the game must put up the full stake. If he does so it is not necessary for him to speak, except as provided in Law 33.

33. A player must speak and announce his intention if he has previously put up a counter or counters, or if he puts up other than the exact amount, or if he is raising the stake.

34. A person who puts up more than the minimum amount is assumed to be playing for the minimum unless he announces the contrary.

35. If the original stake has been raised, the player who put it up may abandon his hand, forfeiting the amount put up, or may make up his stake to the increased value, or may again raise the stake. Each player in turn has similar rights.

36. Betting before the draw ceases when all players have put up the amount necessary to compete, or have abandoned their hands.

37. A person who abandons his hand after having entered the game on account of a subsequent raise leaves his counters on the table and they become the property of the winner of the hand.

The Draw

38. When the betting before the draw is complete each of those still in the game is entitled to discard any or all of his cards and draw others in their places.

39. The dealer gives cards from the top of the pack, each player receiving the number of cards for which he asks in order starting on the dealer's left.

40. A player taking cards must ask distinctly for the number he wants, and discard that number from his original hand. When helping himself the dealer must state aloud the number he takes.

41. A player asking for cards may alter his request only if he does so in the same breath, or before the dealer has removed cards from the pack in response to his request.

42. A player must reply to a question as to how many cards he has drawn, provided that the question is put by a player still in the game and before the last card in the draw is given. The dealer must state at any time the number of cards he has drawn himself if questioned. Otherwise, no information may be given.

43. If any card is found faced in the pack when cards are given for the draw it must be placed amongst the discards after having been shown and named to all the players.

44. If one or more cards are exposed by the dealer when giving cards for the draw the player may not take the exposed card or cards, but must wait until all the other players, including the dealer, have been helped. He then receives a card or cards from the top of the pack in place of the exposed card or cards. The player retains any other cards given to him but not exposed.

45. A card is not deemed to have been exposed by the dealer if before it is faced it touches the player for whom it is intended, whether given in the deal or in the draw. No card given by the dealer to himself is an exposed card.

46. If there is any doubt about the actual cards given to a player it is the duty of the dealer to decide. Players must abide by his decision.

47. In giving cards for the draw the dealer must not give the bottom card of the pack. If there are not sufficient cards to help everyone, then the bottom card and the cards already discarded by other players are mixed together by the dealer, who shuffles the pack so formed and hands it to the player on his right to cut. After it has been cut the dealer resumes giving cards for the draw.

48. A player demanding cards in the draw should at the same time discard the number he wants. If he omits to do so and cards are given in order and picked up by another player, he cannot subsequently object and must be assumed to have asked for the number actually given him.

49. A player who demands cards and at the same time discards is not penalized if the wrong number is given him, provided he points out the error before picking up the cards given. If, meanwhile, another player has picked up cards given in the draw, the adjustment must be made after the giving of cards to all the players in the game is complete,

either by placing unseen in the discard the card or cards given in excess or by giving from the top of the pack a card or cards to make up the deficit.

After the Draw

50. At plain poker the first player to speak after the draw is the player who first entered the hand. He may either check, signifying that he does not raise the stake, or he may raise the stake.

51. If the first player checks the others may also check, and there is a showdown, no further stake being put up.

52. Any player who raises the stake may do so in accordance with Law 91. He may double the amount of the stake already put up, provided that the amount of the raise does not exceed eight chips.

53. When a player does not wish to see a raised stake he abandons his hand, leaving in the pool all the counters that he has put up.

54. When a bet has been raised, any other player still in the game may call the bet by putting up the amount of the raised bet, or may again raise the bet.

55. When the last raised bet has been called, and there is no further betting, there is a showdown. The pool is taken by the player with the hand which ranks highest.

56. The first to speak after the draw, if he checks or bets before picking up the cards given him in the draw, is entitled to the pool if the check or bet is not called, provided he was dealt the correct number of cards originally.

57. Except as provided in Law 56, the hand of a player with the wrong number of cards in the final showdown is dead.

58. In the showdown each person in the game must expose his hand face upwards on the table so that no card is touching any other card.

59. If there is any dispute about the value of a hand in the final showdown a person who has not exposed his hand as described in Law 58 is assumed to have been in the wrong.

The Rank of Hands

60. Hands rank in the following order:

Royal Flush. Ace, King, Queen, Jack, Ten, of the same suit.

Straight Flush. Five cards of the same suit in sequence, not being a Royal Flush. The Ace ranks low.

Fours. Four of a kind and an odd card.

Full Hand. Three of a kind and a pair.

Flush. Five cards of the same suit, not being a Royal or Straight Flush

Straight. Five cards in sequence, not being a Royal or Straight Flush. The Ace may rank high or low.

Threes. Three of a kind and two odd cards.

Two Pairs. Two pairs and an odd card.

One Pair. One pair and three odd cards.

No Pair. Hands not containing a pair or better.

61. When two or more hands of the same description meet, and are higher than any other hand, there is a tie if all five cards are of the same rank; otherwise the hand which ranks highest is as follows:

Straight Flushes and Straights. The hand with the highest card except that Five, Four, Three, Deuce, Ace, ranks lowest.

Fours. The hand with the highest fours.

Full Hand. The hand with the highest threes.

Flush. The hand with the highest card. If the highest card is the same, the hand with the next highest card, and so on.

Threes. The hand with the highest threes.

Two Pairs. The hand with the highest pair. If the highest pair is the same, the hand with the next highest pair. If both pairs are the same, the hand with the highest odd card.

One Pair. The hand with the highest pair. If two hands have the same highest pair, that with the highest odd card; if these are the same, the hand with the next highest; and so on.

Hands with Less than a Pair. The hand with the highest card. If the highest cards are the same, the hand with the next highest card; and so on.

Jack Pots

62. When a jack pot is played every player contributes two chips, and the amount so subscribed forms a pot. There are no antes. The cards are dealt as in plain Poker.

63. The player on the left of the dealer is the first to speak. He may open the pot provided his hand is as good as a pair of Jacks, or better. If he decides not to open, each player in turn, beginning on his left, has the right to do so.

64. If no player opens the pot the pot is sweetened by every player contributing one half-chip. The deal then passes and each player in turn again has the right to open the pot.

65. On each occasion when the pot is not opened, a further sweetener of one half-chip is added to the pot.

66. After the pot has been opened every player starting on the left of the opener has the right to enter the pot, or to increase the opening

stake. This includes players who have previously refused to open. The betting before the draw may then proceed as in plain Poker, subject to Law 91.

67. When all players taking part in the pot have put up the necessary stake, and the others have withdrawn, cards are given for the draw as in plain Poker.

68. The player who starts the betting after the draw is the opener. He may either check or raise the bid. The betting then proceeds as in plain Poker, subject to Law 91.

69. A player who opens a jack pot must not discard so as to split his opening qualification without announcing that fact. If he announces that he is splitting his openers he may draw as he likes, provided that he is able to establish that he possessed the necessary qualifications for opening. If he splits his opening qualification without making such an announcement he is assumed not to have had openers.

70. The opener of a jack pot must expose his full hand after the pot has been won.

False Openers

71. Should a player open without the proper qualification his hand is dead and all he has put into the pot is forfeited.

72. Should any player have come into play against the false opener, the pot shall be played for just as if it had been properly opened.

73. When a pot has been falsely opened and play proceeds, the pot is won by the hand of highest rank in the final showdown regardless of whether that hand could have opened the pot or not.

74. Where there is no competition against the opener in the final showdown, either because nobody else has entered the pot or because nobody has called the opener's check or bet, and it is found that the opener has not the necessary qualifications, the pot must be played for again. Any player may withdraw the amount he has put in subsequent to the pot being opened except the opener himself, who leaves in all he has contributed.

75. When there has to be a re-play in accordance with the last rule the opener is dealt out of the pot and may not take part in the game until the pot has been finally won.

76. There is no penalty for falsely opening a pot, except as provided above. The opener does not have to replace the pot.

Freak Pots

77. A freak pot is played after the jack pot is finished. In a freak pot the four Deuces are known as freaks and are treated as Jokers.

78. Subject to Law 79, a player with one or more freaks in his hand may treat such freak or freaks as having the value of any card not in his hand, except that two freaks may not both represent the same card.

79. The value of hands rank as in plain Poker, but there is a new description of hand known as fives. This is held when the cards in the hand, other than freaks, are all of the same value.

80. A hand containing five ranks below a Royal Flush, but above a Straight Flush.

81. The laws for opening, sweetening, entering, and raising the bid in freak pots are the same as for jack pots, except that no opening qualification of any kind is required.

82. In giving cards for the draw in a freak pot Law 47 does not apply. The dealer must give the bottom card of the pack.

83. If there are not enough cards to give any player the number he wants he may, if he wishes, abandon his hand and take back his entry chips.

Misère Pots

84. A misère pot is dealt after a freak pot. The object is to get a hand which ranks lower in value than any other hand. Such a hand takes the pot on the final showdown.

85. The cards rank the same as in plain Poker, except that the ace is always considered to be the lowest card and never the highest.

86. If a card is exposed in dealing a misère pot Law 12 does not apply. There must be a fresh deal, subject to Law 45.

87. In giving cards for the draw Law 39 is modified. No player may discard more than three cards.

88. The laws for opening, sweetening, entering, and raising the bid are the same as in jack pots, except that no opening qualification of any kind is required.

The Stake

89. The first player to speak at plain Poker may put up a stake of not less than four nor more than eight chips.

90. A player opening a pot must put up a stake of four chips.

91. A person raising a stake may do so by any sum from a half a chip up to the amount of the stake already put up, provided that in no case may he increase the stake by more than eight chips.

92. The amount contributed by a player before a pot is opened is not to be considered part of his stake.

93. The counters in front of a player must not be less than, and if possible should be exactly, the amount for which he is liable.

94. A player must not interfere with the counters of another player, nor take change from the pool. A player who disregards this rule is assumed to be in the wrong should any dispute occur.

Speaking Out of Turn

95. If a player out of turn speaks, or indicates otherwise that he will or will not call, raise, open a pot, or take part in the hand, his speech or indication is cancelled. The right reverts to the proper player. When it comes to the turn of the offender he is subject to Laws 96 to 99.

96. If a player out of turn passes, abandons his hand, refuses to call a bet, or otherwise indicates that he withdraws, his hand becomes dead.

97. If a player out of turn refuses to open a pot he is debarred from opening when his turn comes, but he may compete if the pot is opened by another.

98. If a player out of turn makes a bet, when his turn comes:

(*a*) If no bet has been made meanwhile he must make the bet he made out of turn.

(*b*) If a smaller bet has been made he must raise to the extent of the bet made out of turn.

(*c*) If an equal bet has been made he must call.

(*d*) If a larger bet has been made he may call or raise, or he may withdraw on forfeiting an amount equal to the bet made out of turn.

99. If a player out of turn announces that he will play, or puts up a stake, or opens a pot, or calls, or raises a bet, Law 98 applies, so far as may be to the altered circumstances.

Imperfect Pack

100. If a pack of cards is discovered to be imperfect, the deal in the course of which the discovery is made is cancelled, and all stakes made in the course of the subsequent play are withdrawn. There must be a fresh deal by the same dealer. Previous play is not affected.

Etiquette

There are certain breaches of the laws for which no penalties are imposed, partly because of the difficulty in enforcing them, and partly because the good sense of players should render such penalties unnecessary. There are also certain standards of play generally observed by club players, although not specifically laid down. The following may be mentioned:

It is a recognized principle of Poker that a player should not discuss the contents of his hand, or suggest by any statement or mannerisms whether it is good or bad. He has a free hand in the betting only.

A player who makes a mistake which he corrects in time, or makes any other breach of the rules, or makes any remark about his hand, should avoid raising the stake.

Disputes arising between players should be settled, if possible, by the players involved. If they arrive at an agreement no other player should interfere.

Players should not demand a ruling on a point of law unless it is essential for the continuance of the game.

In respect of a matter already finished, a player with a grievance may bring it before the Committee subsequently.

Players should recognize that it is not easy for most players to see an exposed hand unless it is spread out fully in the way required by Law 58.

Speech is not as a rule necessary, but where required it should be clear and without ambiguity.

Where there is a doubt about words used by a player his own statement about the words he used should be accepted.

The dealer should at all times be particularly alert. It is his business to control the game, and to be clear about all questions of fact.

It is of the utmost importance that no player should throw his cards out of turn. The effect of doing so, while it brings him no advantage, may radically alter the play of others, and operate unfairly to their disadvantage.

It is unfair knowingly to open a jack pot without the proper qualification. A player who does so inadvertently should announce his mistake as soon as he discovers it.

A player who is out of the game should not retain cards in his hand, unless he has opened a jack pot. The practice of doing so in other cases is apt to mislead players still in the game.

The dealer, when giving cards for the draw, should await the player's discard, so as to ensure giving the right number.

A player intending to play should do so as soon as a table is formed, and should not await the arrival of other players.

A player has full discretion to bet his cards as he likes and should never be criticized for betting or failing to bet.

Brag

This very old card game is similar to Poker in its essential principles. For example (1) the best hand (as determined by certain rules) wins; (2) the players can bet on the respective merits of their hands; and (3) the hands are not exposed if the player making the best bet is not 'seen'. So, as in Poker, there can be an element of bluff. But it is a far cry from Brag to Poker as I shall show.

The ordinary game of Brag is a three-card game played with a full pack. The Ace of Diamonds, the Knave of Clubs and the Nine of Diamonds are known as 'braggers'. They are, in effect, Jokers. And each of them can represent any other card.

To begin the game the dealer puts up any stake to the agreed limit. (Incidentally, this, like Poker, is a game which is pointless unless played for stakes.) Three cards are dealt to each player and each in turn must either put up at least as much as the dealer's stake or retire. Successive players may raise the stake and any player staking an amount that no one else will meet takes the pool without exposing his hand. Any player, however, who is 'called' or 'seen' must expose his hand, and the best hand takes the pool.

The following is the order of value of the hands:

(1) Three natural Aces (the Ace of Diamonds ranks as a natural in a Three-Ace hand).

(2) Three Aces including one or more 'braggers', e.g. any one Ace, the Knave of Clubs and the Nine of Diamonds.

(3) Three natural Kings.

(4) Three Kings including one or more 'braggers'; and so on down to three Twos.

After threes come pairs from Aces downwards; a natural pair taking precedence over one which includes a 'bragger'. If two players have similar pairs, the player holding the highest third card wins. And if no player has a pair, the highest single card.

If two players have equal cards preference goes to the elder hand, i.e. the player who is the first of the two to stake.

A second form of the game is Three Stake Brag. In this game three separate and individual stakes are made in respect of each deal. The third card is dealt face upwards and the stake goes to the holder of the highest card. The second stake goes to the holder of the best hand (determined as above). This second stake is likely to increase in the same way as single-stake Brag. The third stake goes to the player whose cards most nearly total 31; Aces count 11 and Court cards 10 each. Thus, an Ace and two Court cards would take or share the stake. A player with a total of less than 31 may draw another card (as in Vingt-et-Un) but if his total then exceeds 31 his hand is dead.

All the hands are exposed before any extra cards are drawn so that each player knows what he is up against.

Seven-Card Rummy

Any reasonable number of players, from two upwards, can take part in this game. Two packs of cards, well shuffled together, are needed. Each player has so many counters to begin with, and before the first deal, an agreed number – say, two from each player – is put into the 'kitty'.

Players cut for deal, lowest card (Ace low) dealing.

Seven cards are dealt, one at a time and face downwards, to each player. The remainder of the pack is placed face downwards on the table with the top card (i.e. the card next to the card last dealt) face upwards beside the stock. This card is the foundation of the 'discard pile'.

Each player in turn (beginning with the player on the left of the dealer) takes a card, which can be either the unseen top card from the stock or the exposed card beside it. He then discards a card from his hand, placing it face upwards on the discard pile. Every player has the same choice: to take either the unseen top card from the stock or the top (exposed) card from the discard pile.

The object of the game is to collect in one's hand certain combinations of cards, namely: sets of three or more cards of the same denomination, e.g. three Tens; three Sevens; four Knaves, etc.; and *sequences* of three or more cards of the same suit, e.g. ♥ 7 8 9 ♠ 5 6 7 8, etc.

All the Twos are Jokers and can be used to represent any other card.

As soon as a player has seven cards in his hand composed entirely of sets or sequences (or both), or has six cards so arranged and one card, not higher than a 7, over, he can put his cards down. It sometimes happens that a player is dealt a hand such as: ♥ 7 6 2, ♥ K, ♦ K, ♣ K, ♠ 3. As he has one sequence (♥ 7 6 2) and one set (♥ K, ♦ K, ♣ K) and a 3 over, he can put his hand down at once, saying: 'Down for Three'.

When a player 'goes down' all the other players put their cards face upwards on the table. Points are scored against any cards in their hands which do not form part of a sequence or set. Court cards have a value of 10; Aces count one; other cards their pip value; a Two which has not been used in a sequence or set counts 15. When a player 'goes down' for (say) 5, any Fives held by other players can be thrown on his 5 and are not scored.

For example, a player with the following hand:

♠ 7 6 5 ♥ A J ♣ 4 3

would, in the event of another player 'going down' for 3, have an adverse score of 15. Nothing is counted against him in respect of his sequence or his 3, and the remaining cards add up to 15.

A player cannot go down immediately he has exchanged a card; he must wait until his turn comes round again.

As soon as a player has gone down, the scores are recorded and the 'kitty' replenished, each player contributing (say) one counter. The deal then passes to the player on the dealer's left.

When a player's score reaches 100 he is out of the game. When there are only two players left it is usual for them to divide the 'kitty' 3 to 1, the player with the lower score taking the larger share.

Kings and Queens

Two full packs of cards are used in this variant of Seven Card Rummy. Any number of players can take part.

Each player is dealt seven cards, face downwards and one at a time, the remainder forming the stock. The top card of the stock is turned face upwards and forms the foundation of the 'discard pile'. All the Twos are Jokers.

The object of the game is to 'go out' as quickly as possible. One is able to go out when one has six cards in one's hand composed of sequences or sets, providing the seventh card is not higher than a 6. Sequences and sets are, as in Rummy, three or more consecutive cards of the same suit, and three or more cards of the same denomination. If all seven cards can be arranged in sequences or sets one can, of course, 'go out for nothing'.

The difference between this game and Rummy is that the Kings and Queens have a special value. If one has a set or sequence which contains a King one can deduct 5 from one's initial score and, if a Queen, 3. Thus, a player who 'goes out for Four' with the following hand:

♠ Q 4, ♥ A K Q, ♦ Q, ♣ Q

will have a score of + 13, not, as in Seven Card Rummy, – 4. He gets a bonus of 17 for the King and four Queens but has to deduct 4 for the odd card.

The value of the cards is as in Seven Card Rummy, i.e. Court cards count 10; Aces, 1; other cards their pip value; and an unused Two counts 15.

As it is possible in Kings and Queens to have a minus score, it is a good plan to start each player at (say) 100. His minus scores (i.e. scores which count against him) are *added* to this total: when it reaches 200 he is counted out. His plus scores (e.g. the score of 13 shown in the above example) are *deducted* from his total, i.e. from 100 it goes to 87.

Counters can be used, as in Seven Card Rummy, to build up a 'kitty', which can either be taken by the last surviving player or divided between the last two.

Sequence Rummy

This game is played with two full packs of cards, including Jokers, well shuffled together. If there are no Jokers, any other two cards may be used to represent them. Any number of players can take part, the ideal numbers being five, six, or seven.

Eight cards are dealt to each player and the remainder are placed on the table, with the top card exposed beside them, to form the stock.

Each player, in turn, can either take the unexposed top card of the stock or all the exposed cards beside it, up to and including any card he is able to play at once. For example, supposing a player holds the following cards:

♠ 7 6 3, ♥ A K, ♦ 5 4, ♣ Q,

and the last three exposed cards are:

♣ 5, ♥ 7, ♠ 5,

he may take these cards, but he must at once put down on the table his sequence, i.e. ♠ 7 6 5.

No player can score anything until he has put down a sequence. When he has done this he may then put down other sequences, sets of three or more, and cards which continue other players' sets or sequences. Thus, a player who holds the above hand may, after he has put down his sequence (♠ 7 6 5), add his own ♣ Q to another player's set of Queens.

Jokers can only be used to represent cards not exposed on the table. Thus, if both ♠ 10's have been played to the table, the Jokers cannot represent the ♠ 10. A player who holds a Joker may, when his turn comes, exchange it for the card it was meant to represent. And if he holds the card the Joker represents he may exchange it for the Joker.

If a player discards a card that he can play, e.g. he discards the ♥ 7 when there is a sequence of ♥ 6 5 4 on the table, he is 'rummied'. Someone calls 'Rummy' and he has to accept a card from each of the other players.

Each player scores for all cards as he plays them. Aces score

15 (except when they are in a sequence of A 2 3, when they count 1); Court cards, 10; other cards, their pip value. Thus, a player putting down ♠ 6 7 8 and adding ♠ 10 to someone else's set of Tens scores 31.

At the end of the deal, which occurs when a player has disposed of all his cards, the cards which remain in players' hands are added up, and deducted from his score. If, for example, the player who put down ♠ 6 7 8, and added ♠ 10 to another player's set of Tens (giving him, as we have seen, a score of 31) still holds ♥ 6 5 3, ♣ 4 2 at the end of the deal, he will have to deduct 20 from his score of 31, leaving him an aggregate score of 11. Jokers, if not played at the end of a deal count 25 against the holder.

Vingt-et-Un (*Pontoon*)

Any reasonable number can play this game, which is very easy to learn. One pack of cards is needed, unless there are more than seven players, in which case two packs are recommended.

One player is Banker. To choose the Banker, each player should draw a card and the holder of the highest takes the Bank.

Vingt-et-Un is played for stakes, though not necessarily for money.

The cards are shuffled and cut and the Banker deals one card face downwards to each player, including himself. The players (except the dealer) look at their cards and each stakes any amount, up to the agreed limit, on his card.

The object of the game is to secure a combination of two or more cards totalling 21. The Ace, in this case, counts either 1 or 11, and each Court card 10. Other cards carry their pip value. Hence the stake originally laid on one's card will depend on one's chances of making 21, or of getting nearer to it than the Banker.

If a player's card is an Ace, he will stake the maximum, as he only needs a Ten or a Court card to have the best possible combination; if his card is a Ten or a Court card he will stake something a little lower than the maximum; Twos and Threes, as will appear later, are also worth a moderate stake. The minimum should be staked on other cards.

When the players have staked, the dealer looks at his card. If he wishes he may double the stake. If he holds an Ace he will certainly do so; and if he holds a Court card or a 2 he will probably do likewise. When the other players are staking they should bear in mind the possibility of their being doubled by the dealer.

The dealer now deals a second card to all the players including himself. If any player now has a 'Natural' (i.e. an Ace and a Court card or a Ten) he exposes his cards at once and is paid three times his original stake by the dealer, unless the dealer himself has a Natural. The player who has a Natural takes the Bank for the next deal.

Any Naturals having been turned up, the dealer asks each player in turn, starting with the player on his immediate left, whether he wants any more cards. These cards can either be bought for as many counters (or as much money) as the player likes (up to the original stake), and are dealt face downwards to him; or they can be 'twisted', i.e. dealt face upwards, so that all the players can see them. A player who has had one or more cards twisted cannot afterwards buy any cards. But a player who has bought one or more cards can have subsequent cards twisted.

As soon as a player has reached 21, or as soon as his total is so near 21 that he does not want to risk taking another card, he says 'stand'. If a card dealt to a player makes his total over 21 he exposes his hand and forfeits his stake.

Some Illustrative Deals

A has been dealt a 10 and a 7; without exposing his cards, he says 'stand'.

B has a 4 and a 10; he says 'twist me one'. His score of 14 is not likely to win, but the chances are seven to six that another card will leave him in the game. It is a 10 and he is out.

C has an Ace and a 3. He staked two counters and now 'buys one for two'. This is another Ace. He now has a good combination and buys another one for two counters. This is an 8. He now has a card twisted. This one is a 7 and he now has five cards totalling 20 which entitles him to receive double his original stake.

When all the players have had the cards they want and those that are out have disclosed the fact, the dealer looks at his two cards. He may now deal himself as many cards as he wishes to bring his total to 21 or as close as possible. If he thinks there are some good scores against him he will try to get 20 or 21, otherwise he will stand at 17 or 18.

Settlement is made in the following way:

(1) Players who have gone 'bust', i.e. exceeded 21, forfeit their stakes.

(2) If the dealer has a Natural he receives a single stake from any other player with a Natural; double stakes from those with 'five and under' or 21; and three times their stake from all the others.

(3) If the dealer has 'five and under', he receives a single stake from other players with 'five and under'; and double stakes from all other players.

(4) The dealer pays three times the original stake to a player with a Natural; double stakes to any player having 21 or 'five and under' and single stakes to any player with a better total than his own. Thus, if he stands at 18, he says 'pay 19.' He receives single stakes from any player with a score equal to or lower than his own. It can be seen that it is a great advantage to hold the Bank.

'Splitting' cards is a variation of the game, which, although a trifle complicated at first, adds to the interest of the game.

If a player is dealt two similar cards, i.e. two Tens or two Eights, etc., he can say 'split' and stake the same amount on each card. A second card is then dealt in respect of both these. The player now has two hands which are played separately as above.

The Banker holds the Bank until someone has a Natural, when it passes to that player, unless the Banker also has a Natural. The Bank does not 'pass' on a 'split' Natural. If a player does not want to take the Bank, he may put it up for auction.

But, as it is of considerable advantage to hold the Bank, a player should not reject it unless he is very short of counters.

Napoleon ('Nap')

This is played with a pack of 52 cards and any number of players from two to seven can take part. The ideal number is four or five.

The pack is shuffled and cut before each deal and the dealer (each player dealing in turn) deals out five cards one at a time to each player. The players look at their hands and each in turn (beginning with the Eldest hand or player on the dealer's left) makes a call or passes.

The calls, in ascending order, are: Two, Three, Misère, Four, Nap, and (where Nap has already been called) Wellington.

The call of Two is an undertaking to take two tricks out of the five; Three, to take three tricks; Four, to take four tricks. Nap is an undertaking to take all the tricks. Wellington, too, is an undertaking to take all five tricks and can only be made where there is already a five-trick offer. There is no further call over Wellington.

Misère is, as in Solo, an undertaking to take no tricks.

The player who makes the highest call leads to the first trick as soon as the other players have passed. The trump suit is the suit of the card which he first plays and the rules are the same as for Whist:

(1) The highest card of the suit led takes the trick. Aces count high.

(2) Players must follow suit whenever possible. If they are unable to do so they may either trump or discard.

(3) The winner of the trick leads to the next one.

At Misère there is no trump suit, otherwise the rules are the same.

Here is an example:

There are five players. E deals and A is Eldest hand.

A holds: ♠ K 5 ♥ J 8 ♣ 6
B holds: ♠ A Q J ♥ 5 ♦ 2
C holds: ♦ A K 10 4 ♣ 9
D holds: ♥ A K Q 9 3
E holds: ♣ A K Q 8 7

A passes. B calls 'Two'; C, 'Three', D, 'Nap'. E can now call 'Wellington' and, of course, lands his contract.

It is usual to play Nap for stakes, the caller paying or receiving from each of the other players. Thus, at Penny Nap, a player calling Three receives 3d from each of the other players if he makes three (or more) tricks, and pays 3d to each of them if he fails. If the call is Two he pays or receives 2d; if Misère, 3d; if Four, 4d.

If the call is Nap the caller usually pays 6d to each player if he fails and receives 10d from each if he succeeds in taking all the tricks.

The Wellington stakes are double those at Nap.

Catch the Ten

(SCOTCH WHIST)

Any number from two to eight can play this game. Usually a shortened pack of 36 cards is used, the Twos, Threes, Fours and Fives having been taken out.

If there are eight players, the Sixes are removed (making a 32-card pack), and if there are five or seven players the Six of Spades only is removed (making a 35-card pack).

Usually each player plays against each, but it can be played in partnership; thus, if there are six players, there can either be two partnerships of three (sitting alternately) or three partnerships of two. If there are eight players there may be either two 'sides' of four or four partnerships of two.

The cards are dealt in the following manner. If there are two players, each will have eighteen cards. These are dealt singly in three packets of six to each player. Each of these packets of six cards is a separate hand and is played out independently; a player does not look at his second or third packet until the first has been played out. Where there are three players, each has two packets of six cards. Where there are more than three players one hand only is dealt. The number of cards is nine, seven, six, five, or four according to the number of players.

The last card is turned up to indicate the trump suit.

The ranking of the cards is as in Whist, the Ace being the highest card, except that the Knave in the Trump suit is the highest card of all.

Players must, of course, follow suit whenever possible.

The object of the game is to take as many tricks as possible especially those which contain certain *scoring cards*. The *scoring cards* are the honour cards of the trump suit. The Knave of trumps scores 11 points (this must go, of course, to the player who was dealt this card); the Ten of trumps scores 10 points; and the Ace, King and Queen of trumps score 4, 3, and 2 points respectively.

There are always, therefore, 30 points to be distributed in respect of these five cards. Also, at the end of each hand, one point is scored for every card over the original number dealt to a player or side. Thus, in a two-handed game, a player who at the end of the first hand has taken four tricks has two cards in excess of the six he started with, and scores two points.

The Four Knaves

This may be played by any number from four to seven. If, however, there are seven players the dealer deals to the other six players and misses his own turn.

It is played with a Piquet pack, i.e. a pack of 32 cards, the Twos, Threes, Fours, Fives, and Sixes having been removed from a full pack.

The cards are dealt singly beginning with the player on the dealer's left. So, if there are four players, each will have eight cards; if there are five players, two will have seven each and the other three six each; if there are six players, two will have six each and the other four, five each. This discrepancy does not matter in the slightest.

The player on the dealer's left leads to the first trick. There is no trump suit and the players must follow suit when possible. The trick is won by whoever plays the highest card of the suit and the winner leads to the next trick.

The object is to avoid taking a trick with a Knave in it. A player who does so places the Knave face upwards on the table in front of him.

The Knave of Spades counts 2 points against the player who 'wins' it and the Knaves of Hearts, Diamonds, and Clubs 1 point each. As soon as anyone has lost 10 points he is out of the game. Thus, if there were seven players to begin with, it is now reduced to six and so on until there is only one player left with a score of less than 10. If stakes are being played for he takes the pool.

Cheat

This game can be played by any number of players. Two packs of cards are needed (or, if there are more than eight players, three.)

The cards are shuffled and dealt out as far as they will go.

The player on the dealer's left leads. He plays any card from his hand, placing it face downwards on the table, at the same time, naming its denomination. For example, he may play a 3 face downwards on to the table saying 'Three'. The next player now has to play a 4 face downwards on to the table. If, however, he has no 4 in his hand he plays any card he likes, still saying 'Four'.

Play continues in this way, 5 following 4, 6 following 5, and so on. Ace follows King, and 2 follows Ace.

The object of the game is to get rid of the cards in one's hand as quickly as possible. One may do this in the above manner or even, if one can do it undetected, by putting down two cards at once.

Any player may challenge another, if he thinks that the card played is not the one nominated, by calling 'Cheat'. The card is then turned up and, if it in fact is the one nominated, the challenger has to take all the cards on the table. If the challenge proves to be right then the player who tried to 'cheat' has to take them. Suppose, for example, a player calls 'Seven' and plays a King, and another player challenges him, the player challenged must take all the cards so far played.

After a challenge the player sitting next to the one who was challenged begins another round, playing any card he likes to the table.

Rockaway

This is a game for any number of players, using two packs of cards well shuffled together.

Seven cards are dealt to each player and the remainder are placed in the centre of the table with one card face upwards beside them. This card is the 'kitty' card.

The object of the game is to get rid of one's cards as quickly as possible by discarding them on to the 'kitty' card in any of the following ways:

(1) a card of the same suit as the 'kitty' card;

(2) a card of the same denomination as the 'kitty' card;

(3) any Ace (Aces being Jokers).

For example, suppose the 'kitty' card is the ♦ 7; the first player can discard (1) any Diamond; (2) any Seven; (3) any Ace. Let us say that he discards the ♠ 7, the next player can now discard (1) any Spade; (2) any Seven; (3) any Ace. If an Ace is discarded (say) the ♥ A, then only an Ace or a Heart can be discarded.

If a player is unable to discard he has to take a card from the stock, and must continue to do so until he picks up a card that he can play. When the stock is exhausted a player who cannot discard just misses his turn.

The deal is ended when one player has played all his cards. The other players then total up the pip value of the cards remaining in their hands. These are scored against them as in Rummy. Aces count 15; Court cards 10; and remaining cards their pip value.

Racing Demon

The essence of this game is speed. One pack of cards for each player is needed. It is advisable to use old cards as they are apt to get damaged and, for reasons which will become apparent later, each pack should be distinctive.

Each player shuffles his cards and, when everyone is ready, deals out thirteen cards in a stack in front of him, turning it over so that the cards are face upwards in a pile with only the top card exposed. Then he lays four cards face upwards in a row.

This game should be played at a large table so that there is plenty of room left in the centre after the players have arranged their cards in front of them.

One of the players should act as starter, and at the word 'Go' each player puts into the middle of the table any Aces which are exposed in his row; if the top card of his stack is an Ace this may be played as well. Now any Twos of the same suit as the Aces already on the table are played to the Aces; exposed Threes are played on to the Twos, and so on, building up each suit from the Ace. The packs from which the cards are played are immaterial. For example, if the player sitting opposite you has put down the ♣ A and you have the ♣ 2 exposed in your row, you slap it on to the Ace as quickly as possible as there may be several other players with the ♣ 2 exposed. The player to get his card there first wins.

When a player has played a card from his row of four cards he fills up the space with the top card from his stack of thirteen. When he has no card in front of him that he can play he starts turning over the cards in his hand, three at a time, playing any appropriate cards to the centre of the table as he comes to them, at the same time filling in the spaces in his row with cards from his stack.

As well as doing this a player may get rid of his stack by building on the cards in the row in descending sequence of cards of alternating colours, i.e. black Nine on red Ten; red Queen on black King. When this is done only the last card of each sequence can be played to the table. For example, in a sequence of red Nine, black Eight, red Seven, only the red Seven can be played.

There are two objects in this game; (1) to get rid of the stack of thirteen (either by playing them direct to the table or by playing them to the row of four cards); and (2) to put as many cards as possible into the centre of the table.

Scoring is as follows: when a player has got rid of his thirteen cards, he says 'Out'. All play stops. The cards that have been played to the table are sorted out (that is why each player must have a distinctive pack) and returned to their respective owners. Each player's score is the number of cards which he put into the centre of the table *less* the number of cards left in his stack of thirteen. Thus, a player who put twenty-one cards in the centre, but who has four cards left in his stack, scores 17.

Commit

This is played with one pack of cards from which the ♦ 8 has been removed, and any number of players can take part from two to eight.

The cards are dealt, face downwards, as far as they will go. (As the deal passes after each hand has been played, it does not matter that every player may not have the same number of cards.)

The object of the game is to get rid of one's cards as quickly as possible.

The player sitting on the dealer's left places any card he likes in the middle of the table, at the same time calling out its name.

Suppose the first card played is the ♣ 3. The player who holds the ♣ 4 puts it on the table, at the same time naming it. This goes on until the ♣ K is reached. This is a 'stop' card and whoever plays it can then play any card he chooses.

Note that the ♦ 7 is a 'stop' card as well as the ♦ K. And the ♦ 9 can be played by anyone who holds it at any time he likes; at the same time he calls out 'Commit'. This stops that particular sequence and the player can then start another one.

Where a suit has been opened with a card higher than an Ace, the card immediately below it is a 'stop' card. For example, if a sequence starts with (say) ♠ 10, it will run to the ♠ K and stop. And if another sequence starts with the ♠ 4 it will run to the ♠ 9 which has become a 'stop'.

As soon as a player has got rid of all his cards he says' Out', and the other players pay him one counter in respect of each of the cards they still hold; the holder of an unplayed ♦ 9 has to pay two counters in respect of this card.

Great Expectations

This game bears a great resemblance to the well-known game of 'Keno'. It is very simple to play and there is no element of skill in it.

Each player is given so many counters. The pack is then dealt out as far as it will go, as follows:

If there are five players, each receives ten cards and there are two over.

If there are six players, each receives eight cards and there are four over.

If there are seven players, each receives seven cards and there are three over; and so on. The odd cards are successively auctioned to the players by the dealer; the player who offers the most chips for a card gets it.

The dealer now takes a second pack, well shuffled, and deals the five top cards from it on to the table in front of him face downwards. Now each player pays his stake to the dealer as follows:

Where there are three players, each pays 8 counters.

Where there are four players, each pays 6 counters.

Where there are five players, each pays 5 counters.

Where there are six or seven players, each pays 4 counters.

Where there are eight, nine or ten players, each pays 3 counters.

Where there are three, four, six, or eight players the 24 counters are distributed on the five cards in the following way: 1 on the first card, 2 on the second, 4 on the third, 7 on the fourth, 10 on the fifth.

Where there are five players the 25 counters are distributed: 1, 2, 4, 8, 10.

Where there are seven players the 28 counters are distributed: 1, 3, 5, 8, 11.

Where there are nine players the 27 counters are distributed: 1, 3, 4, 8, 11.

Where there are ten players the 30 counters are distributed: 1, 3, 5, 9, 12.

The proceeds of the auction may be added to the stakes at the dealer's discretion.

When the stakes have been laid on the cards, the dealer deals out the remainder of the second pack, one card at a time, calling out what it is as he does so. The player who holds that card puts it down in front of him. In this way the forty-seven useless cards are disposed of and the game begins to get really exciting. When these forty-seven cards have been dealt, the first of the five hidden cards is turned up. The player who holds the corresponding card claims the stake, and so on with the other four.

Parliament

This game, which is also known as 'Sevens' or 'Card Dominoes', can be played by any number from three to eight using one pack of cards; or, if there are more than eight players, two packs well shuffled together.

The whole pack is dealt, one card at a time and face downwards. The fact that the players may not have the same number of cards is immaterial.

The object of the game is to get rid of one's cards as quickly as possible. The player who is 'out' first either wins the game or scores a certain number of points.

To begin the game the dealer asks: 'Who has the Seven of Diamonds?' This is the key card, and the player who holds it puts it down in the centre of the table, face upwards. Now the player on his left can (if he holds one of them) play either the ♦ 8, the ♦ 6 or another Seven. If he plays a Seven he places it alongside the ♦ 7, if it is the ♦ 8 or the ♦ 6 he places it endways to the ♦ 7. The next player now has a choice of six cards to play. If, by chance, he has no card to play, he says 'Go' and play passes to the player on his left.

Although this is a very simple game there is scope for some skill. For example, suppose you are able to play the ♦ 10 and the ♣ Q, and you also hold the ♦ J, obviously you will play the ♦ 10 because this will enable you to play the ♦ J when your turn comes round again.

Minoru

Originally this game required a special cloth and a number of lead horses, but it can be played just as well with a pack of cards, a large piece of paper and a piece of chalk.

First of all, mark the sheet of paper as follows:

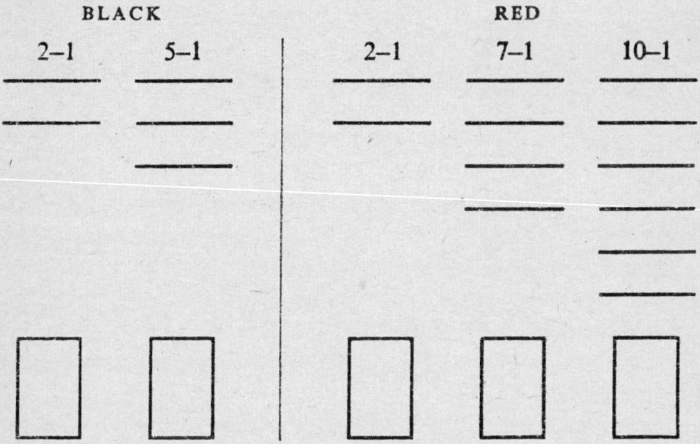
BLACK
RED
2–1
5–1
2–1
7–1
10–1

Allow enough space above each of the columns and on the 'Black' and 'Red' for the stakes to be placed.

The Banker is chosen either by cutting for the lowest card or by choice. Each player should hold the Bank for six deals.

Each player now backs the 'horse' he fancies, putting his counters above the appropriate column, and the race begins.

The Banker deals out five cards – face downwards – on each of the five squares. He then deals out one card at a time, face upwards, below the 'horses'.

The 'horse' immediately above the highest card (Ace high) moves up to touch the first line. Then five more cards are dealt in the same manner, the 'horse' above the highest card moving up. And so on until one 'horse' reaches the top line and wins. The Banker pays out the odds as shown.

Obviously the horses in the columns with only two lines are more likely to win as they only have to move twice.

Instead of backing a horse, or perhaps as well as, players can back Black or Red. In this case the Banker pays even money. If the winning horse is on the right of the dividing line, he pays on Red and, if on the left, on Black.

If possible counters of different colours should be used, each colour representing a different coin. The odds are almost correct mathematically but with a very slight advantage to the Banker.

Chase the Ace

Any number of players can take part in this simple game.

Each player is given three counters, each of which represents a 'life'. When a player has lost his three counters he is out. The winner is the survivor.

One card is dealt to each player. The object of the game is to avoid holding a low card, Ace being the lowest, and King the highest. card. Spades rank higher than Hearts; Hearts than Diamonds; Diamonds than Clubs. So the highest card is the King of Spades and the lowest card the Ace of Clubs.

The players look at their cards; any player who has been dealt a King places it face upwards on the table. These players cannot be asked to exchange cards. Now, beginning with the player to the dealer's left, each player can either say 'stand' or exchange his card (face downwards) with the player to his own left, unless that player has exposed a King. Hence a low card is passed round the table until it reaches a player who has given an even lower one in exchange. He will, of course, 'stand'.

When it comes to the dealer's turn, he exposes his card and he can then either 'stand' or cut from the pack in front of him.

All the cards are then shown and the holder of the lowest card forfeits a counter.

Authors

This is a very simple game (with no literary connexions whatsoever) not unlike 'Happy Families'.

Any number up to eight or nine can take part. The cards are dealt, one at a time, as far as they will go. It doesn't matter that all the players may not have the same number.

The object of the game is to collect sets of four cards of the same denomination, e.g. four Aces; four Tens; and so on.

The player on the left of the dealer begins. He can ask any player, chosen at random, for any card he likes. He must, however, hold at least one card of the same denomination. For example, a player with the following hand

♠ K Q 4, ♥ Q, ♦ 3 2

can ask another player for a Queen as he holds two of them. If the player he asks has in fact a Queen in his hand he has to hand it over; if he doesn't he may then ask any player for a card. So it goes on.

As soon as a player has collected a set he places it face downwards on the table. Each set counts one point. At the end of the game (an agreed number of deals) the player with the most points wins.

If a player, on completing a set, has no more cards in his hand, he is finished as far as that deal goes and the player from whom he took his last card now has the right to ask for one from someone else.

A player who is observant will do better at this game than one who is not. For example, supposing one holds the ♥ 10 and the ♣ 10 and another player asks for and gets the ♠ 10 from someone else, one is certain of getting both the ♠ 10 and the ♦ 10 from this player when one asks for it.

Oh! Well

This game can be played by three, four, five, six, or seven players. When there are three players, the bottom card of the pack is removed, but not disclosed; when there are four, the whole pack is used; when there are five, six, or seven players, two, four, and three cards respectively are removed.

The remaining cards are dealt, the last card to be dealt (to the dealer himself) is exposed, and the suit of this card is declared trumps.

The player on the left of the dealer now says how many tricks he thinks he will be able to make. If he thinks he can't make any at all, he says 'None'. Now all the players in turn call, stating the number of tricks they think they can make. The calls are recorded on the score-sheet.

The player on the dealer's left leads, and the game proceeds along the same lines as Solo Whist or Nap; that is to say that players must follow the suit led, if they are unable to do so they can either trump or discard a card of a different suit.

The winner of the trick leads to the next one and so on, each player in turn, starting always on the left of the dealer, playing until the hand is completed. The tricks of each player are then counted and the player who has made the exact number of tricks he nominated receives a bonus of 10 points as well as a point for each trick.

A player who has made either more or less tricks than he nominated gets 1 point for each trick but no bonus. The player to score 100 first wins the game.

If the game is being played for money, either players put a certain sum into the kitty at the beginning and the winner takes it all, or players pay the differences at so much a point.

When there is any number other than four playing it is essential to return the discarded cards to the pack at the end of each hand, shuffle it well and then remove the bottom card or cards. If this is not done these cards become known and a great deal of the interest is lost.

Although it may seem to be a good plan to declare 'None' as

...rry out because, ...will combine

...eady made that ...nake you take one

...part in this lively (and noisy) ...shuffled, are required. A trump ...pack, after which seven cards are

...is to win tricks containing Twos; ...Knaves. They are mentioned in this ...g tricks, Twos rank higher than Aces; ...an capture the Ace of the same suit. When ...t the end of the game Twos count more than ...s follows:

...ach Two	11 points
...each Ace	10 points
...r each King	5 points
...or each Queen . . .	4 points
For each Knave . . .	3 points

...us, a player who has won tricks containing a Two, an Ace ...d a Knave will score 24 points.

The player on the left of the dealer leads to the first trick. Players must follow suit whenever possible, otherwise they may trump or discard a card of another suit. The winner of a trick leads to the next one. If two players play identical cards (e.g. two ♦ Q) the player of the second one is assumed to have played the higher card. So it is important to note what winning cards are out.

After playing to a trick each player draws a card from the top of the pack, which is placed in the centre of the table after the deal. If, after the draw, a player finds that he has in his hand

a King and a Queen of the same suit, he
same time laying his King and Queen face
Trump suit now changes to the suit in w
'Pip-Pipped', and he scores 50 points for do

If a player has been dealt a King and Que
(other than trumps) he can 'Pip-Pip' at once,
changes before the first trick has been pla
players find that they have a King and a Quee
than trumps, they both score 50 points and the tru
to that of the player who called 'Pip-Pip' last.

A player can 'Pip-Pip' twice in the same suit p
both Kings and Queens. He cannot pair his Kings
the two Queens in turn.

A player need not 'Pip-Pip' as soon as he finds he
and Queen of the same suit, if he thinks it would be a
not to; but by not doing so he runs the risk of losing
bonus.

When the number of cards in the centre of the tab
than the number of players taking part, drawing ceas
remaining cards are turned face upwards and do not c
anybody. The tricks in hand are then played out.

Hoggenheimer

This game is played with a Piquet pack, i.e. thirty-two cards, t
Twos, Threes, Fours, Fives, and Sixes having been removed fro
a full pack, and one other card (say) the ♣ 2.

The cards are shuffled and cut by the player on the Banker's left. He then deals out thirty-two cards, face downwards, in four rows of eight.

The game consists in turning up each card one by one, putting it in its appropriate place, and turning up the card that occupied that space. In the course of the game, therefore, any Aces are placed in the first column; the Ace of Spades going in the top left-hand corner, with the Ace of Hearts below it and so on. In the last column the Sevens will be placed, as they turn up, the ♣ 7 going in the lowest right-hand corner.

Now players can back single cards, groups of two or four cards, complete rows or columns of cards to turn up before the ♣ 2, up to an agreed amount. For example, a player who has backed the ♦ Ace will receive the amount he has staked if the ♦ Ace turns up. If he has backed the ♦ Ace, K and they turn up he will receive twice his stake; if he has backed all the Aces, four times his stake; all the Spades, eight times his stake.

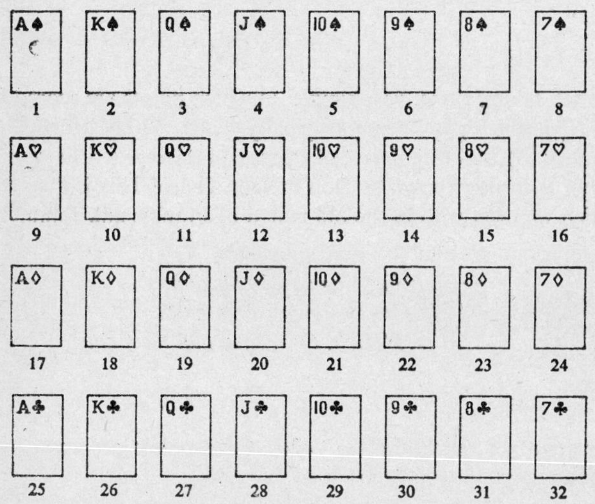

When all the stakes have been laid, the banker turns up the thirty-third card. If it is the ♣ 2 he takes all the stakes and the bank passes to the next player.

But let us suppose that this thirty-third card is the ♣ 9. The banker will place it in its appropriate place, i.e. space 30 on the diagram and turn up the card that was there. Suppose that this card is the ♦ 7. He will place it in the space marked 24 and turn up that card. This continues until the ♣ 2 turns up, then the Banker collects any stakes placed on cards that have not turned up and pays out on those that have turned up, according to the scale set out above.

The deal ends when the ♣ 2 is turned up and the Bank passes to the next player.

Brief Notes on Other Card Games

I have dealt as fully as possible with all card games which command a wide measure of support. The notes which follow are designed to indicate the general character of such other games as have distinctive names and more or less well-defined rules.

ALL FOURS

A trick-taking game, very simple, in which points are scored for (1) *High* (the highest trump originally dealt); (2) *Low* (the lowest trump); (3) *Jack* (the Knave of trumps); (4) *Game* (tricks won in play). It is also known as Don or Don Pedro. This is the game which we meet with in the old ballad of Frankie and Johnny:

Johnny was ever a gambler;
Gambling was always his aim;
The last words Johnny ever spake
Were: 'High, Low, Jack and the Game'.

ALL FIVES

A variant of the above, in which extra points are scored for winning certain trumps in play.

ANIMALS

The nursery game of Animal Grab played with playing cards. Each player selects some denomination (e.g. the Tens) and an animal name for the Ten (e.g. Cat). When two Tens are turned up, the first player to call *Miaow* secures the appropriate cards.

BACCARAT

One of the two major games played in casinos (the other being Chemin de Fer). It is a game of pure chance, sums being staked cumulatively by the players on either side of the table on the outcome of the cards dealt by a banker (seated at the head of the table) to the players at his right and left, and to himself. There is no point in my going into the game in detail; if you visit a casino you will learn how it is played in a few minutes; in this country it is illegal.

BANGO

There are various forms of this game, which resembles the numbers game (Keeno or Bingo). Five cards are dealt face upwards to each player; the remaining cards are then dealt face upwards to the centre of the table. As each card is dealt a player holding a card of the same denomination places a chip on it. The first player to get a chip on all his cards calls *Bango* and scoops the pool.

BIERSPIEL

A trick-taking game in which each player, unless he pays a forfeit, undertakes to take at least one of five tricks. If he succeeds he gets one-fifth of the pool for each trick he takes. If he fails he is penalized.

BLACK JACK

A variant of the avoidance game, Black Widow (see below), in which the Knave of Spades, instead of the Queen, carries the appropriate penalty.

BLACK WIDOW

Essentially the same game as my Black Maria, already described as the best card-game for three, except that only the Queen of Spades and the Hearts carry penalties. Also, if a player takes all the penalty cards, there is no penalty against him, but 26 is scored against each of the other players.

BOODLE

A variant of Newmarket (see below) in which the cards are all dealt out, one more hand being dealt than there are players. This hand is dealt face upwards and, before looking at their cards, players stake an agreed number of chips on one or more of the cards exposed. These exposed cards correspond to the 'luxuries' in Newmarket.

BOSTON

An elaborate variation of Solo Whist. At one time it was fashionable in America, but I have never heard of its being played in this country.

CALABRASELLA

A three-handed trick-taking game played with a pack of forty cards. Twelve are dealt to each player; the fourth (dealt face downwards as a 'widow') is available to whoever first elects to play against the other two. Certain cards have defined values which accrue to those who take the tricks containing them.

CALYPSO

A partnership game for four players which requires a special cloth and other gadgets. It is played with four ordinary packs having identical backs. Each player has his own trump suit. The object is to build Calypsos: sequences containing all thirteen cards of a suit. Thus Calypso belongs essentially to the Rummy family.

CASSINO

A game for two or four players, too complex to describe in detail. Four cards are dealt to each player; four to the table. The cards dealt to the table are exposed. Each player in turn plays a card face upwards, his objectives being to pair cards with those on the table; to 'build' combinations having the same aggregate pip value; to take in the Great Cassino (♦ 10) or Little Cassino (♠ 2). Like Cribbage, the game calls for a knowledge of arithmetic.

CHEMIN DE FER

Essentially the same game as Baccarat, and likewise an illegal game in this country. The difference between 'Shemmy' and Baccarat is that in the former game the banker bets against each player individually and the bank frequently changes hands.

COLONEL

Two-handed Coon-Can, and thus a member of the Rummy family. Each player is dealt ten cards originally; may lay down sets and sequences as the game proceeds; may play to sets and sequences already on the table; and must declare he is going down before making his last discard.

COMMERCE

There are many varieties of this game, which bears some resemblance to Poker. Each player endeavours, by exchanging cards successively for cards played (in previous exchanges) to the table, to secure a winning hand; he then 'knocks' and the rival hands are exposed. The final hands rank in the order: (*a*) Threes (three Aces beating three Queens, and so on); (*b*) Sequences (A K Q the highest sequence; 3 2 A the lowest; (*c*) Point, i.e. the greatest number of pips in one suit.

CONCENTRATION

This is not in the strict sense a card game at all; it could be played equally well with the cards used for Snap or Happy Families. All the cards are spread face downwards on the table; each player in turn exposes two and, if they make a pair, collects them; otherwise they are turned face downwards again. The point of the game is, of course, that players with good visual memories are bound to do better than players who are just drawing cards at random; the closing stages of the game produce interesting tactical situations.

COON-CAN

One of the original Rummy games, in which ten cards are dealt to each player. Two full packs are used, plus Jokers, which can represent any card. Sequences and sets may be laid on the table as formed (in which case other players can contribute to them); and, if the Joker is part of an exposed sequence or set, a player having the card which the Joker represents may make the appropriate exchange. Cards left in hand count against those holding them; the Joker counts 15, the Ace 11.

DONKEY

A nursery game for any number of players. Before the deal, counters numbering one less than the players are placed on the table within reach of all. Each starts with four cards, passing one in turn to the player to his left. As soon as a player has four of a kind he grabs a counter from the table; the others all endeavour to grab one; the player who gets no counter is the Donkey.

DUTCH BANK

One of the simplest of gambling games. A card is dealt face downwards to each player; then all the cards are exposed. The dealer (who is banker) pays to players who have a higher card than his own and receives from players who have lower or equal cards.

DUTCH WHIST

For four players. Hands are played out in sequence (*a*) as at ordinary Whist; (*b*) at No Trump; (*c*) at Nullos; (*d*) with a trump suit nominated by the player to the dealer's left.

ÉCARTÉ

An old but no longer fashionable game for two. It is played with a Piquet pack, the ranking order of the suits being K Q J A 10, etc. Five cards are dealt to each player with which, after one or more have been exchanged, he endeavours to take tricks. There are various complications which make the game more interesting than this bare outline suggests.

EUCHRE

At one time America's most popular game, now superseded by Contract Bridge and Pinochle. It is a trick-taking game, with a trump suit, played with a Piquet pack. Each player is originally dealt five cards. It has some resemblance to Ecarte, in that the main object of the game is to win three of the five tricks.

FAN TAN

The name causes some confusion. Chinese Fan Tan is a pure gambling game in which players bet on the number of cards left in part of a pack that has been cut. The name Fan Tan is also given to Parliament (q.v.).

FARO

A somewhat elaborate banking game requiring a special apparatus; not legal unless played in strict privacy.

FIVE HUNDRED

A game for three players, of American origin, which appears to derive from Euchre but incorporates some of the points of Whist.

GERMAN WHIST

A form of Whist for two. The trump suit is decided by cutting. Each player is dealt thirteen cards originally and the top card of the stock is exposed. Non-dealer leads to the first trick; the winner of the trick gets the top card. The other player takes the next one without showing it. When the stock is exhausted each player will have thirteen cards, and these are played, trick by trick; these are the thirteen tricks that count.

GIN RUMMY

A form of Ten Card Rummy which for a while was immensely popular but was then superseded by Canasta. A player may 'knock' when the cards are ten or under. 'Gin' is going out with no remainder. Scoring rules vary. The most popular method is one in which the results of the first deal and all subsequent deals are scored in one column, the results of the second and subsequent deals in another column, and the results of the third and subsequent deals in a third column. A player is 'blitzed' if he fails to score in all three columns; the score against him in any column in which he fails to score is doubled. Game is usually 150 up.

GREEK HEARTS

A variation of Hearts (see below) for four or more players. The Queen of Spades and the Hearts are the penalty cards, but a player who takes all of them gets a bonus of 150 points as against each of the other players.

HEARTS

The basic 'avoidance' game. The penalty cards are the Queen of Spades (15 points against the winner) and the Hearts (one point each).

KALABRIASZ

A somewhat complicated game with a variety of rules and a great many different names. It is played all over Europe and its extraordinary terminology suggests its mixed origins. It is a trick-taking game with various declarations, and has affinities with both Piquet and Euchre.

NEWMARKET

A 'stop' game, with next to no element of skill. Four 'luxuries' are exposed on the table (usually one Ace, one King, one Queen, and one Knave). The remainder of the hand is then dealt out; if there are three players four hands are dealt, one being unexposed. Before the deal, stakes are placed on the 'luxuries' in any manner agreed. The player on the dealer's left sets the ball rolling by playing the lowest card of any suit. Whoever has the next one must play it, and so on till a 'stop' is reached, the missing card being in the unexposed hand. After a stop another suit can be led. Eventually one of the 'luxuries' is reached and the player who plays the preceding card takes all the money staked on it. If no one holds the card which secures a luxury, or if a player has gone out (played all his cards) before it is reached, the money staked on it stays there and may eventually reach a sizable sum.

OLD MAID

A nursery game. One of the Queens is removed from the pack. Cards are dealt out; passed from hand to hand; the object is to collect pairs. Eventually all will be paired except the odd Queen; the holder of this is the 'old maid'.

PINOCHLE

The American form of Bezique played with a pack of 48 cards: two each of the A K Q J 10 9 of each suit. The scoring differs from that of Bezique but it is essentially the same game.

SKAT

A complicated but not very exciting game, of German origin, and played extensively in the U.S.A. It is impossible to give even a rough idea of it in less than a thousand words.

SLOBBERHANNES

Another 'avoidance' game. Penalties are incurred by (*a*) taking the first trick; (*b*) taking the last trick; (*c*) taking the trick which contains the Queen of Clubs.

THIRTY-ONE

Players are dealt three cards each; they discard and draw as in the Rummy games. Ace counts 11; Court cards 10 each; other cards their pip value. The object is to secure three cards in one suit with a total value of 31: this at once wins the kitty. Or any player may 'knock' if he thinks he has the highest valued hand.

Patience

Patience games are for the most part games for one player only (hence their American name, Solitaire). The player, having no opponent against whom he can pit his wits, sets himself the task of attaining a prescribed result by arranging and rearranging, in accordance with the conditions of his game, the cards drawn in sequence from a well-shuffled pack. In some Patiences the result depends almost entirely on chance; in others a high degree of skill is required to plan one's play to the best advantage. Hundreds of Patiences have been invented; I reproduce here a selection of those which are fairly well known. The number of possible games is limitless; anyone who is familiar with a pack of cards and is reasonably ingenious can invent as many as he likes for himself.

Patience can also be made a competitive game for two (or any greater number) of players. Suppose there are two players. Get some third person to shuffle a pack thoroughly, and then to arrange the cards in a second pack in exactly the same sequence. Then give one pack to each player. The winner is the one who gets the better result.

The Vocabulary of Patience Games

Certain recognized terms will be used throughout the descriptions which follow. These apply to all Patience games.

FOUNDATIONS. These are the cards set out originally, upon which other cards will be played, in sequence, in accordance with the rules of the particular game.

ASCENDING SEQUENCE. Cards played from the Ace (or any other card) upwards, e.g. A 2 3, etc., or 8 9 10, etc. Unless otherwise prescribed, an Ascending Sequence goes 'round the corner', e.g. Q K A 2 3, etc.

DESCENDING SEQUENCE. The reverse of a Ascending Sequence, e.g. 9 8 7, etc., 3 2 A K Q, etc.

DEPOTS. Depositories in which cards not eligible for Foundations may be placed, in accordance with the rules of the particular game.

SPACE. A space becomes available when there are no cards left in a depot. It may then be used as a clearing-house for the transference of cards from one depot to another.

STOCK. Some Patiences make provision for dealing cards to a stock as well as to depots and foundations.

RUBBISH HEAP. Cards not played otherwise are, if the rules of the game permit, played face upwards to a 'rubbish heap'.

EXPOSED CARD. A card not covered or overlapped by another and therefore, as a rule, playable.

ONE-PACK PATIENCES

Miss Milligan

(Played with a full pack of fifty-two cards.)

OBJECT. To build in ascending sequence of suit on four foundations.

PROCEDURE. Seven cards are dealt, face upwards, to form seven depots. The cards of the depots are exposed cards. As soon as an Ace appears it is played to one of the foundations; then the 2 of the same suit is played on, when available, and so on.

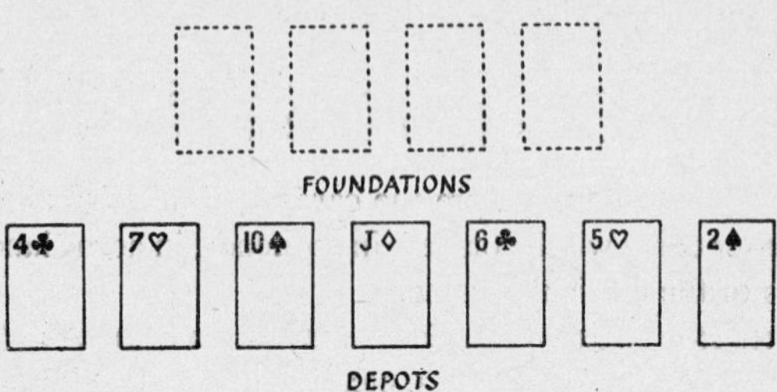

Exposed cards are played in ascending sequence of suit to foundations, or in descending sequence of alternating colour to depots. Thus, if the seven cards first dealt are as shown, the ♠ 10 may be played on to the ♦ J; the ♣ 6 on to the ♥ 7; the ♥ 5 on to the ♣ 6; the ♣ 4 on to the ♥ 5. These cards are placed so that they overlap; the player can then see exactly what cards are available, and plan accordingly. An available space can only be filled by a king, on which Q, J, 10, etc., can in due course be deposited.

A complete sequence may be moved as it stands from one depot to another, but part of a sequence may not be moved (except, of course, the top, or 'exposed', card, which can be moved at any time).

When the first seven cards have been dealt with as described above, deal seven more cards, one into each vacant space, and one on to the exposed cards of each of the other depots. Then continue play as before.

This process is continued until all cards have been dealt out.

A point may be reached where the Patience is 'blocked': all cards have been dealt out and no adjustment will release cards required for building one's ascending sequences. If the Patience 'comes out', however, the four sequences will have been completed from the Ace up to the King.

If two players have played this game competitively, starting with identically arranged packs, the winner is the player whose four foundation piles have the higher aggregate pip total (count King 13, Queen 12, and so on). This principle can be made applicable to all competitively played Patiences.

Fort

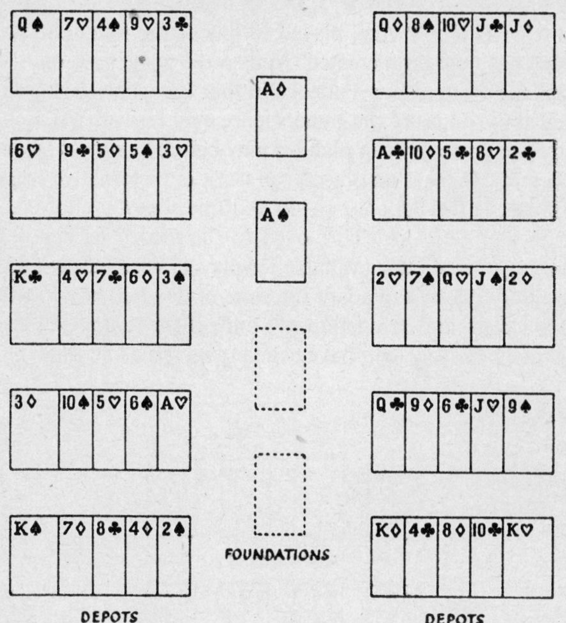

OBJECT. To build in ascending sequence of suit on the four foundations.

PROCEDURE. Before shuffling the pack, take out any two Aces and play them to two of the foundations. The other two Aces will be played when they become available.

Deal the remaining fifty cards to ten depots, each of five overlapping cards. The exposed cards are the top one in each depot. These may be played to a foundation in ascending sequence of suit; to another depot in either ascending or descending sequence of suit; or to the 'space' which becomes available when all the cards of a depot have been played.

Thus, in the example shown, the ♦ 2 and ♦ 3 can at once be played on the ♦ Ace. Now the ♠ Q, J, 10, 9 can be successively played on the ♠ K.

Now the ♥ Q and ♥ J can be played on to the ♥ K. The ♥ 6 and ♥ 5 will go on the ♥ 7; the ♠ 6 on the now exposed ♠ 7. This releases the ♥ Ace, played to one of the foundations, and a space has now been created. And so the game goes on.

This is an interesting Patience in that the whole set-up is disclosed at the outset of the game. Hence a player with a sufficiently good visual memory can plan his play before he moves any cards at all, and (if time is no object) can work out alternative schemes.

MERCI. If the Patience is blocked one *merci* is allowed. One card in any depot can be moved to the top of its depot, thus becoming immediately available for play. (I need hardly add that the solitary player can adapt the rules of any Patience to suit his own interests and temperament; and, if he is not playing the game competitively, can have as many *mercis* as he likes!)

Single Rail

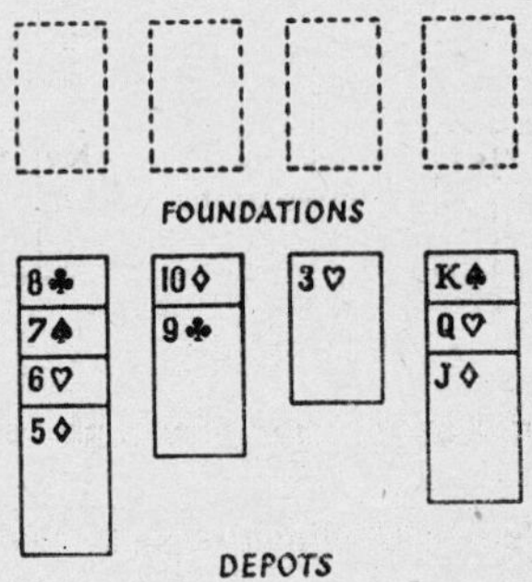

OBJECT. To build in sequence, irrespective of suit, on the four foundations.

PROCEDURE. Four cards are dealt, face upwards, to a row of four depots.

Aces dealt to depots, or exposed in play, are played to the four foundations. Any 2 can be played on any Ace; any 3 on any Two; and so on.

Having dealt the first four cards, continue to deal; playing any card, lower in sequence than the one exposed, to a depot, and the remainder to a rubbish heap. Only the top card of the rubbish heap ranks as an exposed card.

Suppose, in the game shown, that the top card of the rubbish heap is a 3 and that an Ace is the card next dealt. The Ace is played to a foundation; then the 2 can be played from the rubbish heap; then the ♥ 3. Now a space is created to which one can play either the next card in the rubbish heap or the next card from the pack.

MERCI. Take any one card from the rubbish heap for play to a foundation or depot.

The Windmill

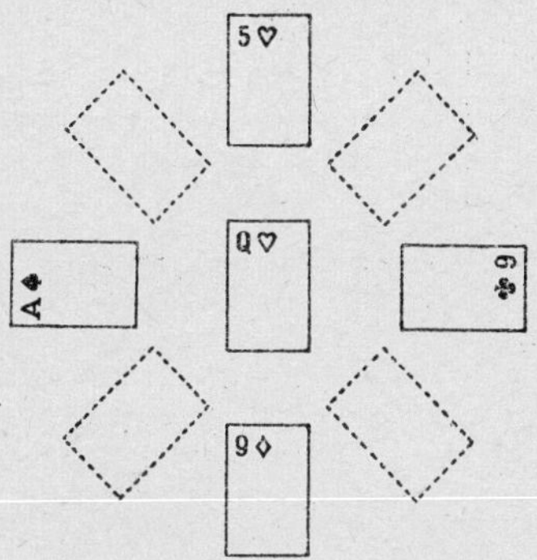

LAY-OUT OF DEPOTS AND FOUNDATIONS
Foundations are denoted by dotted lines

OBJECT. To build on Ace foundations in ascending sequence of suit.

PROCEDURE. Five depot cards are dealt as shown. The foundations (Aces) are placed as indicated to form the Windmill. In this example the ♠ Ace can at once be transferred to a foundation, creating a space to which another card is dealt. If no Ace is dealt in the first five cards, take one from the pack; re-shuffle, cut, and continue.

Having dealt the first five cards and played one Ace, continue to deal, playing any 4 on the ♥ 5, any J on the ♥ Q, and so on and other cards either to a space or to a 'rubbish heap'.

When all cards have been dealt, and as many as possible played to foundations and depots, pick up the rubbish heap, shuffle, and redeal. In the redeal no rubbish heap is allowed. If all cards cannot now be played to foundations, depots, or spaces the Patience is blocked.

Gradations

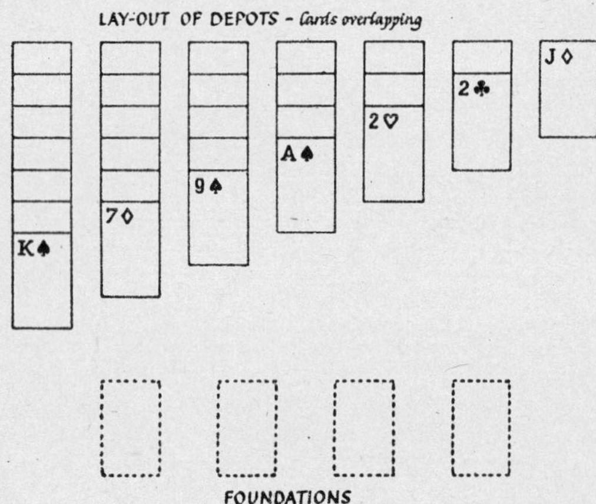

OBJECT. To build in ascending sequence of suit on the four foundations.

PROCEDURE. Deal out the first twenty-eight cards as shown to form seven depots. In the first depot six cards are dealt face downwards, then one face upwards; in the next depot five cards face downwards, then one face upwards, and so on. Only the cards dealt face upwards are exposed. When one of these is played to a foundation or depot the next one is turned face upwards.

In the example given, the ♠ Ace is at once played to a foundation and the card below it exposed. Exposed cards can be played, in ascending sequence of suit, to foundations; in descending sequence of alternating colour, to depots. Thus, if the card below the ♠ Ace is the ♠ 2 or another Ace, it will be played to a foundation; if the ♥ Q, ♣ 6, etc., to a depot.

When available cards have been played and those which now become available turned face upwards, continue to deal. Cards not playable to foundations, depots, or spaces are played face upwards to a rubbish heap.

When the pack has been exhausted the rubbish heap is turned face downwards and redealt. This time no 'rubbish heap' is allowed.

Simplex

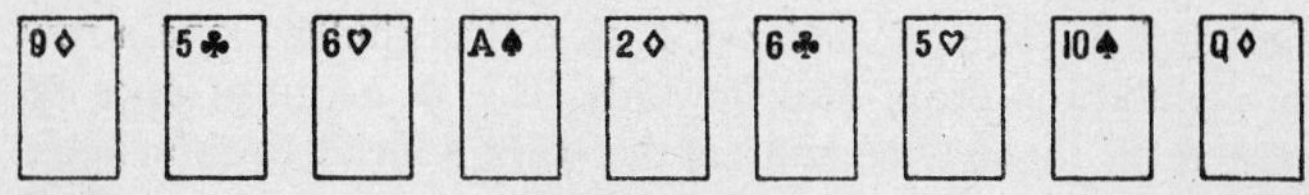

FOUNDATIONS

OBJECT. To eliminate all the cards by completing sets of four cards of the same denomination.

PROCEDURE. Nine cards are dealt to foundations as shown. If two (or more) are of the same denomination (e.g. the two Fives and the two Sixes) one 5 is played on to the other 5, one 6 on to the other 6, and cards are dealt to the two vacant spaces. The above procedure is then repeated.

Continue dealing, playing any card of a denomination shown to the appropriate foundation or to a space, and the remainder, face upwards, to a rubbish heap. The top card of the rubbish heap is playable as soon as a space occurs.

As soon as one denomination is completed (four Kings, four Sixes, etc.) it is thrown aside and a space becomes available. Hence if four sets are completed it must be possible to eliminate all the cards.

This is a simple Patience, demanding little skill, and only the one deal is allowed.

Labyrinth

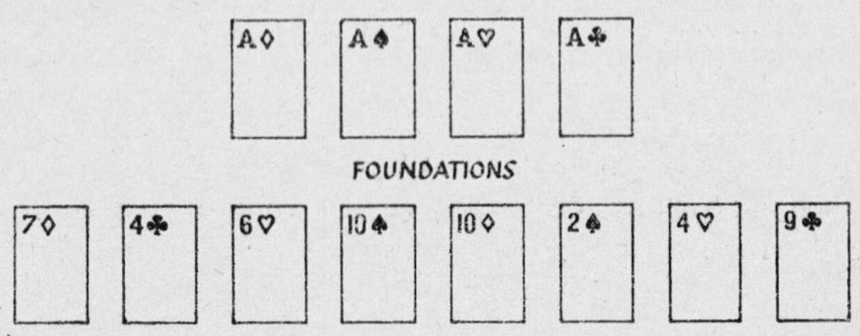

OBJECT. To build in ascending sequence of suit on the four Ace foundations.

PROCEDURE. The four Aces are placed as shown to form foundations. The remainder of pack is then shuffled, and a row of eight cards dealt, face upwards. The ♠ 2 can at once be played on the ♠ Ace and another card is dealt to the vacant space. If this is a playable card (e.g. the ♦ Ace or ♠ 3) it goes to a foundation and the space is filled again.

When all available cards have been played another row of eight cards is dealt, below the first one. Now there are two rows from which cards can be played, and in which spaces can be filled from the pack.

Next, a third row is dealt. Now the cards in the second row cease to be available; but, if a space occurs in the top or bottom row, the adjacent card from the middle row can be moved into it and becomes exposed. Spaces in the middle row are left unfilled.

When the possibilities of three rows are exhausted a fourth row is dealt. As before, only the cards in the top and bottom row are exposed. But a card can be moved from one of the interior rows to a vacant space below or above it.

Finally, a fifth row and sixth row (if necessary) are dealt, and cards moved as required into vacant spaces.

If, after all this, the Patience is blocked, any one card can be taken from any row for play to a foundation. Only the one deal is allowed.

TWO-PACK PATIENCES

Kings. (*Played with two full packs of fifty-two cards*)

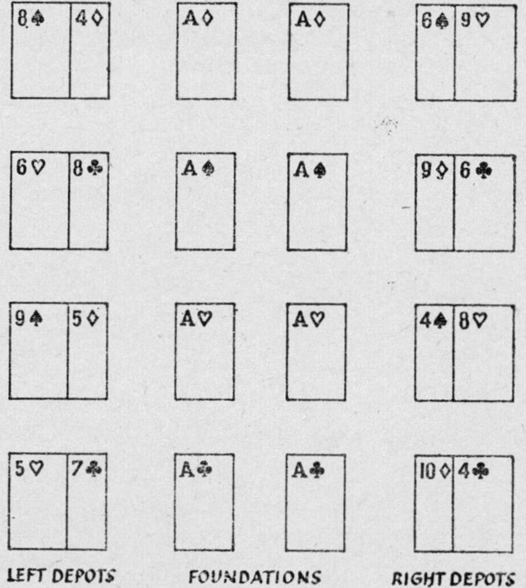

OBJECT. To build in ascending sequence, irrespective of suit, on the eight Ace foundations.

PROCEDURE. Take out the eight Aces and set them out, as shown, as foundations. Shuffle the remaining cards and deal eight depots of two cards each, four to the left of the Aces, four to the right. The eight top cards of the depots are exposed.

Until all the cards have been dealt, an exposed card can only be played to a foundation from the depot adjoining it, i.e. each foundation has its own depot. After playing to foundations such cards as are available (any 2 on an Ace, and so on) deal cards singly to each depot; the card dealt becomes the top card.

When all the cards have been dealt, the rules become less strict. The exposed cards of a depot can be played (*a*) to any foundation (ascending sequence), (*b*) to any depot in either ascending sequence (irrespective of suit); (*c*) to any space. A space can be left vacant if desired.

Only one deal is allowed.

French Blockade

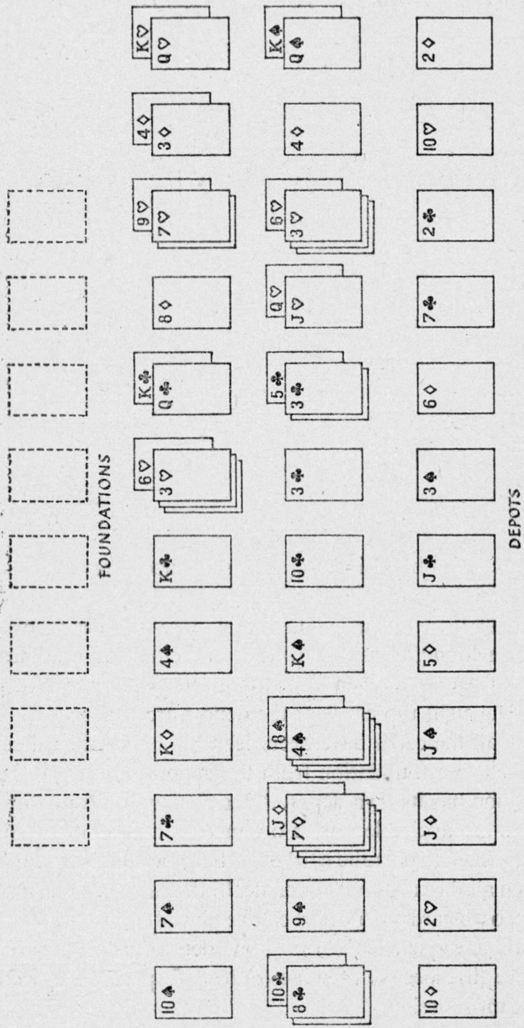

OBJECT. To build on the eight Ace foundations in ascending sequence of suit.

PROCEDURE. Begin by dealing a row of twelve depot cards, face upwards. Any Aces are played to foundations; then Twos, Threes, etc., and spaces are filled by dealing further cards.

When available cards have been played a second row of twelve cards is dealt. These cards 'blockade' the cards immediately above them. Thus (in the example shown) the ♠ 7 in Row 1 cannot be played until the ♠ 9 below it has gone. Or, when Row 3 has been dealt, the ♠ 9 remains until the ♥ 2 has been played.

Exposed cards (depot cards not blockaded) can be played, not only to foundations, but to other exposed cards (not to blockaded cards) in descending sequence of suits.

When play is finished a complete round of depot cards must be dealt before play begins again.

OBJECT. To build in ascending sequence of suit on the eight Ace foundations.

PROCEDURE. Deal the first thirty-six cards as shown. Aces as dealt go at once to the eight foundations.

There are now eight vertical depots. The bottom card of each depot is exposed and can be played, as opportunity occurs, to a foundation.

Exposed cards may also be played to spaces or, in descending sequence of suit, to other depots provided they are played to depots which do not contain more cards than the depot from which they are taken.

Cards played in sequence on a depot card, however, all count as one card. They should be so arranged that the top and bottom card of the sequence can be seen.

Single cards only may be moved, not sequences – except, of course, that all the cards in a sequence can be played successively to a foundation.

When the first thirty-six cards have been set out and any possible plays effected, deal the remaining cards. They go (*a*) to foundations; (*b*) to depots; (*c*) if otherwise unplayable, to a rubbish heap. They are dealt to the rubblish heap face upwards and its top card is exposed.

Harp

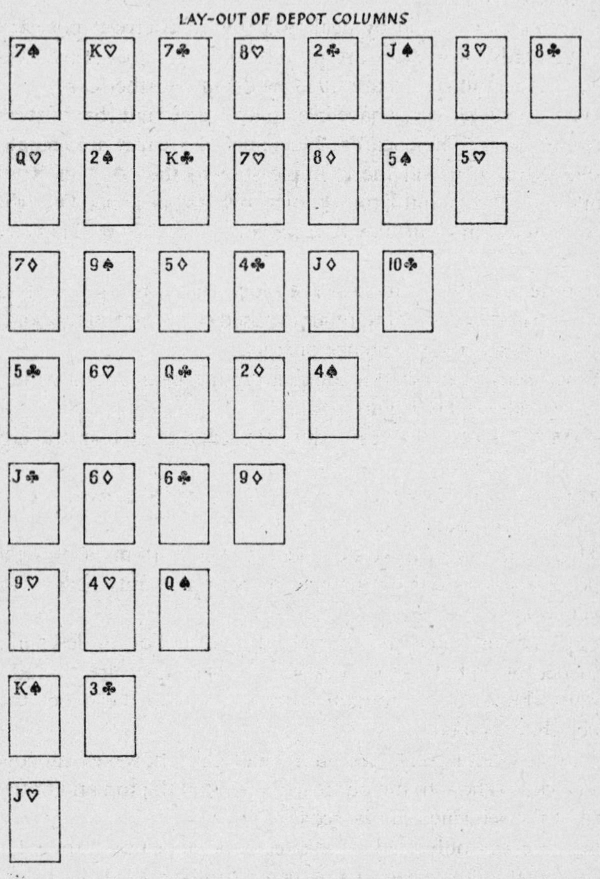

One redeal is allowed; the rubbish heap cards are turned face downwards and redealt without shuffling. Unplayable cards are again dealt to a rubbish heap, and this time may overlap one another to enable one to plan one's play. Even so, this Patience may well fail to come out.

Thirteen

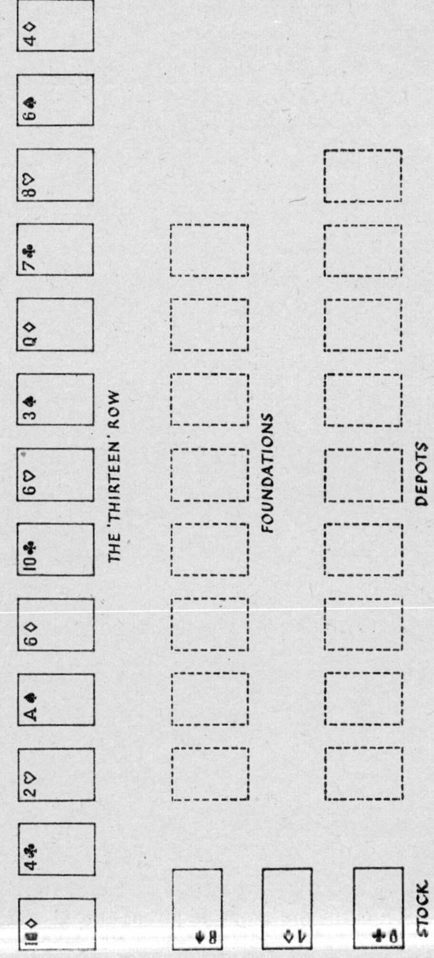

OBJECT. To build in ascending sequence of *alternating colour* on foundations. If the foundation card is other than an Ace (e.g. a 6) an Ace of a different colour will be played on the King and the sequence terminates with a 5.

PROCEDURE. Deal a row of thirteen cards as shown. Then deal three 'stock' cards; any one of these may be taken as a foundation card and laid out as the first of the eight foundations. Suppose the 9 is chosen; all the remaining foundations will be Nines. If two or three Nines are dealt both or all three will be played as foundation cards. The remaining two stock cards (if three of different denominations are dealt) become depot cards, and more depot cards are dealt to bring the total number up to nine.

The following are exposed cards: (*a*) the top card of each of the nine depots; (*b*) the right-hand card (only) of the 'thirteen' row; (*c*) the top card of the rubbish heap.

Exposed cards may be played (as already explained) in ascending series of alternate colour on foundations; in descending series of alternate colour (5 4 3 2 Ace, King, etc.) on depot cards. If not otherwise playable they go, face upwards, to a rubbish heap.

There are no spaces in the 'thirteen' row. Its cards disappear one by one. Spaces in the depots are filled from the rubbish heap.

Only one deal is allowed.

Streets

OBJECT. To build in ascending sequence of suit on foundations.

PROCEDURE. Begin by dealing a row of ten depot cards; then ten more overlapping them; ten more; and ten more. There are now ten vertical depots, the top card of each being exposed.

Exposed Aces, and Aces exposed in play, are at once taken as foundations. Thus (in the example given) the ♥ Ace, and then the ♥ 2 and ♥ 3, can at once be played.

When available cards have been played the remaining cards are dealt; they go to the foundations; to the depots (where they are played in descending sequence of alternating colour); or, face

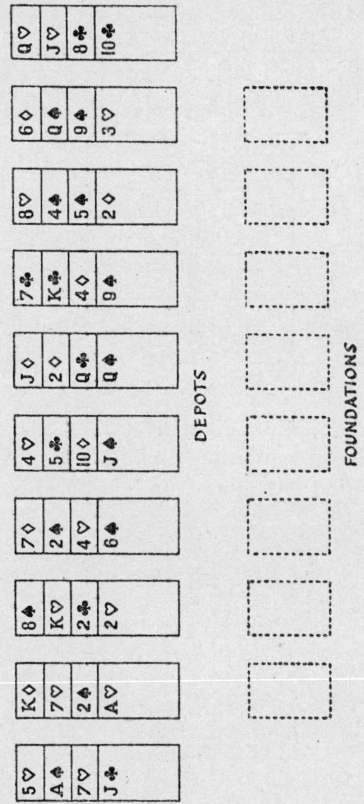

upwards, to a rubbish heap. The top card of the rubbish heap is exposed.

Spaces *may* be filled by exposed cards; but they should be kept vacant if possible to allow other cards to be freely moved about.

Algerian

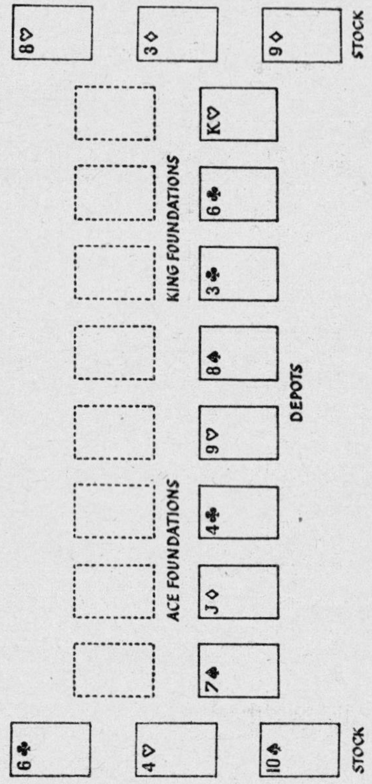

OBJECT. To build, in ascending sequence of suit, on the four Ace foundations and, in descending sequence of suit, on the four King foundations.

PROCEDURE. A row of eight depot cards is dealt; then six stock packets of four cards each, placed at the side of the depots.

One Ace and one King of each suit are taken, as they are dealt, to form the eight foundation cards. (Thus the ♥ K would be immediately removed and made a foundation card.)

Exposed cards are the top cards of the stock packets, and cards of depots not overlapped by other cards.

Exposed cards may be played (in ascending or descending suit sequence respectively) on Ace or King foundations and in either ascending or descending suit sequence on depots. In playing them to depots the sequence may at any time be changed; e.g. one can play 6 7 8 9 8 7 6 5, etc.

A King may be played on an Ace, or an Ace on a King.

Cards may only be moved singly from the depots.

A space in a depot may be filled by any exposed cards. A space in the stock may not be filled as long as there are any cards in hand.

When all available cards have been played deal two cards, face upwards, to each depot. The second of these now becomes the exposed card of the depot. When only eight cards are left they are dealt singly to depots.

When all the cards have been dealt a space in the stock packets may be filled by an exposed card, but no other cards may be played on to it.

Only one deal is allowed.

PATIENCE GAMES FOR TWO

(Played with two full packs of cards)

Duplex

OBJECT. The cards are built on the foundations in ascending sequence of suits. The player wins who first gets rid of all the cards in his stock, depots and rubbish heap.

PROCEDURE. The two packs are shuffled together; then each player takes half of them. Each deals thirteen cards, face upwards, as his stock and then four depot cards. The players are so seated that they can play cards to both depots; between the depots will be placed the eight Ace foundations.

The player whose stock has the higher card plays first (if equal, they cut). He moves all Aces from the eight depots, or from his

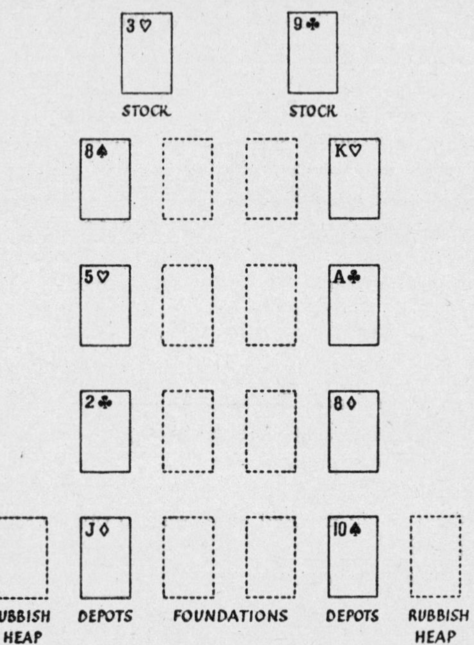

own stock (not his opponent's) to foundations, and continues with any other available cards. He can play exposed cards also (*a*) in descending sequence of suit on any of the depots, or (*b*) in either ascending or descending sequence of suit on his opponent's stock or rubbish heap; (he naturally will not prejudice his chances by playing them on his own). He may not, however, take cards from his opponent's stock or rubbish heap.

The first player continues to play available cards, and to deal when available cards are exhausted until he deals an unplayable card, which starts his rubbish heap. Play now passes to his opponent who continues in the same way.

When all cards have been dealt each player in his turn may play any exposed depot card or the top card of his own rubbish heap. If a space occurs in a depot it is filled by a card from the player's own stock. When the stock cards are exhausted it may be filled by any exposed card.

The player wins who has first got rid of his stock, depots and rubbish heap. If both have cards left when there are no more playable cards exposed the player wins who in stock, depots, and rubbish heap has the smaller number of cards unplayed.

This is an amusing game with considerable scope for the exercise of skill. For example, one will plan not only to build on the foundations but to play as many cards as possible to one's opponent's side of the table.

Double Demon

(Played with two full packs of cards)

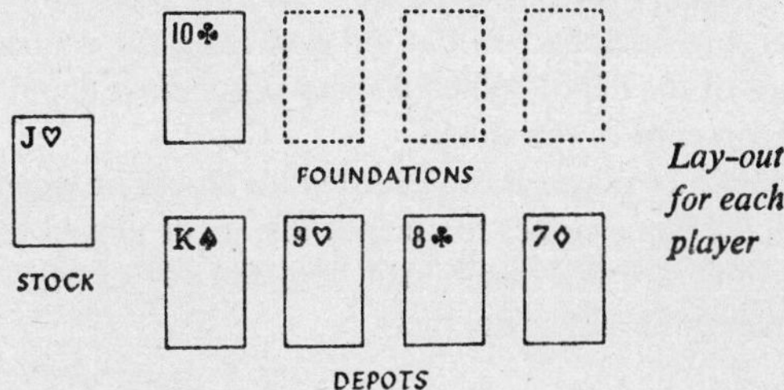

Lay-out for each player

OBJECT. Cards are built on foundations in ascending sequence of suit and each player's object is to contribute the larger number of such cards.

PROCEDURE. Each player starts with his own pack; they must have distinctive backs. Each having shuffled his pack (which should be cut by his opponent) deals thirteen cards, face upwards, to a stock, and four depot cards. The player whose stock card is of higher value plays it to one of the foundations, and cards of the same value will, as exposed, be the basic cards of the remaining seven foundations. Cards will be played on these in ascending sequence of suit.

In the example shown, the higher stock card was a 10. All Tens now become foundation cards; the sequence will proceed J Q K Ace 2 3, etc. It ends, of course, with the 9.

The players deal and play simultaneously, each confining his attentions to his own stock, depots and rubbish heap, but playing cards to all eight foundations.

Exposed cards are the top cards of depots, the top card of the stock, and every third card dealt to the rubbish heap when other cards become unplayable, as the cards to the rubbish heap are dealt in batches of three. But, when only two cards are left in a player's hand, they are dealt singly and both may, if eligible, be played.

When all cards are dealt pick up the rubbish, turn it face downwards, and redeal. This process continues until no more cards can be played.

A player can play cards not only to foundations, but to his own depots in descending sequence of alternating colour. A sequence can be transferred as it stands from one depot to another, provided that its bottom card is next in sequence to the top card of the depot. When a space occurs in a depot it is filled by the top card of the stock.

When either player has exhausted his stock, or when both are 'stuck', the game comes to an end. The cards played to the eight foundations are then examined, and the player wins who has contributed the larger number.

Patience addicts who have exhausted the possibilities of the games given here, and seek new worlds to conquer, will find a further selection of Patiences in my *Card Games*. These are:

One-Pack Patiences: Castles in Spain; Monte Carlo; Mystery; Pas Seul; Raglan; Six by Six; Thirty.

Two-Pack Patiences: Alternations; As You Like It; Carlton; Deauville; Demon; Forty-Nine; Lady Palk; Les Huits; Milligan Harp; Red and Black; Reform; Regiment; Royal Parade; Squadron; Sultan; Triangle; Triple Line.

And in the English edition of Culbertson's *Card Games Complete* are to be found yet more Patiences (of American provenance): Accordion; Beleaguered Castle; Calculation; Canfield; Clock; Four Seasons; Hit or Miss; Klondike; La Belle Lucie; Spider.

Games of Encounter

Draughts

DRAUGHTS (known in America as Checkers) is sometimes regarded as a sort of poor relation of Chess. The latter game, it is true, is a great deal more difficult than Draughts; to learn to play Chess of the highest class takes years of study and practice; and in Russia, if not elsewhere, mastery of the game ranks high among recognized social activities and carries rich rewards. Draughts has no such standing, in Russia or anywhere else. All the same it is a fine game which no one can play well without giving much thought to its principles and their application; the strategy and tactics involved are different in kind from those familiar to Chess players; and it has a substantial and fascinating literature. I first realized its possibilities when, as a schoolboy, I played some games against an ex-world champion; he set up a position in which (as he demonstrated) he had announced a win in a maximum of 53 moves.

THE RULES OF DRAUGHTS

The game is played (like Chess) on a board chequered black and white of 64 squares. The board is so placed that each player has a black square in the corner of the board immediately to his left.

When diagrams of games are printed, however, black and white are, for the sake of clarity, reversed. In any actual game the squares shown as white would be black and *vice versa.*

Each player, to begin with, has twelve 'men' which, at the beginning of the game, are placed as in Fig. 1. In Fig. 2 are shown the 32 black squares (white in the diagram) to which the moves of the player are confined. They are numbered for purposes of reference. The moves in the game are recorded, very simply, by indicating the square whence a man has moved and the square to which its move has been made.

The object of the game is so to fix one's opponent that he cannot make a move; if one succeeds in doing this one has won the game; if neither player succeeds the game is drawn. A high proportion of games between good players are draws.

BLACK

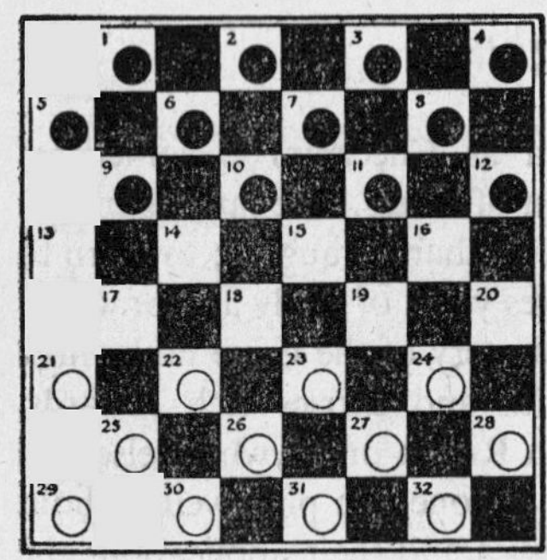

WHITE

FIG. I

BLACK

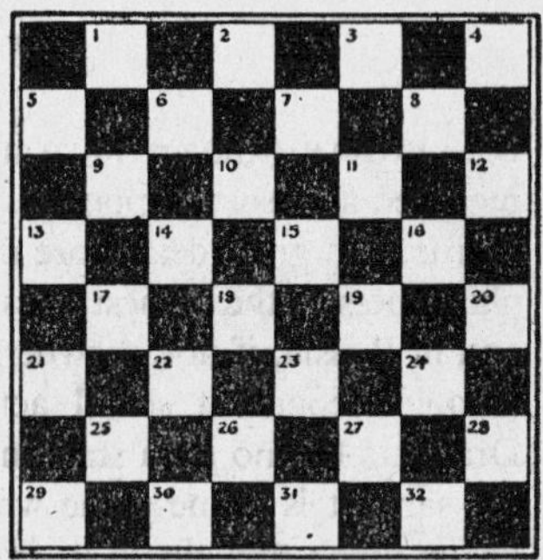

WHITE

FIG. 2

Here are two situations (Figs. 3 and 4) which could – however improbably – arise in play, in both of which Black (whose turn it is to move) has a lost game. In Fig. 3 his twelve men are still on the board, but (as we shall see) he cannot move one of them. In Fig. 4 each side has six men on the board. As, again, we shall see, Black must lose five of them in succession, after which he cannot move at all. In such a position anyone but a novice would, of course, abandon the game.

BLACK

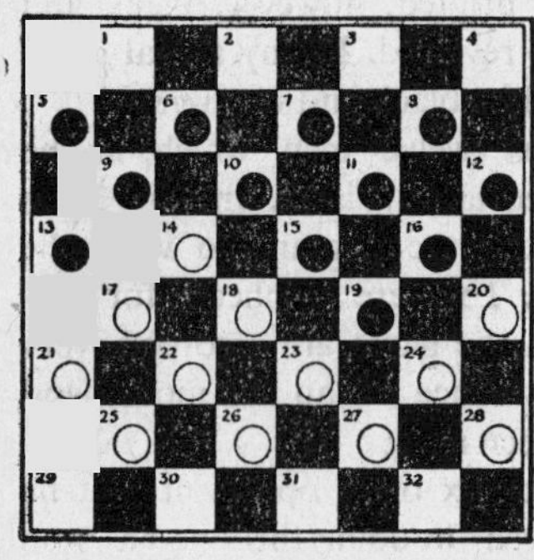

WHITE

FIG. 3

BLACK

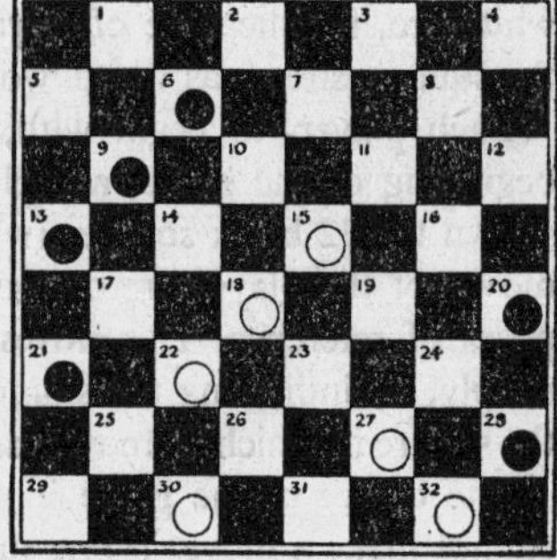

WHITE

FIG. 4

The players move alternately, Black making the first move. Two kinds of moves are possible. (1) A man can be moved forward and diagonally if the square to which he wishes to move is vacant. (2) If the adjacent diagonal square is occupied by the opponent, but the next square on the same diagonal is vacant, a man must jump over the opponent's piece (capturing it *en route*) and land on the vacant square. The piece captured is removed from the board. If there is a second piece which can be captured in this way it not only can, but must, be taken.

Figs. 5 and 6 illustrate these moves.

Fig. 5 shows a game in which each player has so far made three moves. It is now Black's turn. His *possible* moves are 9 – 13; 9 – 14; 10 – 14; 11 – 16; 12 – 16. Of these moves, 9 – 14 and 12 – 16 would be suicidal; the former presents White with two men (18 – 9 – 2) and the latter with one (19 – 12).

In Fig. 6 each player has lost one man. Black, who had intended to play 10 – 15, has mistakenly played 11 – 15. Now White has the option of playing 18 – 11 – 2 or 18 – 11 – 4, in either case capturing two men and (as will be explained) 'crowning' one of his own.

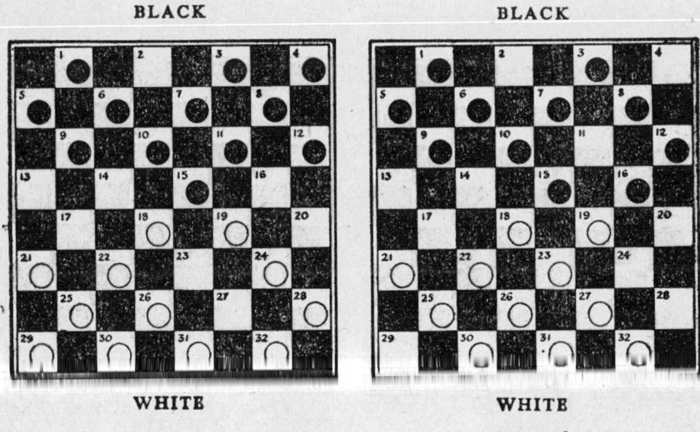

FIG. 5　　FIG. 6

When a man reaches the eighth rank (the opposite side of the board from that on which he started) he becomes a 'king' and is 'crowned'. This means that a man already removed from the board is placed on top of him. A king is much more powerful than a man. His moves are the same, but he can go backwards as well as forwards. How powerful he is is shown in Figs. 7 and 8.

In Fig. 7 Black has just moved. He has three kings and two men against one king and three men; he should have won easily. But, instead of playing 16 – 20, he has played 16 – 19. White wins immediately. He plays 23 – 16, capturing the man which has just moved. Black must now recapture, playing 12 – 19. And now White plays 24 – 15 – 6 – 13 – 22, leaving Black with nothing on the board.

Fig. 8 shows an even more spectacular success for White. He is lamentably inferior in material (he has three kings and one man against four kings and two men) but his opponent – blissfully unaware of the doom now impending – has just played 5 – 9. White's riposte is 10 – 6. Black must take this man (1 – 10) and White captures the whole of the opposing forces 'at one fell swoop'. (7 – 14 – 21 – 30 – 23 – 14 – 5). Coups of this character are frequently staged against players deficient in technique.

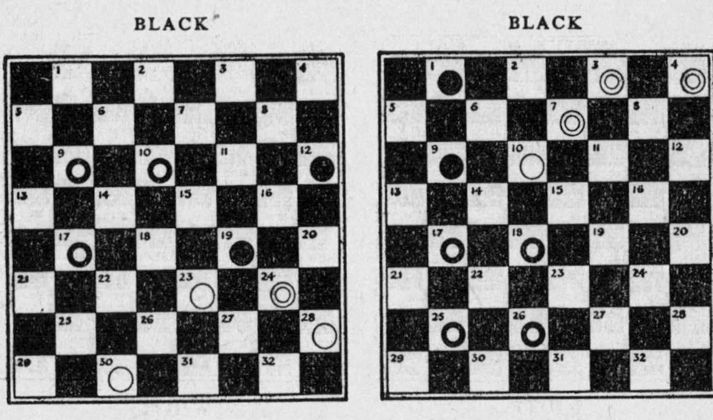

FIG. 7

FIG. 8

The Capture and the 'Huff'

As already mentioned, a player who can capture a piece (man or king) must do so. If his opponent's move gives him the choice of two captures, he can choose either; nor does he have to make a move which captures two (or more) of his opponent's pieces if there is an alternative move which offers him only one. But if an opponent's move offers a sequence of two or more pieces he must take them all. If a man (not a king) ends a sequence of two or three captures on the eighth rank, so becoming a king, and could – if it had started as a king – make yet another capture, the newly crowned king cannot make it until the next move.

A player who can take an opposing piece and fails to do so lays himself open to the penalty of the 'huff'. This means that his opponent can remove from the board the man or king which should have made the capture. The 'huff' does not rank as a move; Black (say) fails to take a piece which is open to capture; White now removes the offending man from the board and then makes his own move.

But a player is not bound to huff his opponent, for sometimes to do so would disadvantage him. He has three options: (1) to huff; (2) to insist on his opponent withdrawing his last move and making a move he could properly have made; (3) without huffing, to allow his opponent's last move to stand.

Figs. 9 and 10 illustrate these points.

Fig. 9 is a complex position in which Black, by one bad move, virtually throws the game away. He plays 11 – 15. Now White has three options. He can play (*a*) 18 – 11 – 2 (not 18 – 11 only); or (*b*) 20 – 11 – 2 (not 20 – 11 only); or (*c*) 19 – 10.

White must choose the first of these options. 18 – 11 – 2 wins easily: White gets two men for nothing. But (*b*) and (*c*) are alike disastrous. If White plays 20 – 11 – 2, Black is left with a choice of moves, of which the best is 15 – 22 – 31. White must now play 27 – 24. And Black's reply is 31 – 27, with a won game.

And if White is so careless as to play 19 – 10, his downfall is spectacular. Black's riposte is 7 – 14 – 21 – 30, collecting three men. Now White must play 20 – 11, and Black next plays 8 – 15 – 22 – 31, collecting three men more!

This example illustrates how full of pitfalls the game is.

In Fig. 10 White also has a winning game. It is his move and he plays 23 – 19. Black must take the man offered (16 – 23). White now takes three of Black's men in two ways: 27 – 18 – 11 – 4 or 26 – 19 – 10 – 3. If he chooses the latter his man becomes a king at 3, but the newly crowned king cannot immediately take the man at 8.

If, when White plays 23 – 19, Black fails to capture but plays (say) 15 – 18, White can (*a*) insist on Black withdrawing this move and playing 16 – 23; or (*b*) 'huff' Black, removing the man at 16 and then making his own move; or (*c*) allow Black's move to stand and play 19 – 12 – 3.

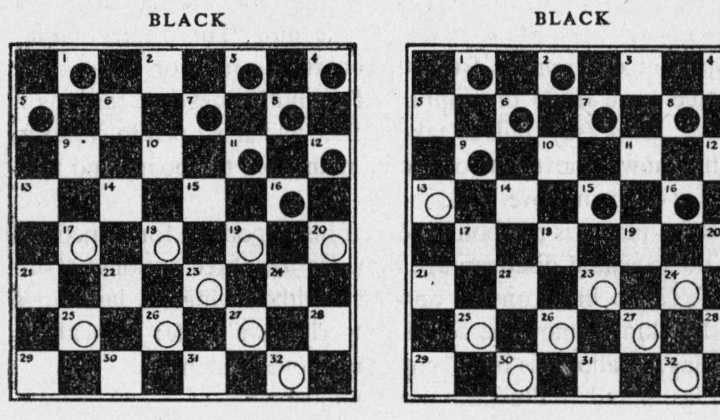

FIG. 9 FIG. 10

Illustrative Games

The rules of Draughts (as expounded above) can best be illustrated by reference to actual games. I have only space however for one or two. My first game develops on classical lines and proceeds uneventfully to an agreed draw. But the play is worth studying. Games more or less identical with this one must have occurred in tournament play over and over again.

This is one marked difference between Chess and Draughts. One very seldom gets two games at Chess which are identical beyond a certain point in the opening. But there is less scope for originality or variation at Draughts: so much so that, in some tournaments, competitors may not choose their opening moves but must play whatever openings are imposed by a random draw.

Position after White's 5th move

BLACK

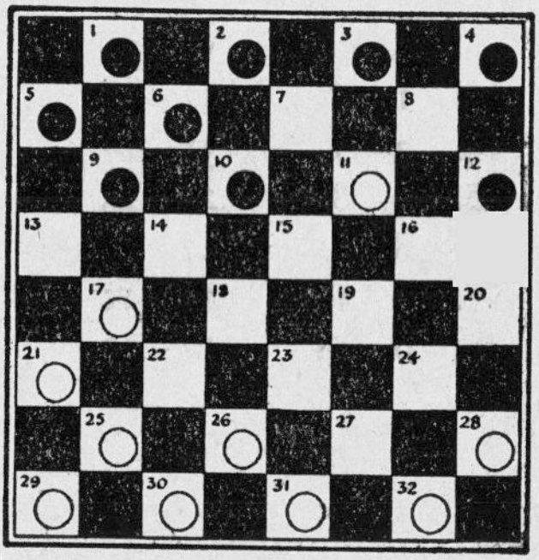

WHITE

FIG. 11

	BLACK	WHITE
1.	11 – 15	23 – 19
2.	8 – 11	22 – 17
3.	11 – 16	24 – 20
4.	16 – 23	27 – 11 (a)
5.	7 – 16	20 – 11

(a) Taking two men.

Position after White's 12th move

BLACK

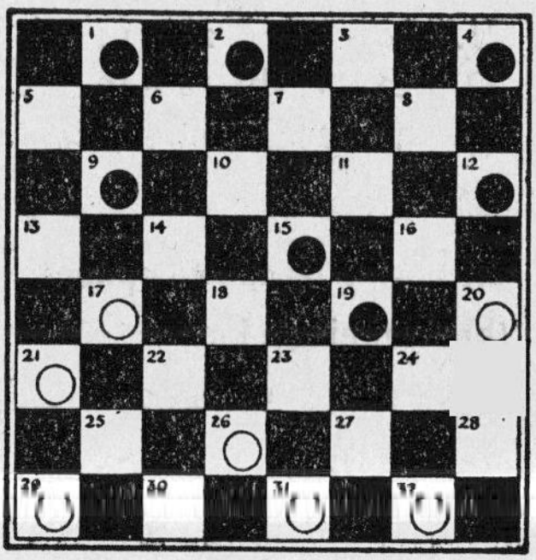

WHITE

FIG. 12

6.	3 – 7	25 – 22
7.	7 – 16	22 – 18
8.	9 – 14	18 – 9
9.	6 – 22 (a)	26 – 17
10.	5 – 9	28 – 24
11.	10 – 15	24 – 20
12.	16 – 19	30 – 26

(a) Taking two men.

	BLACK	WHITE
13.	1 – 6	32 – 28
14.	2 – 7	31 – 27
15.	4 – 8	29 – 25
16.	8 – 11	27 – 24
17.	7 – 10	25 – 22
18.	9 – 14	17 – 13

Position after White's 18th move

BLACK

WHITE

FIG. 13

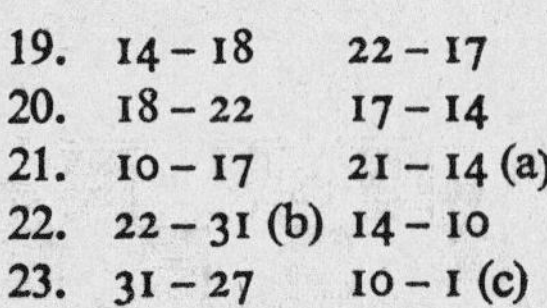

19.	14 – 18	22 – 17
20.	18 – 22	17 – 14
21.	10 – 17	21 – 14 (a)
22.	22 – 31 (b)	14 – 10
23.	31 – 27	10 – 1 (c)

(a) Giving Black two options.

(b) Crowning a king.

(c) Crowning a king.

Position after White's 23rd move

BLACK

WHITE

FIG. 14

Position after White's 30th move

BLACK

WHITE

FIG. 15

	BLACK	WHITE
24.	19 – 23	1 – 6
25.	15 – 18	6 – 10
26.	18 – 22	10 – 7
27.	11 – 15	7 – 10
28.	15 – 18	10 – 15
29.	23 – 26	15 – 10
30.	27 – 23	24 – 19
31.	23 – 16	20 – 11
32.	22 – 25	10 – 14
33.	18 – 22	13 – 9
34.	25 – 30	9 – 6

Draw agreed.

Final Position

BLACK

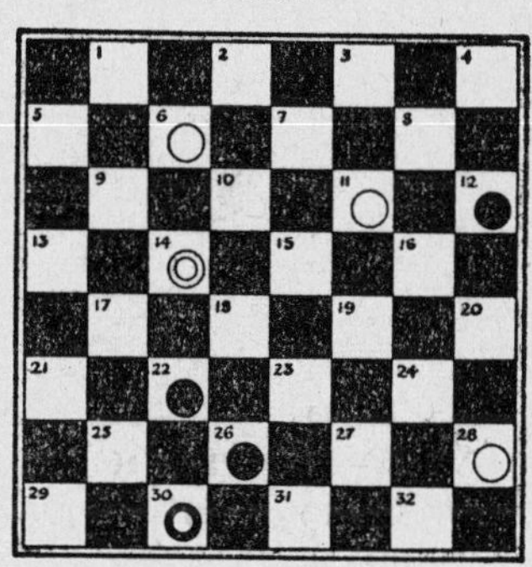

WHITE

FIG. 16

My second game is a more complex and more exciting example of the battle of wits to which a game of Draughts gives rise. The first twenty moves or so follow a classical pattern, but eventually Black makes a bad mistake and loses.

	BLACK	WHITE
1.	11 – 15	23 – 19
2.	9 – 14	22 – 17
3.	7 – 11	25 – 22
4.	11 – 16	26 – 23
5.	5 – 9	17 – 13
6.	3 – 7	29 – 25
7.	1 – 5	22 – 17

Position after White's 7th move

BLACK

WHITE

FIG. 17

8.	8 – 11	31 – 26
9.	16 – 20	19 – 16
10.	12 – 19	23 – 16
11.	14 – 18	26 – 23
12.	18 – 22	25 – 18
13.	15 – 22	23 – 18
14.	22 – 25	17 – 14

Position after White's 14th move

BLACK

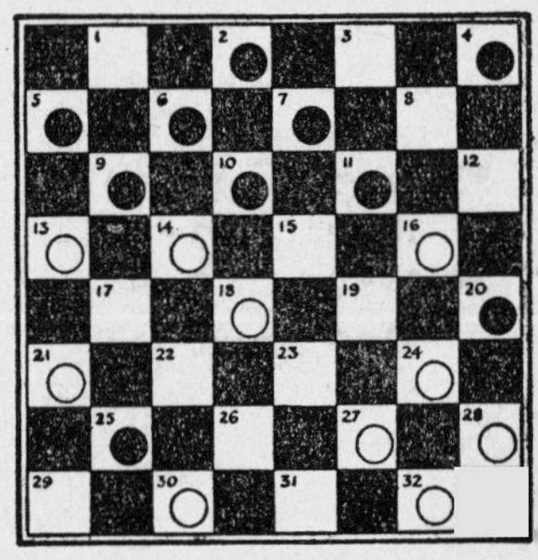

WHITE

FIG. 18

	BLACK	WHITE
15.	10 – 17	21 – 14
16.	11 – 15	18 – 11
17.	9 – 18	30 – 21
18.	18 – 22	21 – 17
19.	22 – 26	24 – 19
20.	26 – 30 (k)	19 – 15
21.	30 – 26	17 – 14
22.	26 – 22	13 – 9

Position after White's 22nd move

BLACK

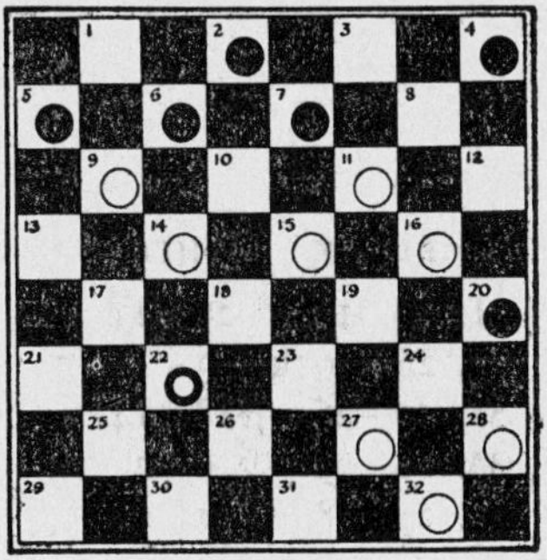

WHITE

FIG. 19

23.	6 – 13	15 – 10
24.	22 – 17	10 – 3 (k)
25.	17 – 10	11 – 7
26.	2 – 11	16 – 7
27.	10 – 15	7 – 2 (k)
28.	13 – 17	3 – 7
29.	17 – 22	2 – 6
30.	22 – 26	7 – 10

Position after White's 30th move

BLACK

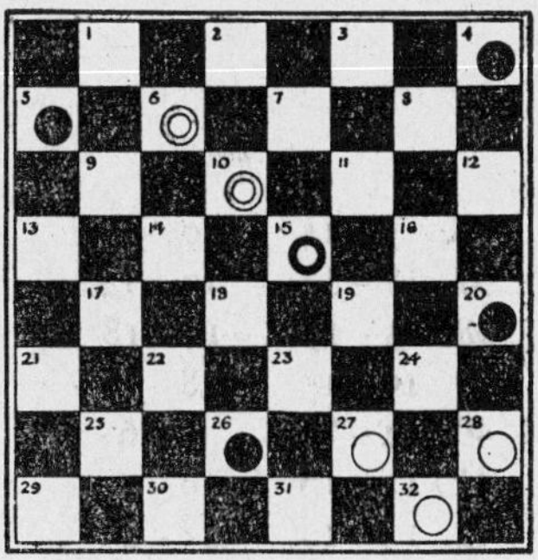

WHITE

FIG. 20

	BLACK	WHITE
31.	15 – 11	27 – 23
32.	26 – 30 (k)	23 – 18
33.	30 – 26	18 – 14
34.	26 – 23	6 – 2
35.	23 – 18	14 – 9

Position after White's 35th move

BLACK

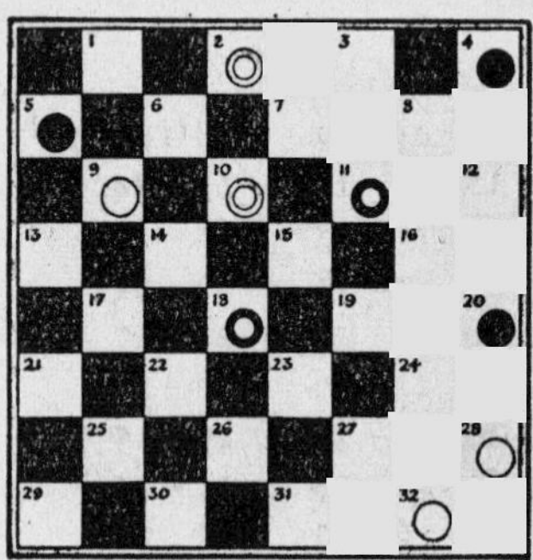

WHITE

FIG. 21

36.	5 – 14	10 – 17
37.	18 – 15	17 – 14
38.	15 – 19	14 – 18
39.	19 – 15	18 – 23
40.	4 – 8	2 – 6
41.	11 – 16	6 – 9
42.	15 – 19	23 – 27

Position after White's 42nd move

BLACK

WHITE

FIG. 22

	BLACK	WHITE
43.	8 – 12	9 – 14
44.	19 – 15	27 – 31
45.	15 – 19	14 – 18 (a)
46.	16 – 11	31 – 27
47.	19 – 23	18 – 22
48.	23 – 19	27 – 24 (b)

White delivers the coup de grâce

BLACK

WHITE

FIG. 23

(a) Both players, exhausted by a tense struggle, were losing their grip on the game. This move of White's is a bad blunder.

(b) But Black misses his opportunity and falls into White's trap. The game, as Fig. 23 shows, ends spectacularly. Black must play 20 – 27, and White (32 – 23 – 16 – 7) gets three pieces for one.

My third illustrative game is also built upon a classical foundation. Expert players will recognize its opening moves.

	BLACK	WHITE
1.	11 – 16	23 – 18
2.	16 – 20	24 – 19
3.	8 – 11	19 – 15
4.	10 – 19	18 – 14

Position after White's 4th move

BLACK

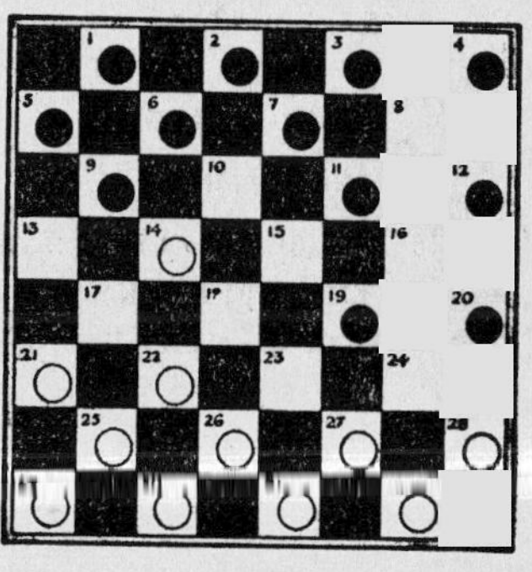

WHITE

FIG. 24

	BLACK	WHITE
5.	9 – 18	22 – 8
6.	4 – 11	27 – 24
7.	20 – 27	31 – 8
8.	12 – 16	8 – 4 (k)
9.	16 – 20	26 – 23
10.	3 – 8	4 – 11
11.	7 – 16	25 – 22

Position after White's 11th move

BLACK

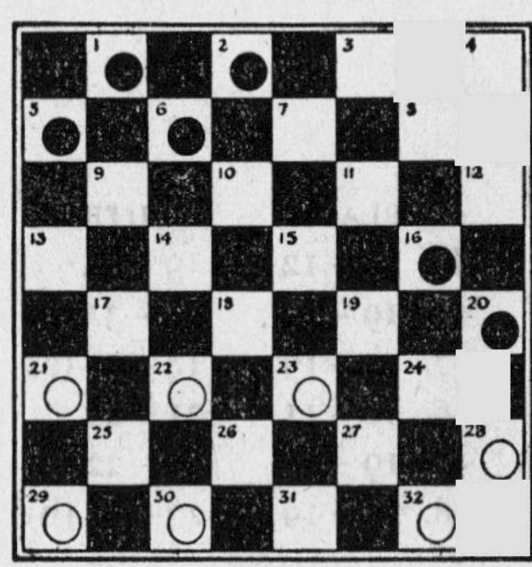

WHITE

FIG. 25

12.	2 – 7	22 – 18
13.	5 – 9	18 – 15
14.	9 – 14	15 – 11
15.	7 – 10	11 – 7

Black resigns.

White is about to crown another king and Black has no hope of penetrating his defences.

Black resigns

BLACK

WHITE

FIG. 26

These three games will, I hope, give some idea of the subtlety and complexity of Draughts, and of the pitfalls in which it abounds. The beginner cannot hope to get very far until he has learned to look out for such pitfalls, has some idea of the essentials of Draughts strategy, and has trained himself to look as far ahead as his mental capacities permit.

It is also worth while to study the various opening moves, and to familiarize oneself with at least the more probable situations of the end game. Hundreds of such situations have been exhaustively analysed by experts, and a good player will build up his middle game with a favourable end-situation in view.

OPENING MOVES

There are maybe fifty recognized openings, but a dozen or so of these far transcend the remainder in popularity. Here is a synopsis of them, with the names under which they have become familiar. It will be noticed that in every case but one Black's first move is 11 – 15: a move towards the centre of the board, which offers the widest scope for subsequent development.

OPENING		BLACK	WHITE
	1.	11 – 15	23 – 19
Laird and Lady	2.	8 – 11	22 – 17
	3.	9 – 13	
Glasgow	2.	8 – 11	22 – 17
	3.	11 – 16	
Old Fourteenth	2.	8 – 11	22 – 17
	3.	4 – 8	
Defiance	2.	9 – 14	27 – 23
Fife	2.	9 – 14	22 – 17
	3.	5 – 9	
Souter	2.	9 – 14	22 – 17
	3.	6 – 9	
Wilter	2.	9 – 14	22 – 17
	3.	7 – 11	

Will o' the Wisp	2.	9 – 13	
Single Corner	1.	11 – 15	22 – 18
	2.	15 – 22	25 – 18
Second Double Corner	1.	11 – 15	24 – 19
Maid of the Mill	1.	11 – 15	22 – 17
	2.	8 – 11	17 – 13
	3.	15 – 18	
Dyke	1.	11 – 15	22 – 17
	2.	15 – 19	
Cross	1.	11 – 15	23 – 18
Ayrshire Lassie	1.	11 – 15	24 – 20
	2.	8 – 11	28 – 24

Bristol	1.	11 – 16	24 – 20
	2.	16 – 19	

Space does not permit the further analysis of these openings, which in most cases has been carried out very thoroughly. If you have not access to the work which has been done on them, you can find out quite a lot about them by setting up the various positions and trying to find out how both Black and White can most profitably deploy their forces.

GENERAL PRINCIPLES

My advice to the beginner would be as follows:

1. Try to build up, and maintain, a strong centre. It may look safer to park one's men at the two sides of the board; but a man who has only one square to move to is only half as efficient as a man who has two.

2. Try to keep the situation *fluid*. Do not, therefore, commit too many men at the outset to an attack which may fail. Remember that the men in your rear rank have the greatest mobility; so keep them in reserve for as long as possible, without detriment to the development of an effective attack.

3. Try to crown at least one of your men at the earliest possible moment.

4. The moment you have an advantage in numbers, exchange as many more pieces as possible if you can do so without detriment to your game. Ten men should win against nine, but it is more certain that five will win against four, and – given room for development – three cannot fail to win against two. Where good players are reduced to three kings on the one side, and two kings on the other, the weaker party does not bother to continue the game. Learn how to handle this situation. (See below, p. 240.)

5. Above all, try to see, for as far ahead as you can manage, what the possible consequences of your moves, *and of your opponent's moves*, are. Draughts is largely a game of improvized stratagems, cunningly-baited traps. Whenever your adversary makes what looks like a peculiar move, ask yourself: 'Why is he doing that?'

The end-plays which follow illustrate some of the pitfalls which lend the game so much of its charm.

If you set up, and play through, not only the 'basic positions', but the representative endings which follow, you should have a good idea of the technique of the game.

END-PLAYS

(1) *The Four Basic Positions*

All textbooks on Draughts lay stress on the mastery of four positions, which – with variations – tend constantly to recur. They are known as the First, Second, Third, and Fourth positions. Here they are:

The First Position

White to play and win

	WHITE	BLACK
1.	15 – 10	9 – 14
2.	10 – 6	14 – 18
3.	6 – 1 (k)	18 – 23
4.	1 – 6	23 – 27
5.	6 – 10	27 – 32 (k)
6.	11 – 7	32 – 27
7.	7 – 2 (k)	27 – 24
8.	2 – 7	24 – 27
9.	7 – 11	27 – 23
10.	10 – 15	23 – 27
11.	15 – 19	27 – 32
12.	11 – 15	32 – 27
13.	15 – 18	27 – 32
14.	18 – 23	32 – 28
15.	23 – 27	28 – 32
16.	19 – 23	32 – 28
17.	27 – 32	28 – 24
18.	32 – 28	24 – 20
19.	23 – 19	20 – 24
20.	19 – 15	24 – 27
21.	15 – 18	3 – 8
22.	18 – 15	27 – 23
23.	28 – 32	8 – 12
24.	32 – 28	23 – 27
25.	15 – 18	12 – 16
26.	28 – 32	27 – 24
27.	18 – 15	16 – 20
28.	15 – 18	24 – 19
29.	32 – 28	19 – 16
30.	18 – 23	16 – 11
31.	23 – 19	11 – 8
32.	28 – 32	8 – 11
33.	32 – 27	11 – 8
34.	27 – 23	8 – 11
35.	23 – 18	11 – 8
36.	18 – 15	8 – 12
37.	15 – 11 and wins	

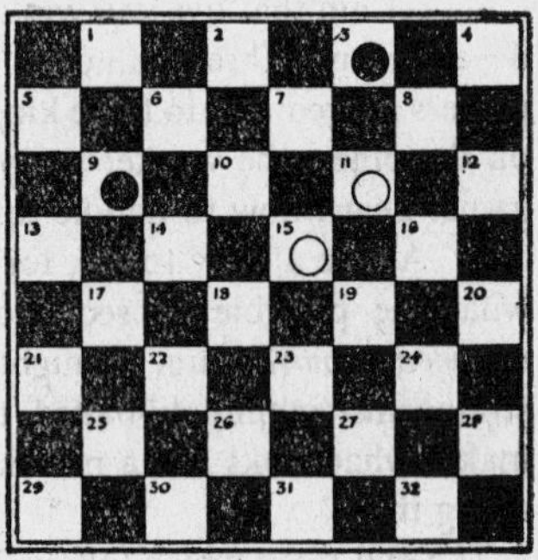

BLACK

WHITE

FIG. 27

A tedious affair, the beginner may think, but it is worth studying carefully, for it illustrates how – with only two kings against a king and a man – White is able to 'winkle out' Black from his refuge in the 'double corner' and secure what is called 'the move' against him. Having 'the move' is all-important in end-play, where each side is reduced to two or three pieces, or perhaps one piece, only. If one has 'the move' one is able to drive one's adversary to a square from which he cannot escape.

Further examples of this vital element in the tactics of the game are given below (pp. 237 ff.).

The Second Position

Black to move and win

This also is a lengthy exercise. Each side has one king and two men, but Black, with the move, has superior mobility.

BLACK

WHITE

FIG. 28

	BLACK	WHITE
1.	1 – 5	8 – 11
2.	5 – 9	11 – 15
3.	9 – 14	15 – 11
4.	14 – 18	11 – 16
5.	18 – 15	16 – 20
6.	15 – 11	20 – 24
7.	3 – 7	24 – 19
8.	7 – 10	19 – 23
9.	10 – 15	23 – 27
10.	15 – 19	27 – 32
11.	19 – 24	32 – 28
12.	24 – 27	28 – 32
13.	27 – 31 (k)	32 – 28
14.	31 – 27	28 – 32
15.	27 – 23	32 – 28
16.	23 – 18	28 – 24
17.	18 – 14	24 – 19
18.	6 – 10	19 – 23
19.	10 – 15	23 – 27
20.	15 – 19	27 – 32
21.	19 – 24	32 – 28
22.	24 – 27	28 – 24
23.	27 – 32 (k)	24 – 28
24.	32 – 27	28 – 32
25.	27 – 24	32 – 28
26.	24 – 19	28 – 32
27.	19 – 15	32 – 28
28.	15 – 10	28 – 24
29.	10 – 6	24 – 19
30.	14 – 10	19 – 24
31.	10 – 15	24 – 28
32.	15 – 19	28 – 32
33.	19 – 24	32 – 28
34.	11 – 16	28 – 19
35.	16 – 23	12 – 8
36.	23 – 18	8 – 4 (k)
37.	18 – 14	4 – 8
38.	6 – 1	8 – 11
39.	14 – 9	13 – 6
40.	1 – 10	11 – 16
41.	10 – 15	16 – 20
42.	15 – 19 and wins	

Black's marching and counter-marching eventually force White into a position where, with only one king each on the board, Black has 'the move.'

It may seem strange to the tiro that so many moves are necessary to resolve what, at first blush, may seem a comparatively simple problem, But in fact what is remarkable is that it has been solved at all. Players not conversant with the exercise which they have (presumably) just worked through would almost inevitably abandon the game as drawn.

The Third Position

Black to move and win

BLACK

WHITE

FIG. 29

	BLACK	WHITE
1.	13 – 9	22 – 18
2.	9 – 6	18 – 22
3.	6 – 1	22 – 18
4.	21 – 25	18 – 15
5.	1 – 6	14 – 17
6.	6 – 2	17 – 14
7.	25 – 22	15 – 10
8.	22 – 26	14 – 18
9.	5 – 9	10 – 6
10.	9 – 13	6 – 10
11.	26 – 31	10 – 14
12.	31 – 27	18 – 22
13.	27 – 23	22 – 25
14.	2 – 7	25 – 22
15.	7 – 11	22 – 25
16.	11 – 15	25 – 22
17.	23 – 27	22 – 26
18.	27 – 24	26 – 22
19.	24 – 20	22 – 26
20.	20 – 16	26 – 22
21.	16 – 12	22 – 26
22.	12 – 8	16 – 22
23.	8 – 3	14 – 9
24.	15 – 10	

and Black wins, for White's kings are now cut off from one another, and the king at 22 can be contained by Black's king at 10.

There are a number of variations of this position, all demanding careful play on Black's part.

The Fourth Position

Black to move and win
or
White to move and draw

(*a*) BLACK TO MOVE

	BLACK	WHITE
1.	28 – 24	32 – 28
2.	24 – 20	28 – 32
3.	22 – 18	31 – 27
4.	23 – 19	27 – 31
5.	19 – 24	32 – 27
6.	24 – 28	27 – 32
7.	18 – 22	31 – 27
8.	22 – 26	30 – 23
9.	28 – 24	27 – 31
10.	24 – 27	31 – 24
11.	20 – 18 and wins	

BLACK

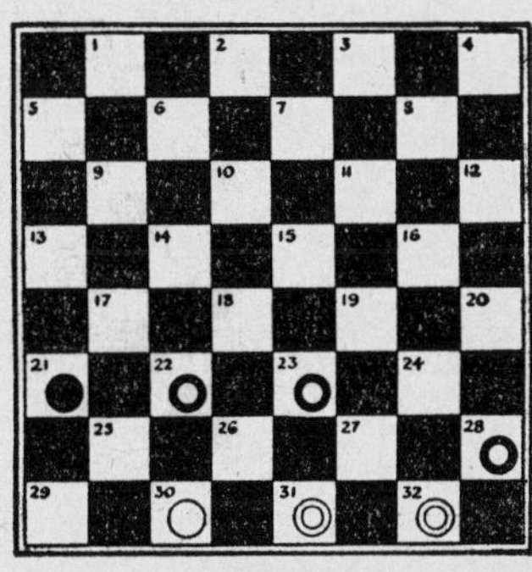

WHITE

FIG. 30

(*b*) WHITE TO MOVE

	WHITE	BLACK
1.	31 – 27	23 – 19
2.	27 – 31	19 – 24
3.	32 – 27	24 – 20
4.	27 – 32	22 – 18
5.	31 – 27	28 – 24
6.	27 – 31	18 – 23
7.	31 – 26	

Black can make no headway against White's defence, and the game is drawn.

(2) *Securing 'the Move'*

As I have mentioned (p. 235), one's chances of success in a position that can be analysed with certainty may turn on whether one has 'the move' or not. By 'the move' is not meant 'turn to play', but a position in which, if one plays properly, one can be certain of winning. Thus, in Fig. 31, if it is Black's turn to play, he also has 'the move'. He plays 10 – 15, and that is the end of White. Similarly, if it is White's turn to play, he has 'the move'; he plays 23 – 18. This is the simplest possible example.

If these two men were kings, the game would be drawn, whoever's turn it is to play. For either player can escape defeat by retreating to the double corner.

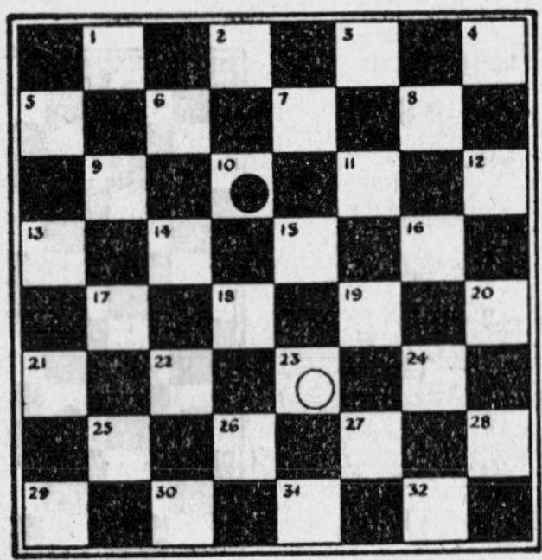

FIG. 31

That is why, in the end-game, one must be on the look-out for situations in which retreat to the double corner is impossible. In Fig. 32, Black cannot win against White. But, if it is White's turn to play, he has the move and must win.

FIG. 32

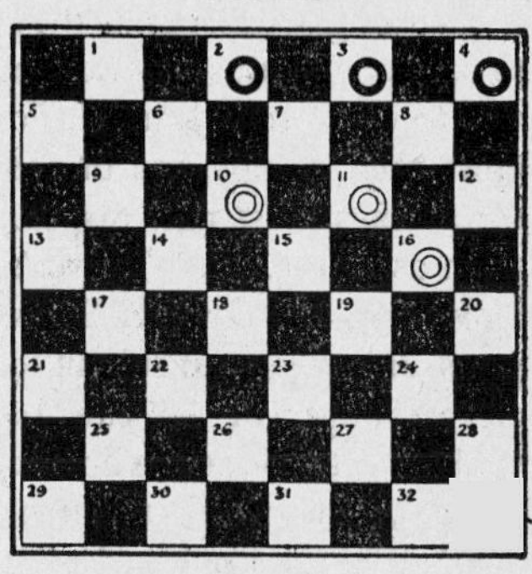

WHITE

FIG. 33

Fig. 33 shows another simple situation. If it is White's turn to play, he wins, obviously, by 16 – 12. If it is Black's turn to play, White loses. For Black plays 3 – 8; White plays 11 – 15; now Black plays 8 – 11, winning one of White's kings.

Fig. 34 is very amusing. Here Black deliberately co-operates in a trap laid by White, since he sees that he will have 'the move' at the critical moment of the game, White (to move) plays 30 – 26. Black plays 7 – 11. White, ignoring the implications of this move, plays 26 – 23. Black plays 19 – 26, and White must now play 31 – 8, collecting three of Black's men but putting three of his own out of action. And now Black, with 'the move', plays 2 – 6, and White's remaining king is doomed.

BLACK

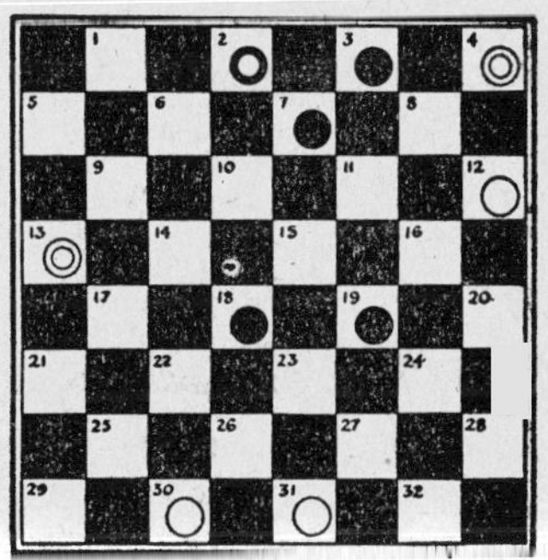

WHITE

FIG. 34

(3) *Three Kings Against Two*

Two kings cannot draw the game against three, and it is useless to continue, in this situation, against a competent opponent. The way to win is soon learned. To stand any chance, the two kings must each occupy one of the double corners. The player with three kings must now dispose them as in Fig. 35. Whoever's move it is, and however Black plays, either he must submit to an exchange, or he can be winkled out of one of his double corners, or immobilized there; while White's two remaining kings deal with the other double corner. Black cannot escape.

FIG. 35

(4) *Some Representative End-play Situations*

Some of these end-plays were (so far as I know) first published by Sturges. To these I have added a few *jeux d'esprit* of my own.

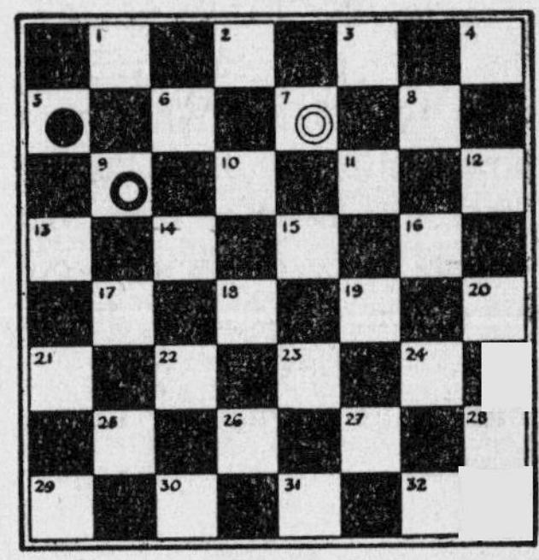

FIG. 36

1. *White to move and draw*

WHITE	BLACK
7 – 10	9 – 13
10 – 14	13 – 9
14 – 10	

FIG. 37

2. *White to move and win*

WHITE	BLACK
32 – 27	28 – 32
27 – 24	19 – 28
26 – 23	

3. *White to move and win*

WHITE	BLACK
27 – 32	28 – 24
23 – 18	24 – 28
18 – 15	28 – 24
32 – 28	24 – 27
15 – 18	12 – 16
28 – 32	27 – 24
18 – 15	24 – 28
15 – 11	16 – 19
32 – 27	28 – 32
27 – 31	19 – 23
11 – 15	32 – 28
15 – 19	

FIG. 38

4. White to move and win

WHITE	BLACK
9 – 6	1 – 10
2 – 6	

White gets two pieces for one. This is one of those familiar traps against which players should always be on their guard.

BLACK

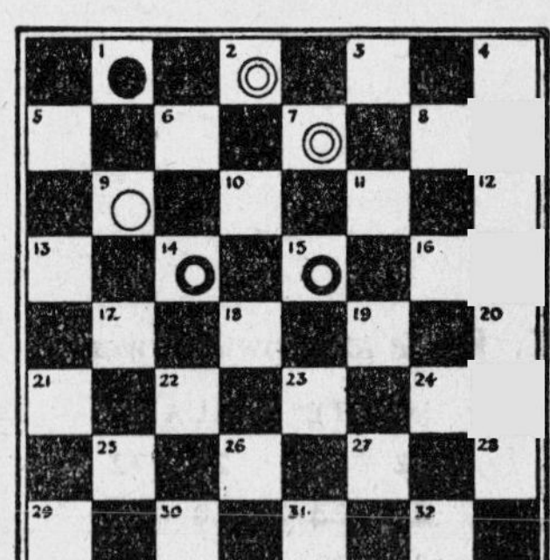

WHITE

FIG. 39

5. White to move and win

WHITE	BLACK
19 – 24	20 – 27
18 – 22	

Black's kings are immobilized by their own henchman.

BLACK

WHITE

FIG. 40

BLACK

WHITE

FIG. 41

6. *White to move and win*

WHITE	BLACK
32 – 27	23 – 32
26 – 23	19 – 26
30 – 23	

Another variant of the bottling-up technique.

BLACK

WHITE

FIG. 42

7. *White to move and win*

WHITE	BLACK
10 – 7	15 – 8
2 – 6	3 – 10
6 – 24	

White has 'the move'.

If White plays 2 – 6 instead of 10 – 7, or Black 3 – 10 instead of 15 – 8, the result is exactly the same.

8. White to move and win

WHITE	BLACK
30 – 25	21 – 30
8 – 11	30 – 23
11 – 27	

Black's remaining king is doomed.

BLACK

WHITE

FIG. 43

9. White to move and win

WHITE	BLACK
11 – 7	3 – 19
16 – 21	

A pretty development of the typical end-game trap. White gets three pieces for two, immobilizes Black's last man, and so wins at a stroke what seems to be a lost game.

BLACK

WHITE

FIG. 44

10. Black to move, White to win

BLACK	WHITE
6 – 10	19 – 23

A nice riposte to what looks like an effective move by Black. If he takes the two kings now on offer, he loses both of his own.

FIG. 45

11. White to move and win

WHITE	BLACK
26 – 22	18 – 25
19 – 16	12 – 19
11 – 8	4 – 11
7 – 23	30 – 26
23 – 21	

FIG. 46

12. White to move and win

WHITE	BLACK
24 – 19	16 – 23
22 – 18	23 – 14
17 – 1 (k)	

Now White's king can contain Black's man at 4, while his remaining man has the move against Black's man at 5. White will crown his man first. Black can get a king too; but, just the same, he is doomed.

BLACK

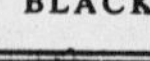

WHITE

FIG. 47

13. White to play and win
'Circular Tour'

White's position does not look particularly promising, but he polishes Black off in six moves

WHITE	BLACK
21 – 17	22 – 13
16 – 19	23 – 16
31 – 27	32 – 23
30 – 25	29 – 22
14 – 9	13 – 6

BLACK

WHITE

FIG. 48

Black's six kings are now located as in Fig. 49, and one move disposes of them all.

Note. This position is based on actual play. I have not seen more than six kings taken in one move, though theoretically it is possible to take nine (Fig. 50). Various routes are open to the White King, e.g. 10 – 3 – 12 – 19 – 26 – 17 – 10 – 19 – 28.

FIG. 49

FIG. 50

14. *Black to move; he plays 27 – 31. White will now play and win.*

BLACK	WHITE
27 – 31	26 – 22
18 – 25	17 – 22
10 – 26	28 – 24
20 – 27	19 – 15

FIG. 51

The final position is shown in Fig. 52. The whole of Black's forces are immobilized.

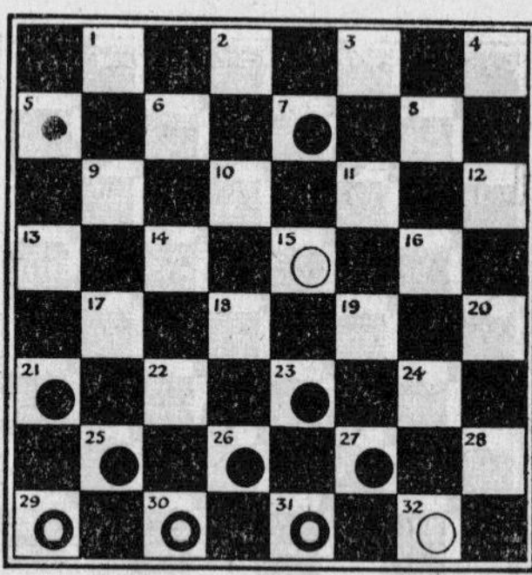

FIG. 52

Backgammon

Technically, Backgammon is a racing game. That is to say, each player's object is not to capture or immobilize his adversary's pieces, but to be the first to reach a defined objective. It is an old game, and an interesting one. It is also, I believe, the only game played with dice that has (so far) avoided interference from our chaotic and unintelligible gaming laws.

Backgammon is played on a special board, represented (as seen from above) in Fig. 1. Each player has fifteen 'men' similar to (though smaller than) draughtsmen. At the beginning of the game they are arranged as in Fig. 1. The object of the game is to move one's men along a prescribed route to the far confines of the board, and finally off the board, in terms of a series of prescribed moves. The moves that one can make depend on the outcome of throwing two dice. The fascination of the game lies in one's capacity, not only to move one's own men, but to obstruct the moves of one's opponent.

The board is divided into two compartments or 'tables',

divided by a bar. The men are set out originally, as shown in the diagram, on the twenty-four 'points' indicated. White's are moving counter-clockwise; Black's, clockwise. Each player's initial position is duplicated by his opponent's. Thus, each has five men in his own 'home table' (these men have only a short distance to go); three men in his own 'outer table'; five men in his opponent's 'outer table'; two men, as far away from home as possible, in his opponent's 'inner table'.

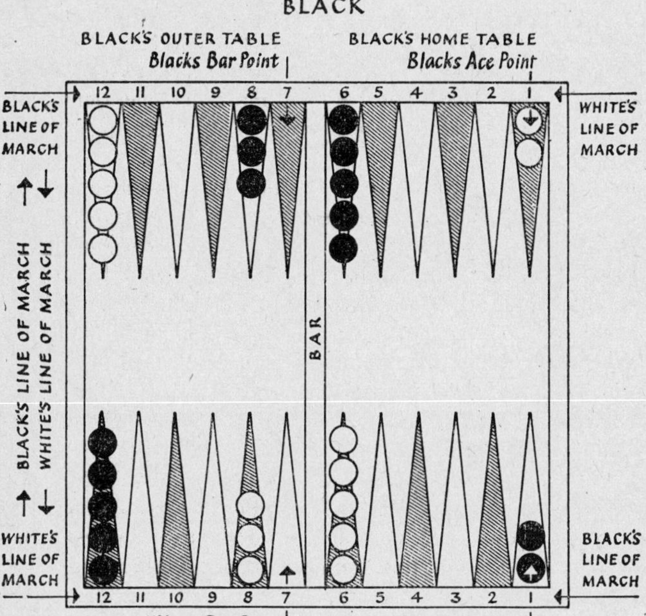

II

The players are seated as in the diagram, facing one another. To decide who shall play first, each throws one die. The player making the higher throw plays first; if there is a tie, they throw again. The player who wins now makes the first move, for which he must adopt both the numbers thrown. Suppose, for example, that White has thrown a 4 and Black a 3. For his first move, White can either move one of his men four places forward, and another one three places forward, or, adding the numbers 4 and 3, he can move one man only seven places forward. What he would probably do (since these initial moves are more or less hallowed by custom) is to play one man from his opponent's twelve point to his own nine point, and another to his own ten point.

From now onwards each player in turn throws both his dice, and moves in accordance with their dictates. A throw of 6 and 5, for example, enables him to move one man six places forward and the other five places forward; or to move one man only eleven places forward. He has not, however, absolute freedom; he cannot move to a point which is occupied by two (or more) of his opponent's men. Hence a situation may well arise where a throw is useless; in this event, the player must just miss his turn. On the other hand, a throw may yield a countervailing advantage. If a player has one man only on a given point, this constitutes a 'blot', and his opponent, throwing a number which will enable him to bring a man to that point, is said to 'hit' the 'blot'. When that occurs, the opponent's man is removed to the 'bar' which divides the two compartments of the board, and he cannot make another move until he can launch the man on the bar once again on his wearisome journey.

For the purpose of re-entering a man on the bar, the combined numbers thrown may not be used. Thus, one has a man on the bar and throws 3 – 2. One can move him to one's opponent's three point, if vacant (one can even hit a blot if he has only one man there); or to his two point; but one cannot move him to one's opponent's five point.

Success in hitting an enemy 'blot' plays a big part in the fluctuating fortunes of the game. It may, as the result of a single throw, convert an unpromising position into a hopeful one.

Let us now revert to the throw of the dice. The most profitable throws are doubles; 1 – 1, 2 – 2, and so on. For a double throw gives one doubled chances. Suppose, for example, that one throws 5 – 5. One can move each of one's men ten places; or one man fifteen places and another one five places; or one man twenty places. Provided, that is, that none of the relevant points is blocked (i.e. occupied by two or more of the adversary's men). Thus, if one threw 5 – 5, and the point five moves away were occupied by the enemy, one could not make any move at all.

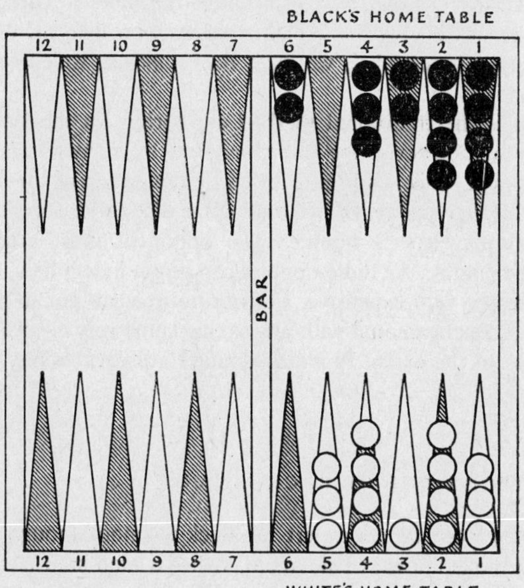

Bearing off

FIG. 2

Bearing Off. When a player's men are all in his own home table, he is ready to 'bear them off', i.e. remove them from the board. He has not won the game until they are all removed. To 'bear off' a man, a number must be thrown which carries a man at least one place further than one's own ace point. Thus, in Fig. 2, both players are ready to 'bear off'. Suppose it is Black's throw, and he throws 6 – 5. He can bear off one man from the six point. For the 5 throw, all he can do is to move the other man on his six point to his ace point. If, however, White throws 6 – 5, he can bear off two of the men on his five point.

Scoring. Backgammon (unlike Draughts and other games of pure skill) is normally played for stakes. The first player to bear off all his men wins. But, if the loser has failed to bear off any of his men, this is a *Gammon* and double the stake is paid. And, if the loser has one or more men remaining on the bar, or in his opponent's inner table, we have *Backgammon*, which carries a triple stake.

Such is the traditional method of scoring. In the last thirty or so years, however, the game has – like so many others – been streamlined. This has been effected by the device of the *optional double*. Either player, before casting his dice (after the game has started) may say 'I double'. His opponent must accept the double or retire. As these doubles can go on indefinitely, a game can become very expensive. I advise my readers not to play for stakes at Backgammon without making some very clear arrangement as to the extent to which doubles are permissible.

THE TECHNIQUE OF BACKGAMMON

I do not pose as an expert on Backgammon, though I have played the game with enjoyment. It has a high skill factor, but very little has been written about it which affords more than elementary guidance; the best players are informed, not by books, but by their own accumulated experience. But there are two or three basic principles which the beginner should assimilate:

(1) Learn the odds against any particular blot being hit by an opponent. There are thirty-six possible throws of two dice:

6 – 6	6 – 5	6 – 4	6 – 3	6 – 2	6 – 1
5 – 6	5 – 5	5 – 4	5 – 3	5 – 2	5 – 1
4 – 6	4 – 5	4 – 4	4 – 3	4 – 2	4 – 1
3 – 6	3 – 5	3 – 4	3 – 3	3 – 2	3 – 1
2 – 6	2 – 5	2 – 4	2 – 3	2 – 2	2 – 1
1 – 6	1 – 5	1 – 4	1 – 3	1 – 2	1 – 1

So it is	25	to	11	against a blot being hit from which an opponent's man's distance is			1 point	
,, ,,	24	,,	12	,,	,,	,,	2 points	
,, ,,	22	,,	14	,,	,,	,,	3	,,
,, ,,	21	,,	15	,,	,,	,,	4	,,
,, ,,	21	,,	15	,,	,,	,,	5	,,
,, ,,	19	,,	17	,,	,,	,,	6	,,
,, ,,	30	,,	6	,,	,,	,,	7	,,
,, ,,	30	,,	6	,,	,,	,,	8	,,
,, ,,	31	,,	5	,,	,,	,,	9	,,
,, ,,	33	,,	3	,,	,,	,,	10	,,
,, ,,	34	,,	2	,,	,,	,,	11	,,
,, ,,	33	,,	3	,,	,,	,,	12	,,
,, ,,	35	,,	1	,,	,,	,,	15	,,
,, ,,	35	,,	1	,,	,,	,,	16	,,
,, ,,	35	,,	1	,,	,,	,,	18	,,
,, ,,	35	,,	1	,,	,,	,,	20	,,

Some of these figures – especially the throws that yield moves of 4, 6, 8, 12 points may appear puzzling.

A move of 4 points can be made in fifteen ways as follows:

4–6 4–5 6–4 5–4 4–4 3–4 2–4 1–4
4–3 1–3 4–2 2–2 4–1 3–1 1–1

A move of 6 points can be made in seventeen ways:

6–6 5–6 4–6 3–6 2–6 1–6 6–5 1–5 6–4
2–4 6–3 3–3 6–2 4–2 2–2 6–1 5–1

A move of 8 points in six ways:

2–6 3–5 4–4 5–3 6–2 2–2

A move of 12 points in three ways:

6–6 4–4 3–3

This table brings out the fact that a man of yours is most vulnerable when one of the enemy's men is six points away. You should make every effort to move him or to bring up another man to the same point.

(2) Learn what I may call the recognized opening moves, i.e.

the moves that should be made after your first throw. Most of these have been established for many years.

Throw	*The recognized move*
1 – 1 ('Aces')	Two men from your 6 point to your 5 point and two from your 8 point to your bar point.
1 – 2 ('Deuce Ace')	One man to your 11 point; one to your 5 point.
1 – 3 ('Trois Ace')	Two men to your 5 point.
1 – 4 ('Quatre Ace')	One man to your 9 point; one to your 5 point.
1 – 5 ('Cinque Ace')	One man from your 12 point to your 8 point and one from your 6 point to your 5 point.
1 – 6 ('Six Ace')	Establish your bar point by playing one man from your 12 point and one from your 8 point.
2 – 2 ('Deuces')	Two men to your 4 point; two to your 11 point.
2 – 3 ('Trois Deuce')	One man to your 5 point; one to your 11 point.
2 – 4 ('Quatre Deuce')	Two men to your 4 point.
2 – 5 ('Cinque Deuce')	One man to your 11 point; one to your 8 point.
2 – 6 ('Six Deuce')	One man to your 12 point; one to your 5 point ($6 + 2 = 8$).
3 – 3 ('Double Trois')	There are three possibilities: (1) Two men from your 12 point to your bar point. (2) Two men to your 5 point; two to your opponent's 4 point. (3) Two men to your 5 point; two to your 3 point.

3 – 4 ('Quatre Trois')	One man to your 10 point; one to your 9 point.
3 – 5 ('Cinque Trois')	Two men to your 3 point.
3 – 6 ('Six Trois')	One man to your adversary's 10 point
4 – 4 ('Double Quatre')	Alternative moves: (1) Two men to your 5 point. (2) Two men to your adversary's 5 point; two to your 9 point.
4 – 5 ('Cinque Quatre')	One man to your 9 point; one to your 8 point.
4 – 6 ('Six Quatre')	One man to your adversary's 11 point.
5 – 5 ('Double Cinque')	Two men from your adversary's 12 point to your 3 point.
5 – 6 ('Six Cinque')	One man to your adversary's 12 point.
6 – 6 ('Sixes')	Two men to your bar point; two to your adversary's bar point.

You should set up the pieces and try out these various moves.

(3) Backgammon is like Chess in that, to succeed, one must have a flexible plan of campaign. One has no idea what one's opponent is going to do. But the game differs from Chess in that every move, and therefore the future of such plans as one may have formulated, is subject to the arbitrament of chance. To lay down the law about one's second move, therefore, would involve analysing every possible reply to each of one's opening moves: 441 separate situations. So far as I know, no writer has attempted this Herculean task.

I would only say, therefore, in general terms, that you want to find the right balance between caution and enterprise. Do not risk the exposure of too many 'blots', but do not be afraid to risk a blot if the man moved is well placed for the next throw. Remember that an attacking game is, on the whole, more likely to succeed than a defensive one. If you can establish, early in the game, your own bar point and five point, you are in a good defensive position; and can begin to plan the advancement of your men as a whole. Do not completely isolate your rear runners, or they may be pinned down in such a way that the loss of the game becomes almost inevitable.

But there is always hope at Backgammon – the chance of a series of favourable throws while your opponent is in the doldrums – just as there is always the chance that you will be dealt a straight flush at Poker.

The Chess War Game

I have not attempted to deal with Chess in this book. As a game, it stands in a class by itself. Its records go back for centuries; it has a literature which far exceeds that of all other games put together; and – at any rate in Russia and her satellite countries – it can be made the basis of a spectacular career. I could do little more, then, than outline its mechanics: a waste of space when so many good introductions to Chess are available, notably Mr Golombek's admirable Penguin. Chess is my favourite game and I don't like omitting it, but common sense must prevail.

The Chess War Game, however, is on quite a different footing. Chess *Kriegsspiel* – Chess played against an opponent whose moves can only be deduced when the two forces make contact – has been played for a good many years. But the game I give here is not orthodox *Kriegsspiel*. I invented it during World War I, when it was played with much enthusiasm, and a fair standard of attainment, by a number of officers in my brigade. Since then I have introduced it to many other players, and its reception has been uniformly favourable. It demands a knowledge of the moves made on a chessboard, but no technical knowledge of Chess whatever. So anyone who has mastered the moves can start the War Game from scratch, and, if he has an aptitude for it, stands as good a chance of winning as has any experienced Chess player.

The objective in this game is the same as in Chess: to *mate* the opposing King. The King cannot be captured; he is *mated* when an opposing piece commands the square on which he stands (he is then said to be *in check*) and he cannot get out of check: he cannot move to an adjacent square; there is no piece which can be interposed; and the piece which has checked him cannot be taken. If one's King is not in check, but there is no move which one can lawfully make, the game is a draw; the game is also drawn if neither side has the material to force a win.

Apart from the King, all pieces can be captured; a piece is captured and removed from the board when an opposing piece moves to the square on which it stands. A move cannot be made if it exposes one's own King to check. And that, apart from the moves made by the various pieces, is all we need to know.

The King's Move

The King can move to any adjacent square, and can capture a piece which is situated there provided it is not defended. But he cannot move into check.

The King's Move

He can move to any of the eight squares indicated.

FIG. 1

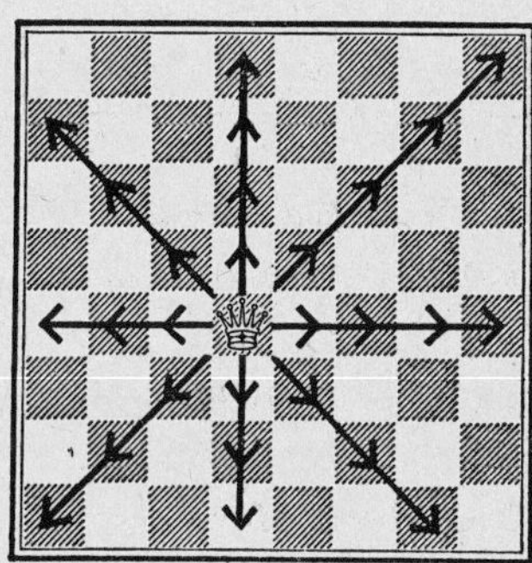

The Queen's Move

The Queen in the centre of the board covers 27 squares.

FIG. 2

The Queen's Move

The Queen is by far the most powerful piece. She can move in a straight line in any direction, as long as she has an unobstructed path.

The Rook's Move

Rooks are also known as Castles. The Rook can move along an unimpeded path either vertically or horizontally, but not (as the Queen can) diagonally as well.

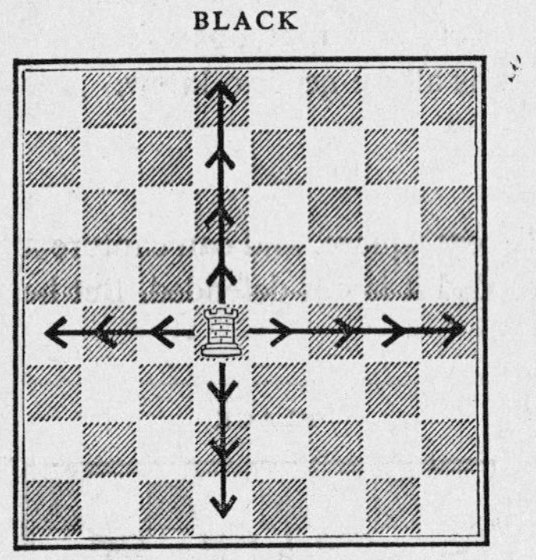

The Rook's Move

The Rook here covers 14 squares.

FIG. 3

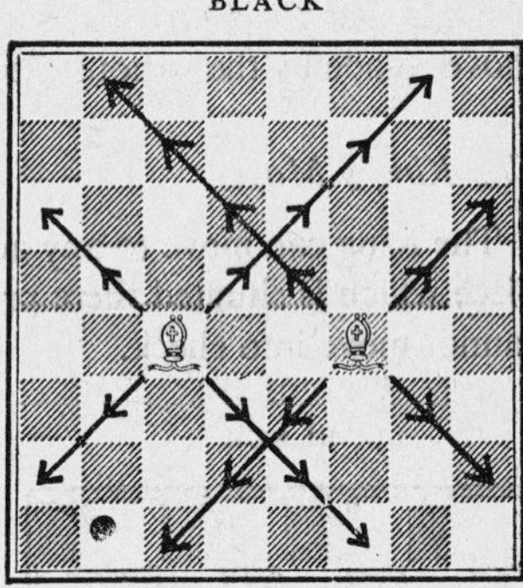

The Bishop's Move

Here the Bishop covers 11 squares. His maximum is 13.

FIG. 4

The Bishop's Move

The Bishop, *per contra*, can only move diagonally. He never 'changes colour'. In the War Game, as in Chess, each side starts with one Bishop standing on a black square, and another one standing on a white square.

The Knight's Move

This move tends to puzzle beginners, but it is very quickly mastered. The Knight can 'jump over' opposing pieces. He moves to the opposite diagonal of a rectangle 3 squares × 2. The diagram will, I hope, make this clear.

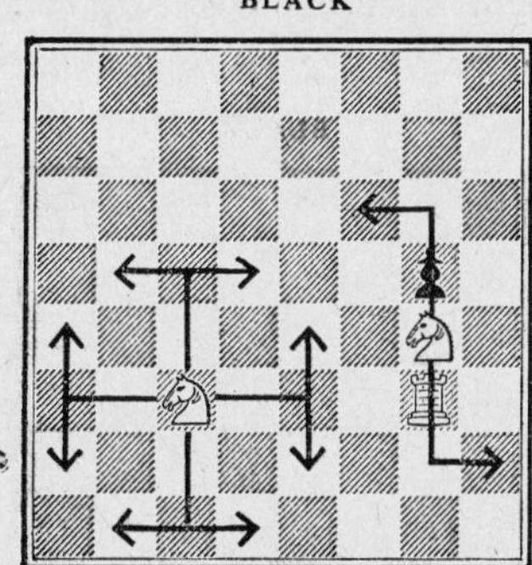

The Knight's Move

He can move to any of the eight indicated squares, and this regardless of the position of the opponent's pieces.

FIG. 5

The Pawn's Move

The Pawn at A can go forward one or two squares. So can the Pawn at B. The Pawn at C can only move forward one square. The White Pawn at D cannot move forward but can take the Pawn on the adjacent file.

FIG. 6

The Pawn's Move

In Chess all Pawns start on the second row. In Kriegsspiel they can start anywhere.

A Pawn, when not capturing a piece (or pawn) moves forward one square at a time. But a Pawn which starts on one's back row or second row may, if one chooses, go forward two squares when it is first moved. In capturing, however, a Pawn moves diagonally: one square forward to the right or the left.

A Pawn cannot move backwards. It must go steadily forwards. But, if it attains the eighth rank, it can be exchanged for any other piece. This privilege makes Pawns a good deal more important in the War Game than in ordinary Chess.

There are two moves used in Chess which are not made use of

in the War Game: the 'castling' of the King, and the taking of a Pawn by another Pawn *en passant.*

BLACK

WHITE

Checkmate

Black's King is mated by White's Queen.
White's King is mated by Black's Knight ('smothered mate').

FIG. 7

BLACK

WHITE

Stalemate

The Black King is not in check, but cannot move.
The same is true of the White King.

FIG. 8

BLACK

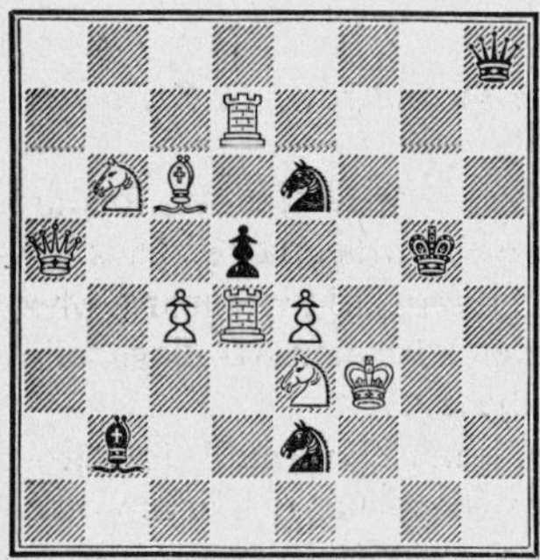

WHITE

FIG. 9

Captures

An unlikely (but not impossible) position illustrating captures.

Black's Pawn can be taken by no fewer than eight pieces: the Queen; two Rooks; Bishop; two Knights; two Pawns.

White's Rook (at Q 4) can be taken by Black's Queen, Bishop, both Knights.

There is no other capture on the board, for Black's pawn is 'pinned'; it cannot move without 'discovering' check.

Notation of Games

There are two recognized ways of recording games. I have used that which, though the more cumbersome, is also the more familiar. White's moves are recorded by reference to his own side of the board, and so are Black's. The diagrams below show the designations of the sixty-four squares from the point of view of each player.

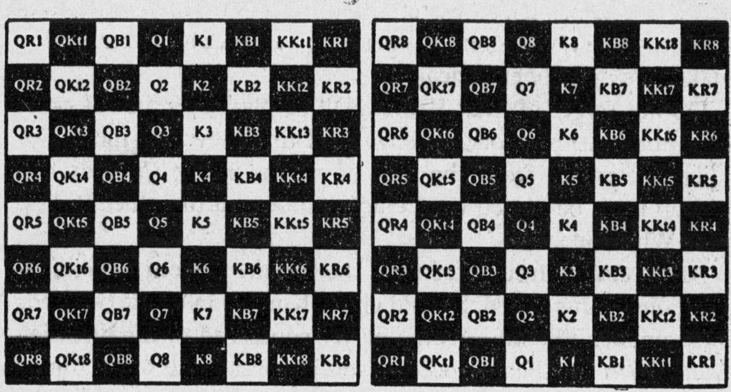

FIG. 10

HOW THE WAR GAME IS PLAYED

Three players are necessary: the two combatants and an Umpire. The players are seated back to back – or, at any rate, where they can't see one another's boards – and each has a table with (preferably) a full-sized board and his own set of men. The Umpire should have a pocket-sized board (not essential, but mistakes are almost certain to occur if he hasn't one) on which he records the moves of both players. If he is prepared to keep a record of the game, so much the better.

White moves first. Before the game begins, the players decide where they are placing their Kings. Each player can put his King where he likes – as also the rest of his pieces – *on his own half of the board.* The Umpire notes the position of the Kings and tells each player where his opponent's King is situated. Thus, he may announce: 'White's King is at his King's Bishop's second; Black's at his Queen's Rook's Square.'

Now the players have (say) ten minutes in which to arrange the rest of their pieces. Each will try to find a formation well suited to the defence of his own King and to the launching of an effective attack. This is where the War Game differs completely from Chess. Every arrangement of one's men can differ radically from any that one has tried before, and this – combined with the fact that, to begin with, one is operating completely in the dark – makes play purely empirical.

Do not forget (*a*) that Pawns may be placed on any of one's four ranks (so may one's pieces), and that they may move two squares forward from the first or second rank; (*b*) that one Bishop must be placed on a black square and the other Bishop on a White one.

At the end of the allotted time, the Umpire sets out both initial positions on his board. Should either King be in check (which is most unlikely) he informs the player concerned of the direction from which the check proceeds, and he must make some adjustment (other than moving his King) which nullifies the check.

The game now begins. Each player indicates to the Umpire (usually without speaking) what move he wishes to make; he does this by making the actual move and looking interrogatively at the Umpire. If he can't make the first move he tries, he suggests another; and the interrogation of the Umpire continues till a legitimate move is found. This move must be made. The Umpire then says 'White has moved.'

Since one's immediate object is to find out where one's opponent's pieces are, the planning of one's trial moves plays a large part in the game. One should try to get as many negative replies as possible – without, in the course of doing so, risking a valuable piece – before one makes a move which one expects to be feasible.

When a move is made which neither checks the opposing King nor effects a capture, the Umpire simply says 'White has moved' (or 'Black has moved'). If the opposing King is checked, the

Umpire says 'White has moved and Black's King is in check.' This is all the information vouchsafed to White, but Black is told – or, rather, the Umpire indicates on his (Black's) board – the direction from which he is threatened. If diagonally, the threat may come from a Queen, Bishop, or Pawn – Black is not informed which – and it may, of course, be a discovered check. (The Umpire must be constantly on the look-out for the accidental 'discovery' of check.) If a move captures an opposing piece, the Umpire announces (say) 'White has moved and has taken the piece at Black's King's Bishop's fifth.' He reports the capture as that of a 'piece' whether it is, in fact, a major piece or pawn.

To make this clear, let me show how the Umpire handles the opening moves of my second Illustrative Game.

White's first move is QP×P (the symbol × means 'takes') The Umpire announces: 'White has moved, and has taken the piece at Black's Queen's Bishop's fourth.' He makes the appropriate move on his own board and, if asked, may indicate to Black which piece has been taken.

Black's first move, in reply, is KtP×P. The Umpire announces 'Black has moved, and has taken the piece at White's Queen's Bishop's fifth.'

Now White makes his second move (P – B4) and the Umpire simply announces: 'White has moved.'

You may think, reading all this, that the whole process is unbearably slow. But, in fact, with competent players and a brisk and experienced Umpire, it takes very little time: much less time than 'serious' Chess, where a player in difficulties may 'huddle' for perhaps twenty minutes!

You may also think that it must be supremely difficult, operating in the dark, to bring any game to a satisfactory conclusion. Here again you would be quite wrong. After a few games, one rapidly learns how to draw conclusions from the various moves that have been made, and so gradually to construct a mental picture of the position of one's adversary's forces. It is, of course, permissible for White to place the Black pieces on his own board, in any way that he wishes, if this will help him to visualize the situation. Personally, I don't often do this until the closing stages of the game, as one is apt to forget that the pieces one has located may have moved to other squares in the course of the next few moves.

That the enemy's King can be tracked down and mated with comparatively little difficulty is illustrated by the two games which follow. These are both games from actual play, played by comparative beginners. I suggest that you should play them through, and endeavour to discover along what lines the two protagonists' minds were working.

Illustrative Game I

BLACK

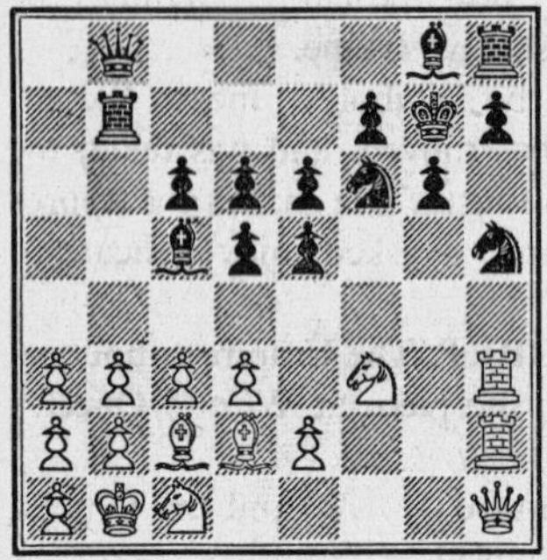

WHITE

FIG. 11

Initial Dispositions

Take a look at the initial position (Fig. 11). White has a forest of pawns, supported by a Bishop and Knight, protecting his King. On the King's side, he is prepared to attack in force. No fewer than five of his pieces – the Queen, both Rooks, a Bishop and a Knight – can be brought to bear on his adversary's KR2.

Black's deployment is more conventional. Five Pawns and a Bishop occupy the centre. (The Bishop would be better placed at R2.) The King is not too strongly defended; but, if attacked, can probably retreat to KB Sq.

WHITE	BLACK	
1. P – Q4	P×P	It is not clear why White did not place his Pawn at Q4 originally. Presumably, when the time limit expired, he had not quite decided on his plan of attack. Had his Pawn been at Q4, his first move might have been P×B.

2. P×P	B – R2	
3. B – B3	Kt – B5	Hazardous! The Knight is unsupported.
4. Kt – Kt5	Kt×R	Black had guessed something of White's dispositions.
5. Kt×Kt	Kt – Kt5	R×Kt would have been a more logical move for White.
6. Kt – Kt5	Kt×R	A second, and unanticipated, blow. Moreover, White dare not risk the Queen by re-taking.
7. P – K4	Kt – Kt5	
8. P – K5	P×P	
9. P×P	Kt×P	
10. B×Kt ch (See Fig. 12)	P – B3	Black, like White, is not voluntarily risking his Queen.

BLACK

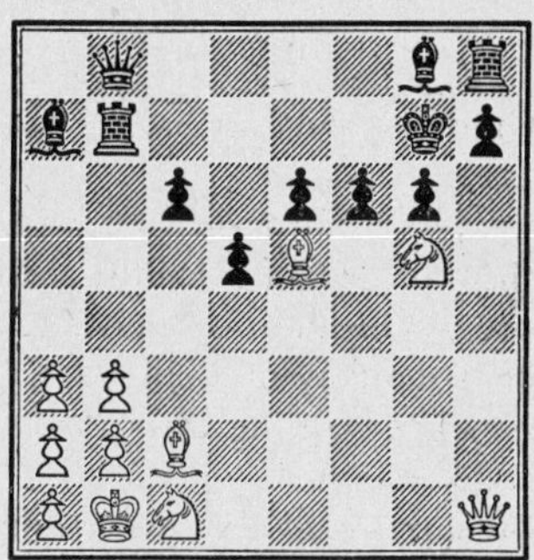

WHITE

Position after Black's 10th move

FIG. 12

White went into a considerable huddle before making this 20th move. He has lost more pieces than he had anticipated, and Black (though he does not know this) has three pieces left against

WHITE	BLACK
11. B × Q	B × B

White expected to find a major piece at his Kt8.

WHITE	BLACK
12. Kt – B3	P – K4
13. Kt – Q3	P – Q5
14. Kt – B5	P – K5
15. Kt × QP	P – B4
16. Kt(Q4) – K6 ch	K – B3
17. P – Kt4	B × Kt
18. Kt × B	K × Kt
19. B × P	P × B
20. Q × P ch (See Fig. 13)	

BLACK

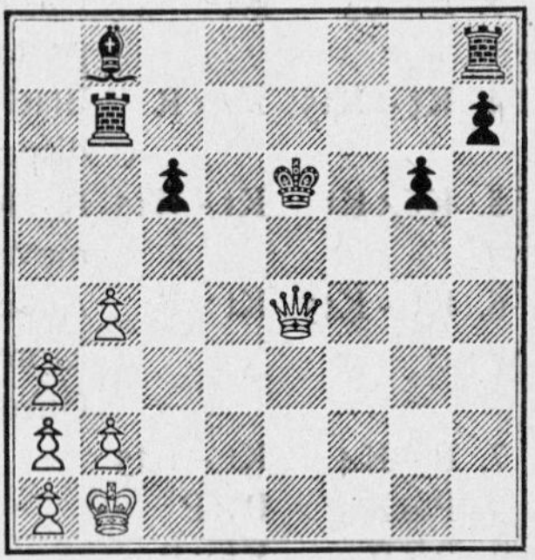

WHITE

Position after White's 20th move

It is no part of White's plan to exchange Pawns here.

FIG. 13

his Queen. But White's phalanx of Queen's side Pawns will now come into the game.

These moves look very absurd when the game is played out on one board. Play them on separate boards, and the ideas behind them become more intelligible. At the same time, there is a certain *naïveté* about the play on both sides. White and Black alike are too keen on advancing their Pawns to pay enough attention to their adversaries.

This is, of course, a common fault with beginners. It is just as important to try and visualize what one's adversary may be doing as it is to plan one's own moves. Black's Rook at QKt2 had been there from the beginning of the game; his Bishop went to QR2 at his 21st move; yet it had not occurred to him to try to find out whether White was attacking on this side of the board. The consequence? All three of Black's pieces are lost in a matter of as many moves.

White, after a bad start, reaped the benefit of his initial dispositions. Black failed to exploit early successes. At the end

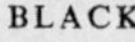

20. K – Q3
21. Q – Kt2 B – R2
22. P – R4 P – B4
23. P – Kt5 R(R1) – QKt1
24. P – R5 P – R3
25. P – R4 P – R4
26. P – R6 P – Kt4
27. P – R5 P – R5
28. P – Kt6 P – Kt6

(See Fig. 14)

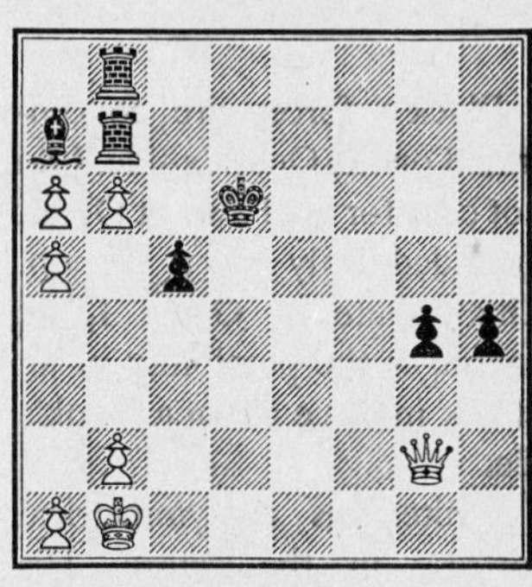

WHITE

Position after Black's 28th move

FIG. 14

of the game he should have gone ahead with one pawn, instead of trying to queen two. One Queen, in this game, stands a fighting chance against two; though White's two Queens were cautiously handled and should have won anyway.

BLACK

	WHITE	BLACK
29.	P × R	R × P
30.	Q × R	P – R6
31.	P × B	P – Kt6
32.	P queens (R8)	P – R7
33.	Q(1) – Q5 ch	K – K2
34.	Q(2) – KKt8	P – Kt7
35.	Q(2) – K6 ch	K – B1
36.	Q(2) – B7 mate	

(See Fig. 15)

WHITE

Finale

FIG. 15

Illustrative Game II

Black's forces are concentrated on his Queen's side. I do not care for his Pawn at QKt4, defended only by a Bishop. Like White in Game I, he envisages the possibility of an attack in force along a Rook's file.

White has a symmetrical fortress in the centre. His Rooks, oddly enough, are on the same file as Black's. I would expect White to get the better of the earlier exchanges.

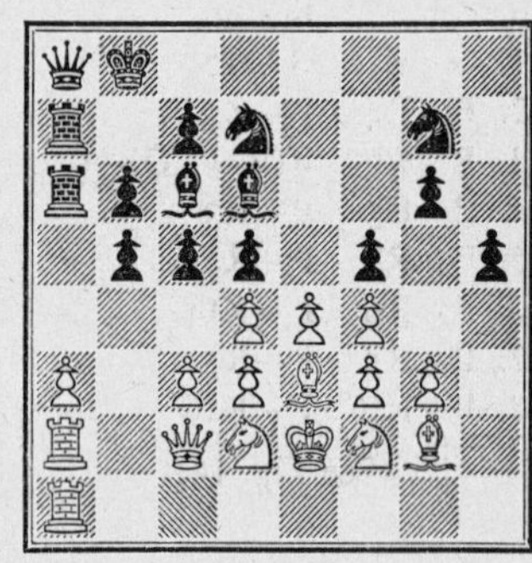

Initial Position

FIG. 16

	WHITE	BLACK	
1.	QP × P	KtP × P	Black's Pawn at Kt4 is now pinned if there happens to be a White Rook on the Knight's file.
2.	P – B4	P – Q5	
3.	P – R4	P × B	This came as a surprise to White, who went into a huddle before making his next move.
4.	K × P	P – Kt4	Waiting to be attacked on the Queen's side.
5.	RP × P (*a*)	R × R	(*a*) See Fig. 17.
6.	R × R	R × R	
7.	Q – Kt Sq	R – R2	A successful foray by Black.
8.	P × B dis ch	K – B1	
9.	P × Kt ch	K × P	
10.	Q – KR1	Kt – K3	
11.	P – K5	P × P	
12.	P × P	(See Fig. 18)	

BLACK

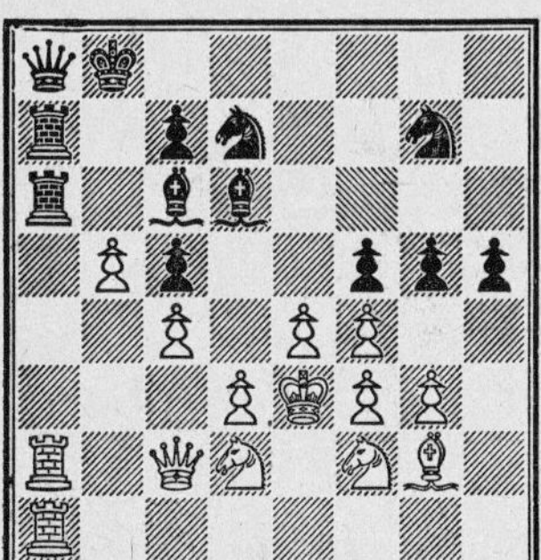

WHITE

Position after White's 5th move

FIG. 17

BLACK

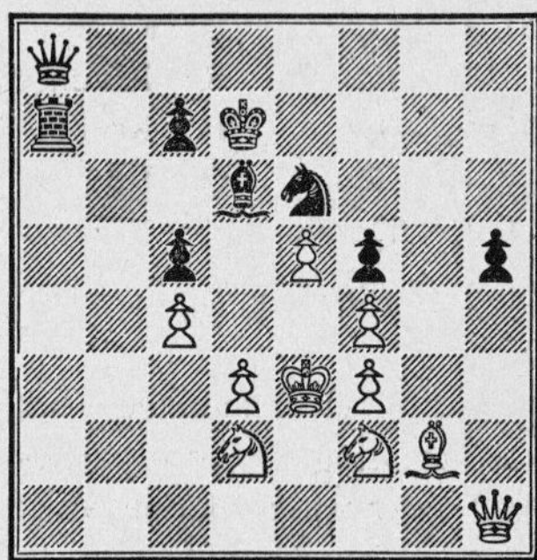

WHITE

Position after White's 12th move

FIG. 18

	WHITE	BLACK
12.		B – B1
13.	Kt(B2) – K4	B – R3
14.	Kt – Kt3	Kt × P

(See Fig. 19)

	WHITE	BLACK
15.	P – Q4	P × P ch
16.	K × P	R – R5
17.	Kt × P	Kt – K3 ch
18.	K – B3	Q – R4 ch
19.	K – Q3	Q – Kt5

(See Fig. 20)

BLACK

WHITE

Position after Black's 14th move

FIG. 19

At this point White had been outplayed; he is in a most parlous position. Had Black risked 19. Q × Kt ch, K – K4, 20. R × P ch, mates in two moves. But Black choses the wrong moment to be cautious.

20.	Q – QKt1	B × Kt
21.	Q – B2	R – R6 ch
22.	K – K2	R – K6 ch
23.	Kt × R	Q – B6
24.	Q – Q3 ch	

(See Fig. 21)

These last exchanges had been exciting for both parties. And the position is one which afforded much amusement to the Umpire. Black plays:

24.		Q – Q5

Had he played instead Kt – Q5, giving check, he can win White's Queen the next move.

	WHITE	BLACK
25.	K × B	K – K2
26.	P – B4	Q – Kt3
27.	P – B5	P – B4
28.	P × B6 ch	K – K1
29.	B – K4	Kt – B5
30.	B – B5	P – R5
31.	Q – Q7 ch	K – B1
32.	Q – K7 ch	K – Kt1
33.	Q – Kt7 mate	

(Fig. 22)

BLACK

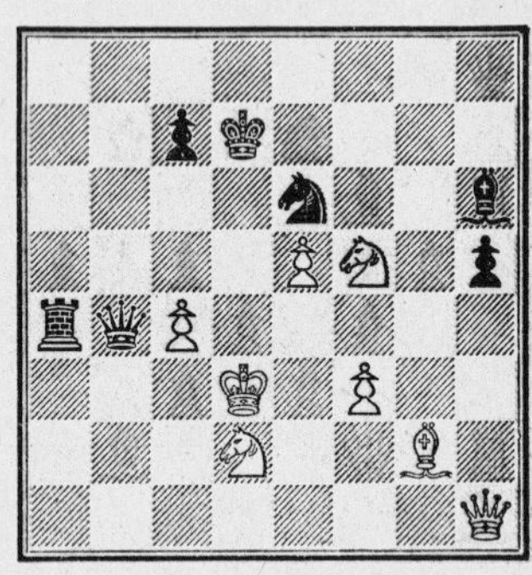

WHITE

Position after White's 19th move

FIG. 20

Black's attack has failed. He is a piece and a pawn down. He retires to the defensive.

BLACK

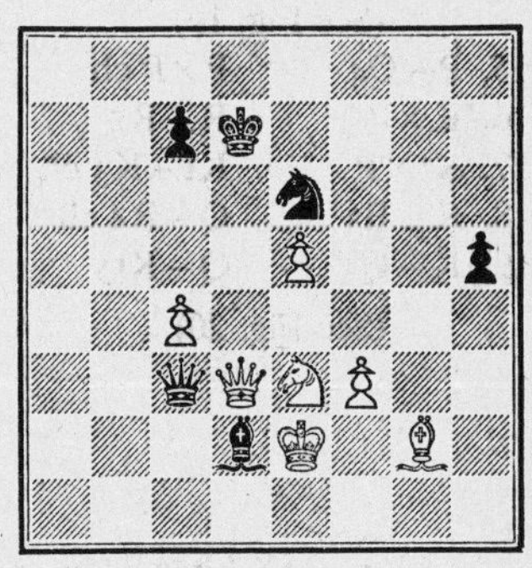

WHITE

Position after White's 24th move

FIG. 21

This is another game of fluctuating fortunes; of well-planned moves alternating with ill-judged hazards; of both caution and boldness exercised at the wrong moments.

The game was played through afterwards on one board – as, indeed, every game should be – and the *post-mortem* provided much entertainment. Take another look at Figs. 17 – 21. These show what possibilities there were for both players, given a little more imagination, or a slightly better grasp of the position. Black comes near to winning after his 15th move. He suspects that the White King is at Q4, and correctly plays R – R5. But, to his disappointment, the Rook fails to give check, and White is just able to extricate himself from an unpromising position. Black's 24th move was perhaps the turning-point of the game. He did not realize, when he played Q – Q5, that his Bishop was no longer defended. White promptly pounced upon it with his King. The loss of this Bishop marks the end of Black's all-but-successful foray. Now White contrives as pretty an ending as is possible when one is operating in the dark.

Note that White uses his King to advantage. The King is the one piece that can operate as a 'scout'; provided that he can get away if threatened he can often do good work in the centre of the board.

BLACK

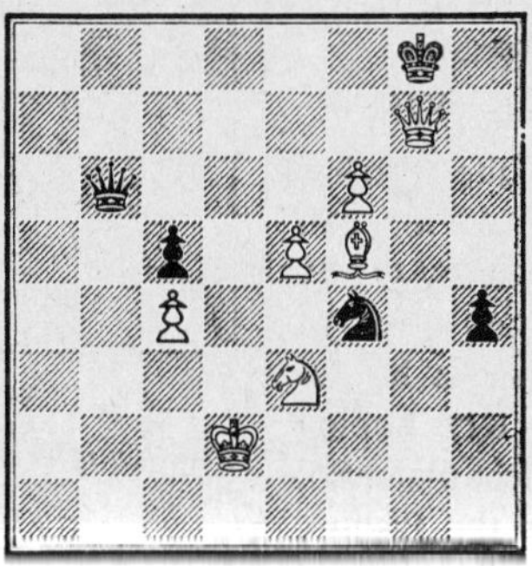

WHITE

Finale

FIG. 22

Illustrative Game III

This game was given to me by the Umpire who gleefully recorded the moves.

Initial positions (Fig. 23). White planned an all-out attack on the King's side. Black had constructed what he thought was an impregnable citadel.

BLACK

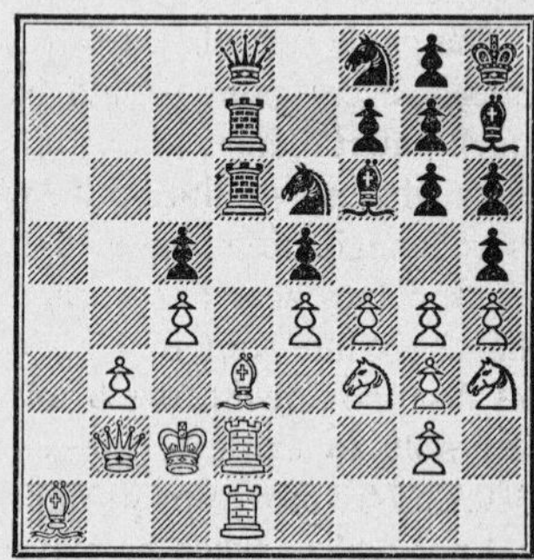

WHITE

Initial Dispositions

FIG. 23

	WHITE	BLACK
1.	P – KKt5	P × KtP
2.	RP × P	B × P
3.	P × B	Kt × P
4.	Kt(R3) × Kt	Q × Kt(rash)
5.	Kt × Q	P – B3
6.	R – KB Sq	P × Kt
7.	R(Q2) – B2	P – Kt5
8.	R × Kt	R – KB3
9.	R – R8 (exploratory)	R(Q2) – KB2
10.	Q × P	R – B1
11.	R(R8) × R	R × R
12.	R × R	P – R5
13.	P × P	P – Kt6

(See Fig. 24) White, who has a fair idea of the position, can now of course mate by Q × P. But White did not want to jeopardize his Queen: he decided to play B – Kt7, hoping that this might effect mate. So, to make way for the Bishop, he played 14. Q – Kt5.

Stalemate!

BLACK

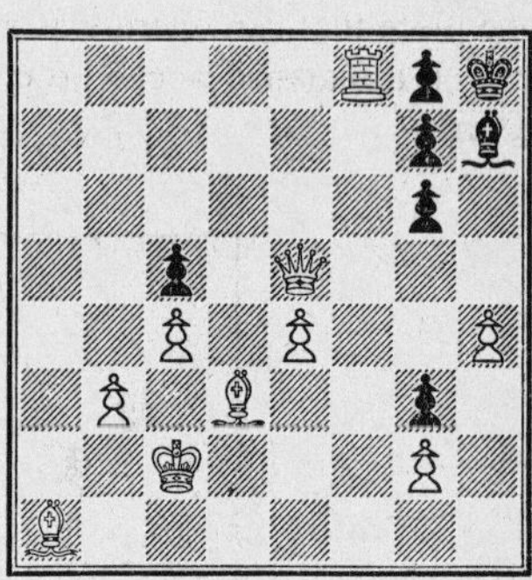

WHITE

Position after Black's 13th move

FIG. 24

Naval War Game

THE RULES

This game is played on squared paper, the area within which battle takes place being 21×21 squares, i.e. 441 squares in all. The general idea is that the opposing forces (Red and Blue) have fleets which have taken shelter in adjacent archipelagos. Each is endeavouring to bomb the other's ships. The player wins whose surviving ships, at the end of the game, have the greater point-value.

At the beginning of the game, each player is allotted 160 points. These he allocates among ships, planes, artillery, and A-A guns. He *must* spend at least 60 points on ships, and at least 60 points on aircraft, A-A guns and artillery. The remaining 40 points he can dispose of as he likes.

Ships

These are of five types:

(1) AIRCRAFT-CARRIERS, represented by a square 2×2. They cost 4 points each.

(2) BATTLESHIPS, represented by four squares in line. They also cost 4 points each.

(3) CRUISERS, represented by three squares in line. They cost 3 points each.

(4) DESTROYERS, represented by two adjacent squares. They cost 2 points each.

(5) SUBMARINES, represented by a single square. One point each.

All ships, of course, are at sea. The entire area of 441 squares is sea, save in so far as either player introduces land. This he can do to any extent he likes.

The ships can be placed where one wishes, battleships, etc., lying either horizontally or vertically. But no ship may be in contact with another ship; it is not even permissible to have a corner of one ship touching the corner of another.

Bombers and Reconnaissance Planes may be carried on

Aircraft-Carriers, each plane occupying one square. Atom-Bombers and A-A guns must be located on land. Artillery (used for firing salvoes) is not specifically located anywhere, and cannot, therefore, be put out of action.

Land

A unit of land is 3 × 3 squares, i.e. nine squares altogether. Units of land may adjoin one another.

Aircraft

These are of three types:

(1) ATOM-BOMBERS. An Atom-Bomber costs 10 points. It cannot be shot down by an A-A gun. An Atom-Bomber directed to any particular square destroys the enemy ships, planes, etc., on that square and on the twenty-four squares surrounding it (i.e. everything within a square 5 × 5). No player may buy more than six Atom-Bombers.

(2) BOMBERS. A Bomber costs 3 points. It destroys enemy ships, planes and guns, within a square 3 × 3 (nine squares in all), of which the square to which it is directed is the centre. It can be shot down by an A-A gun if it is directed to one of the nine squares of which that gun is the centre.

(3) RECONNAISSANCE PLANES (R.P.). These cost one point each. An R.P. cannot do any damage, but – unless shot down by a gun – can report the enemy's exact dispositions within the nine squares of which the square to which it is directed is the centre.

A-A Guns

These cost one point each. They can bring down Bombers or R.P.'s directed to any one of the nine squares of which the gun is the centre. An A-A gun can only be used once; thereafter it is out of action.

Artillery

A salvo of three shots costs one point. The three shots can be directed to any three squares, however far apart. Whatever is located on a square to which a shot is directed, is destroyed.

To be Put Out of Action

A ship must be completely sunk. A Bomber, despatched without reconnaissance to a particular square, may find an enemy Battleship is partly within the area that it covers. The report from the opponent would be 'two hits on a Battleship' or 'one hit on a Battleship'. Now whoever has scored these hits must endeavour to locate the Battleship, and, with another Bomber or a salvo, sink it.

In the first of the illustrative games which follow, Red has a Cruiser partly sunk at S 6 – 7. Blue did not have the resources to locate it and complete its destruction.

HOW THE WAR GAME IS PLAYED

To begin with, each player has two charts of 21 × 21 squares; the squares are identified by reference to letters and numbers: the top left-hand square is A 1. (See the illustrative games which follow.) He is allowed an agreed time (say, twenty minutes) in which to decide how to lay out his 160 points and make his dispositions. Before this is done, the players toss for first move.

As long as both sides have offensive forces (planes or artillery) at their disposal, they move in turn. But one player's resources are almost sure to be exhausted before the other's. The latter then plays on until his offensive material is also exhausted.

The players then compare their own charts, on which they made made their initial dispositions; they will have marked which of their vessels have been sunk. The point-values of the unsunk ships (1 square = 1 point) are then compared, and the player with the higher aggregate wins.

The second chart, with which each player begins, is used by him to record what he learns from his R.P.'s (if any) and from such other information as he is given.

A player must mark on his own chart where he is placing 3 × 3 squares of land; where his ships are; where his planes and A-A guns are. Where a ship is sunk, or partially sunk, he should record the fact by blackening in the whole or part of it; when he despatches a plane or uses an A-A gun he should record the fact by placing a ring round it. He cannot just despatch *any* plane; it must be one of which the position is specifically marked on his chart, for planes, like ships, are liable to destruction. He should also note at the foot of his chart how many planes, A-A guns, and salvoes he is starting with, and ring them as they are used.

Finally, two players, who are taking the game seriously, may, if they wish, keep a record of each move, such as is shown in the illustrative game which follows. This will facilitate a *post-mortem*, which can be extremely interesting.

Note. In the record which follows, each player notes from which squares planes are despatched and where the A-A guns are located of which he makes use. He does not, of course, give this information to his opponent.

And so to our illustrative games.

Illustrative Game I

Red's Dispositions (see Fig. 1)

Red decides to spend 80 of his points on ships and 80 on attack and defence. He buys:

6 Battleships	24 points
8 Cruisers	24 points
10 Destroyers	20 points
12 Submarines	12 points

He marks 14 units of land (nine squares each) on his chart, and invests his remaining points as under:

12 R.P's	12 points
8 Bombers	24 points
24 A-A guns	24 points
20 salvoes	20 points

His dispositions are interesting. His biggest concentration of ships (to a total of 27 points) is in the SW. corner of the chart, and here he masses 17 of his 24 A-A guns. This plan, as we shall see, works out very well. Blue has 6 R.P's shot down in this area, where Red only loses 2 of 7 Cruisers.

Game I

FIG. I

Red's Dispositions

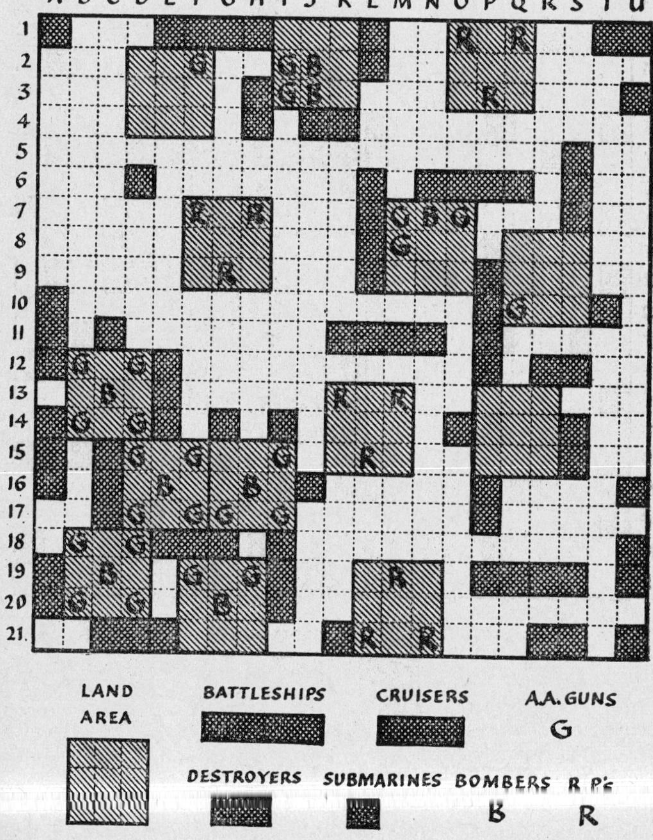

Game I

FIG. 2

Blue's Dispositions

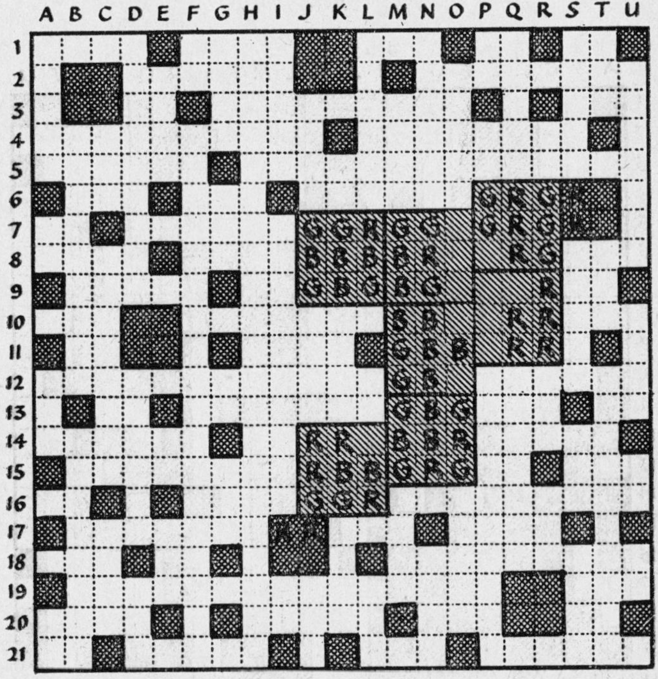

Blue's Dispositions. (*See Fig. 2*)

Blue spends only 72 points on ships. He buys:

6 Aircraft-Carriers	24 points
48 Submarines	48 points

He only marks 7 squares of land, on which he masses his R.P.'s and Bombers, heavily defended by A-A guns. Four R.P.'s however are on Aircraft-Carriers.

He has 88 points left for offensive and defensive material:

16 Bombers	48 points
20 R.P.'s	20 points
20 A-A guns	20 points

He spends nothing on salvoes, which is a bad mistake; a few salvoes would have enabled him to sink economically the ships he had located.

Apart from this blunder, Blue's plan has merit, and he is somewhat unlucky to come off as badly as he does. His idea is that Red may well attack in the centre, will find it heavily defended, and will erroneously assume that his ships are concentrated there. In fact, he has a large number of widely-dispersed submarines, which it is not worth while defending with guns; also (what is more dubious) 4 undefended Aircraft-Carriers. But he is unfortunate in that, at the end of the game, Red – taking 'pot-shots' with his salvoes – sinks an Aircraft-Carrier and 7 Submarines.

The Play	*Red's Moves*	*Blue's Response*	*Blue's Moves*	*Red's Response*
MOVE NO.				
1	R.P. (G 9) to K 11	Sub. at L 11	R.P. (I 17) to F 6	Land at FG 7 R.P. at F 7
2	R.P. (F 7) to K 6	Shot down (K 7)	R.P. (L 7) to J 11	B'ship at K 11
3	R.P. (H 7) to K 6	Shot down (J 7)	R.P. (J 17) to M 14	Land at LM 13, 14, 15, R.P's at M 13, L 15
4	R.P. (M 13) to K 6	Land at JKL 7	R.P. (J 15) to H 17	Shot down (G 17)
5	R.P. (L 15) to M 8	Shot down (M 7)	R.P. (J 14) to H 17	Shot down (I 17)

The Play	*Red's Moves*	*Blue's Response*	*Blue's Moves*	*Red's Response*
6	R.P. (K 13) to Q 11	Land at PQR 10, 11, R.P's at QR 10, 11	R.P. (Q 10) to H 17	Land at GHI 16, 17, Bomber at H 16 Cruisers at G 18, I 18
7	Bomber (H 16) to R 11	Three R.P's destroyed	R.P. (R 9) to K 19	Land at L 19,8 20
8	R.P. (L 21) to Q 14	Sub. at R 15	R.P. (L 16) to E 19	Shot down (D 18)
9	R.P. (N 21) to E 15	Sub. at E 16	R.P. (N 15) to E 19	Shot down (D 20)
10	R.P. (L 15) to D 12	A.-C. at DE 11	R.P. (K 14) to E 19	Shot down (F 19)
11	R.P. (P 3) to D 7	Subs. at C 7, E 6, E 8	Bomber (N 11) to F 19	Cruiser sunk
12	R.P. (O 1) to C 3	A.-C. at BC 2, 3 (Lucky!)	R.P. (O 14) to B 16	Cruisers at A 15, 16 and C 15, 16, 17 (Also lucky; but Blue never got around to sinking them.)
13	R.P. (Q 1) to M 19	Sub. at M 20	R.P. (S 7) to E 12	Shot down (D 12)
14	Bomber (C 19) to F 3	Sub. sunk	R.P. (S 6) to E 12	Land D 12, 13 Cruiser at E 12, 13
15	Bomber (J 2) to I 3	One hit on an A.-C.	R.P. (Q 7) to N 8	Shot down (M 8)
16	Bomber (N 7) to M 3	Sub. sunk	R.P. (Q 8) to K 8	B'ship at L 7, 8, 9
17	Bomber (C 13) to P 2	Two subs. sunk	R.P. (N 8) to I 4	Shot down (I 3)

The Play	*Red's Moves*	*Blue's Response*	*Blue's Moves*	*Red's Response*
18	Bomber (J 4) to S 3	Two subs. sunk	R.P. (Q 6) to I 5	Dests. at H 4, J 4
19	Bomber (E 16) to S 7	A.-C. sunk (Lucky!)	Bomber (N 13) to P 17	Dest. sunk
20	Bomber (G 20) to S 19	Two hits on an A.-C.	Bomber (N 14) to S 19	Two hits on a B'ship
	(See Fig. 3, showing Red's chart of Blue's position at this stage.)			
21 to 25	Five salvoes (fifteen shots) which sink A.-C's at BC 2, 3 and DE 10, 11, and seven Subs. at C 7, E 6, E 8, E 16, L 11, M 20, R 15		Bomber (J 8) to R 7	One hit on B'ship; two hits on Cruiser
			Bomber (K 8) to O 5)	B'ship sunk
			(Fig. 4 show's Blue's chart after his 22nd move.)	
			Bomber (L 8) to S 11	Dest. sunk
			Bomber (M 8) to S 15	Dest. sunk
			Bomber (M 9) to R 20	Dest. sunk; one hit on a B'ship
26 to 40	Fifteen salvoes (forty-five shots) which sink A.-C.'s at QR 19, 20 and JK 1, 2, and seven more Subs. at A 6, 9, 11, 15, 17, 19 (Red works systematically along A) and G 5 (Fig. 6 shows Blue's situation at the finish.)		Blue has eight Bombers left; 26 to 33, he sinks three B'ships at KLMN 11, PQRS 19, L 6, 7, 8, 9; one Cruiser at I 18, 19, 20; two Dests. at H 3, 4, JK 4; one Sub. at K 21 (Fig. 5 shows Red's situation at the finish.)	

Game I

FIG. 3

Red's Chart of Blue's Dispositions after 20 moves

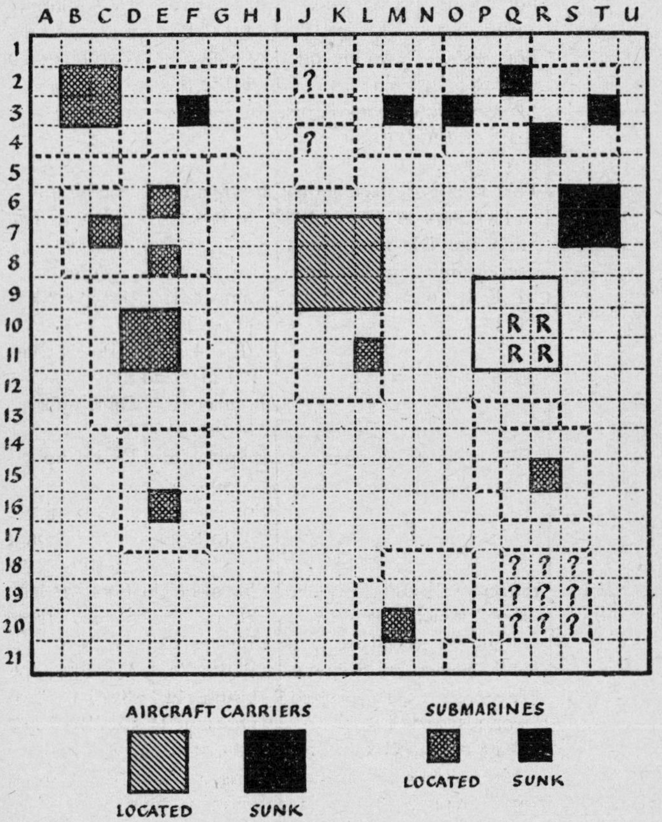
A B C D E F G H I J K L M N O P Q R S T U
1
2
3
4
5
6
7
8
9
10
11
12
13
14
15
16
17
18
19
20
21
?
?
R R
R R
? ? ?
? ? ?
? ? ?
AIRCRAFT CARRIERS
LOCATED
SUNK
SUBMARINES
LOCATED
SUNK

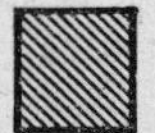

Game I

FIG. 4

Blue's Chart of Red's Dispositions after 22 Moves

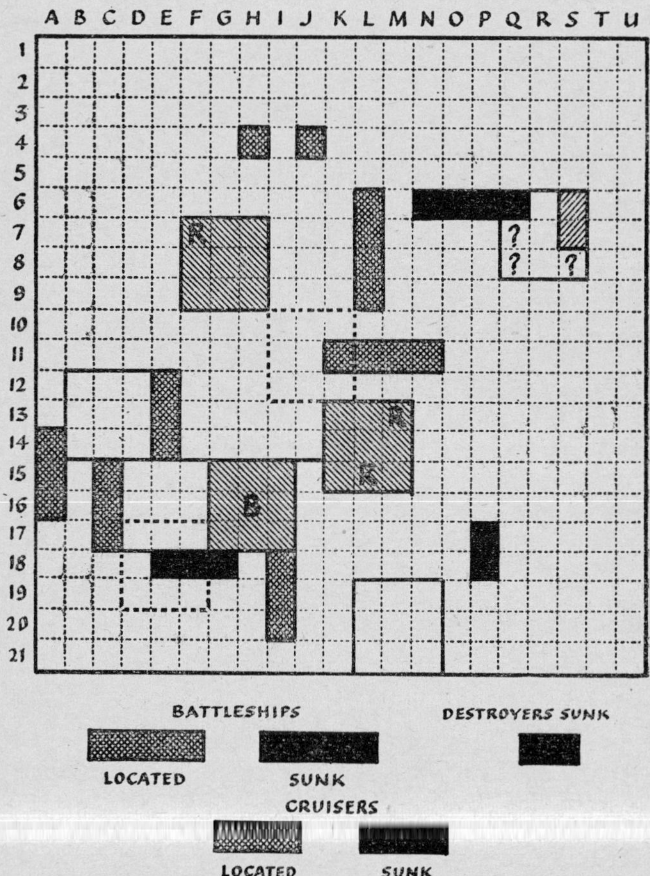

The final positions are compared (Figs. 5 and 6) and checked by the players' records.

RED	*Begins with*	*Remains with*	*Points*
Battleships	6	2	8
Cruisers	8	6	18
Destroyers	10	4	8
Submarines	12	11	11
			—
			45

BLUE	*Begins with*	*Remains with*	*Points*
Aircraft-Carriers	6	1	4
Submarines	48	28	28
			—
			32

So Red, who has played the better game, wins by 45 points to 32.

To what factors can Red's success be attributed? Partly – since in this game, as in war itself, there is an element of chance – to the luck being on his side. But, luck apart, he can claim:

(*a*) That his initial dispositions were sensible. To concentrate one's ships, as Red concentrated his, involves certain risks. For example, Blue might have bought Atom-Bombers, and might have elected to attack the area in which Red had parked seven of his Cruisers. That would have been unlucky. But, against any attack save that of Atom-Bombers, the Cruisers are well defended: eight of Blue's Reconnaissance Planes were shot down.

(*b*) That his attacking force was well balanced. Seven of his R.P.'s collected useful information, and all of his eight Bombers inflicted damage on the enemy. There remained 20 salvoes with which to sink craft located but not destroyed by Bombers. Blue was seriously disadvantaged by not having made a corresponding investment.

(*c*) That he was able to build up a fairly satisfactory – though, of course, an incomplete – picture of Blue's dispositions.

Game I

FIG. 5

End of Game : Red's Losses

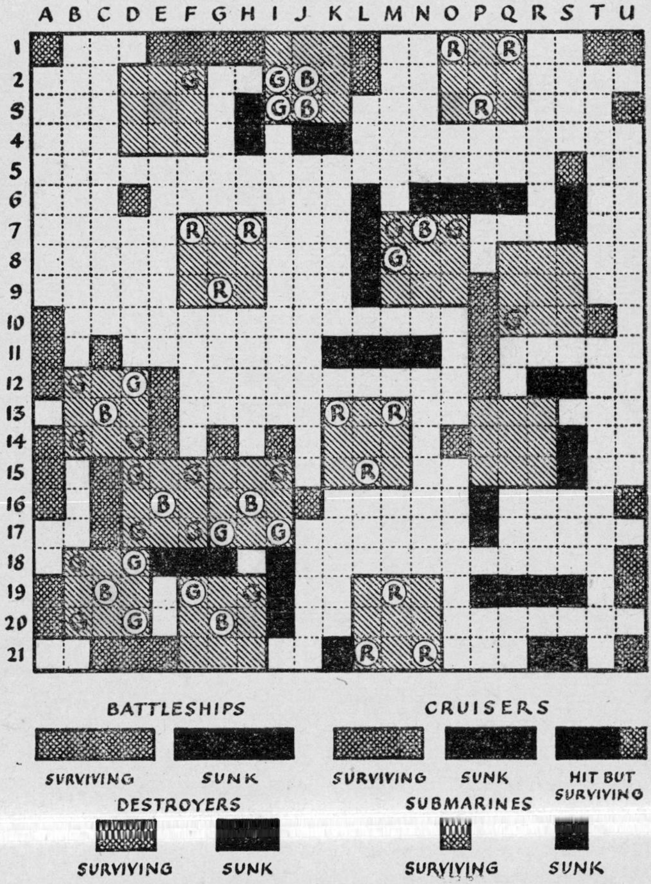

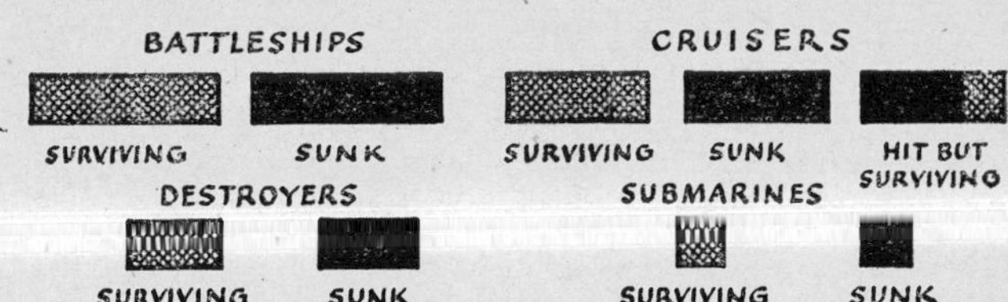

Game I

FIG. 6

End of Game: Blue's Losses

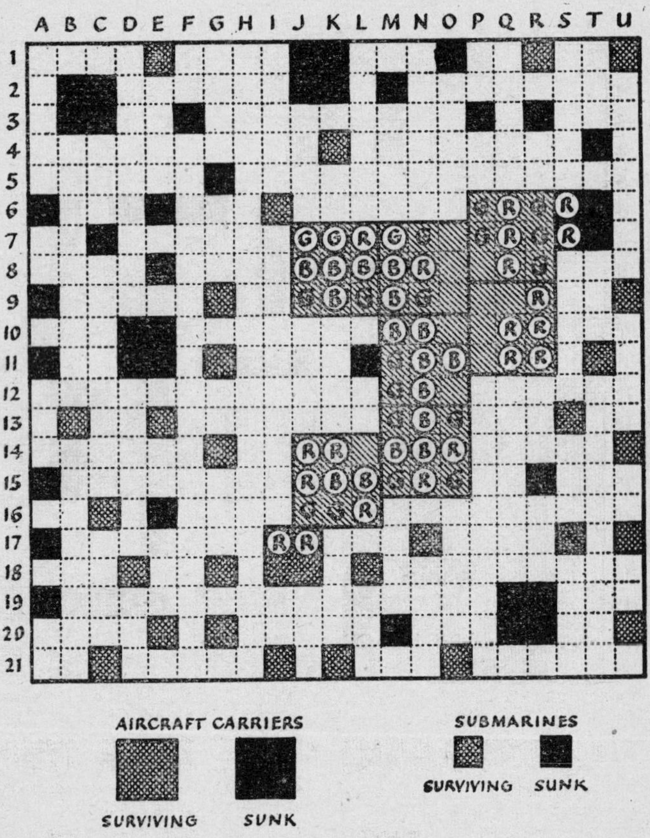

AIRCRAFT CARRIERS

SURVIVING SUNK

SUBMARINES

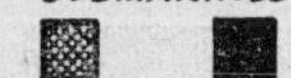

SURVIVING SUNK

Illustrative Game II

In the game just given, neither player had thought it worth while to buy Atom-Bombers. But now Blue, who again lost the toss, had decided to go all out for success with this formidable weapon. He planned for 6 Atom-Bombers, fortified by offensive and defensive weapons to the value of another 40 points. Red, meanwhile, had spent 100 points on ships.

Red's Dispositions (Fig. 7)

Red invested in 15 Battleships (60 points); 10 Cruisers (30 points); 10 Submarines (10 points). They were 'staggered' fairly evenly about Red's target area. Since it is impossible to defend so many ships, Red's further investment consisted of 16 R.P's (16 points), 10 Bombers (30 points), 6 Guns (three placed as 'bait' M 5, O 5, M 7) (6 points), and 8 salvoes (8 points). Red calculated that his meagre attacking strength would be more than compensated for by the difficulty of sinking so many ships.

Blue's Dispositions (Fig. 8)

Blue massed his Atom-Bombers (60 points) in opposite corners of his area, with 13 A-A guns (13 points) to defend them. His further attacking force consisted of 6 R.P's (6 points) and 7 Bombers (21 points). Once again he did not buy any salvoes.

His naval force consisted of 20 Destroyers and 20 Submarines. He hoped that his Atom-Bombers, which, collectively, can cover 150 squares, would dislocate Red's forces sufficiently to give him good winning chances.

In this game the relative values of one's offensive and defensive material are (I think) very nicely balanced. Consider the 10 points which one pays for an Atom-Bomber. This will obliterate 25 enemy squares – but may yet do no damage at all. And, if their despatch is preceded by that of R.P's, there is the dual risk (*a*) that the R.P's will be shot down, and (*b*) that the Atom-Bombers, if not despatched quickly, may be destroyed on the ground. (Blue's concentration of his Atom-Bombers is very unwise, as I remark later.) So whether it is worth while to spend 10 points on an Atom-Bomber where, alternatively, one can buy two Bombers and four R.P's, is anybody's guess.

Game II

FIG. 7

Red's Dispositions

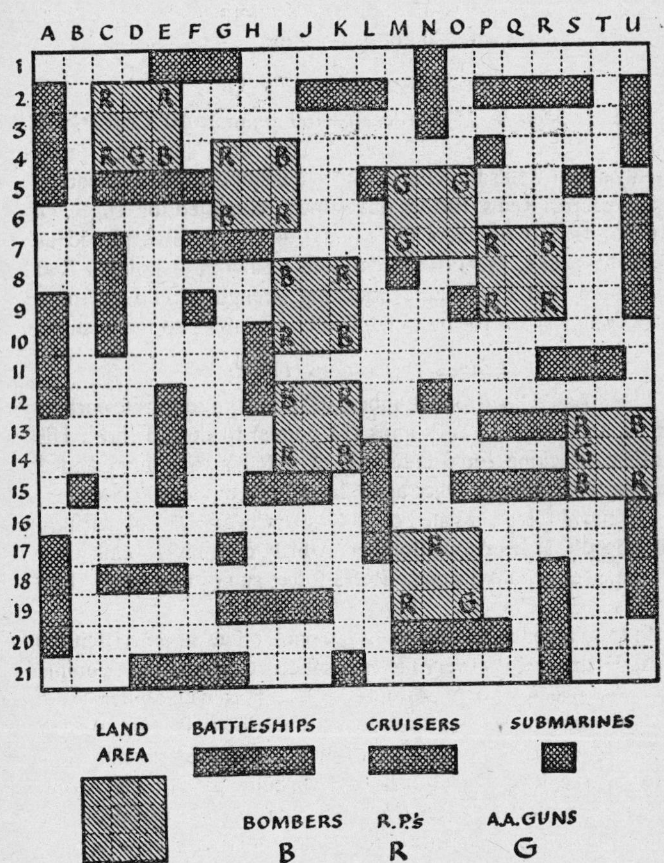

Game II

FIG. 8

Blue's Dispositions

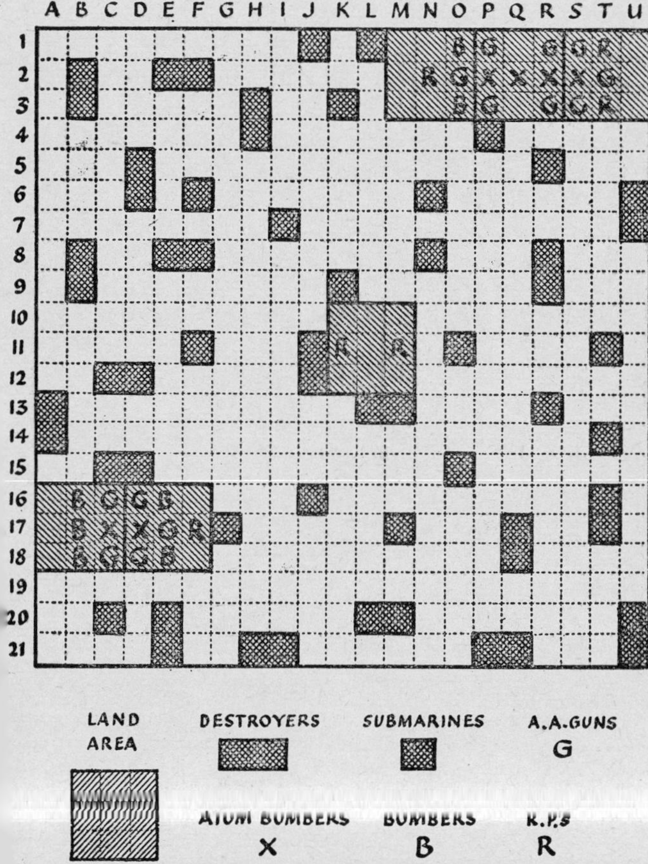

Game II

FIG. 9

Blue's Chart of Red's Losses and Dispositions after 12 moves

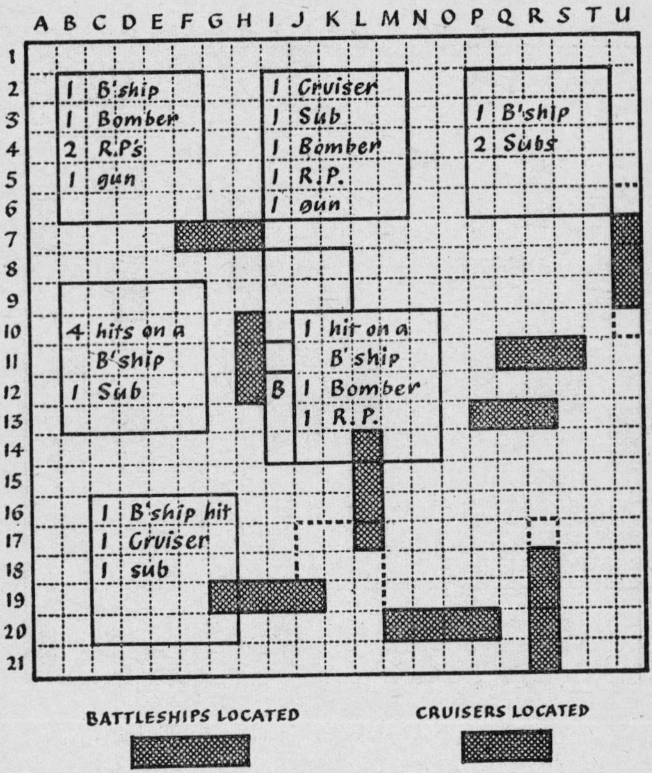

A B C D E F G H I J K L M N O P Q R S T U

1
2
3
4
5
6
7
8
9
10
11
12
13
14
15
16
17
18
19
20
21

1 B'ship
1 Bomber
2 R.P's
1 gun

1 Cruiser
1 Sub
1 Bomber
1 R.P.
1 gun

1 B'ship
2 Subs

4 hits on a B'ship
1 Sub

B

1 hit on a B' ship
1 Bomber
1 R.P.

1 B'ship hit
1 Cruiser
1 sub

BATTLESHIPS LOCATED

CRUISERS LOCATED

Game II

FIG. 10

Red's Chart of Blue's Dispositions after 15 moves

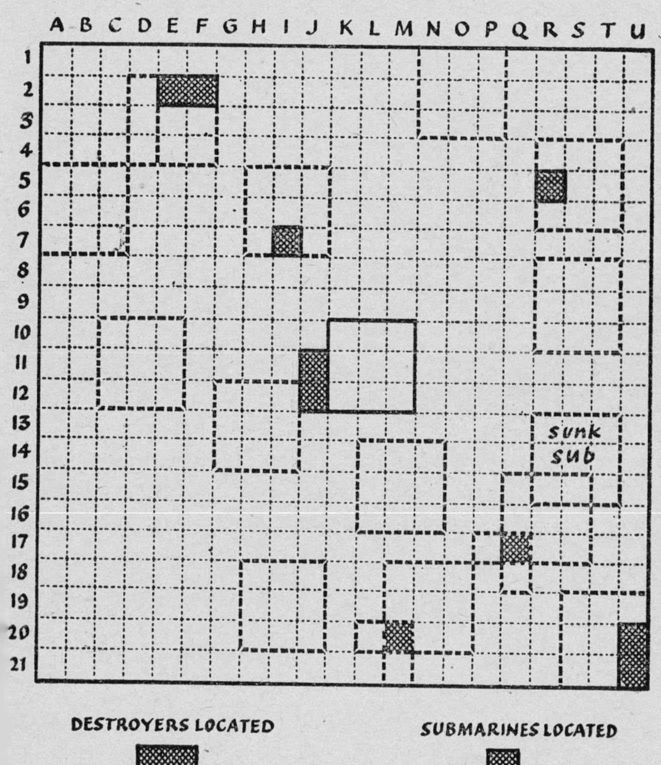

The Play	*Red's Moves*	*Blue's Response*	*Blue's Moves*	*Red's Response*
MOVE NO.				
1	R.P. (E 2) to S 5	Sub. at R 5	A.-Bomber (C 17) to D 4	One B'ship sunk, one Bomber, two R.P's and one gun destroyed
2	R.P. (G 4) to O 2	Shot down (P 1)	A.-Bomber (P 2) to R 4	One B'ship and two Subs. sunk
3	R.P. (P 7) to T 9	Open sea	A.-Bomber (D 17) to K 4	One Cruiser and one Sub. sunk, one Bomber, one R.P. and one gun destroyed
4	R.P. (K 8) to H 13	Open sea	A.-Bomber (S 2) to D 11	One Sub. sunk, four hits on B'ships
5	Bomber (K 10) to S 14	Sub. sunk	A.-Bomber (Q 2) to L 12	One hit on a B'ship, one Sub. sunk, one Bomber and one R.P. destroyed
6	Bomber (S 15) to I 19	No damage	A.-Bomber (R 2) to E 18	One Cruiser and one Sub. sunk, one hit on a B'ship
7	R.P. (P 9) to N 19	Dest. at M 20	R.P. (F 17) to K 18	B'ships at L 17, J 19
8	R.P. (R 9) to R 16	Dest. at Q 17	R.P. (N 2) to Q 19	B'ships at P 20, R 18, 19, 20

<table>
<tr><th>The Play</th><th>Red's Moves</th><th>Blue's Response</th><th>Blue's Moves</th><th>Red's Response</th></tr>
<tr><td>9</td><td>R.P. (I 14) to T 20</td><td>Dest. at U 20, 21</td><td>R.P. (K 11) to Q 12</td><td>Cruisers at QR 11, PQR 13</td></tr>
<tr><td>10</td><td>R.P. (I 10) to E 3</td><td>Dest. at EF 2</td><td>R.P. (M 11) to T 8</td><td>B'ship at U 7, 8, 9</td></tr>
<tr><td>11</td><td>R.P. (S 13) to B 6</td><td>Open sea</td><td>R.P. (T 1) to H 11</td><td>Land at I 10, I 12, with Bomber, Cruiser at H 10, 11, 12</td></tr>
<tr><td>12</td><td>Bomber (I 12) to D 10</td><td>No damage</td><td>R.P. (T 3) to E 8</td><td>Cruiser at F 7 (Fig. 9 shows what information is available to Blue.)</td></tr>
<tr><td>13</td><td>R.P. (U 15) to I 6</td><td>Sub. at I 7</td><td colspan="2" rowspan="4">(Blue has now only his seven Bombers. He considers how he can best make use of them. With six he sinks the four Cruisers located and two of the B'ships already hit by A.-Bombs. But the seventh Bomber is useless against the remaining B'ships; Blue's information is inadequate. So Blue takes a 'pot-shot' at F 1 and – miraculously – sinks another Cruiser.)</td></tr>
<tr><td>14</td><td>R.P. (N 17) to K 11</td><td>Land at K 10, 11, 12, Dest. at J 11, 12</td></tr>
<tr><td>15</td><td>R.P. (M 19) to M 15</td><td>Open sea</td></tr>
<tr><td></td><td colspan="2">(See Fig. 10. Now Red remains with four Bombers and his eight salvoes (twenty-four shots). He sinks the five Dests. and two Subs. located and also the Dest. at E 20, 21.)</td></tr>
</table>

Result of the Game

RED	*Begins with*	*Remains with*	*Points*
Battleships	15	11	44
Cruisers	10	4	12
Submarines	10	4	4
			—
		Total	60

BLUE			
Destroyers	20	14	28
Submarines	20	17	17
			—
		Total	45

Red wins by 60 points to 45.

Blue's Atom-Bombers have failed him. The snag about these weapons is that they must be used against targets chosen at random, for R.P's are likely to be wasted where enemy ships are concentrated and the Atom-Bombers are themselves vulnerable should the enemy be similarly armed. Blue realized, after the battle, how foolish his concentration of Atom-Bombers had been. He had assumed, with no good reason, that Red would have none. But, if Red had had Atom-Bombers, a shot directed at (say) Q 3 would have left Blue with just 2 Atom-Bombers and 4 Bombers, supported by 5 R.P's, to fight with!

As it was, Blue's 6 Atom-Bombers, which had cost him 60 points, only sank enemy ships to the value of 20 points. This was unlucky. Had his targets been E 3, E 8, I 17, L 3, Q 14 and R 17 he would have sunk ships to the value of 39 points and might well have won the game.

His second mistake lay in supporting his Atom-Bombers with Bombers instead of salvoes. The 21 points spent on Bombers would have yielded 21 salvoes (63 shots): enough to sink the 4 Cruisers and 5 Battleships located (32 shots) and, almost certainly, at least one more Battleship. In this event, Blue would have won by one point.

Game II

FIG. II

End of Game: Red's Losses

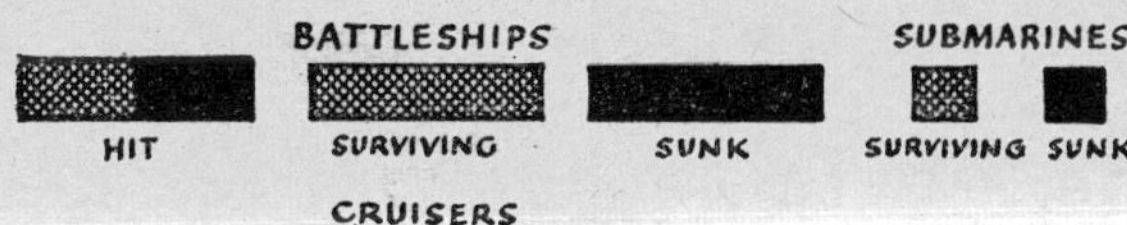

Game II

FIG. 12

End of Game: Blue's Losses

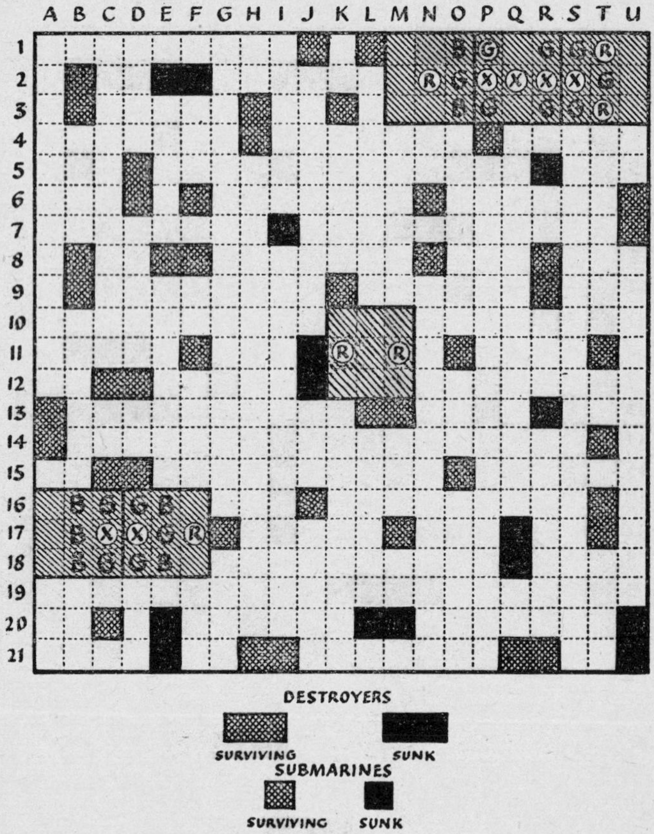

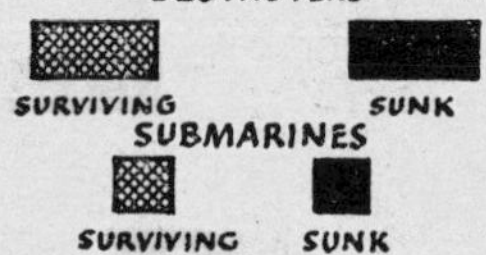

Illustrative Game III

Blue won the toss.

Both players had endeavoured to absorb the lessons of the previous game.

Blue's Dispositions

Blue had decided to persevere with Atom-Bombers, but planned, this time, to employ them in a concentrated attack on the lower half of Red's target area. They would collectively cover 150 of the bottom 220 squares (unless, of course, one or more of them were destroyed). Blue dispersed them as widely apart as possible, and decided to waste no points in trying to protect them. A random shot from a Bomber might destroy one (very long odds against that), and, should an R.P. appear, the Atom-Bomber spotted would immediately take off.

Blue also bought 24 R.P's, which (subject to casualties) could cover 216 of Red's remaining 291 squares. Finally he spent 16 points on salvoes, which would give him 48 shots against located targets.

This left Blue with the minimum 60 points for his outlay on ships. He bought 30 Destroyers.

Red's Dispositions

Red had correctly judged that he might have to meet another Atom-Bomber attack. He decided to invest 100 points in Battleships (25 ships); since, if Blue were relying again on Bombers to support Atom Bombers, it would take two Bombers to sink any one of them. They were somewhat thinly defended by 20 A-A guns. Red's remaining points he invested in 10 R.P's, 6 Bombers, and 12 salvoes (36 shots).

Game III

FIG. 13

Blue's Dispositions

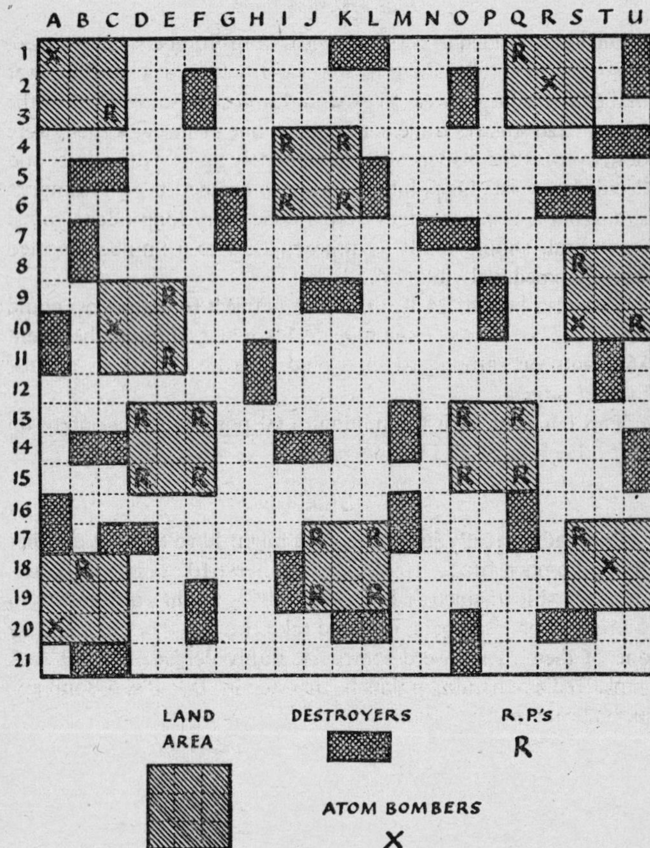

Game III

FIG. 14

Red's Dispositions

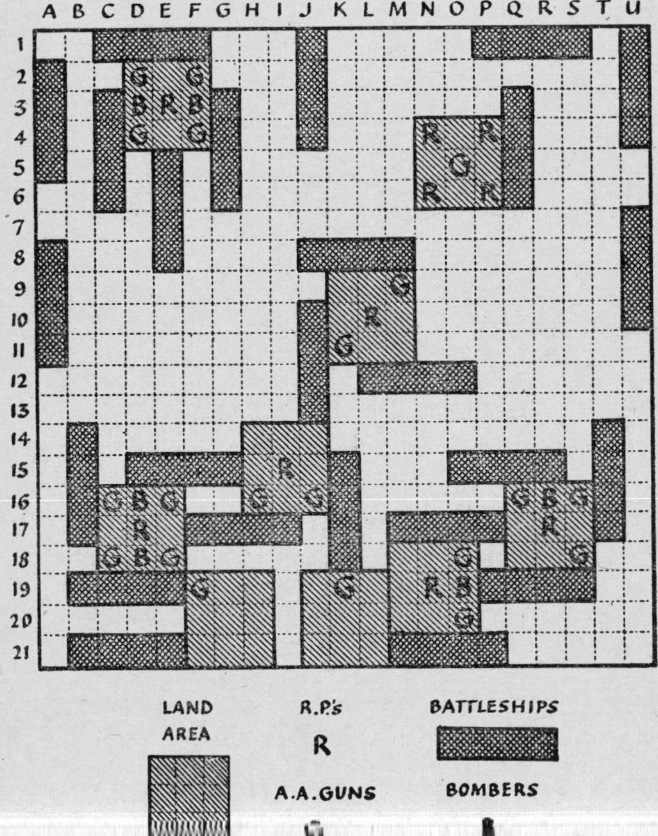

The Play	*Blue's Moves*	*Red's Response*	*Red's Moves*	*Blue's Response*
MOVE NO. 1	A.-Bomber (A 20) to C 19	Two B'ships sunk, one hit on a B'ship, one Bomber, one R.P., and two guns destroyed	Bomber (D 16) to F 9	One R.P. destroyed
2	A.-Bomber (C 10) to 14	B'ship sunk, two hits on a B'ship, two guns destroyed	Bomber (D 3) to T 7	One hit on a Dest., one R.P. destroyed
3	A.-Bomber (T 18) to H 16	Two B'ships sunk, one R.P. and two guns destroyed	Bomber (O 19) to C 9 (Unlucky for Red! The A.-Bomber at C 10 had taken off.)	One hit on a Dest.
4	A.-Bomber (R 2) to M 18	Six hits on B'ships, one R.P. and three guns destroyed	Bomber (R 16) to T 3	One Dest. sunk, one hit on a Dest
5	A.-Bomber (S 10) to R 17	Two B'ships sunk, six hits on B'ships, one R.P. and three guns destroyed	Bomber (F 3) – and his last – to N 9	Open sea
6	A.-Bomber (A 1) to M 13	Three B'ships sunk, one gun destroyed	R.P. (D 3) to B 2	All land, with R.P. at C 3

Let us now take stock of the position (Figs. 15 and 16). Blue's attack, this time, has been overwhelmingly successful. He still has 22 of his R.P's. He succeeds (Fig. 15) in charting all but one of Red's Battleships, and sinks 12 of them, in addition to the 10 already destroyed by Atom-Bombers. So just 3 of Red's ships survive. (Fig. 17.)

Fig. 16 shows Red's chart of Blue's dispositions after the despatch of the sixth Atom-Bomber. All he has left is 5 R.P's and his 12 salvoes (36 shots). With their aid he contrives to bring his 'kill' up to 9 Destroyers. (Fig. 18.)

Result of the Game

BLUE	*Begins with*	*Remains with*	*Points*
Destroyers	30	21	42
RED			
Battleships	25	3	12

So Blue wins overwhelmingly by 42 points to 12.

Whether the best reply to an anticipated Atom-Bomb attack is to buy a number of Battleships is, I think, debatable. Red's argument is fortified by another consideration: that an Atom-Bomb may well partially sink a Battleship to the actual location of which the adversary has no clue, and a ship is not lost until it is wholly sunk. All the same, the better investment, if one expects an Atom-Bomb attack, is probably a large number of widely dispersed Submarines. These can be so distributed that an Atom-Bomb is not likely to sink more than three.

Game III

FIG. 15

Blue's Chart of Red's Dispositions after his 28th move

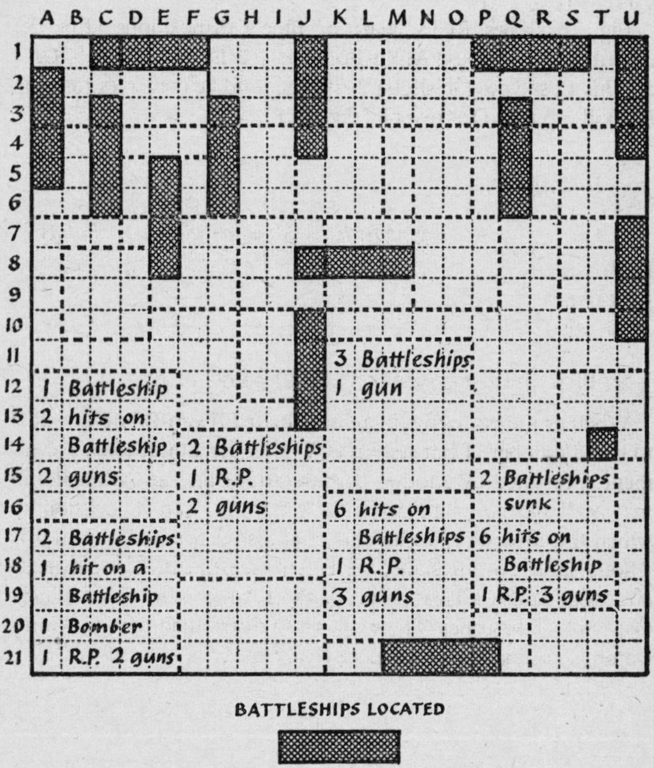

A B C D E F G H I J K L M N O P Q R S T U

1 2 3 4 5 6 7 8 9 10 11 12 13 14 15 16 17 18 19 20 21

1 Battleship
2 hits on Battleship
2 guns

2 Battleships
1 hit on a Battleship
1 Bomber
1 R.P. 2 guns

2 Battleships
1 R.P.
2 guns

3 Battleships
1 gun

6 hits on Battleships
1 R.P.
3 guns

2 Battleships sunk
6 hits on Battleship
1 R.P. 3 guns

BATTLESHIPS LOCATED

Game III

FIG. 16

Red's Chart of Blue's Dispositions after his 6th move

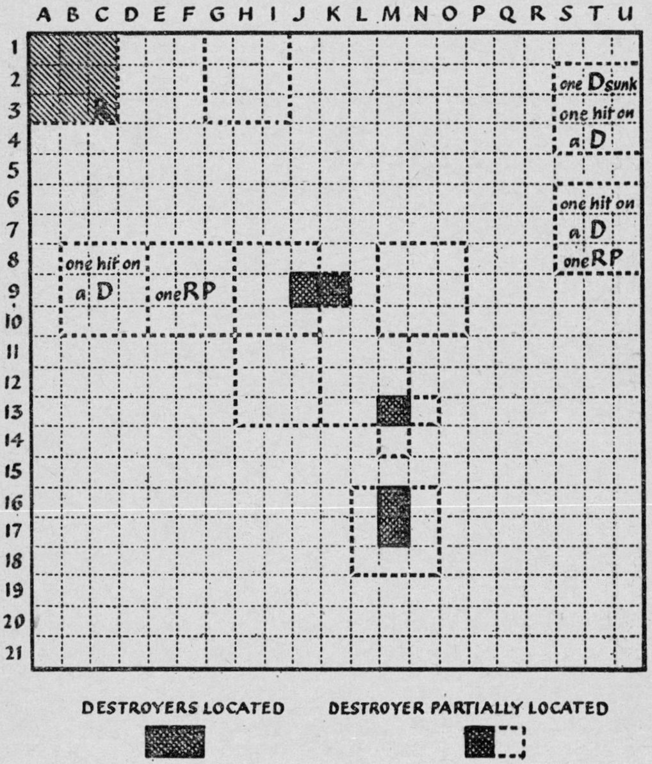

A B C D E F G H I J K L M N O P Q R S T U

1 2 3 4 5 6 7 8 9 10 11 12 13 14 15 16 17 18 19 20 21

one D sunk
one hit on a D

one hit on a D
one RP

one hit on a D

one RP

DESTROYERS LOCATED

DESTROYER PARTIALLY LOCATED

Game III

FIG. 17

Blue's Losses

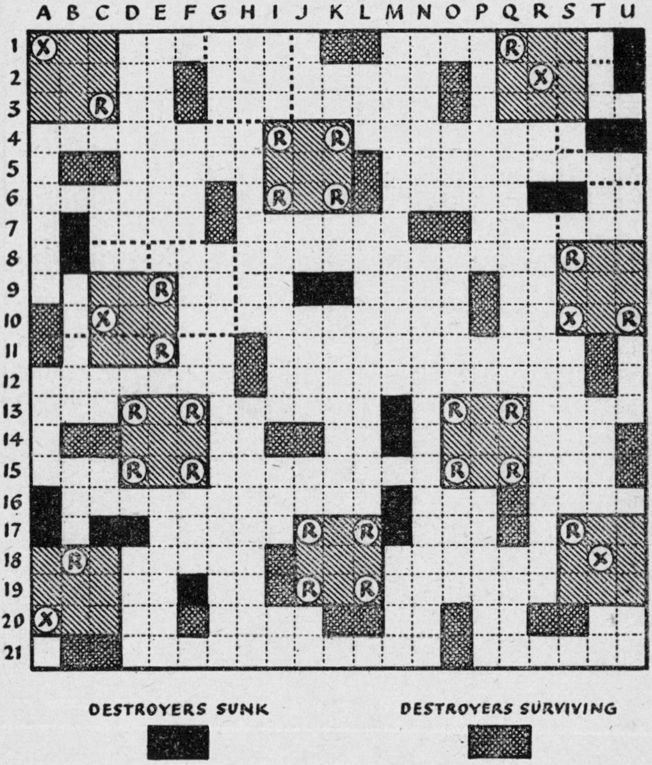

DESTROYERS SUNK

DESTROYERS SURVIVING

Game III

FIG. 18

Red's Losses

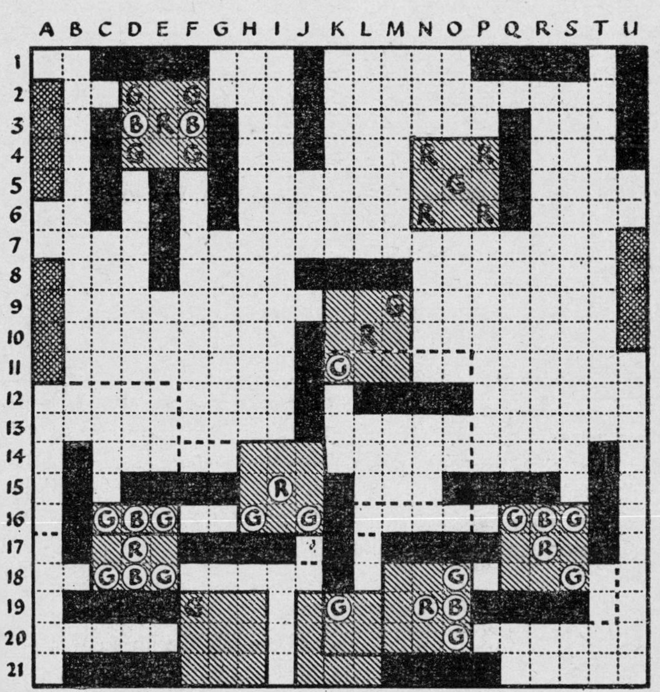

BATTLESHIPS SUNK

BATTLESHIPS SURVIVING

Illustrative Game IV

Before the fourth (and last) of their series of four games, both Red and Blue did some more hard thinking. Blue's plan in the third game had proved overwhelmingly successful. But there is an answer to every plan, and Blue tried to put himself in Red's place. One answer, of course, would be for Red to adopt the same tactics as Blue, but that would turn the game into a 50 – 50 gamble, with half a dozen Atom-Bombers on each side taking pot-shots at the enemy target area. Blue felt sure Red would try for something more effective. He decided that Red's best answer to his Atom-Bomber plan would be to concentrate his ships, so that the success of the Atom-Bombers would be more 'chancy' than ever, and to defend them with A-A guns against reconnaissance after all the Atom Bombs had been released.

And this is exactly what Red did do.

Blue's Dispositions (Fig. 19)

Blue (who had won the toss) decided he must have more ships to give himself a greater safety-margin, and also more R.P's, to allow for casualties. This meant fewer Atom-Bombers: he reduced the number to four (40 points). He also bought 30 R.P's and 18 salvoes. This left 72 points for ships: 18 Destroyers and 36 Submarines. They were dispersed evenly over the target area, with no protection against enemy planes.

Red's Dispositions. (Fig. 20)

Red had planned his defence on precisely the lines envisaged by Blue. He invested 84 points in ships – 14 Battleships, 6 Cruisers and 10 Submarines – and so grouped them as to make it unlikely that any one Atom Bomb would do a great deal of damage. They were defended against reconnaissance by 24 A-A guns. Red's offensive force consisted of 30 R.P's and 22 salvoes, which would give him 66 shots against located targets.

There was, of course, no certainty that Blue would again use Atom-Bombers, but Red's plan is likely to be equally effective against any other attack.

And this time, as we shall see, luck was in his favour.

Game IV

FIG 19

Blue's Dispositions

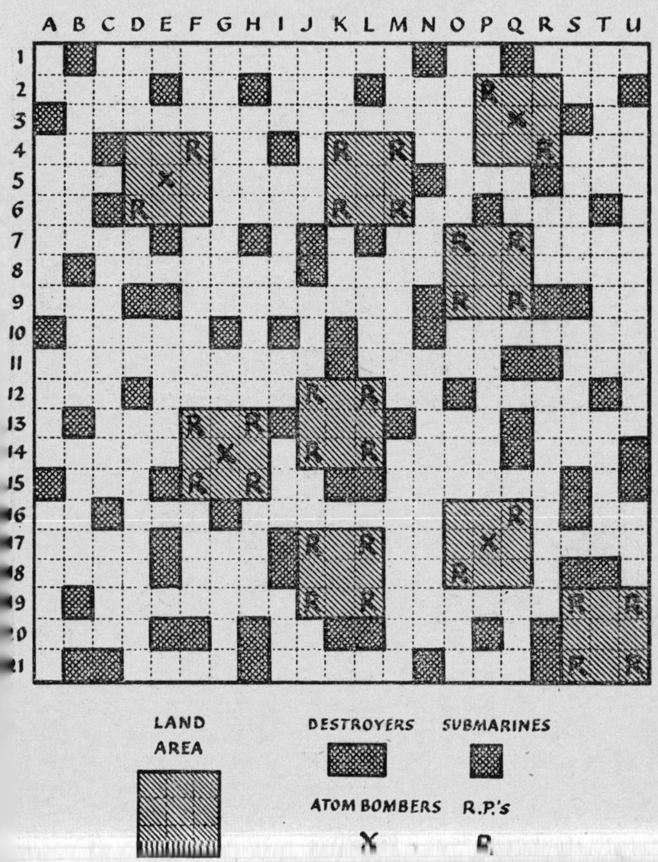

Game IV

FIG. 20

Red's Dispositions

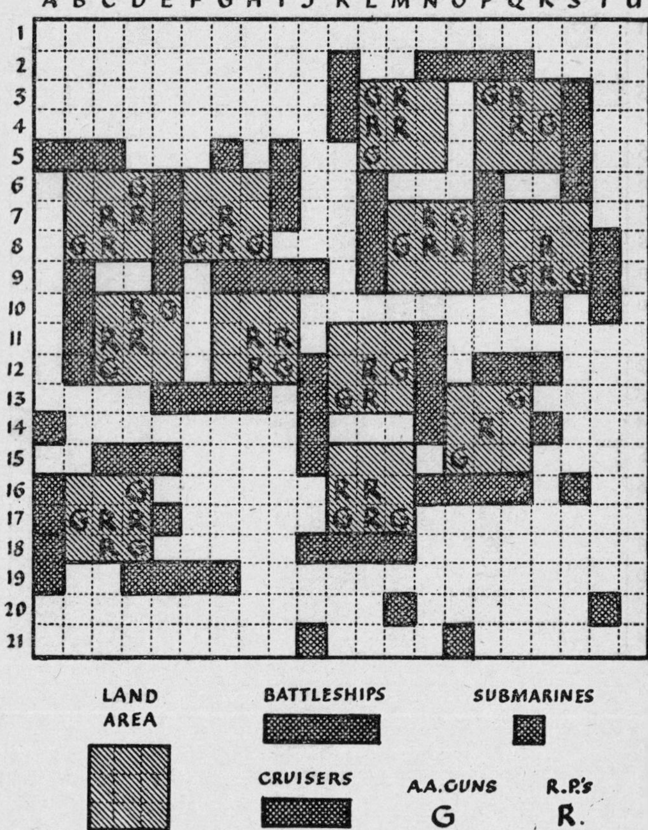

The Play	*Blue's Moves*	*Red's Response*	*Red's Moves*	*Red's Response*
MOVE NO.				
1	A.-Bomber (E 5) to K 13	One B'ship sunk, three R.P.'s and three guns destroyed	R.P. (L 16) to R 4	A.-Bomber at Q 3, R.P. at R 4, Subs. at R 5, S 3
2	A.-Bomber (Q 3) to K 8	One B'ship sunk, two hits on a B'ship and two hits on a Cruiser, one gun destroyed	Salvo: R 4, R 5, S 3	Two Subs. sunk, one R.P. destroyed
3	A.-Bomber (G 14) to F 18	One B'ship and one Sub. sunk, one R.P. and two guns destroyed	R.P. (C 17) to M 7	Land at LM 6, R.P. at M 6, Subs. at L 7, N 5
4	A.-Bomber (P 17) to O 18	One B'ship and one Sub. sunk, one hit on a B'ship, one gun destroyed	Salvo: L 7, M 6, N 5	Two Subs. sunk, one R.P. destroyed

The Atom-Bombers have barely justified their cost. An expenditure of 40 points may not have cost Red more than 18 points' worth of ships.

Blue is now in a losing position (and suspects as much). He has twenty-eight R.P's left with which to try to locate 68 points' worth of ships; but he is certain to lose a number of them. Red has twenty-four R.P's against 70 points worth of ships which are entirely undefended.

As no R.P's were destroyed on the ground, during the exchanges which follow, I have not recorded from which squares they were despatched.

The Play	*Blue's Moves*	*Red's Response*	*Red's Moves*	*Red's Response*
MOVE NO. 5	R.P. to K 17	Shot down	R.P. to J 9	Dests. at J 8, K 10, Sub. at I 10
6	R.P. to K 17	Land at KL 16, 17, B'ship at JKL 8	R.P. to N 13	Subs. at O 12, M 13
7	R.P. to F 13	B'ship at EFG 13	R.P. to R 9	Land at Q 8, 9, Dest. at RS 9
8	R.P. to F 10	Shot down	R.P. to R 12	Dests. at QR 11, Q 13
9	R.P. to F 10	Land at E 10, 11, B'ship at E 9, B'ship at G 9	R.P. to T 15	Dests. at S 15, 16, U 14, 15
10	R.P. to C 7	Shot down	R.P. to S 19	Land at ST 19, 20, Dests. at ST 18, R 20
11	R.P. to C 7	Shot down	R.P. to P 20	Sub. at P 20
12	R.P. to C 7	All land (What a sell for Blue!)	R.P. to M 20	Land at L 19, Dest. at L 20, Sub. at N 21
13	R.P. to C 3	Open sea	R.P. to H 19	Dests. at H 20, I 18
14	R.P. to F 3	Open sea	R.P. to E 19	Dests. at E 18, EF 20
15	R.P. to I 2	Open sea (Where *are* Red's ships?)	R.P. to B 20	Dest. at BC 21, Sub. at B 19
16	R.P. to M 4	Shot down	R.P. to B 16	Subs. at A 15, C 16
17	R.P. to M 4	Shot down	R.P. to C 13	Subs. at B 13, D 12

The Play	*Blue's Moves*	*Red's Response*	*Red's Moves*	*Red's Response*
MOVE NO.				
18	R.P. to M 4	All land (cf. moves 10 – 12)	R.P. to C 10	Dest. at D 9
19	R.P. to Q 4	Shot down	R.P. to C 7	Subs. at C 6, B 8
20	R.P. to Q 4	Shot down	R.P. to B 4	Subs. at A 3, C 4
21	R.P. to Q 4	All land	R.P. to E 2	Sub. at E 2
	(Blue can now see the writing on the wall. While Red is systematically charting his dispositions, he – Blue – has used twelve R.P's and located nothing but land and open sea.)			
22	R.P. to S 7	Land at RS 7, 8, B'ship at S 6, Cruiser at T 8	R.P. to I 3	Subs. at H 2, I 4
23	R.P. to R 12	Shot down	R.P. to M 2	Subs. at M 1, L 3
24	R.P. to R 12	Land at Q 13, Cruiser at QR 12	R.P. to G 6	Sub. at H 7
25	R.P. to T 14	Open sea	R.P. to F 10	Dest. at E 9, Sub. at G 10
26	R.P. to T 19	Sub. at T 20	R.P. to F 13	Land at FG 13, 14
27	R.P. to O 8	Shot down	R.P. to K 15	Land at JKL 14, Dest. at KL 15
28	R.P. to O 8	Land at No 7, 8, 9, B'ship at P 7, 8, 9	R.P. to I 7	Sub. at I 6
			(See Fig. 21. Red has now located all but one of Blue's Dests., and all but ten of his	
29	R.P. to G 7	Shot down		

The Play	*Blue's Moves*	*Red's Response*	*Red's Moves*	*Red's Response*
MOVE NO.				
30	R.P. to G 7	Shot down	Subs. With his twenty remaining salvoes he sinks all the ships located and also the Sub. at A 10 (Fig. 23).)	
31	R.P. to G 7	All land (!)		
32	R.P. to B 18	Shot down		
	(See Fig. 22. Blue's R.P's, owing partly to bad luck, but much more to Red's well-planned defence, have located very few of the enemy ships. Blue's fifty-four shots sink the ones he has located, and 'pot-shots' also sink the B'ship at A 16, 17, 18, 19, and the Sub. at G 5 (Fig. 24).)			

Result of the Game

RED	*Begins with*	*Remains with*	*Points*
Battleships	14	3	12
Cruisers	6	3	9
Submarines	10	3	3
		Total	24
BLUE			
Destroyers	18	1	2
Submarines	36	9	9
		Total	11

So Red emerges from this holocaust the winner by 24 points to 11.

Game IV

FIG. 21

Red's Chart of Blue's Dispositions after 25 moves

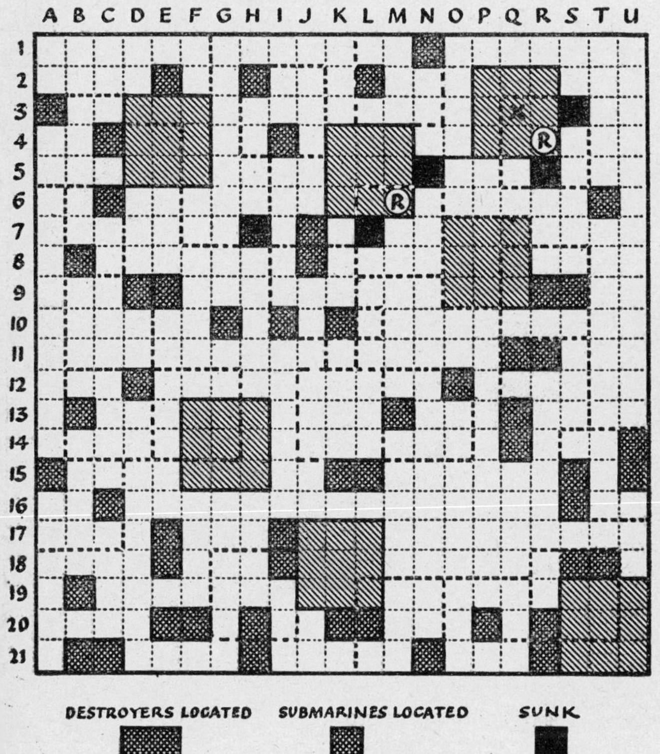

Game IV

FIG. 22

Blue's Chart of Red's Dispositions after 32 moves

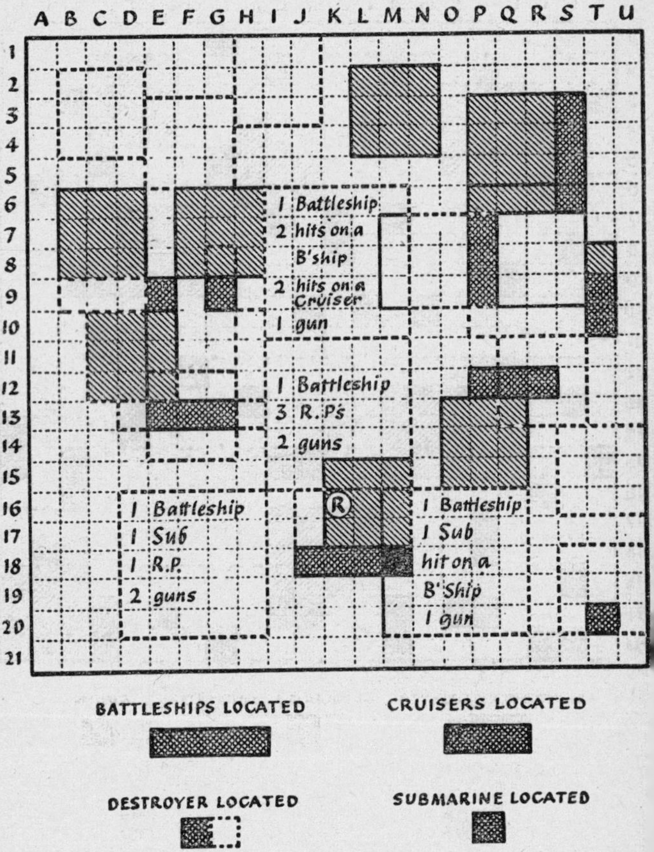

A B C D E F G H I J K L M N O P Q R S T U

1 2 3 4 5 6 7 8 9 10 11 12 13 14 15 16 17 18 19 20 21

1 Battleship
2 hits on a B'ship
2 hits on a Cruiser
1 gun

1 Battleship
3 R.P's
2 guns

1 Battleship
1 Sub
1 R.P.
2 guns

R

1 Battleship
1 Sub
hit on a B'Ship
1 gun

BATTLESHIPS LOCATED

CRUISERS LOCATED

DESTROYER LOCATED

SUBMARINE LOCATED

Game IV

FIG. 23

Blue's Losses

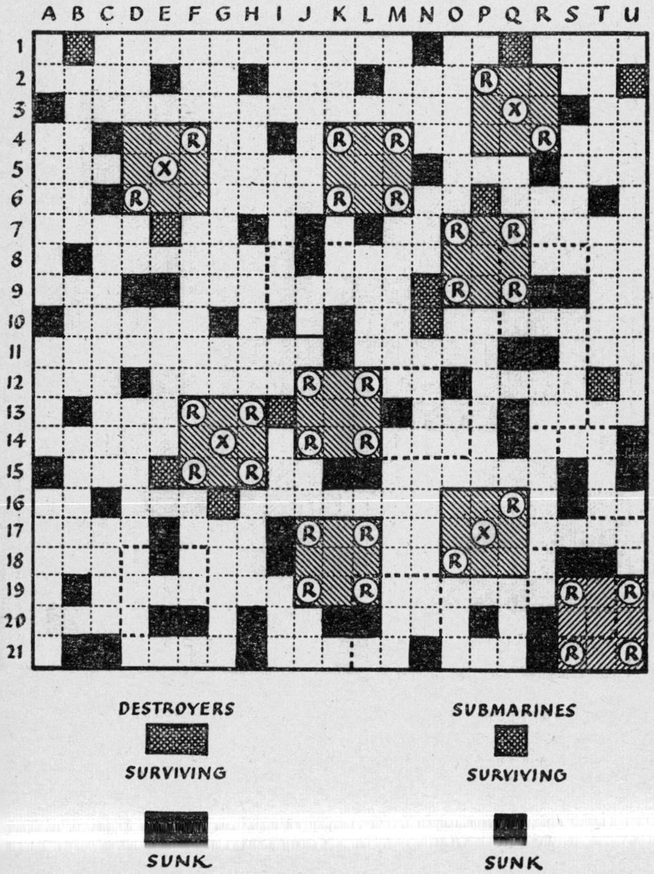

A B C D E F G H I J K L M N O P Q R S T U

1 2 3 4 5 6 7 8 9 10 11 12 13 14 15 16 17 18 19 20 21

DESTROYERS

SURVIVING

SUNK

SUBMARINES

SURVIVING

SUNK

Game IV

FIG. 24

Red's Losses

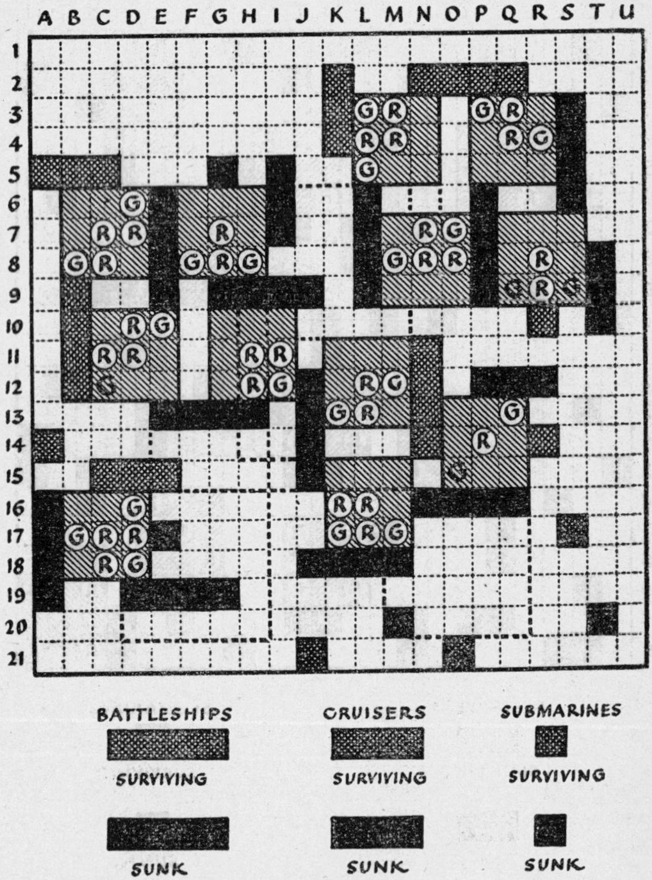

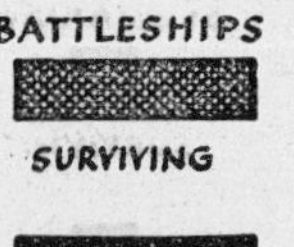

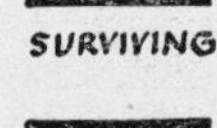

One can't get more than a slight idea of the possibilities of Combat from my four representative games. How best to plan one's dispositions against adversaries of varying temperaments – there's a lot of psychology in the game – can only be learned by experience. Here, however, are two tables which summarize the results of our games:

Table I. Initial Outlay and Final Scores

GAME	EXPENDITURE (IN POINTS) ON WEAPONS							POINT VALUE OF	
	Ships	*Guns*	*R.P's*	*B'rs*	*A-B'rs*	*Salvoes*	*Total*	ENEMY SHIPS SUNK	OWN SHIPS SURVIVING
1. RED	80	24	12	24		20	80	40	45
BLUE	72	20	20	48			88	35	32
				Red won by 45 points to 32					
2. RED	100	6	16	30		8	60	15	60
BLUE	60	13	6	21	60		100	40	45
				Red won by 60 points to 45					
3. RED	100	20	10	18		12	12	60	12
BLUE	60		24		60	16	100	88	42
				Blue won by 42 points to 12					
4. RED	84	24	30			22	76	61	24
BLUE	72		30		40	18	88	60	11
				Red won by 24 points to 11					

Table II. Survival of Ships of Various Types

	PURCHASED	SURVIVED	PERCENTAGE
Battleships (and one A/C)	61	20	33 per cent
Cruisers	24	13	54 per cent
Destroyers	78	40	51 per cent
Submarines	136	72	53 per cent

To draw, from these exiguous data, the conclusion that Battleships don't pay, would be altogether wrong. Red lost 22 out of [illegible] Battleships in the third game. In the other three games 60 per cent of Battleships survived.

Party Games

PARTY GAMES

THERE is no better fun than a Games Party if trouble is taken with its organization. One's programme should be thought out beforehand and the necessary material (e.g. for Quiz games) prepared. And, if there are a number of players, they should be organized in teams; make games, in so far as they are competitive, competitive as between the teams and not between individuals. Then duffers or those who are allergic to games (though the latter shouldn't be invited at all) can let others do the work without making themselves conspicuous.

I have roughly classified my games as:

1. *Getting-together Games*, to start the party off.
2. *Round Games.*
3. *Action Games.*
4. *Word Games.*
5. *Mezzobrow Games.*
6. *Quiz Games.*

Some games fall into more than one of these categories.

Every game listed has its variants; every game will suggest others. I don't think I have ever given a Games Party without producing something new. All the games given here have proved their popularity over and over again.

Getting-Together Games

Here are three ways of starting off a party.

PAIRING CARDS

The 52 cards of an ordinary pack are hidden – but where they can easily be found – in various parts of the room or rooms in which the guests forgather. Each guest is then given a card from another pack, and has to find its mate. As soon as this is produced, the two cards are given to the host, who promptly hands out another one. This is a very brisk game. The team that collects the largest number of pairs wins.

SARDINES

A game primarily for teenagers. One of the party hides, e.g. behind a curtain. The others are then sent in search of him (or her). The first to succeed noiselessly joins him; then the next one; and so on. Eventually there will be so many 'sardines' that further concealment is impossible.

WHO AM I?

Each player has a card pinned to his back, which bears some well-known name: Jack the Ripper; Hercules; Cleopatra; Little Miss Muffet. By questioning others in the vicinity he has to identify himself; he will also, of course, answer questions put by others. The team wins whose members are all identified first.

Action Games

SLAVE MARKET

This is a good game for a large party of young people. Some half-dozen pretty girls are chosen and put up for auction. Each team is given a prescribed number of counters with which to bid for the girls. The nominal object of the game is to secure as many 'bargains' as possible.

KITTIWAKE

Boys and girls (or men and maidens) are paired off. Each of the girls chooses a distinctive 'cry': 'ToWhoo'; 'Miaow'; 'Cuckoo', etc. Their partners are blindfolded; then the girls are lined up at one end of the room and start calling their mates. The team that first finds all its partners wins.

MURDER

One of the most popular of all games. Cards are drawn; whoever draws one specified card is the 'Murderer'; whoever draws another, the 'Detective'. The detective discloses his identity at once; the murderer does not. All now leave the room and roam freely about as much of the house (or flat) as is available. All lights should be turned out. After, say, ten minutes' suspense, the 'murderer' selects a victim, who must count ten and then utter a blood-curdling scream. Meanwhile the murderer makes his get-away. No one but he may move after the murderer's victim has given tongue.

The lights are now turned up and the detective inspects the scene of the 'crime'. Then all assemble in one room. The detective puts three questions to each of the other players, with the exception of the 'corpse'. All but the murderer must answer his questions truthfully; the murderer, of course, may lie. The detective, if he has enough nous, should now be able to say who the murderer is.

CHARADES

Everyone knows this 'dressing-up' game, but not everyone knows how to play charades properly. A word of two syllables should be selected, each syllable of which, as well as the complete word, can be acted. And the action should, if possible, offer a coherent story; though this is perhaps a counsel of perfection. It is not necessary to introduce either the syllables or the word; the scene offered should portray the general idea. Suitable words are *Black-board; Bed-time; Fool-proof; Cold-stream; Wind-fall; Rail-way; Hard-ship; Man-drill; Fox-glove*, etc. The list could be extended indefinitely.

SERGEANT MURPHY

Very good fun. The competitors are lined up like a squad of recruits, and one person is chosen to 'drill' them. He proceeds to give orders; e.g. 'Sergeant Murphy says 'Shun!'; 'Sergeant

Murphy says Right Turn!' and so on. A player who fails to comply is at once told to fall out. Intermingled with the 'Sergeant Murphy' orders are others *not* preceded by 'Sergeant Murphy', either rasped out ('Shun!' or 'Halt!') or offered in a conversational tone ('Stand easy'). Anyone conforming to one of these orders must also fall out; sometimes the entire squad is hoodwinked. The last player to survive is the winner.

PSYCHOLOGY

The players sit in a circle. Each is dealt a card, which he does not show to anyone. The compère keeps a score. Each player announces his card – or rather names any card – and, after he has done so, the compère asks each of the other players whether, in their opinion, he has or has not told the truth. The player then shows his card. Points are scored (*a*) for deceiving others; (*b*) for guessing correctly whether others have told the truth or not. Thus, suppose there are 16 players. Suppose that Mary has told the truth, but 11 players say that she has lied; while Mary herself is correct in her judgement regarding 13 other players. She clocks up 11 + 13 = 24 points; a very good score. The best team aggregate wins.

MUSICAL HATS

Everyone knows Musical Chairs. If you haven't space to play it properly, try Musical Hats. You need one hat less than the number of players originally playing. They are seated in a circle and the hats are passed from player to player; there should be rhythmic music so that this can be done at a uniform pace. The music stops suddenly, and one player will have no hat. He is out, and a hat is taken away from the remainder. And so on, until there is only one survivor.

ORANGES

Team plays against team; if there are four teams, have two rounds and a final. Each team is seated side by side and they should face one another. They extend their legs in front of them so that their feet will support an orange. When both teams are ready, the compère places an orange in the hollow formed by the upturned feet of the nearest player on each side. The oranges have to be passed from player to player all the way down the row and back; and only the feet may be used to pass it. If it falls to the floor the process must start all over again. The team wins whose orange does the double journey most quickly.

Round Games

ADVERBS

This is a very simple game. One person is sent from the room, and the others think of an adverb. The adverb must be one that can suitably be applied to a remark. If the adverb makes sense when added to the following phrase, it will do: 'Yes', he said '. . .'

Let us suppose that the players have chosen 'emphatically' as their adverb. The absent player is recalled and asks each player, in turn, a question. Each has to answer the question in the way that the adverb describes. For example, the questioner asks: 'Are you enjoying this party?' to which the answer, most emphatically, is: 'Yes, indeed. Jolly good party. Best party I've been to for years.'

The questioner may ask as many questions as he wishes but he is only allowed three guesses. If he does not guess the right adverb, he has failed, and someone else is sent out of the room – with, of course, a different adverb.

When choosing the adverb it is as well not to make it too difficult. For example, 'naturally' would be a permissible one to use but it would be much too difficult to guess. Here are some suitable adverbs: *hesitantly*, *angrily*, *softly*, *loudly*, *slyly*, *stupidly*, *contemptuously*, *sarcastically*, *hastily*, *bitterly*. If a difficult word is chosen the questioner may be allowed four or five guesses instead of only three.

Another way of playing Adverbs is for the questioner to ask the players to perform some action in the manner of the adverb. For example, to shake hands with another player, or to offer someone a chair, or borrow a match and light a cigarette. Here are a few adverbs suitable for this variation of the game: *slowly*, *gracefully*, *clumsily*, *ungraciously*, *nervously*, *nonchalantly*, *obsequiously*.

PROVERBS

One member of the party is sent out of the room while the others think of a proverb. This is the most difficult part of the game because it must be a proverb that the person outside is likely to know and, at the same time, it must not contain any word which, when introduced into a sentence, would at once give away the proverb.

When the proverb has been chosen, the party decide who shall answer the first question, who the second, and so on. The player is recalled from outside and asks the person nominated to answer the first question any question he likes.

The reply must contain the first word of the proverb. Similarly, the second answer must contain the second word of the proverb, and so on until the proverb is completed. If the player fails to identify the proverb, he must give it up, and someone else tries to identify another one.

Here is an example: 'One man's meat is another man's poison.'

The questioner, when he returns, is told that the proverb is one of seven words. Here are the questions which he might ask and the answers which might appropriately be given.

Q. Are you enjoying this party?
A. Very much. I've never before been to one quite like it.
Q. Do you play Canasta?
A. No, it bores me. I prefer a man's game: Poker, say, or Bridge.
Q. Have you seen that new play of Anouilh's?
A. Yes, and I don't think much of it. Existentialist tosh! I want something with more meat in it.
Q. Difficult, thinking up these questions, isn't it?
A. Is it? I'd have thought it was just your cup of tea.
Q. What is your favourite beverage?
A. Anything with a kick in it. One of my favourites is Cointreau; another is Kummel; best of all, perhaps, Vodka.

Q. Are you hoping to go abroad this year?

A. I doubt it. When a man's not his own master, it's difficult to make plans.

Q. What do you think of the present Government?

A. Their foreign policy is sensible enough; their domestic policy's poison. I shall back another horse next time.

The last speaker has a difficult job. 'Poison' may well give the show away. He contrives to suggest, however, that the proverb has something to do with a horse.

Other Suggested Proverbs

Give a dog a bad name and hang him.
It's an ill wind that blows nobody any good.
It's a long lane that has no turning.
It's no use crying over spilt milk.
A fool and his money are soon parted.
There's no time like the present.
There's many a true word spoken in jest.
The longest way round is the shortest way home.

ECHOES

The success of this game depends largely on careful and intelligent preparation. The players can compete individually or in teams. It is not a difficult game to play. The compère will call out a definition, such as 'Mad little flower' and the players have to find two words – normally, though not always, an adjective and a noun – which conform to the definition, and which more or less echo each other. The 'echo' which the compère expects is, in this case, 'Crazy daisy'.

It is possible – though unlikely – that a player will suggest a phrase just as good as the one the compère has in mind. If so, it should be accepted (the compère's decision is final). In any case, incorrect answers should not be penalized.

Here are some suggested clues and the corresponding answers:

1. Frozen fat	*Hard lard*
2. Foolish young mare	*Silly filly*
3. Not the first, or second, of our feathered friends	*Third bird*
4. Beloved bird	*Darling starling*
5. A solemn bar of music	*Grave stave*
6. Girl with a heavy basket	*Laden maiden*
7. Norseman on a walking-tour	*Hiking Viking*
8. Jackdaw's cowardly cousin	*Craven raven*
9. Peculiar face-fungus	*Weird beard*
10. An inexpensive look	*Cheap peep*
11. Blushing footman	*Scarlet varlet*
12. Not a new anecdote	*Stale tale*
13. Devastating abuse	*Effective invective*
14. Hirsute elf	*Hairy fairy*
15. Baron, not amused	*Bored lord*
16. Construct emotional warmth	*Fashion passion*
17. Stop, you common condiment	*Halt salt*
18. Haughty gathering	*Proud crowd*
19. Not the taller sister	*Shorter daughter*
20. An exact gadget	*Precise device*
21. Small-type blockhead	*Ruby booby*
22. Inebriated vagabond	*Tipsy gipsy*
23. Tropical bird-talk	*Flamingo lingo*
24. Oddity from Athens	*Greek freak*
25. All-powerful fresh-water fish	*Supreme bream*
26. Impassioned lapwing	*Plover lover*
27. Minister, now out of gaol	*Released priest*
28. Imitation Liebfraumilch	*Mock Hock*
29. Calpurnia's dress material	*Latin satin*
30. Amusement from the hive	*Funny honey*
31. Flaccid crustacean	*Limp shrimp*
32. Mirthful Spanish wine	*Merry sherry*
33. Inefficient sleuth	*Defective detective*
34. More agile incumbent	*Quicker vicar*
35. Well-groomed little dog	*Sleek Peke*
36. Napoleon, hard up	*Stony Boney*
37. Fellow-traveller's tipple	*Pink drink*

38. Unprepossessing statesman — *Sinister minister*
39. Bogus trotter — *Phoney pony*
40. Light-hued gastropod — *Pale snail*
41. Football-team's tame ape — *Villa gorilla*
42. Wrath-quelling nostrum — *Pacific specific*
43. Devilish officer — *Infernal colonel*
44. Unflurried beast of burden — *Cool mule*
45. Fictional shack — *Novel hovel*
46. Half-baked versifier — *Inchoate poet*
47. Son of Venus, not too bright — *Stupid Cupid*
48. An oddity among holy men — *Quaint saint*
49. Bogus reptile — *Fake snake*
50. Big cat, riddled with shot — *Peppered leopard*

'MY AUNT WENT TO TOWN'

This game may either be played as a team game (the last surviving team being the winner) or it may be played by individuals, each having an agreed number of lives to lose. The players sit in a circle and one of them begins by choosing a letter. Here is an example of one round of the game:

A. I choose H. My Aunt went to town and bought a Haddock.

B. My Aunt went to town and bought a Haddock and a Hat.

C. My Aunt went to town and bought a Haddock, a Hat, and a Horse.

D. My Aunt went to town and bought a Haddock, a Hat, a Horse, and a Hankie.

E. My Aunt went to town and bought a Haddock, a Hat, a Horse, a Hankie, and a Harmonica.

F. My Aunt went to town and bought a Haddock, a Hat, a Horse, a Hankie, a Harmonica, and a Hack-saw.

G. My Aunt went to town and bought a Haddock, a Hat, a Horse, a Hankie, a Harmonica, a Hack-saw, and a Hound.

H. My Aunt went to town and bought a Haddock, a Hat, a Horse, a Hankie, a Harmonica, a Hack-saw, a Hound, and a Hyacinth.

I. My Aunt went to town and bought a Haddock, a Hat, a Horse, a Harmonica, a Hack-saw, a Hound, a Hyacinth, and a Hyena.

'I' has missed out the Hankie and loses a point. The next player chooses a letter and the game continues.

CHAIN OF SUGGESTIONS

The players sit in a circle. One of them mentions the first thing that comes into his head; the next player says what that reminds him of and so on. When each player has added (say) three links to the chain, the last player, starting with the last link, must unravel the chain, passing through each suggestion until he reaches the first one. The player who breaks down is out of the game or loses a life. The game proceeds until there is only one player left.

Here is an example:

cigarette	caddy	Crown Jewels
ash	tea	Tower of London
oak	cake	ravens
hearts	soap	rook
clubs	washing	chess
golf	King John	Alice

The last player, starting with Alice, now names all the links to cigarette.

FAMILY SNAP

This is another game that always 'goes over big'. Each player is given a name, as in the appended list; the names should be such as to cause confusion. When everyone knows (or purports to know) his or her name, the compère reads names from a prepared list, artfully introducing other names that haven't been given to anyone. When a name is called out whoever likes to do so can call 'Snap'. If a player 'snaps' his own name before anyone else has done so, he scores one point. If he is the first to 'snap' someone else's name, he scores two points. If he 'snaps' a name that hasn't been given to anyone, he loses three points. The minuses often outweigh the pluses. The best team-aggregate wins.

An example follows.

Names for twelve players:

Mr Johnson Potter	Lady Julia Potts
Miss Susan Summers	Major John Jackson
Capt. Jock Paterson	Miss Janet Porter
Mrs Porter Johns	Mrs Paterson Potter
Sir Jackson Spring	Mr Jack Summers
Miss Pat Springfield	Sir Julius Potterton

Extra names

Lady Jean Porter	Capt. Jack Potter
Mrs Juliet Johnson	Major Jackson Porter
Mr John Summerfield	Miss Juliet Summers

PERSONS AND THINGS

This – believe it or not – is about the most popular of all games, and one of the simplest. It needs a good compère and an assistant who helps to 'spot' who has given the first correct answer, and who also keeps the teams' scores.

Teams should be seated together. The compère explains the game. An illustration or two will make its principle clear. The compère calls out (say) 'Country in Europe'. Then, after a few seconds, (say) 'B'. The first person to shout out 'Belgium' or 'Bulgaria' scores one point for his team. Next the compère may say: 'Quadruped . . . A'; Ape, Ass, Alligator, etc., are all in the running. If there is any dispute, the compère's decision is final.

This game may be made as easy or as difficult as you like. Thus: 'Composer . . . I shall give the second letter . . . O.' Mozart is one obvious answer, but someone is sure to say 'Offenbach'; this carries a penalty. Or the last letter may be given: 'Politician . . .

last letter . . . N.' Eden or Bevan scores; the compère might or might not accept 'Winston'. The difficulty of the 'categories' asked for will, of course, depend on what manner of folk the guests are.

Word Games

These are all competitive games and the players should be organized in teams. They are given a section to themselves because they are all concerned with the meaning, structure or sound of words. There are other word games in this section on Party Games which fall more readily into other categories, and are therefore not included here.

The following selection of word games is by no means exhaustive but it may be that they will suggest a number of others.

HIDDEN WORDS

Although this can be played as a pencil and paper game it is a better game without these accessories. For example, the following sentence: 'How fresh are those apples?' conceals the name of a quadruped: *hare*. When the sentence is seen in print it is not difficult to spot it. But when it is read out aloud, some alertness is needed.

When preparing the sentences the following points should be noted.

(1) The hidden quadruped, poet, or country may be concealed in one word, e.g. 'They packed the china carefully in a crate' contains the word *rat*. It is better, however, to use two or more words to conceal the hidden one.

(2) The simplest names are often the most difficult to find.

(3) Care must be taken not to include two hidden words by mistake.

The game itself is very simple to play. The compère reads aloud the prepared sentences, and points are scored by the player or team who first calls out the hidden name. An incorrect guess may be penalized.

Here are some examples of hidden POETS, PLAYWRIGHTS, NOVELISTS, TREES, FLOWERS, and TOWNS (in the British Isles). There are, of course, many other 'categories' from which words can be taken: QUADRUPEDS, FISH, RIVERS, COUNTRIES, and so on.

Hidden Poets

1. We wake at seven on a Sunday morning just as on any other day of the week.
2. They all got to the top at more or less the same time.
3. The wall was stone and, although he hammered it hard, the nail would not go in.
4. A writer's pen serves him in the same way as a sword serves a soldier.
5. The laundry denied very emphatically having torn the sheet almost to shreds.
6. We watched the car go over the bridge, speed down the road and disappear in a cloud of dust.
7. The dog would follow all errand-boys on bicycles, barking and snapping at their legs.
8. James is so fussy about his food but Mary eats anything and everything, as you know.
9. One farmer will call them 'stacks', another 'ricks'; but they are one and the same thing.
10. A thin, unwilling ray of sunlight came through the heavy clouds.

Hidden Playwrights

1. He sees hawthorn and chestnut trees in bloom even in December.
2. I don't think being so high-minded and legal's worth your while at the moment.
3. If I told him he was a welsher I'd anger him still more.
4. The highest branches of the pine rose several feet above all the other trees.
5. The road runs the whole length of Rydal Water, through some of the loveliest scenery in the Lake District.

6. Believe me, one illness in the family at a time is enough.
7. We have had more than our share of frost and snow this winter.
8. Did you see the Regent's Pavilion when you were at Brighton?
9. You'll come to the source of the Tamar lower down this path.
10. There he was rocking with laughter, holding his ribs, enjoying his own jokes even if no one else did.

Hidden Novelists

1. When I last saw him he was galloping across the field in great style.
2. If you're going, ask Ellen for my scissors, please.
3. Let's agree never, under any circumstances, to do such a thing again.
4. We certainly started off in the car, yet had to finish the journey on foot because it broke down.
5. The aster neat and primrose sweet never bloom together.
6. They are obviously unable to care adequately for us in this hotel.
7. We shall have to go in that tub or rowing boat, as they call it.
8. Won't it roll open again as soon as I put it down?
9. That was the first evensong I've been to in the cathedral.
10. Pleasure and joy certainly are not the same thing.

Hidden Trees

1. My uncle James ranks among our most popular chess players.
2. I do hope Arthur won't catch measles from his brother.
3. When he was at school he was always top in English and History.
4. What a spendthrift the boy is – just like his father.
5. If bacon and butter are still cheap, please buy me a pound of each.
6. He says that one day he will own a very large racing car.
7. Is it small pitchers or tiny ewers that have big ears?
8. He chanced a run of good luck which, of course, didn't come off.

9. Must you always be echoing her words and telling us what she said?
10. They consumed large quantities of beer before continuing their journey.

Hidden Flowers

1. Were you thinking of taking or sending the present to her?
2. As we were coming round Selsey Bill we saw the Isle of Wight.
3. In spite of the torch I despaired of ever finding them in the dark.
4. There they all were, drinking cups of tea and eating Bath buns.
5. I couldn't help wondering whether they were only friends or relations of his.
6. 'He was, at all times, a perfect gent,' I answered.
7. You can't really be prosecuted for trespassing you know.
8. I have never been as terrified in my life as I was at that moment.
9. We understand that the son and heir is to be present at the party next Wednesday.
10. There were several little birds – sparrows, finches and larks – pursued by a hawk.

Hidden Towns (BRITISH ISLES)

1. I think you'll do very well if you get there before tomorrow morning.
2. How restive Stephen is to-day. He can't sit still for a minute.
3. I find that loaves when new have no tough crusts which have to be cut off.
4. Aren't those beeches terribly dangerous in a high wind?
5. They adore a ding-dong fight – the noisier it is, the better they like it.
6. There was a bomb right on the house next door – missed us by inches.
7. He came here for dinner one evening two years ago and has been here ever since.
8. This table is wider by at least two inches than the old one.

9. They say this is the last ball and over, yet it's only ten past six.
10. We shall do all the better for resuming the game later on, after we have rested.

Hidden Poets

1, Keats. 2, Patmore. 3, Meredith. 4, Spenser. 5, Dryden. 6, Bridges. 7, Waller. 8, Yeats. 9, Herrick. 10, Gray.

Hidden Playwrights

1, Shaw. 2, Galsworthy. 3, Sheridan. 4, Pinero. 5, Fry. 6, O'Neill. 7, Rostand. 8, Etherege. 9, Marlowe. 10, Ibsen.

Hidden Novelists

1, Fielding. 2, Gaskell. 3, Greene (Graham) or Green (F. L. or Henry). 4, Cary. 5, Sterne. 6, Reade. 7, Borrow. 8, Trollope. 9, Stevenson. 10, Joyce.

Hidden Trees

1, Larch. 2, Pear. 3, Pine. 4, Aspen. 5, Apple. 6, Willow. 7, Yew. 8, Cedar. 9, Beech. 10, Medlar.

Hidden Flowers

1, Gorse. 2, Groundsel. 3, Orchid. 4, Kingcup. 5, Sorrel. 6, Gentian. 7, Rose. 8, Aster. 9, Iris. 10, Larkspur.

Hidden Towns (British Isles)

1, Dover. 2, St Ives. 3, Newhaven. 4, Chester. 5, Reading. 6, Brighton. 7, Hereford. 8, Derby. 9, Llandovery (or Andover, or Rye). 10, Forres.

WORDS, JUST WORDS

The players are seated in a circle. One player calls out a letter and the next player has one minute (or two, if preferred) in which to call out as many words as he can think of beginning with that letter. Someone should act as umpire to check off the words and eliminate those which are made-up or are plurals of words already mentioned. There should, however, be no stopping in the middle to argue about a word. Each player, at the end of his minute, names a letter for the next player. Letters such as J, Q, and Z should be eliminated for obvious reasons. Indeed, the game might well be played with the following selection only: B, C, D, F, G, H, L, M, N, P, R, S, T, W.

WORD-MAKING

This card game requires a little preparation beforehand. A number of cardboard squares are needed – each about half an inch square – with a letter clearly painted on each. Out of a piece of cardboard measuring 15 in. by 10 in. 600 squares can be cut. The proportion of letters constructed should be based on their respective 'frequencies'. Thus, 600 letters should be proportioned as follows:

E, 100	R, 20	P, 15
A, 50	B, 15	Y, 10
I, 50	D, 15	J, 10
O, 50	G, 15	Q, 10
U, 30	L, 15	Z, 10
T, 25	M, 15	K, 10
S, 25	N, 15	V, 10
H, 25	W, 15	X, 10
C, 20	F, 15	

The players sit round a table with the letters face downwards and well shuffled in front of them. Each player takes a heap of letters (they need not be divided exactly among the players) and, keeping them face downwards places them in front of him. Now each player in turn places a letter face upwards in the centre of the table. (If the players are very young, it is perhaps a better idea for the compère to have all the letters and for him to turn them up one at a time.)

Players now have to try and make a word from the exposed letters. As soon as a player sees a word, he calls it out and arranges the letters face upwards in front of him.

The winner is either the player with the most words in front of him at the end of the game or (better still) the player with the highest number of points; one point being awarded for each letter which is part of a word.

Except when very young players are taking part in this game, three-lettered words should not be allowed. Four, or perhaps five, letters should be the minimum. Plurals and all inflected forms should be barred also. SMALL is permissible but not SMALLER or SMALLEST.

Suppose there are six players, and the first six letters turned up are A, O, G, R, S, N. Someone will quickly spot GROAN or ARGON or ORGAN and will take his word and place it in front of him. (GROANS, of course, is not allowed but SARONG would be, also SNAG and ROAN and, if three-lettered words are allowed, SON, SAG, NAG, GAS, etc.)

To make *Word-making* a more exciting game, *Word-building* and *Word-taking* can be added to it. That is, a player who, by adding one or more exposed letters to another player's word, can make another word from it can 'take' the word. For example, suppose a player has the word BRING in front of him, and the next letters turned up are T, E, H, another player can say: 'BRIGHTEN' and take BRING and the T, E, H and rearrange them in front of him. A player may also take two or more words from another player (or players) if he can make them into one word. For example, suppose one player has STEED and another PRIM, a third player can say 'DISTEMPER' and take them both.

When Word-Taking and Word-Building are being played in addition to the straightforward Word-Making, it is essential that the players should only speak in turn (i.e. immediately after turning up a letter) otherwise more adept players will secure all the words.

LETTER AUCTION

This is an exciting game in which any number of players (from two upwards) can take part. One player is the Auctioneer and has a supply of (say) 100 letters, similar to those used in *Word-Making*, face downwards on the table in front of him; he also has a supply of counters.

The other players have (say) 50 counters each.

The Auctioneer now turns his letters up, one at a time, and auctions them to the other players. Players buy the letters with a view to making complete words with them. When all the letters have been auctioned, points are awarded for every complete word in accordance with an agreed scale.

This scale must be known beforehand, as the 'price' of the letters will depend on it. For example, the Auctioneer agrees to pay, at the end of the game:

5 counters for a 3-lettered word
10 counters for a 4-lettered word
20 counters for a 5-lettered word
30 counters for a 6-lettered word
40 counters for a 7-lettered word

and so on, at the rate of 10 counters for each additional letter in a word.

A letter that is not bid for should be thrown in as an 'extra' with the next one.

Players can do what they like with the letters they have bought; arranging them and rearranging them to get the best value out of them. They may also sell to other players by private arrangement during the auction. And, unless a rule to the contrary is made, two players may combine together and share the counters paid out at the end of the game for their words. The winner is, of course, the player with the most counters.

The decision of the Auctioneer as to what constitutes a permissible word must be final. Suppose, for example, he refuses to pay anything for GERTRUDE on the grounds that it is a proper name, the player may rearrange the letters and make DRUG and TREE, claiming 20 counters for two four-lettered words.

FIRST ANAGRAM GAME

This game, like all the games in this section, can be played either as a team game or by individuals. It can also be played in two ways: either each player has a pencil and paper, and writes down the answer; or a point is scored by whoever calls out the correct answer first.

These are 'classified' anagrams. The compère tells the players beforehand what the anagrams in each group have in common, e.g. they are all anagrams of the names of flowers; of novelists; of statesmen; and so on.

Before reading out the anagram the compère should state the number of letters, e.g. for the first example given below: 'Six letters: LOVEIT.'

In the selection of 'classified' anagrams which follow, it will be noticed that they are all of eight letters, or less. This is because, if the letters are being called out and not written down, it is not easy for non-expert players to remember more.

Group 1 – Flowers

1. LOVEIT (6)
2. BEERHALL (8)
3. GRIMLOAD (8)
4. LETTEN (6)
5. DORICH (6)
6. LOGSBUS (7)

Group 2 – Novelists

1. GLIDEFIN (8)
2. TANUSE (6)
3. KINGLIP (7)
4. LOPETROL (8)
5. SINDECK (7)
6. ADEER (5)

Group 3 – Statesmen

1. OFABLUR (7)
2. LOWPALE (7)
3. LETEAT (6)
4. RAIDLIES (8)
5. GRUBHILE (8)
6. SORRYBEE (8)

Group 4 – Countries

1. NEARLID (7)
2. LAPDON (6)
3. IDCLEAN (7)
4. SHUNROAD (8)
5. FENCAR (6)
6. INITBAR (7)

Group 5 – Birds

1. PROWARS (7)
2. ONCALF (6)
3 BRERLAW (7)
4. AWREATHE (8)
5. GRINSLAT (8)
6. LOWBRAN (7)

Group 6 – Artists

1. ITINAT (6)
2. TONME (5)
3. SITSMATE (8)
4. STIRTOES (8)
5. LIMSAIL (7)
6. LATECUR (7)

There are, of course, many more groups of things or persons from which suitable anagrams can be made, e.g. TREES, POETS, RIVERS, TOWNS, COMPOSERS, BATTLES, etc.

SECOND ANAGRAM GAME

There can be any number of players (or teams) taking part in this game; each player or team competing against the others. Each, in turn, offers an anagram of an agreed number of letters for the others to solve. Whoever solves it first scores a point. Marks may be taken off for wrong guesses and for plurals, which are not allowed. It is agreed that three rounds shall be played, with words of five, six and seven letters respectively.

There are six players: *A*, *B*, *C*, *D*, *E*, and *F*. And the first round might go like this:

A. 'CAPEL'. After a moment's thought *E* says, 'PLACE', scoring one point.

B. 'ASIER'. *A* says, 'RAISE', and *F*, 'ARISE'. *A* got his in first and wins a point.

C. 'STRIF'. *A* gets in first with this one, too, 'FIRST' and scores another point.

D. 'SOPER'. Simultaneously *E* and *F* say, 'POSER'. *D* whose decision is final awards them half a point each.

E. 'PLEAP'. *C* says 'APPLE' first, and wins a point.

F. 'CLATH'. *B* gets this one first, 'LATCH', and is awarded one point.

The score at the end of this round is therefore: *A*, 2; *E*, 1½; *B*, 1; *C*, 1; *F*, ½; *D*, 0. Now the players go into the second round, each in turn offering a word of six letters.

GHOSTS

A spelling game, with much scope for ingenuity. The first player names a letter; each in turn adds to it. Whoever ends a word of more than three letters, loses a life. One may not use proper names; parts of verbs other than the infinitive, or plurals. A player who can think of no continuation may challenge his predecessor; the latter loses a life if he cannot name his word. There is great art, if one is in a hole, in producing, with a poker face, what sounds like a proper word, and so avoiding a challenge. Let us just play a round.

Mabel: C.
Jean: H.
Charles: A.
Toby: N.
Anne: N.
Stephen: E.
Richard: R.
Helen: I.
Francis: I challenge that!
Helen: CHANNERING.
Francis: There's no such word.

Umpire (with dictionary): Of course there isn't. Helen loses a life. What was your word, Richard?

Richard: I hadn't one. (Laughter from all, except Helen.)

CROSSWORD CLUES

If you like party games you probably like solving Crosswords. Here then is a game which is almost certain to be popular. The compère reads out – for solution by individuals or teams – what might be a 'crossword clue'. The clue itself is preceded by a statement of the number of letters in the word. Three points should be given for the first correct solution, and one point deducted for a wrong one.

A list of suitable clues follows. The required word should not, as a rule, be one of more than nine letters. It is essential – if this game is to give satisfaction – that there should not be any possible alternative answer to the clue.

For this reason, a high proportion of the suggested clues are anagrams – with, in addition, the meaning of the required word.

EXAMPLES

Four letters

1. Her land is a State of the American union.
2. The wisest herb?
3. Measure a city besieged in the Crusades.
4. Stop – in reverse.
5. What brings back the nuts?
6. Moral decapitation.
7. Type of bowler whose ball nips back?
8. What a bore this costume could be!
9. He gets a penny.
10. Made to be a lady of consequence?

Five letters

11. Here's a town in Surrey.
12. An entrance of precious stone?
13. Met no impressionist artist?
14. What's not needed can still make a stew.
15. What I took from Japan?
16. A Greek upper chamber?
17. No ale is unaccompanied.
18. How send a mountain range?
19. The girl could provide a horn.
20. A follower of Willy?

Six letters

21. The fruit of a royal house.
22. His bar is not far from London.
23. Tries a lampoon?
24. Subtle style in women's fashions.
25. Street with four posts.

26. No stag for this Frenchman.
27. Proust in Brussels?
28. Sieve which presents a conundrum.
29. Her Tom has a word for her.
30. Miss Alcott's women.

Seven letters

31. No smart variation.
32. Find a bouquet for yon sage.
33. The well-dressed suitor's suit is.
34. The spectre of a kingly power.
35. Topical seat of authority.
36. Played by Dickens on the hearth?
37. Mary's might be Myra.
38. Fictional letter and pimpernel.
39. The lady changes her seat.
40. Tramples a relative by marriage.

Eight letters

41. Ten hours' confusion.
42. A headline of mere rats.
43. His memory makes him an ideal choice for the panel.
44. Meet Ross – in a western shire.
45. Just the playwright to make Enid rash.
46. The way they go to the everlasting bonfire.
47. Sing about the hill – it's not worth much.
48. The world's most famous yard.
49. Can Pa use a domestic utensil?
50. Proverbially, it is as it does.

Nine letters

51. Rotten herb on game.
52. Puzzle showing ill-temper.
53. Source of hypocritical tears.
54. His Conservatives are full of dates.

55. Island cereal for mythical goat.
56. Jutting leap in sun.
57. Old boy, highly successful at stud.
58. Give us any moon without a name.
59. No hoe on my blissful fortnight.
60. Fail the lad in his examination.

Phrases

61. Why the timid man wears two pairs of socks? (4, 4).
62. What Cupid does when threatened with imprisonment? (6, 2, 10).
63. In which we do not see ourselves as others see us (7, 5).
64. The proverbial miss (2, 4, 2, 1, 4).
65. 'O, what a fall was there, my countrymen' (6-6).
66. Was this the girl photographer's answer when the wrong guy proposed? (2, 3, 8).
67. Not a tall girl, but oh, so delectable! (5, 3, 5).
68. The ventriloquist serenades his partner? (2, 3, 9, 4).
69. Janus – as Bunyan might have described him (6, 4, 4).
70. Percy, the pride of North London (9, 7).
71. Not the same thing as a battle of flowers (3, 4, 2, 3, 5).
72. Lot, unlucky in the prize ring? (7, 4).
73. They seem to have no use for oratory (3, 4, 7, 6).
74. Lack of logic, but excess of flesh, perhaps (13, 6).
75. What puzzles you is, as I'll show you, elementary (2, 4, 6).
76. An early version of the telephone directory? (3, 4, 2, 7).
77. What no line can hope to say to its parallel? (7, 2, 4, 3).
78. Mendacity under the counterpane? (5, 2, 3).
79. On which moccasins were fashioned? (3, 4, 2, 3, 8).
80. Is this where the spiv concealed himself? (5, 3, 7).

Answers to Crossword Clues

1. Mary(land).
2. Sage.
3. Acre.
4. Pots.
5. Stun.
6. (M)oral.
7. Spin.
8. Robe.

9. He-a-d.
10. Dame.
11. Esher.
12. Agate.
13. Monet.
14. Waste.
15. Tokio.
16. Attic.
17. Alone.
18. Andes.
19. Norah.
20. (Willy)nilly.
21. Orange.
22. Potter.
23. Satire.
24. Bustle.
25. Tester.
26. Gaston.
27. Sprout.
28. Riddle.
29. Mother.
30. Little.
31. Transom.
32. Nosegay.
33. Pressed.
34. Sceptre.
35. Capitol.
36. Cricket (on the Hearth).
37 Anagram.
38. Scarlet.
39. Theresa.
40. Steps-on.
41. Southern.
42. Streamer.
43. Elephant.
44. Somerset.
45. Sheridan.
46. Primrose (path).
47. S-hill-ing.
48. Scotland (Yard).
49. Saucepan.
50. Handsome.
51. Bad-mint-on.
52. Cross-word.
53. Crocodile.
54. His-Tories.
55. Capri-corn.
56. Peninsula.
57. Grand-sire.
58. Anonymous.
59. Honeymoon.
60. Plough-boy.
61. Cold feet.
62. Laughs at locksmiths.
63. Looking-glass.
64. As good as a mile.
65. Humpty-Dumpty.
66. In the negative.
67. Short and sweet.
68. Oh, you beautiful doll.
69. Facing both ways.
70. Tottenham Hotspur.
71. The Wars of the Roses.
72. Knocked down.
73. Our Dumb Friends League.
74. Undistributed middle.
75. My dear Watson.
76. The Book of Numbers.
77. Pleased to meet you.
78. Lying in bed.
79. The Last of the Mohicans.
80. Under the counter.

Mezzobrow Games

These are for reasonably well-educated folk with an I.Q. of not less than, say, 110. That should cover most of the purchasers of this book!

ALIBI

Two players are sent out of the room. They have to think up an 'alibi' for a stated period of one hour. They are supposed to have been together, e.g. lunching, or on a railway journey. At the end of ten minutes allowed them for consultation, the first of them comes in and is asked to say what he and his partner were doing during the stipulated hour. He is then cross-examined, either by 'learned counsel' or by the whole party. Then the second player comes in and is subjected to the same ordeal. Discrepancies in the two narratives are spotted, of course, and, if they are glaring discrepancies, the alibi fails and another pair have a go.

CONVERSATIONS

Two selected players go out of the room. They are asked to come in separately when the rest of the party have thought up their 'sentences'. Then each is told what his role and 'sentence' is.

'George, you are Major Wapshott, late of the Indian Army. Your sentence is: *And, dammit, she was under the bed all the time.*' (George goes out, and Marian comes in.)

'Marian, you are Mrs Wheedle, relict of our much lamented Vicar. Your sentence is: *You know how maddening these paper patterns can be.*'

George now comes in again. Major Wapshott is presented to Mrs Wheedle, as it might be at a garden party. The two sit down, and embark on a courteous, intelligent, and leisurely 'conversation'. But each – unhurriedly and in as natural a way as possible – must endeavour, as soon as possible, to introduce his or her 'sentence'. Marks are awarded, not for getting there first, but for ingenuity and 'style'.

HYDE PARK

A number of slips of paper are put into a hat by the compère. Each bears the subject of a three-minute speech from a tub at Hyde Park Corner. Competitors draw from a hat, and have (say) five minutes in which to think up their speeches.

Suggested Subjects

The prospects of the race.
Do alligators make good mothers?
Should parents be allowed to read comics?
Stalemate.
Why I dislike these parties.
Any port in a storm.

THREE-WORD VERSES

Each competitor writes three words on separate slips of paper; these are put into a hat. Then they are well-shuffled, each competitor draws three words, and is given ten minutes in which to write a verse containing the three words he has drawn. The winner is decided by a show of hands, or in any other way mutually agreed.

Suppose there are eight competitors. Here are their twenty-four words:

COUGAR PALINODE PYROMANIAC HATTER SCABIOUS DODECAGONAL HE-MAN EYESORE CLEOPATRA SOUTHEND PSYCHOPATH GRINGO REACH-ME-DOWN WHATNOT URANIUM BEZIQUE HONEYMOON CALYPSO MISANTHROPE BEARSKIN MONACO SYZYGY MUMPS KIPPERS

Prize-winning effort:

'I went to the shop of a hatter called Pop,
A bowler to purloin,
For all I possessed was a reach-me-down vest
And one dodecagonal coin.'

Quiz Games

Quizzes are so popular nowadays that no 'mezzobrow' party, at any rate, would be complete without one. The catch is, that they require careful preparation; one must be sure that one's answers are correct. I offer here material that may form the basis of four Quiz games: A General Quiz, Quotations, Misquotations, and 'Lives of the Great'. Specialized quizzes can, of course, be devised for specialized parties; e.g. a Musical Quiz (where passages played from records must be identified); an Art Quiz, where reproductions of pictures are handed round; a Film Quiz (with 'stills') and so on.

A Quiz can be played either verbally, the first player to give the right answer winning, or players being asked questions in turn; or as a pencil and paper affair.

GENERAL QUIZ

100 Questions

1. Can you think of four meanings of the name Pluto?
2. 'A little stout, vivacious lady, very plainly dressed, not much dignity or pretension about her.' Who is speaking of whom?
3. What games are played by: (*a*) Free Foresters; (*b*) Barbarians; (*c*) Pegasus?
4. What connexion is there between the second and sixth Presidents of the United States?
5. A hundred years ago what is now a South American republic was an empire. Can you name the empire and its ruler?
6. 'Gin-and-water is the source of all my inspiration.' Who makes this remarkable (and mendacious) statement?
7. Who or what is Sothis?
8. Where is the Cesarewitch run, and over what distance?
9. (*a*) Who slept under the dresser?
   (*b*) Who said he was going to dine with some men?
   (*c*) Who could bicker uphill?
10. A solid figure, which could be inscribed in a sphere, has twelve identical faces. What is the shape of each face?

11. Four successive Prime Ministers were all old Etonians. Can you name them?

12. Who were sisters under their skins?

13. What is a halogen?

14. What are the titles of the heads of these Oxford colleges?: (*a*) Lincoln; (*b*) Balliol; (*c*) Merton; (*d*) Christ Church; (*e*) Magdalen.

15. What was the value, and what the colour, of our earliest postage stamps?

16. What three British mammals, other than bats, live mainly on insects?

17. What are the present-day names of (*a*) Uriconium; (*b*) Verulamium; (*c*) Camulodunum?

18. What are the family names of the holders of these dukedoms?: (*a*) Rutland; (*b*) Bedford; (*c*) Marlborough; (*d*) Devonshire; (*e*) Westminster.

19. 'Anything awful makes me laugh. I misbehaved once at a funeral.' Who writes thus, and to whom?

20. 'Let us now praise famous men.' What is the source of this familiar quotation, and what is the remainder of the sentence?

21. Who was the first British, and who the first American, author to win the Nobel Prize for Literature?

22. Who or what is the Taoiseach?

23. What common plants are the sources of these drugs?: (*a*) aconitine; (*b*) digitalin; (*c*) hyoscyamine.

24. What filly, and in what year, won the Oaks, the St Leger, the Two Thousand Guineas and the One Thousand Guineas?

25. Came you name: (*a*) the Mystery Cat; (*b*) the Theatre Cat; (*c*) the Cat About Town?

26. (*a*) 'Three vertical bands: red, white, red.' (*b*) 'Three horizontal bands: red, yellow, red.' Of what States are these the national flags?

27. 'An utterly shallow and wretched segment of a human creature, incapable of understanding Anything in the ultimate conditions of it.' Who takes this depressing view of whom?

28. What Poet Laureate died in 1850, and who succeeded him?

29. Two famous musicians were born in 1685. Who were they?

30. What are the names of the brightest stars in each of these constellations?: (*a*) Cygnus; (*b*) Taurus; (*c*) Leo; (*d*) Ursa Minor.

31. Cobweb and Peas-blossom are two members of a well-known quartette. Where does this quartette appear, and who are its other members?

32. 'If I had no duties, and no reference to futurity, I would...' What would Dr Johnson have done?

33. Where are the Cape Verde Islands, and to whom do they belong?

34. In what novels do we encounter these characters?: (*a*) Mr Stiggins; (*b*) Mr Pumblechook; (*c*) Sir Joseph Bowley; (*d*) Noah Claypole; (*e*) Tom Pinch.

35. 'His daughter came out to meet him with timbrels and with dances: and she was his only child.' Who was the father?

36. Ten statesmen served Queen Victoria as Prime Minister; how many of them can you name?

37. What is the meaning of these heraldic adjectives?: (*a*) couchant; (*b*) gardant; (*c*) passant; (*d*) rampant; (*e*) sejant.

38. Can you name, in their proper order, the states which lie (*a*) on the right bank of the Mississippi, and (*b*) on its left bank, as it flows towards the sea?

39. Who was on the throne when each of the following was written?: (*a*) *The Canterbury Tales;* (*b*) *Romeo and Juliet;* (*c*) *Paradise Lost;* (*d*) *Robinson Crusoe;* (*e*) *Don Juan.*

40. Can you name: (*a*) Polonius's daugher; (*b*) Prospero's daughter; (*c*) Leonato's niece; (*d*) Shylock's daughter; (*e*) the wife of Leonatus Posthumus?

41. What are the better-known names for (*a*) Diptera; (*b*) Coleoptera; (*c*) Lepidoptera?

42. 'If poetry comes not as naturally as the leaves to a tree, it had better not come at all.' Who says so?

43. What happened to the 'sea-green incorruptible' on the 'tenth day of Thermidor'?

44. 'What shall be done unto the man whom the king delighteth to honour?' Who said this to whom?

45. To what gods or goddesses did the Romans dedicate these plants?: (*a*) oak; (*b*) olive; (*c*) laurel; (*d*) myrtle; (*e*) vine.

46. Who was born at Woolsthorpe on Christmas Day 1642?

47. What common association have the names Muzio, Evans, Allgaier?

48. Five of these plants belong to the rose family: cinquefoil; peony; lady's mantle; dahlia; agrimony; medlar; tormentil. Which are the two exceptions?

49. What is the better-known name of Cho-Cho-San?

50. Who rode these horses? (*a*) Agnes; (*b*) Black Bess; (*c*) Copenhagen.

51. 'Thy love to me was wonderful, passing the love of women.' Who is the speaker, and where do these well-known words occur?

52. 'He was naturally learn'd; he needed not the spectacles of books to read Nature; he looked inwards, and found her there.' Whose opinion of whom is this?

53. What two mammals lay eggs, and where are they to be found?

54. 'Who's there?' What play opens with this challenge, and who is the challenger?

55. Japan has no fewer than five cities with a million or more inhabitants. How many of them can you name?

56. Who composed the music for these ballets?: (*a*) *Les Biches* (*The House Party*); (*b*) *Daphnis and Chloe;* (*c*) *Le Train Bleu;* (*d*) *Petrouchka.*

57. The longest reign in British history was, as everyone knows, Queen Victoria's. What were the next three longest reigns in our history? And what European monarch reigned a good deal longer than Queen Victoria?

58. Miranda, Ariel, Oberon, and Titania are well-known characters in Shakespeare. What else have they in common?

59. Of which States of the American Union are these the 'popular' names?: (*a*) the North Star State; (*b*) the Lone Star State; (*c*) the Old Dominion; (*d*) the Empire State; (*e*) the Pelican State.

60. Charles, John Wilkes, and William – who all had the same surname – were respectively a social investigator, an actor and assassin, and a militant social reformer. What was their surname?

61. Who said, of what Order of Chivalry, that he 'liked it because there was no damned merit about it'?

62. Who were the fathers of: (*a*) King Henry I; (*b*) Electra; (*c*) Donalbain; (*d*) Mary, Queen of Scots; (*e*) Hector; (*f*) Perdita; (*g*) Charles James Fox; (*h*) Queen Victoria?

63. A spaniel belonging to a Victorian poetess is the subject of a well-known literary biography. Who was the poetess? What is the dog's name? And who wrote about them?

64. Who was the last British king to style himself 'King of France'?

65. Who claimed to have 'sung a king out of three kingdoms', and with what song?

66. A full-sized orchestra normally includes four 'woodwind' instruments. What are they?

67. What is, in round figures, the nominal (and phenomenal) total of the National Debt?

68. Wordsworth, in his sonnet *Scorn Not the Sonnet*, mentions seven immortal 'soneteers'. Can you name them?

69. 'There is such a thing as a man being too proud to fight.' Who said so, and when?

70. What English shires, in addition to Yorkshire, are divided into two or more counties for administrative purposes?

71. Who was the first woman to be elected to the House of Commons; and when? And who was the first woman member to take her seat?

72. They 'were lovely and pleasant in their lives, and in their death they were not divided: they were swifter than eagles, they were stronger than lions.' Who were they?

73. When does a racehorse become a yearling?

74. 'When I want to read a novel I write one.' Who said so?

75. Which of the following are fish? Or, if not fish, what are they?: (*a*) porpoise; (*b*) sackbut; (*c*) squid; (*d*) squab; (*e*) pilchard; (*f*) pilcorn; (*g*) pickerel; (*h*) piddock; (*i*) dolphin.

76. 'Just for a handful of silver he left us.' (*a*) Of what poem is this the first line; (*b*) who wrote it; (*c*) to whom is it supposed to refer?

77. Who or what are Honshu, Hokkaido, and Kyushu?

78. Who or what are Hokusai, Hiroshige, and Kunisada?

79. What island calls itself Island?

80. What was the 'Spirit of St Louis'?

81. 'There was a man in the land of Uz . . .'. What narrative begins with these words?

82. 'Exult O shores, and ring O bells!
    But I with mournful tread
  Walk the deck my Captain lies,
    Fallen cold and dead.'

Who is 'my Captain', and who wrote the poem?

83. What have the following in common: the Earl of Carrick, the Baron Renfrew, and the Duke of Rothesay?

84. These are the closing lines of three plays. What plays are they?

(*a*) 'Myself will straight aboard; and, to the state,
This heavy act with heavy heart relate.'

(*b*) 'Come the three corners of the world in arms,
And we shall shock them: nought shall make us rue.
If England to itself do rest but true.'

(*c*) 'So call the field to rest; and let's away,
To part the glories of this happy day.'

85. 'He had a head which statuaries loved to copy and a foot the deformity of which beggars in the street mimicked.' Who writes this of whom?

86. When did Trinity House receive its charter, and what are its principal functions?

87. What is the link between a Russian hero and a nickel coin?

88. What takes place: (*a*) when there is an eclipse of the sun; (*b*) when there is an eclipse of the moon?

89. Why has the flag of the United States forty-eight stars and only thirteen stripes?

90. Which of the following are insects: wasp, mosquito, greenfly, woodlouse, cockchafer, spider, ladybird.

91. What is the operatic connexion between a Swedish nightingale and a devil?

92. Who dwelt in the land of Nod?

93. What three quite different connotations has the phrase 'triple crown'?

94. When it is twelve noon in London, what time is it in Togoland?

95. Where is the largest clock-face in the British Isles?

96. In what year and where did Oxford first meet Cambridge in a rowing contest?

97. What is a dodecagon? What common object has dodecagonal faces?

98. 'Why is a raven like a writing desk?' Who put this riddle? And, when asked the answer, what was his reply?

99. Which of the famous novelists of the Victorian era (*a*) began life in a blacking warehouse, (*b*) was a clerk in the General Post Office, (*c*) edited the *Cornhill Magazine*, (*d*) was twice Prime Minister, (*e*) received the Order of Merit?

100. 'I am always glad to explain my faith to anyone, and above all to the Bishop of Rome.' Who said so, and when?

General Quiz: Answers

1. (1) One name for the Greek god of the underworld; (2) The outermost (and smallest) planet of the solar system; (3) A Walt Disney character; (4) The war-time 'Pipe Line Under The Ocean'.

2. Charlotte Brontë of Queen Victoria (1843).

3. (*a*) Cricket; (*b*) rugger; (*c*) soccer.

4. John Adams, second President, was the father of John Quincy Adams, sixth President.

5. Brazil; Pedro II.

6. Lord Byron.

7. The Dog Star (better known as Sirius).

8. Newmarket; two and a quarter miles.

9. (*a*) Edward the Confessor; (*b*) Sir Christopher Wren; (*c*) Sir Walter Raleigh (*Biography for Beginners*).

10. A regular pentagon.

11. Gladstone; Rosebery; Salisbury; Balfour.

12. The Colonel's Lady and Judy O'Grady (Kipling: *The Ladies*).

13. A chemical element which, combined with a metal, forms a salt (fluorine; chlorine; bromine; iodine).

14. (*a*) Rector; (*b*) Master; (*c*) Warden; (*d*) Dean; (*e*) President.

15. One penny; black.

16. Shrew; mole; hedgehog.

17. (*a*) Wroxeter; (*b*) St Albans; (*c*) Colchester.

18. (*a*) Manners; (*b*) Russell; (*c*) Spencer-Churchill; (*d*) Cavendish; (*e*) Grosvenor.

19. Lamb, to Southey.

20. Ecclesiasticus, xliv, 1; 'and our fathers that begat us'.

21. Rudyard Kipling (1907); Sinclair Lewis (1930).

22. The Head of the Government of Eire.

23. (*a*) Monkshood (or wolfbane); (*b*) foxglove; (*c*) henbane.

24. Sceptre; 1902.

25. (*a*) Macavity; (*b*) Gus; (*c*) Bustopher Jones (T. S. Eliot).

26. (*a*) Peru; (*b*) Spain.

27. John Ruskin, of John Stuart Mill.

28. William Wordsworth, succeeded by Alfred (Lord) Tennyson.

29. Bach and Handel.

30. (*a*) Deneb; (*b*) Aldebaran; (*c*) Regulus; (*d*) Polaris (the Pole Star).

31. In *A Midsummer Night's Dream* (fairies attendant on Queen Titania). The other two are Moth and Mustard-Seed.

32. 'I would spend my life in driving briskly in a postchaise with a pretty woman, but she should be one who could understand me and would add something to the conversation.'

33. Off the west coast of Africa; Portugal.

34. (*a*) *The Pickwick Papers;* (*b*) *Great Expectations;* (*c*) *The Chimes;* (*d*) *Oliver Twist;* (*e*) *Martin Chuzzlewit.*

35. Jephthah (Judges, xi, 34).

36. Melbourne; Peel; Lord John (Earl) Russell; Derby; Aberdeen; Palmerston; Disraeli (Beaconsfield); Gladstone; Salisbury; Rosebery.

37. (*a*) Lying down. (*b*) facing the observer; (*c*) walking past; (*d*) on the hind legs; (*e*) in a sitting posture.

38. (*a*) Minnesota (also left bank); Iowa; Missouri; Arkansas; Louisiana (also left bank). (*b*) Wisconsin; Illinois; Kentucky; Mississippi.

39. (*a*) Richard II; (*b*) Elizabeth I; (*c*) Charles II; (*d*) George I; (*e*) George III.

40. (*a*) Ophelia; (*b*) Miranda; (*c*) Beatrice; (*d*) Jessica; (*e*) Imogen.

41. (*a*) Flies; (*b*) beetles; (*c*) butterflies and moths.

42. John Keats (in a letter).

43. The 'incorruptible' (Maximilien Robespierre) was guillotined on the 10th Thermidor (28 July 1794).

44. Ahasuerus to Haman (Esther, vi, 6).

45. (*a*) Jupiter; (*b*) Minerva; (*c*) Apollo; (*d*) Venus; (*e*) Bacchus.

46. Isaac Newton.

47. They are opening gambits in Chess.

48. Peony and dahlia.

49. Madam Butterfly.

50. (*a*) Mary, Queen of Scots; (*b*) Dick Turpin; (*c*) the Duke of Wellington.

51. David; I Samuel, xxvi, 23.

52. Dryden's, of Shakespeare.

53. The Platypus (or Ornithorhynchus) and the Echidna (or Spiny Ant-eater). They are both to be found in Australia.

54. *Hamlet;* Bernardo.

55. Tokyo; Osaka; Nagoya; Kyoto; Kobe.

56. (*a*) Francis Poulenc; (*b*) Maurice Ravel; (*c*) Darius Milhaud; (*d*) Igor Stravinsky.

57. George III; Henry III; Edward III; Louis XIV.

58. They are all satellites of Uranus.

59. (*a*) Minnesota; (*b*) Texas; (*c*) Virginia; (*d*) New York; (*e*) Louisiana.

60. Booth.

61. Lord Melbourne, of the Most Noble Order of the Garter.

62. (*a*) William the Conqueror; (*b*) Agamemnon; (*c*) Duncan; (*d*) James V; (*e*) Priam; (*f*) Leontes; (*g*) Henry Fox, Lord Holland; (*h*) Edward, Duke of Kent.

63. Elizabeth Barrett Browning. Flush. Virginia Woolf.

64. George III.

65. Thomas Wharton, with the song *Lillibullero*, bringing into ridicule the government of James II.

66. Flute, clarinet, oboe, bassoon.

67. £25,000 million.

68. Shakespeare, Petrarch, Tasso, Camoens, Dante, Spenser, Milton.

69. Woodrow Wilson, in May 1915.

70. Cambridge, Hants, Lincoln, Northants, Suffolk, Sussex.

71. Countess Markiewicz, in 1918. Like other Sinn Fein representatives, she did not take her seat. The first woman member to do so was Lady (Nancy) Astor.

72. Saul and Jonathan (II Samuel, i, 23).

73. On 1st January next after it is born. Thus a 'yearling' may not be even a month old.

74. Benjamin Disraeli.

75. The only fish are pilchard and pickerel (a young pike). A porpoise is a mammal; so is a dolphin. A sackbut is a musical instrument somewhat resembling a trombone. A squid is a cephalopod. A squab is a young pigeon or rook. Pilcorn is a variety of oats. A piddock is a rock-boring mollusc.

76. (*a*) *The Lost Leader;* (*b*) Robert Browning; (*c*) Wordsworth.

77. They are the three largest islands of the Japanese archipelago.

78. They are perhaps the most famous of Japanese colour printers.

79. Iceland.

80. The plane in which Charles A. Lindbergh made his famous non-stop flight from New York to Paris, 21 May 1927.

81. The Book of Job.

82. Abraham Lincoln; Walt Whitman.

83. These are titles held by Prince Charles, Duke of Cornwall.

84. (*a*) *Othello;* (*b*) *King John;* (*c*) *Julius Caesar.*

85. T. B. Macaulay of Lord Byron.

86. In 1514. Its principal functions are: (*a*) the administration of lighthouses and lightships, and (*b*) the regulation of pilotage.

87. Freebooter. Russian Hero won the Grand National in 1949, and the famous Nickel Coin in 1951. The great Freebooter won in 1950.

88. (*a*) The moon is interposed between the sun and the earth; (*b*) the earth is interposed between the sun and the moon.

89. Each star represents a State. The thirteen stripes represent the original thirteen States.

90. All except woodlouse and spider.

91. 'The Swedish Nightingale' (Jenny Lind) created a sensation on her first appearance in this country in Meyerbeer's *Robert le Diable.*

92. Cain (Gen. iv, 15).

93. (*a*) The Pope's Tiara. (*b*) Three crowns are part of the arms of the University of Oxford. (*c*) At Rugby Football the 'Triple Crown' is won when England, Wales, Scotland or Ireland defeats all of the other three in one season.

94. Twelve noon.

95. On Shell-Mex House, overlooking the Victoria Embankment, London.

96. In 1829, at Henley (Hambledon Lock to Henley Bridge).

97. A plane figure having twelve sides. A threepenny piece.

98. The Mad Hatter (*Through the Looking-Glass*). 'I haven't the slightest idea.'

99. (*a*) Charles Dickens; (*b*) Anthony Trollope; (*c*) W. M. Thackeray; (*d*) Benjamin Disraeli; (*e*) George Meredith and Thomas Hardy.

100. Wyclif; 1384.

QUOTATIONS

1. But at my back I always hear
   Time's winged chariot hurrying near.
2. I bring fresh showers for the thirsting flowers
   From the seas and the streams;
   I bear light shade for the leaves when laid
   In their noonday dreams.
3. Never was heard such a terrible curse!
   But what gave rise to no little surprise
   Nobody seem'd one penny the worse!
4. How many things by season season'd are
   To their right praise and true perfection.
5. Their coats were brushed, their faces washed
   Their shoes were clean and neat –
6. She was a phantom of delight
   When first she gleamed upon my sight;
   A lovely apparition, sent
   To be a moment's ornament.
7. When men were all asleep the snow came flying,
   In large white flakes falling on the city brown,

8. O thou art fairer than the evening air,
Clad in the beauty of a thousand stars.
9. How small a part of time they share
That are so wondrous sweet and fair.
10. One man with a dream, at pleasure
May go forth and conquer a crown.
11. A ship, an isle, a sickle moon –
With few but with how splendid stars
The mirrors of the sea are strewn
Between their silver bars.
12. She is not fair to outward view
As many maidens be
Her loveliness I never knew
Until she smiled on me.
13. Since there's no help, come let us kiss and part
Nay, I have done: you get no more of me,
And I am glad, yea glad with all my heart,
That thus so cleanly, I myself can free.
14. Walled round with rocks as an inland island,
The ghost of a garden fronts the sea.
15. Yet some there be that by due steps aspire
To lay their just hands on that golden key
That opes the palace of Eternity.
16. In small proportions we just beauties see
And in short measures, life may perfect be.
17. The hare limp'd trembling through the frozen grass
And silent was the flock in woolly fold.
18. My lines and life are free; free as the road,
Loose as the wind, as large as store.
19. There's a fascination frantic
In a ruin that's romantic;
Do you think you are sufficiently decayed?
20. Night's candles are burned out, and jocund day
Stands tiptoe on the misty mountain tops.
21. The best laid schemes o' mice an' men
Gang aft a-gley.

22. Diseases desperate grown,
By desperate appliances are reliev'd
Or not at all
23. Our birth is but a sleep and a forgetting;
The Soul that rises with us, our life's Star,
Hath had else where its setting,
And cometh from afar.
24. How happy could I be with either,
Were t'other dear charmer away!
25. Who hath not seen thee oft amid thy store?
Sometimes whoever seeks abroad may find
Thee sitting careless on a granary floor,
Thy hair soft-lifted by the winnowing wind.
26. They are not long, the weeping and the laughter,
Love and desire and hate;
I think they have no portion in us after
We pass the gate.
27. Forget not yet the tried intent
Of such a truth as I have meant.
28. Through wood and dale the sacred river ran,
Then reached the caverns measureless to man,
And sank in tumult to a lifeless ocean.
29. I am gone into the fields
To take what this sweet hour yields.
30. Oh, solitude! Where are the charms
That sages have seen in thy face?
Better dwell in the midst of alarms,
Than reign in this horrible place.

Quotations: Answers

1. Marvell: *To His Coy Mistress.*
2. Shelley: *The Cloud.*
3. Barham: *The Jackdaw of Rheims.*
4. Shakespeare: *The Merchant of Venice.*
5. Carroll: *The Walrus and the Carpenter.*
6. Wordsworth: *She was a Phantom of Delight.*
7. Bridges: *London Snow.*

8. Marlowe: *Faustus.*
9. Waller: Song: *Go Lovely Rose.*
10. O'Shaughnessy: Ode: *We are the Music Makers.*
11. Flecker: *A Ship, an Isle, a Sickle Moon.*
12. Hartley Coleridge: Song: *She is not Fair.*
13. Drayton: *Sonnets.*
14. Swinburne: *A Forsaken Garden.*
15. Milton: *Comus.*
16. Jonson: *A Pindaric Ode on the Death of Sir H. Morison.*
17. Keats: *The Eve of St Agnes.*
18. Herbert: *The Collar.*
19. Gilbert: *The Mikado.*
20. Shakespeare: *Romeo and Juliet.*
21. Burns: *To a Mouse.*
22. Shakespeare: *Hamlet.*
23. Wordsworth: Ode: *Intimations of Immortality.*
24. Gay: *The Beggar's Opera.*
25. Keats: *To Autumn.*
26. Dowson: *Vitae Summa Brevis.*
27. Wyatt: *Steadfastness.*
28. Coleridge: *Kubla Khan.*
29. Shelley: *To Jane: The Invitation.*
30. Cowper: *Verses Supposed to be Written by Alexander Selkirk.*

MISQUOTATIONS

1. Build me a willow cabin at your gate,
And call upon my soul within the house
2. Tell me not in mournful numbers
Life is but an idle dream
3. Come to the stolen waters
    And leap the guarded pale
And pluck the flower in season
    Before desire shall fail.
4. Oh, Tiber! father Tiber!
    To whom the Romans pray,
A soldier's life, a soldier's arms,
    Take thou in charge this day!

5. She left me wondering why my soul
    Was sad that she was glad
6. Full many a rose is born to blush unseen,
    And waste its sweetness on the desert air
7. So, we'll go no more a roving
    So late into the night
   Though the heart be still as loving,
    And the stars be still as bright
8. Sleep that knits up the tangled sleave of care,
   The death of each day's life, sore labour's bath,
   Balm of hurt minds, great nature's second course
9. There's a breathless hush in the Close tonight –
    Ten to make and the match to win –
   A bumping pitch and a fading light,
    An hour to play and the last man in.
10. Splashing and paddling with hoofs of a goat,
   And breaking the golden kingcups afloat
    With the dragon-fly on the river.
11. Music, when soft voices die,
   Lingers in the memory –
   Odours, when sweet violets sicken
   Live within the sense they quicken
12. To rouse the soul by tender strokes of art,
   To raise the genius, and to mend the heart
13. Wanting is – what?
   Summer redundant,
   Autumn abundant,
   – Where is the blot?
14. They lunched on mince, and slices of quince,
   Which they ate with a runcible spoon
15. Her shoes beneath her petticoat,
   Like little moles, crept in and out,
    As if they fear'd the light
16. Sport that haggard Care derides,
   And Laughter holding both his sides.
   Come, and trip it as ye go
   On the gay fantastic toe.

17. The Moving Finger writes; and having writ,
Moves on: nor all thy Reverence and Wit
Shall call it back to cancel half a Line
Nor all thy Tears wash out a Word of it.
18. Ye ancient spires, ye antique towers,
That crown the wat'ry glade
19. Unkempt about those hedges blows
An unauthenticated rose
20. And yet anon repairs his languish'd head,
And tricks his beams, and with new spangled ore,
Shines in the forehead of the morning sky

Misquotations: Answers

1. For *build* read *make* (Shakespeare: *Twelfth Night*).
2. For *idle* read *empty* (Longfellow: *A Psalm of Life*).
3. For *pluck* read *pull* (Housman: *Last Poems*).
4. For *soldier's life* and *soldier's arms* read *Roman's life* and *Roman's arms* (Macaulay: *Horatius*).
5. For *wondering* read *marvelling* (Thompson: *Daisy*).
6. For *rose* read *flower* (Gray: *Elegy Written in a Country Churchyard*).
7. For *stars* read *moon* (Byron: *So, We'll Go No More a Roving*).
8. For *tangled* read *ravell'd* (Shakespeare: *Macbeth*).
9. For *fading* read *blinding* (Newbolt: *Vitai Lampada*).
10. For *kingcups* read *lilies* (Elizabeth Barrett Browning: *A Musical Instrument*).
11. For *lingers* read *vibrates* (Shelley: *To –. Music When Soft Voices Die*).
12. For *rouse* read *wake* (Pope: *Prologue to Addison's Cato*, 1).
13. For *autumn* read *blueness* (Browning: *Wanting – is what?*).
14. For *lunched* read *dined* (Lear: *The Owl and the Pussy-Cat*).
15. For *shoes* read *feet;* for *moles* read *mice;* for *crept* read *stole* (Suckling: *Ballad. Upon a Wedding*).
16. For *haggard* read *wrinkled;* for *gay* read *light* (Milton: *L'Allegro*, 1.).
17. For *Reverence* read *Piety;* for *call* read *lure* (Fitzgerald: *Omar Khayyam*).

18. For *ancient* read *distant* (Gray: *Ode on a Distant Prospect of Eton College*).
19. For *unauthenticated* read *English unofficial* (Brooke: *The Old Vicarage, Grantchester*).
20. For *languish'd* read *drooping;* for *shines* read *flames* (Milton: *Lycidas*).

LIVES OF THE GREAT

This is a 'mezzobrow' game which is, in effect, a Quiz. You won't want to play it if you're not interested in people, or reasonably well-informed; but, if you are, it can give quite a lot of pleasure. It requires – as will be obvious from the examples – careful preparation.

The examples given can, of course, be used, if those taking part are not familiar with this book!

The rules are very simple. The compère reads aloud each of a selected number of 'lives' and whoever first gives the right answer scores three points. For a wrong answer, one point should be deducted.

Alternatively, this can be played as a pencil and paper game. Then those playing – who can, of course, be organized in teams – write down their answers as the 'lives' are successively read out.

EXAMPLES

1. An English painter, best known perhaps for his portraits, was born in 1727. One of his most famous portraits – that of the Duchess of Devonshire – was stolen in 1876 and was not recovered for several years.

2. Perhaps the most popular of nineteenth-century composers was born in Italy in 1858. The scene of his best-known opera is Japan.

3. A famous writer of fables – perhaps the best-known of all such writers – died about 2,500 years ago. The Lion and the Mouse, the Fox and the Crow, the Hare and the Tortoise, are familiar characters from his stories.

4. This famous scholar and theologian was born in the eleventh century. The tragic story of his love for a young girl, whom he secretly married, has attracted the interest of many writers; among them George Moore and Alexander Pope.

5. This English king was born about 1,100 years ago. Although a large part of his reign was spent in successfully fighting the Danish invaders of this island, he also founded schools and translated Latin manuscripts into English. He is buried at Winchester.

6. One of the most famous of English statesmen became Prime Minister at the age of twenty-four. For the greater part of his long term of office Britain was at war with Napoleon and when he died, at the age of forty-six, the end of the struggle was still in the dim distance.

7. This was not the most popular of Victorian novelists – his sales were far exceeded by those of one of his contemporaries – but he is still read with admiration and affection. Among his creations are Major Pendennis, Captain Costigan and the immortal Becky Sharp.

8. One of the greatest of classical composers, a native of Bonn, first became known at the end of the eighteenth century. His compositions include nine symphonies, some of which have not been, and are not likely to be, excelled. In later life he became totally deaf and could never 'hear' in the accepted sense, some of his finest creations.

9. The earliest of British martyrs was a Roman soldier who became a Christian convert and died for his faith. Later King Offa built a monastery to his memory at a town called Verulamium, which now bears the martyr's name.

10. A Knaresborough schoolmaster was arrested at Lynn in 1759 for a murder committed some fourteen years earlier; was found guilty, and was executed. His story is the subject of a novel by Lord Lytton and a poem by Thomas Hood.

11. This brilliant man, the father of one of the most famous of our contemporaries, entered Parliament in 1874. With the aid of a few colleagues he conducted war against both government and opposition. For a short time he was Chancellor of the Exchequer.

12. To recall this lady, it is perhaps sufficient to quote the poet

Tennyson's tribute: 'Sea-king's daughter from over the sea.' She came to England to be married in 1863 and died in 1925, having survived her husband by some sixteen years.

13. A Bishop of Winchester and Lord Chancellor was also a great scholar and educationist. Towards the end of the fourteenth century he founded a college at Oxford and, a few years later, the great school whose motto is *Manners Makyth Man.*

14. A king of Macedon is among the best-known figures of the ancient world. Most of us have heard how he is said to have tamed his famous horse. Successfully conquering and subduing one enemy after another, he founded a city in Egypt which is named after him; and died at the age of thirty-three.

15. A nineteenth-century novelist of Italian descent was born in Paris, where he spent most of his life. His novels were very successful and gave a realistic picture of contemporary France. He is best remembered, however, for the part he took in the Dreyfus case and it was largely due to his efforts that Dreyfus was ultimately vindicated.

16. An eighteenth-century writer of great versatility was a member of the circle graced by Dr Johnson, Sir Joshua Reynolds, and David Garrick. Among his writings are an elegiac poem, *The Deserted Village;* a novel about a country parson; and a comedy of manners which is still frequently performed.

17. This young man, writer, courtier, and soldier, was nephew to the Earl of Leicester. He died in battle while still in his early thirties and has become the epitome of all that was best in the Elizabethan age.

18. Queen Victoria's favourite poet was the son of a Lincolnshire parson. He was made Poet Laureate on the death of Wordsworth, and was ultimately raised to the peerage.

19. A civil servant, through his great ability and industry, worked his way up from comparative poverty to affluence during the seventeenth century. He is best remembered for his diaries which give us an objective account of his highly entertaining private life.

20. A supremely successful military commander lived to take an active part in politics for more than thirty years after he had fought his last battle. He was raised, by successive stages, to a

dukedom; and the name of a London railway terminus commemorates the most famous of his victories.

21. This lady of humble birth and great beauty became the wife of the British Ambassador at Naples. Here she met Lord Nelson who fell in love with her. He had hoped that the nation, which owed so much to him, would provide for her after his death, but his hope was not fulfilled.

22. A French scientist, best known as a bacteriologist, died in 1895. His work was mainly directed towards the curing of deadly diseases, in particular hydrophobia. A famous institute in Paris is named after him.

23. A British composer, born in 1842, began by writing oratorios, but soon – in collaboration with an equally talented librettist – was principally engaged in writing light opera. A long series of successful productions was the outcome of this partnership.

24. A well-known character in the history of Rome was a protégé of Julius Caesar's; he attained power after the latter's assassination. Involved in a series of civil wars, his fortunes declined; he was defeated in battle and committed suicide. He appears in two of Shakespeare's plays.

25. A novelist born in 1867, became in the early years of this century one of the most successful exponents of his craft. His finest novels are concerned with the life and interests of one highly specialized industrial area. He died in 1931.

26. An English landscape painter, elected to the Royal Academy before he was thirty, was to become one of the most discussed artists of his day. John Ruskin, in particular, championed his cause with great energy. He died in 1851, leaving a vast volume of work and an immense fortune.

27. A nineteenth-century biologist was a member of a family which has produced many notable men. His career began, modestly enough, with a voyage of scientific exploration, of which he published a record. Some years afterwards, he launched a theory which was to revolutionize contemporary thought on the subject of the origins of man.

28. An impressive literary career was that of a nineteenth-century poet and novelist who, from first to last, was writing for

some fifty years. His novels, particularly *The Egoist*, were widely read in their day. He died, much honoured, in 1909.

29. A musician, though of German nationality, spent most of his life in this country. His compositions are, for the most part, oratorios, many of which are still regularly performed. He died in 1759.

30. A great Parliamentarian and leader of the Irish Nationalists in the House of Commons, became involved in a domestic scandal and eventually disrupted his own party in 1890. He is also remembered as the plaintiff in an action for libel which won him heavy damages from *The Times*.

Lives of the Great: Answers

1. Thomas Gainsborough (1727–88).
2. Giacomo Puccini (1858–1924). The opera referred to is, of course, *Madam Butterfly*.
3. Aesop (620–560 B.C.).
4. Peter Abelard (1072–1142), lover of his gifted pupil Heloise.
5. Alfred the Great, king of Wessex (848–900).
6. William Pitt, the younger (1759–1806).
7. William Makepeace Thackeray (1811–63). Author of *Pendennis*, *Vanity Fair*, and many other novels.
8. Ludwig van Beethoven (1770–1827).
9. St Alban.
10. Eugene Aram (1704–59).
11. Randolph Churchill (1849–95), father of Sir Winston Churchill.
12. Princess Alexandra of Denmark (1844–1925), daughter of Christian IX of Denmark, and bride of Prince Albert Edward, afterwards Edward VII.
13. William of Wykham (1367–1404). His twin foundations are New College (1379) and Winchester College (1387).
14. Alexander the Great (356–323 B.C.). The legend is that he tamed the horse Bucephalus, who was frightened by his own shadow, by riding him directly towards the sun.
15. Émile Zola (1840–1902). He precipitated the re-opening of the Dreyfus case by his challenging pamphlet *J'accuse*.

16. Oliver Goldsmith (1728–74). The novel is *The Vicar of Wakefield*, and the play, *She Stoops to Conquer*.
17. Sir Philip Sidney (1554–86). He was killed at the battle of Zutphen.
18. Alfred, Lord Tennyson (1809–92). He succeeded Wordsworth as Poet Laureate in 1850.
19. Samuel Pepys (1633–1703). He became ultimately Secretary to the Navy.
20. The Duke of Wellington (1769–1852). The name of the London railway terminus is, of course, Waterloo.
21. Emma, Lady Hamilton (1765–1815).
22. Louis Pasteur (1822–95).
23. (Sir) Arthur Sullivan (1842–1900).
24. Marcus Antonius (Mark Antony) (83–30 B.C.). He appears, of course, in Shakespeare's *Julius Caesar*, and *Antony and Cleopatra.*
25. (Enoch) Arnold Bennett. His best novels – in particular the *Clayhanger* trilogy – are concerned with the Five Towns.
26. J. M. W. Turner (1775–1851). His work is vindicated in Ruskin's *Modern Painters.*
27. Charles Darwin (1809–82). His writings include *The Voyage of the 'Beagle'* and, of course, *Origin of Species.*
28. George Meredith (1828–1909).
29. George Frederick Handel (1685–1759).
30. Charles Stewart Parnell (1846–91). The scandal referred to was Captain O'Shea's petition for divorce, in which Parnell was cited as co-respondent.

NOTES

NOTES

NOTES

NOTES